KEYS TO COLLEGE STUDYING

BECOMING A LIFELONG LEARNER

Carol Carter

Joyce Bishop

Sarah Lyman Kravits

EDITORIAL CONSULTANT

Dr. Jerome V. D'Agostino

Assistant Professor of Educational Psychology
University of Arizona
Specialist in Measurement, Assessment, and Evaluation

Prentice
Hall

Upper Saddle River, New Jersey
Columbus, Ohio

Library of Congress Cataloging-in-Publication Data

Carter, Carol.
    Keys to college studying : becoming a lifelong learner / Carol Carter, Joyce Bishop,
Sarah Lyman Kravits ; editorial consultant Jerome V. D'Agostino.
      p.   cm.
    Includes bibliographical references and index.
    ISBN 0-13-030481-6
    1. Study skills. 2. Adult learning. I. Bishop, Joyce (Joyce L.). II. Kravits, Sarah
Lyman.   III. D'Agostino, Jerome V. IV. Title

LB2395.C267 2002
378.1'7—dc21   00-068477

Vice President and Publisher: Jeffery W. Johnston
Acquisitions Editor: Sande Johnson
Editorial Assistant: Cecilia Johnson
Production Editor: Holcomb Hathaway
Design Coordinator: Diane C. Lorenzo
Cover Designer: Kiwi Design
Cover Art: Lisa Henderling, SIS/Images.Com
Production Manager: Pamela D. Bennett
Director of Marketing: Kevin Flanagan
Marketing Manager: Christina Quadhamer
Marketing Assistant: Barbara Rosenberg

This book was set in Janson by Aerocraft Charter Art Service. It was printed and
bound by R. R. Donnelley, Harrisonburg. The cover was printed by Phoenix Color.

Copyright © 2002 by Prentice-Hall, Inc., Upper Saddle River, New Jersey 07458. All rights reserved. Printed in
the United States of America. This publication is protected by Copyright and permission should be obtained from
the publisher prior to any prohibited reproduction, storage in a retrieval system, or transmission in any form or by
any means, electronic, mechanical, photocopying, recording, or likewise. For information regarding permission(s),
write to: Rights and Permissions Department.

Prentice Hall

10 9 8 7 6 5 4 3 2 1
ISBN 0-13-030481-6

Contents

Chapter 8   Listening and Memory   197

TAKING IN AND REMEMBERING INFORMATION

PART III   NOTES, RESEARCH, AND WRITING   231

INTERPRETING AND EXPRESSING IDEAS

Chapter 9   Taking Lecture Notes   233

RECORDING THE IDEAS OF OTHERS

Chapter 13   Showing What You Know   347

TAKING OBJECTIVE, ESSAY, AND ORAL EXAMINATIONS

Chapter 14   Quantitative Learning   373

BECOMING COMFORTABLE WITH MATH, SCIENCE, AND TECHNOLOGY

Chapter 15 Moving Ahead 399

**MAKING TODAY'S STUDY SKILLS THE FOUNDATION
FOR TOMORROW'S SUCCESS**

Skill Building, Chapters 12–15 419

Preface

STUDY SKILLS FOR LIFE

Daniel B., an undergraduate student we know, was recently offered a summer internship in the global investment banking division of one of the country's largest financial institutions. Although the corporate recruiters thought he was highly qualified, Daniel doubted his own ability, worrying that as a liberal-arts major he lacked the basic knowledge and skills to succeed in a business setting. He had never worked with spreadsheets, graphed financial data, or spoken the specialized language of his business colleagues. While he was familiar with classic novels through his college literature courses, he knew little about capital markets and derivatives. He was so filled with self-doubt that he nearly rejected the internship offer.

The company recruiters were well aware of Daniel's knowledge "deficits" when they offered him the position. However, from talking with references listed on his resume and with Daniel himself during the interview, they realized that he had a quick mind, superior critical-thinking and study skills, and a willingness to learn, all of which were reflected in excellent grades. They were convinced that he would be able to master everything he needed to know for the internship, especially since the program included a week of intensive training classes designed to get everyone up to speed. After a few weeks of hard work, Daniel acquired the skills he needed—and was now moving ahead of many of the other interns in his ability to analyze and apply complex business concepts to unique problem-solving situations.

This true story defines the importance of having solid study and critical-thinking skills in the 21st century. It also illustrates the mission of the first edition of *Keys To College Studying: Becoming a Lifelong Learner.* Like Daniel, you may find yourself doubting your specific knowledge and skills when, for example, you change majors, get a new boss, or change careers. However, the study skills and critical-thinking skills that you learn in this book will help you succeed in college as they prepare you for the challenge of continuous learning throughout your career and life.

Your Study-Skills Tool Bag: What's Important in This Book

This text contains some essential elements that help you achieve diverse goals:

STRATEGIES FOR SELF-MANAGEMENT. Before you can be a successful learner, you need to set the stage for learning in a way that maximizes your abilities. Part I helps you develop self-management through learning styles, self-awareness, goal setting, and time management. It also provides strategies for helping you become a critical thinker. Critical thinking will allow you to take your study skills to a higher level of achievement.

CORE STUDY SKILLS FOR SCHOOL, WORK, AND LIFE. The text focuses on skills that will take you successfully through your classes—and beyond. Each skill is presented in comprehensive terms, showing you what you need to know in order to succeed in school as well as how you will use the skill in the working world and in your personal life. These skills include reading, listening, taking notes, memory, library and internet research, vocabulary building, writing, test taking, math and technology skills, and many more.

TESTING-FOCUSED EXERCISES. At the end of each chapter and each part, a variety of exercises appear that are designed to reinforce knowledge and build test-taking skills. Included are:

- Multiple-choice, true/false, fill-in-the-blank, and matching questions
- A vocabulary-building exercise featuring challenging words from the current media
- Strategic thinking and teamwork exercises

A Real-Life Approach to the Needs of Real-Life Students

Keys to College Studying acknowledges who you are right now and the stresses and pressures you may face. Acknowledging that each student is in a unique life situation, the text includes information such as ways to study with children around, time management advice for working students, and vocabulary-building approaches for students from around the world. *Keys to College Studying* focuses on the individual—you—helping to reduce study-related stress as it emphasizes the development of skills that will help you handle change.

TAKE ACTION: BE A PROACTIVE LEARNER

You are responsible for your education, your growth, your knowledge, and your future. If you know yourself, choose the right paths, and follow them with determination, you will earn the success that you deserve. The best we can do is offer some great strategies, ideas, and structures that will help you study effectively; ultimately, it's up to you to use them. You've made a terrific start by choosing to pursue an education—now take advantage of all it has to give you. Pay yourself the biggest compliment by studying hard, having faith in yourself, and staying focused on your long-term goals.

Acknowledgments

This book has come about through a heroic group effort. We would like to take this opportunity to acknowledge the people who have made it happen. Many thanks to:

- Dr. Jerome V. D'Agostino, Assistant Professor of Educational Psychology at the University of Arizona and a specialist in assessment, measurement, and evaluation, for his careful review of the chapter and part assessments and his sound advice that led to their improvement.

- Michael Jackson, for his writing samples and advice.

- Our reviewers, for their insight, feedback, and guidance: Elaine Wright at the Department of Learning Assistance, Division of Academic Support, University of Southern Maine; Nancy G. Wood, University of Arkansas at Little Rock; Donna Wood, Southwest Tennessee Community College; Debbie Gentile, Mississippi Community College; Sue Knepley, Red Rocks Community College; Lynn Clemons, El Camino College; Michael McClay, University of Delaware, Academic Services Center; Lindsay Lewan, Arapahoe Community College; and Bill Hoanzl, El Camino Community College.

- The Prentice Hall folks who helped to develop the manuscript: Katharine Grassi, Julie Hildebrand, David Gillespie, Sally McPherson, Jennifer Woodle, and Dave Visser.

- Dr. Frank T. Lyman, for his invaluable advice on the text and for his generous permission to use and adapt his Thinktrix critical thinking system.

- Marjorie Freilich-Den, Sheri Garrou, Ross T. Labaugh of California State University at Fresno, and Bobbie Stevens of University of Texas at Arlington, for their reviews of the revised material on library research.

- Our Publisher Jeff Johnston, for his interest, commitment, and leadership with the Student Success list.

- Our terrific editor, Sande Johnson.

- Our fabulous production team, including JoEllen Gohr, Pam Bennett, Gay Pauley, and typesetters Aerocraft Charter Art Service.

- Our marketing gurus, especially Marketing Manager Christina Quadhamer and her assistant Barbara Rosenberg, who put a great deal of thought into how to market this book and position it for students' needs.
- Jeff and Margo McIlroy, for their unyielding support in a variety of capacities.
- Kate Lareau, for all of her energy and enthusiasm for student success.
- Frank Mortimer and Marilyn Phelps for their work on the website and technology.
- The Prentice Hall representatives and the management team led by Gary June, who have shown tremendous support for the success of students of all ages.
- Robin Baliszewski, President of Education, Career, and Technology, for her support and interest in this discipline.
- Our families and friends, who have encouraged us and put up with our commitments.
- We extend a very special thanks to Judy Block, an invaluable member of the team, whose contributions of extensive research and creation of new material were essential.

Finally, for their ideas, opinions, and stories, we would like to thank all of the students and professors with whom we work. Joyce in particular would like to thank the thousands of students who have allowed her, as their professor, the privilege of sharing part of their journey through college. We appreciate that, through reading this book, you give us the opportunity to learn and discover with you—in your classroom, in your home, on the bus, and wherever else learning takes place.

KNOWLEDGE, SKILLS, AND PREPARATION

WHERE THE FUTURE BEGINS

PART

I

CHOOSE

Imagine the feeling you will have as you graduate from the program you're beginning. Unlike in past years, graduation is now an entry point for lifelong learning and a passport to the knowledge economy. Learning in the twenty-first century has been transformed into a continual process—throughout your working life and beyond—that relies on the study skills you acquire and refine during your college years. These skills are the best tools you have to succeed in life and throughout your career.

This chapter will give you an overview of what today's education offers you and why particular ideas and skills will be essential for your success. At the end of the chapter, you will be able to answer these questions:

- How do you become a lifelong learner?
- How do you become a strategic learner?
- How can you get ready to study?

LIFELONG LEARNING
REACHING YOUR POTENTIAL
IN THE TWENTY-FIRST CENTURY

> *"A journey of a thousand miles must begin with a single step."*
>
> **Laotzu**

How Do You Become a Lifelong Learner?

In his book, *TechnoTrends—24 Technologies That Will Revolutionize Our Lives,* futurist Daniel Burns describes a tomorrow that is linked to continuing education: "The future belongs to those who are capable of being retrained again and again," he said. "Think of it as periodically upgrading your human assets throughout your career. . . . Humans are infinitely upgradeable, but it does require an investment" in lifelong learning.[1]

KNOW WHY LIFELONG LEARNING IS IMPORTANT

Today's trends showcase the enormous changes taking place in your world. Here are some that will make lifetime learning a reality for you in the years ahead:

- *Knowledge in nearly every field is doubling every two to three years.* That means that if you stop learning, for even a few years, your knowledge base will be woefully inadequate to keep up with all the changes in your career.

- *Technology is changing how you live and work.* Experts can only guess at the ways in which the Internet will shape communication and improve productivity in the next 20 years. Technological advances, like those you are seeing today, will require continual learning and will be the mechanism through which learning takes place.

- *Our economy is moving from a product and service base to a knowledge and talent base.* Tomorrow's jobs will depend on what you know and your ability to learn more every day.

- *Personal choices are becoming more complex.* The responsibility to make certain critical decisions is becoming yours alone. For example, years ago most companies provided employee pensions that guaranteed income after retirement. Now you probably have—or one day will have—an Individual Retirement Account (IRA), in which you make decisions for your own retirement based on your knowledge of investments.

All of these signs point to the need to become *lifelong learners*—individuals who embrace learning as a mechanism for improving their lives and careers. Developing flexibility and seeing companies as learning organizations will help you learn throughout your life.

DEVELOP AND MAINTAIN FLEXIBILITY

The vast majority of Americans see lifelong learning as important in their own lives. In a recent survey of workers, ages 18 to 24, conducted by the country's leading labor union, the American Federation of Labor and Congress of Industrial Organizations (AFL-CIO), 85 percent of the respondents viewed education and training as the nation's top economic priority, and nine out of ten believed that the key to career advancement is ongoing education and training.[2]

Lifelong learning requires *flexibility*—an attitude that defines how you approach the challenge of change and continual learning in school and at work. Flexibility implies that you:

EMBRACE CHANGE, RESPONDING TO IT WITH ANTICIPATION RATHER THAN FEAR. Every step in life that takes you off dead center has an element of risk. Your ability to view risk-taking as necessary for personal growth and success is crucial. In making the decision to pursue higher education, for example, you showed a willingness to accept the challenges school placed before you—even if you risked disappointment and perhaps failure. Your motivation for change is positive and compelling; you want to succeed in school and in life.

BECOME SELF-DIRECTED. You realize that you will guide yourself through much of the learning process. According to training expert Bruce Tulgan, "gathering, processing, analyzing, and interpreting information—and deciding what to retain and what to discard—will be an integral part of how you operate" in the world of school and work.[3] In this new, flexible environment, you are in charge.

SEE YOURSELF AS PART OF A BIGGER PICTURE. Change is happening to you and to everyone else. In addition to the technological, economic, and personal changes described previously, change is happening on a cultural, social, and business level. Consider how each change affects you as well as your family, your community, your nation, and your world. For example:

- Our culture is changing rapidly as the face of America includes more people of color, immigrants, and single parents. Look around you;

you may see this diversity at school or work. Think of what that implies for our country as a whole.

- Our social interactions are changing as a result of the Internet. At school, students now communicate with each other and their instructors via e-mail and form friendships with people who share common interests but who may live thousands of miles away.
- Business is changing as products and services are being bought and sold on the Internet and as companies take on the responsibility for helping employees continue to learn.

ACCEPT THAT YOU WILL PROBABLY CHANGE JOBS—AND EVEN CAREERS—SEVERAL TIMES IN YOUR LIFE. Although your parents and grandparents may have held the same job for their entire careers, most of today's workers will voluntarily seek new career opportunities as their interests, needs, and lifestyles change. In fact, the National Research Bureau reports that currently the average employee changes jobs every three to four years—a record high in the U. S. Even more startling, it is estimated that a 22-year-old college graduate in the year 2000 will have an average of eight employers in his first 10 years in the workplace.[4] One result of this high level of change is that every time you decide to start a new career, you'll need new knowledge and skills.

For example, a lawyer may start her career working long hours in the trusts and estate-planning department of a major law firm. Wanting more independence to raise her children, she may study for her license as a stockbroker, a career that allows a flexible schedule. Seeing a growing need to help people manage investments, she takes online courses to become a certified financial planner, a step she hopes will add to her independence and earning power. Ultimately, she becomes a financial author and lecturer. Those who are most successful at changing careers link what they already know to what they want to become. In this case, there are interconnecting threads between careers in law, investments, financial planning, and writing and communication.

EXPERT INSIGHT

Study What You Love— and Embrace Technology

It doesn't matter what your degree is. If you study what you love and embrace technology, you'll be successful in the marketplace. I've known students who forced themselves to master technology—even when their instructors didn't require it. They set themselves apart as being willing to take this challenge, and now they have multiple job offers, sometimes at salaries that are twice what their peers are making. There are so many companies that can't find people with this knowledge.

DAN COOPER, MARIST COLLEGE

ACCEPT THAT ECONOMIC SHIFTS MAY FORCE YOU TO MOVE FROM ONE JOB TO ANOTHER. Economic forces have moved the bulk of manufacturing jobs to foreign soil where labor costs are cheaper. In addition, new technologies have made millions of jobs obsolete. For example, it wasn't that long ago that live telephone operators answered calls to business offices. Today, almost all companies use automated voice mail systems. Jobs of the past are being replaced by knowledge-based jobs that ask workers to think critically to come up with workable solutions. Successful workers in such jobs continually learn new information and apply their knowledge to workplace solutions.

VIEW ORGANIZATIONS AS LEARNING CENTERS

There is a good chance that after you finish school, you will be part of a company organization that recognizes the need for lifelong learning. Many modern organizations invite change, working to foster an environment where individuals look for new and better ways of working rather than running around the same track year after year. In this context, organizations—workplaces that focus on unique goals and objectives—take different forms:

- *Corporations and companies.* Corporations, such as Coca-Cola, American Express, and Amazon.com, and small companies, such as accounting firms, Internet retailers, and landscaping businesses, are for-profit organizations that produce goods and services for different markets with the goal of increasing company and shareholder value.

- *Not-for-profit organizations.* Not-for-profit organizations, such as some hospitals, charities, and private educational institutions, employ millions of workers who often work in the same types of jobs as their counterparts in corporations. For example, you may choose to work in the accounting department of your local hospital or branch of Habitat for Humanity or do the same type of work in the accounting department of a major computer software manufacturer.

- *Federal agencies.* Government departments are also workplace organizations. Whether you work as a communication specialist in your state's department of education, a researcher at a public university, or a nurse, with an expertise in sexually transmitted diseases, for the Federal Centers for Disease Control, you will be working in a structured organization that expects—and often requires—lifelong learning.

All of these organizations may hold classes to help employees maintain a customer focus and improve teamwork skills; they may also direct employees to Web-based instructional materials that explain new computer software or government regulations that affect business practices. Organizations are realizing that the *way* they teach new information may be the key to *how well* employees learn it. One-way lectures are being replaced with collaborative learning teams who discuss and problem solve. In addition, Web-based interactive instruction is the fastest growing learning approach.[5] If you can become comfortable working on teams and learning via the Web while you are in school, you will have an important advantage when you begin your career.

Mastering change and becoming a flexible learner starts with a shift in focus from *what* you learn to *how* you learn. Focusing on the *how* of learning emphasizes the skills that are examined in this text, including reading effectively, building vocabulary, studying and mastering new content, gathering data from visual aids, improving listening and memory, taking effective notes, researching, and writing. You need solid study skills to learn all of the information that is set before you on the job and to apply the knowledge you acquire through critical thinking.

If you currently have a part- or full-time job while attending school to earn extra money, you may be puzzled by this emphasis on lifelong learning and learning organizations. Your confusion is understandable if your job has little or no relation to your career goals and dreams. If you are flipping burgers at a fast-food restaurant or answering phones for a department office at your college, studying will not help you do better work or feel more satisfied. And it will certainly not convince you that you are part of a learning organization.

Seeing the value of lifelong learning and making sense out of the concept of a learning organization requires that you understand that there are major differences between *jobs* and *careers*. Your part-time work as a department store cashier is a job; being a menswear buyer for the same department store after you graduate is a career. Similarly, being a teller at your neighborhood bank is a job; being a compensation and benefits manager in the bank's human resources department is a career, requiring college and graduate degrees as well as continual learning. Table 1.1 compares some of the major differences between jobs and careers.

When you enter a career, the more you turn your focus to the *how* of learning, the more you will become a strategic learner, a person who sees learning as a way to grow.

How Do You Become a Strategic Learner?

If *strategy* is "a plan of action designed to accomplish a specific goal," *strategic learners* learn in a focused way, becoming actively engaged in new learning situations that will help lead them toward their goals. Working alone—and with others—they use their current knowledge to solve problems. They also monitor their field to discover information gaps and then set out to fill those gaps quickly and correctly.

Important differences between a job and a career. **TABLE 1.1**

QUESTIONS YOU MAY ASK	POSSIBLE ANSWERS FOR YOUR JOB	POSSIBLE ANSWERS FOR YOUR CAREER
What are my short-term goals?	To earn money to pay bills and buy extras	To earn money for necessities and luxuries; to learn basic career skills; to meet people in my field; to develop interpersonal communication skills
What are my long-term goals?	None	To define my specific career interests and path; to continue to learn about new technologies and other changes that impact my field; to develop my interpersonal, communication, and managerial skills; to advance to higher level positions that pay more and are more challenging
Will my success depend on continued learning?	No	Yes, because no matter what career path I choose, I will be expected to keep up my knowledge and skills to help my organization remain competitive
What financial success can I expect?	Minimum wage, or close to it, with limited chance for a major increase	The sky is the limit, depending on my goals and dreams, motivation, talents, and continued learning
Will I be satisfied with my work?	Probably not, although I will appreciate my weekly paycheck	I may be very satisfied if I choose the right career path and work to meet my potential

Why is strategic learning helpful? On the one hand, *not* learning strategically—that is, learning only what is required by your major or job description, and not actively making plans about how to continue your learning—can be problematic. You may find that you aren't prepared to move into a field that you want, or that you are stuck at a particular level in a field you have already entered. You may find that your skills are suddenly out-of-date or not needed. This can have negative affects on your finances, lifestyle, self-image, motivation, and more.

On the other hand, strategic learning will help you to make the most of your valuable time and effort. If you continually seek information about what you want and need to learn, and make plans for how you will learn it, your skills and knowledge are likely to be in demand. Workers who are wanted and needed are happier, more motivated, and more creative.

By developing strategic learning skills and attitudes and examining obstacles to strategic learning, you increase your chances of success in your college studies and in your career.

DEVELOP STRATEGIC SKILLS AND ATTITUDES

According to psychologists and authors Claire Ellen Weinstein and Laura M. Hume, strategic learners have the *will and self-awareness* to learn, the *skill* to accomplish their goals, and the *self-regulation* to monitor their progress.[6]

THE WILL AND SELF-AWARENESS TO LEARN. This attitude links the desire to make effective learning skills part of your life with knowledge of personal strengths and weaknesses. In this area, strategic learners:

- *Value effective study skills and strategies* and see their connection to life success. Through this book, you will learn all kinds of strategies, from which you can choose the ones that suit you best. You will also learn that your efforts are not wasted as you discover how your skills will serve you far beyond the classroom.

- *Have the self-esteem and confidence to believe that they can learn effective study methods.* Self-esteem underpins all of your achievements (see the section on self-esteem later in this chapter).

- *Have analyzed their personal learning styles* and pinpointed appropriate study methods. In Chapter 2, when you analyze your learning style (your particular way of taking in and retaining information), you will explore study techniques that tap into your strengths as well as strategies to help you build your weaker areas.

THE SKILL TO ACCOMPLISH STUDY GOALS. Strategic learners are good at what they do because of their focus on skill building. They:

- *Develop effective study and learning strategies* and apply these strategies to the work they do in college.

- *Recognize that critical thinking is the foundation for effective studying.* The heart of critical thinking is questioning information. Strategic learners solve complex problems by asking the right questions and searching for solutions. Although it may sound complicated, critical thinking is something you do already, every day. You will explore critical thinking in detail in Chapter 4.

- *Welcome the input of others*—classmates, team members, and coworkers—to gather and study information and come up with creative solutions. They understand that studying and problem solving with others is crucial to their success.

- *Use technology to aid their studying,* including computers for word processing and data analysis and the Internet for research and instant communication.

- *Know how to prepare effectively for exams* to show themselves and others what they know.

THE SELF-REGULATION TO MONITOR AND MANAGE THE PERSONAL LEARNING PROCESS. Self-regulation means knowing where you are in relation to your goals and being able to make mid-course corrections if you get off track. Here strategic learners are able to:

- *Define specific short- and long-term goals* and manage their time in order to complete their work on schedule. Chapter 3 explains how to define and achieve goals and how to manage time effectively.
- *Evaluate how well they do in achieving their study goals* by being receptive to feedback from instructors, employers, and exams. Opening your mind to the perceptions of others will help you grow and learn.

EXAMINE OBSTACLES TO STRATEGIC LEARNING

Different parts of your internal environment (e.g., attitudes, state of mind, stress level, mental and physical health) and external environment (e.g., physical surroundings, family and friends, responsibilities) may affect your ability to become an effective strategic learner. Everyone experiences such obstacles—your task is to address them, considering how to overcome them in order to achieve your learning goals.

The following statements will help you develop a general picture of whether any internal or external obstacles are getting in your way. For each statement rate yourself on a scale of 1 to 5, with 1 meaning "absolutely not" and 5 meaning "absolutely yes."

____ You are aware of your personal learning style, and you tailor your study skills to take advantage of your strengths and minimize your weaknesses.

____ You have made a commitment to lifelong learning, feeling that knowledge will enrich your career and life in the years ahead.

____ You see the connection between the effective study skills you learn today and your career success.

____ You set effective short- and long-term study goals that will help you manage your workload.

____ You manage your time effectively and control your tendency to procrastinate.

____ You are taking steps to reduce study stress by coming up with ways to deal with family demands and work responsibilities that get in the way of your study efforts.

____ You understand the components of critical thinking and use critical-thinking skills to get the most from your work.

____ You take a systematic approach to reading, learning and mastering technical content, listening and memory, note taking, research, writing, and test taking that will enable you to get the best results.

Whatever your answers to these questions, know that you will uncover approaches and solutions in this text that will help you develop your strategic-learning ability. The questions simply give you an overview of your starting point; with that knowledge, it will be easier to determine where you need to go. To begin, you may find some helpful information in the following success strategies.

How Can You Get Ready to Study?

Striving for success in your studies takes effort. It requires motivation, commitment, responsibility, self-esteem, and teamwork. Furthermore, it depends on your ability to embrace change. How you approach studying helps you to gather and retain knowledge today and in the years ahead.

GET MOTIVATED

Motivation refers to the process of being moved to action by a want or need. Such wants or needs are called *motives* or *motivators*. Some are biological (food, shelter), some are psychological and social (achievement, connection with others, autonomy), some are external (money, power), and some are internal (creativity, self-improvement, personal fulfillment).

Each person has his or her own unique set of motivators. Furthermore, what motivates any given person can change from situation to situation or even from day to day. For example, pressing financial needs might motivate you to choose a major that is linked to a lucrative career area. Later, as you progress in your major and find that you really like one particular area, a need for personal fulfillment might motivate you to specialize in that area. When a close family experiences a health emergency, the need to stay connected with that person might even motivate you to put academic progress on hold while you attend to your family situation.

Motivation is a key ingredient in fulfilling goals. It requires energy to build and maintain, and it can falter from time to time. How can you build motivation or renew lost motivation?

- *Spend time reflecting on why your goal is meaningful to you.* Remind yourself about what you wanted and why that goal is still important.

- *Make a decision to take one step toward your goal.* Sometimes feeling overwhelmed by a goal immobilizes you. Don't worry about tomorrow. Focus on the step you can take today.

- *Examine and deal with your obstacles.* What's getting in your way? Decide to examine and remove your obstacles. For example, if health issues are distracting you from your studies, schedule an appointment with your doctor.

- *Begin or begin again.* Open that book or start that assignment. If you can just get yourself started, you'll feel better. A law of physics,

Newton's first law of motion, says that things in motion tend to stay in motion and things at rest tend to stay at rest. *Be a thing in motion.*

For example, to pass an early-morning writing class that you've already failed once, you decide to implement particular strategies. First, you promise yourself that you will go to every class and turn in your work on time. Second, you make a commitment to write daily in a journal. Finally, you promise yourself a reward if you get at least a B minus in the course. Your motivation centers around self-improvement and financial security: Passing this course is necessary to continue your education, and the writing skills you learn will help you get a good job when you graduate.

MAKE A COMMITMENT

How do you focus the energy of motivation? Make a commitment. Commitment means that you do what you say you will do. When you honor a commitment, you prove to yourself and others that your intentions can be trusted. A committed person follows through on a promise.

Commitment requires that you set goals that are *specific* and *realistic*. For example, a vague and far-reaching decision to ace every course in your major might intimidate you into staying motionless on the couch. However, a decision to get a B or above in a specific course, or to pass every course in a particular semester, might be more realistic. Break any goal into manageable pieces, naming the steps you will use to achieve it. Chapter 3 provides more information about successful goal setting.

How do you go about making and keeping a commitment?

- *State your commitment concretely.* It's hard to commit to something by saying "I'm going to pass this course" because you haven't set yourself clear tasks. Be specific: "I'm going to turn in the weekly essay assignments on time."

- *Get started and note your progress.* The long road of commitment can tire you out. Looking for improvements along the way, no matter how small, can keep you going.

- *Renew your commitment regularly.* You're not a failure if you lose steam in a few weeks or even a few days; it's normal. Recharge by reflecting on the positive effects of your commitment and what you have already achieved.

- *Keep track of your commitment.* Find ways to remind yourself of your commitments. Keep a list of them in your date book or on your computer. Talk about your commitments with friends and family.

For example, you might make this commitment: "I will write in my journal every night before going to sleep." You make journal entries for two weeks, then evaluate what positive affects this daily practice has had on your writing ability. You might boost your commitment by telling a partner or housemate to check on you.

Making and keeping your commitments helps you keep a steady focus on your most important goals. It gives you a sense of accomplishment as you experience gradual growth and progress.

BE RESPONSIBLE

Being responsible is all about living up to your obligations, those that are imposed on you as well as those that you impose on yourself. Through action, you prove that you are responsible, or "response-able," able to respond. When something needs to be done, a responsible person does the work—as efficiently as possible and to the best of his or her ability.

Responsibility has definite benefits. For one, you make a crucial impression on others. You earn the trust of your instructors, supervisors, relatives, and friends. People who trust you may give you increasing responsibility and opportunities for growth because you have shown you are capable of making the best of both. Trust builds relationships, which in turn feed progress and success. Even more important is the self-respect that emerges when you prove that you can live up to your promises.

When you complete class assignments on time or correct errors, you demonstrate responsibility. You don't have to take on the world to show how responsible you can be. Responsibility shows in basic everyday actions: attending class, turning in work on time, and being true to your word.

When you use your motivation, commitment, and responsibility to take action, you promote healthy self-esteem.

BUILD SELF-ESTEEM

Often, a strong belief in their value and capabilities can help lead people toward their goals. Belief, though, is only half the game. The other half is action and effort to help you feel that you have *earned* your self-esteem. Rick Pitino discusses the necessity of earning self-esteem in his book *Success Is a Choice:* "Self-esteem is directly linked to deserving success. If you have established a great work ethic and have begun the discipline that is inherent with that, you will automatically begin to feel better about yourself."[7] Building self-esteem, therefore, involves both thinking positively and taking action.

Think Positively

Attitudes influence your choices and affect how you perceive and relate to others. A positive attitude can open your mind to learning experiences and inspire you to take action. One•of the ways to create a positive attitude is through positive self-talk. When you hear negative thoughts in your mind, "I'm not very smart," replace them with positive ones, "It won't be easy, but I'm smart enough to figure it out." Try to talk to yourself as if you were talking to someone you care a lot about. The following hints will help you put positive self-talk into action:

- *Stop negative talk in its tracks and change it to positive talk.* If you catch yourself thinking, "I can never write a decent paper," stop and say to yourself, "I can do better than that and next time I will." Then think about some specific steps you can take to improve your writing.

- *Replace words of obligation—which rob you of power—with words of personal intent.*

  | I should | *becomes* | I choose to |
  | I'll try | *becomes* | I will |

  Words of intent give you power and control because they imply a personal decision to act.

- *Note your successes.* Even when you don't think you are at your best, congratulate yourself on any positive steps. Whether you do well on a paper, get to class on time all week, or have fewer mistakes on this week's paper than last week's, each success helps you believe in yourself.

It can be very difficult to think positively. If you have a deep-rooted feeling of unworthiness, you may want to see a counselor. Many people have benefited from skilled professional advice.

Take Action

Although thinking positively sets the tone for success, it cannot get you there by itself. You must give those positive thoughts life and support by taking action. Without action, positive thoughts can become empty statements or even lies.

Consider, for example, a student in a freshman composition class. This student thinks every possible positive thought: "I am a great student. I can get a B in this class. I will succeed in school." And so on. Then, throughout the semester, this student misses about one-third of the class meetings and turns in some of her papers late. At the end of the course, when she barely passes the class, she wonders how things went so wrong when she had such a positive attitude.

This student did not succeed because she did not earn her belief in herself through action and effort. You cannot maintain this belief unless you give yourself something to believe *in*. By the end of a semester like this, positive thoughts look like lies. "If I am such a great student, why did I barely make it through this course?" Eventually, with no support, the positive thoughts disappear, and with neither positive thoughts nor action, you will have a hard time achieving any level of success.

Positive thoughts are like seeds. Don't just scatter them on the soil: take action—plant them, water them, and feed them, and they will grow and be fruitful. Here are some ways to get yourself moving:

- *Make action plans.* Be specific about how you plan to take action for any given situation. Figure out exactly what you will do, so that "I am a great student" is backed up by specific actions to ensure success. Then, once you decide on your action, use your energy to just do it.
- *Build your own code of discipline.* To provide a framework for the specific actions you plan to take, develop a general plan to follow, based on what actions are important to your success. Construct each day's individual goals and actions so that they help you achieve your larger objectives.
- *Acknowledge every step.* Even the smallest action is worth your attention because every action reinforces a positive thought and builds self-esteem.

The process of building and maintaining self-esteem isn't easy for anyone. Only by having a true sense of self-esteem, though, can you achieve what you dream. Make the choice to both believe in yourself and take the actions that anchor and inspire that belief.

Self-esteem is a large part of what enables you to relate to others comfortably and successfully. With a strong sense of self-worth, you will be able to develop productive relationships with the diverse people that are an increasing part of your world.

BUILD TEAMWORK SKILLS

Think of the path of your accomplishments, and you will find that rarely do you achieve anything using only your own efforts. Your success at school and at work depends on your ability to cooperate in a team setting—to communicate, share tasks, and develop a common vision.

- You deal with the challenges of day-to-day life in a *family/community team*, with the help of parents, siblings, relatives, and friends.
- You achieve work goals in a *work team*, with supervisors, coworkers, and consultants.
- You learn, complete projects, and pass courses as part of an *educational team*, with instructors, fellow students, tutors, administrators, and advisors.

Teams gain strength from the diversity of their members. In fact, diversity is an asset in a team. Consider a study group for a particular course. Each person has a different style of note taking and a different perspective, but by combining their abilities the students can build a knowledge base that they would not have been able to achieve alone. The more diverse the team members, the greater the chance that new ideas and solutions will surface, increasing the chances of solving problems.

Chapter 12 will go into more detail about how to effectively study with others and why working in a group will benefit you. Also, at the end of each part, a teamwork exercise will help to build your communication, coopera-

EXPERT INSIGHT

A century ago, most people in the United States had jobs on farms or in factories. They worked with their hands and their backs. Today, most people aren't engaged in this kind of physical labor. They work with ideas and symbols in what has become an information revolution. The twenty-first century economy will reflect this shift in the basic definition of work. The value of workers today lies in their thinking rather than in their movement.

JOHN MACIONIS, PROFESSOR OF SOCIOLOGY, KENYON COLLEGE

Redefine Work in the Information Age

tion, and critical-thinking skills as you work with others to accomplish a goal. In the meantime, as you begin to get to know the students in your classes and begin to work with them in particular situations, use these strategies to maximize team success:

- Open your mind and accept that different team members have valuable roles and that no one person can do everything alone.
- Be assertive about sharing your opinions and ideas—you are as valuable as anyone else on your team, and your input is important.
- Welcome the new information and ideas that others offer. Hold off on judgments until you have taken the time to listen carefully and consider the possibilities.
- Know yourself; choose ways to contribute to the team that make the most of your strengths.
- Evaluate any idea based on how it improves a situation instead of focusing on the person who had the idea. Successful teams use what works, no matter who came up with the suggestion.

Diversity is a theme that touches every part of your life, including your education. This book addresses student diversity by presenting examples that suit different study styles and needs.

The focus on diversity is one side effect of the enormous changes going on today. Constant change is one of the few givens of modern life.

EMBRACE CHANGE

As Russian-born author Isaac Asimov said, "It is change, continuing change, inevitable change, that is the dominant factor in society today. No sensible decision can be made any longer without taking into account not only the world as it is, but the world as it will be."[8] Change will often throw you for a loop with little or no warning. As you saw earlier in the chapter, you cannot stop change from happening, but you can embrace change through awareness and by making active, conscious choices about how to handle the changes that come your way. Be an *agent of change* so that you can benefit and grow from it rather than being trampled by it.

Being an agent of change means being aware of change, adjusting to what it brings, and sometimes even causing change yourself. Every choice now will affect what happens down the road—and, conversely, you can trace what happens to you back to actions taken (or not taken) in the past. Start now to be in charge of your choices.

For example, say that your school is planning to cancel a number of sections of a course that you need, which would result in your not being able to take the course in time for graduation. You could be a *victim* of change—you could take the class another time, figure you'll have to graduate later, and suffer other consequences of the change such as putting off full-time employment. Or, you can be an *agent* of change by speaking to your academic advisor about using another class to fulfill this requirement, gathering students who need the class and petitioning to keep those sections open, or finding an internship that will substitute for the class. In this way you have made the most of change.

Whether you have experienced tough changes or not, actively causing a particular change may help you. Consider how you might benefit from a different class or change of major, a change of living location, or any other change, large or small. Finally, seek continual change and improvement in your education. Take to heart this quote from a student in Mississippi: "Without an education in the year 2000, we the people will be in serious trouble. Because now everything is moving forward fast and without an education you will be moving nowhere."[9] Let your ability to make change happen keep you on the move in college and in your career. Remember, as a lifelong learner, you're in charge of your present and your future. Make the most of it.

In Chinese writing, this character has two meanings: One is "chaos"; the other is "opportunity." The character communicates the belief that every challenging, chaotic, and demanding situation in life also presents an opportunity. By responding to challenges in a positive and active way, you can discover the opportunity that lies within the chaos.

Let this concept reassure you as you begin college—either as a recent high school graduate or a student returning later in life. You may feel that you are going through a time of chaos and change. Remember that no matter how difficult the obstacles, you have the ability to persevere. By building your study skills and preparing to use them throughout your education and career, you can take advantage of every opportunity that comes your way.

Study Skills in Action

Test Competence

MEASURING WHAT YOU'VE LEARNED

MULTIPLE CHOICE. *Circle or highlight the answer that seems to fit best.*

1. Some reasons that lifelong learning is valuable to you include
   A. higher expectations and increasing numbers of students.
   B. the product-and-service-based economy and inflation.
   C. growth of knowledge and advances in technology.
   D. higher life expectancy and new medical advances.

2. In the current working world, many companies operate with a strong focus on
   A. building employee self-esteem and financial know-how.
   B. retaining and promoting employees.
   C. the manager-subordinate and worker-to-worker relationships.
   D. collaborative teams and continuing education.

3. According to Weinstein and Hume, part of being a strategic learner is
   A. having the will and the self-awareness to learn.
   B. knowing both facts and opinions.
   C. planning ahead and shifting career goals.
   D. teamwork and trusting those around you.

4. Internal obstacles to learning may include
   A. instructors.
   B. study environment.
   C. noise and activity.
   D. stress level.

5. Some skills that strategic learners focus on, as reported by Weinstein and Hume, include
   A. self-esteem and being able to think positively.
   B. welcoming the input of others and preparing effectively for exams.
   C. learning styles and being able to relate well to others.
   D. understanding work hierarchies and knowing the difference between a job and a career.

6. A *motivator* is
   A. the ability to achieve a goal.
   B. progress toward a goal.
   C. a decision to move toward a goal.
   D. a want or need that moves a person to action.

7. The direct benefits of responsibility include
   A. earning the trust of others at school, work, and home.
   B. getting motivated to achieve study goals.
   C. improved ability to plan strategically.
   D. moving up at work.

8. According to Rick Pitino, the two primary aspects of *self-esteem* are
   A. thinking positively and positive self-talk.
   B. getting motivated and taking action.
   C. noting successes and using words of personal intent.
   D. thinking positively and taking action.

9. Team success strategies do **not** include
   A. welcoming new information and ideas that others offer.
   B. evaluating an idea without focusing on the person who offered it.
   C. accepting that different team members have valuable roles.
   D. using the same team members every time.

10. Being an *agent of change* means
    A. trying to reduce the amount of change in your daily life.
    B. staying aware of change, adjusting to it, and sometimes causing it.
    C. noting when change happens and thinking critically about it.
    D. working for the government in an official capacity.

TRUE/FALSE. *Place a T or an F beside each statement to indicate whether you think it is true or false.*

1. _____ Most of today's workers will remain in one job for their working lives.

2. _____ Study skills you learn and use at school will help you keep up with new developments in the workplace.

3. _____ A job is another word for a career.

4. _____ Making a commitment focuses the energy of motivation.

5. _____ Words of intent like "I choose" and "I will" imply a personal decision to act.

Brain Power

BUILDING VOCABULARY FITNESS

The paragraphs below are taken from the current media. Read the paragraphs, noting the context of the vocabulary words shown in bold type. Next, for each vocabulary word (reprinted in the left-hand column), highlight the word or phrase in column A, B, or C that is the most similar in meaning. Finally, on a separate sheet of paper, solidify your understanding of these words by using each in a sentence of your own.

When the Supreme Court **confronted** its first Internet case three years ago, the justices received special training from their library staff. The lessons "helped assure each of us that we knew how to use the Net and understood the technical matters at issue," Justice Stephen G. Breyer recalled a few weeks ago at a **symposium** on biomedical research in Cambridge, Mass.

Thus empowered, the Court went on in that case, *Reno v. American Civil Liberties Union*, to produce a **unanimous** decision that struck down the Communications Decency Act on First Amendment **grounds** and established the **primacy** of free speech **principles** in cyberspace.

From "Microsoft Will Test Justices' Prowess" by Linda Greenhouse, *The New York Times*, Sunday, June 4, 2000, BU 1.

Vocabulary Words	A	B	C
1. **confronted**	encountered	fought	instituted
2. **symposium**	group	course	colloquium
3. **unanimous**	inconclusive	diverse	agreeing
4. **grounds**	lawn	basis	argument
5. **primacy**	superiority	strength	role
6. **principles**	rules	rulers	concepts

Strategic Thinking

GETTING THE BIG PICTURE

Answer the following questions on a separate piece of paper or in a journal.

Consider how change has affected your life. What is the biggest change that has happened to you in the past year? What effects did it have on your studies, job, and personal life? How did you respond? Do you feel your response was appropriate or would you do it differently if you had it to do all over again? Finally, what changes do you most need to make to be the best-qualified student while at this institution? To be the best job applicant when you leave?

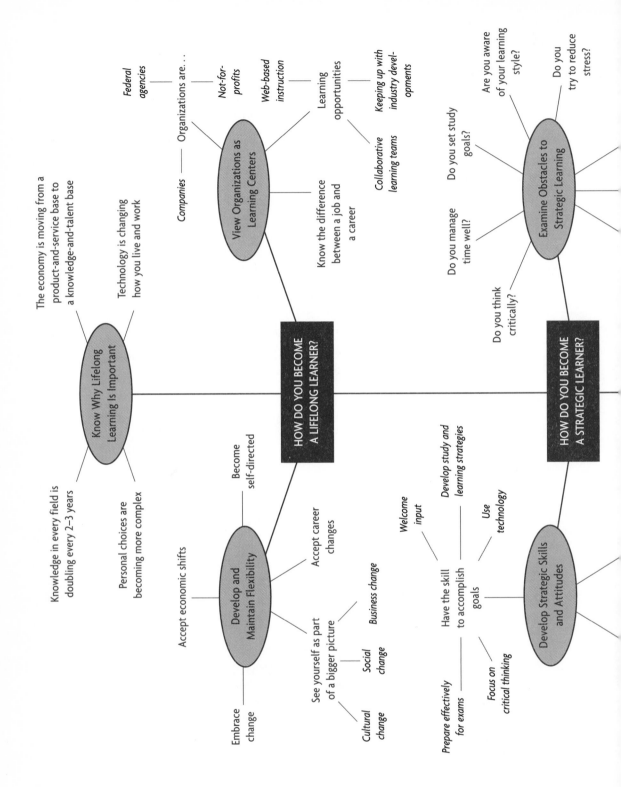

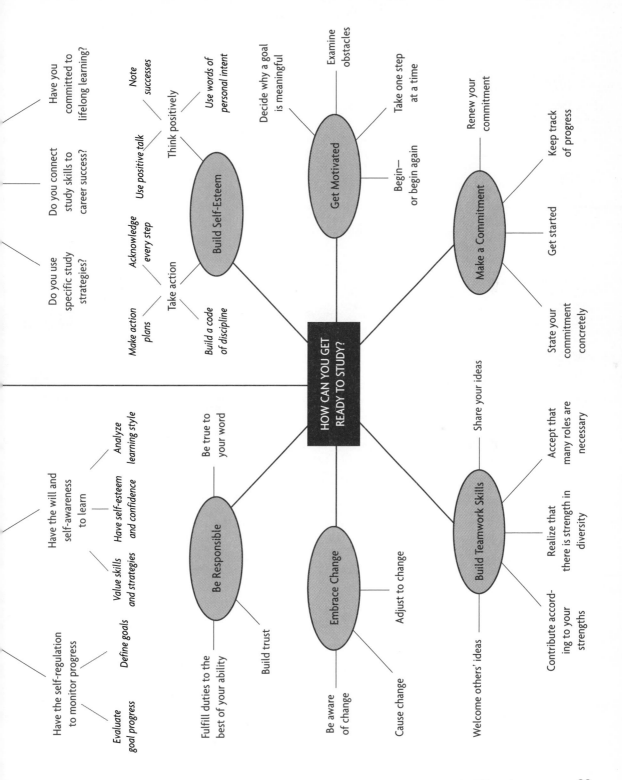

The ability to learn is much more than a college skill. Being a learner for life means that you are able to learn who you are and define what you want, keep pace with rapidly changing workplace technology, stay aware of world developments and how they affect you, and continue to grow as a person. To learn effectively you must understand *how* you learn. The more you know about your learning style, the better prepared you will be to choose a career that makes the most of who you are and what you can do.

This chapter introduces you to two different personal assessments—one focusing on how you take in information, and one that helps you determine how you interact with others. At the end of the chapter, you will be able to answer these questions:

- Is there one best way to learn?
- What are the benefits of knowing your learning style?
- How can you discover your learning style?
- How will knowing your learning style help you in your career?

LEARNING STYLES AND SELF-AWARENESS
KNOWING WHO YOU ARE AND HOW YOU LEARN

> *"To be what we are, and to become what we are capable of becoming, is the only end of life."*
>
> **Robert Louis Stevenson**

Is There One Best Way to Learn?

Your mind is the most powerful tool you will ever possess. You are accomplished at many skills and can process all kinds of information. However, when you have trouble accomplishing a particular task, you may become convinced that you can't learn how to do anything new. Not only is this perception incorrect, it can also damage your belief in yourself.

Every individual is highly developed in some abilities and underdeveloped in others. Many famously successful people were brilliant in one area but functioned poorly in other areas. Winston Churchill failed the sixth grade. Abraham Lincoln was demoted to a private in the Black Hawk war. Louis Pasteur was a poor student in chemistry. Walt Disney was fired from a job and told he had no good ideas. What some might interpret as a deficiency or disability may be simply a different method of learning. People have their own individual gifts—the key is to identify them.

There is no one "best" way to learn. Instead, there are many different *learning styles*—ways in which the mind receives and processes information—each suited to different situations. Each person's learning style is unique. Knowing how you learn is one of the first steps in discovering who you are. Before you explore your learning style, consider how the knowledge you will gain can help you.

What Are the Benefits of Knowing Your Learning Style?

Although it takes some work and exploration, understanding your learning style can benefit you in many ways—in your independent studies as well as in the classroom. Later in the chapter you will explore workplace benefits.

STUDY BENEFITS

Most students aim to maximize learning while minimizing frustration and time spent studying. If you know your strengths and limitations, you can use techniques that take advantage of your highly developed areas while helping you through the less developed ones. For example, say you perform better in smaller, discussion-based classes. When you have the opportunity, you might choose a course section that is smaller or that is taught by an instructor who prefers group discussion. You might also apply specific strategies to improve your retention in a large-group lecture situation.

Following each of the two assessments, you will see information about study techniques that complement the strengths and shortcomings of each intelligence or spectrum. Remember that you have abilities in all areas, even though some are dominant. Therefore, you may see useful suggestions under any of the headings. What's important is that you use what works. During this course, try a large number of new study techniques, eventually keeping those you find useful.

CLASSROOM BENEFITS

Knowing your learning style can help you make the most of your instructors' teaching styles. Your particular learning style may work better with the way some instructors teach and be a mismatch with other instructors. Once you understand the various teaching styles you encounter, you can make adjustments that maximize your learning (remember that an instructor's teaching style often reflects his learning style). After perhaps two class meetings, you can make a pretty good assessment of teaching styles (instructors may exhibit more than one). See Figure 2.1 for some common styles.

Assess how well your own styles match up with the teaching styles. If your styles mesh well with an instructor's teaching styles, you're in luck. If not, you have a number of options.

Students learn better when they know their learning style and adjust their note-taking style to it. For example, when a visual learner is presented with organizational sequences during a class lecture, he can graph the information instead of using more conventional notes. Taking notes according to your learning style helps you process information—when you hear it for the first time and when you go back to study it later on.

ANDREA WORRELL, ITT INSTITUTE

EXPERT INSIGHT

Link Your Note-Taking Style to Your Learning Style

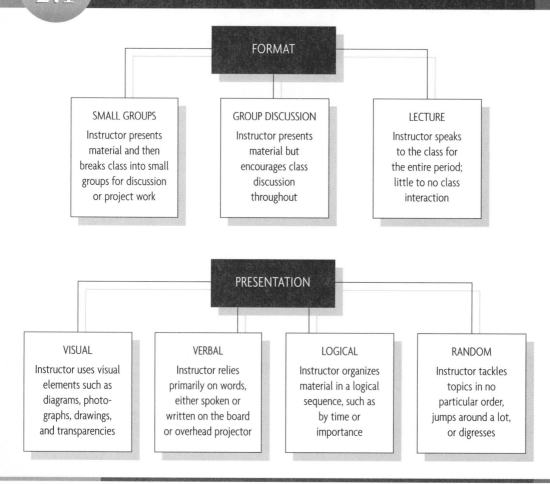

YOU CAN BRING EXTRA FOCUS TO YOUR WEAKER AREAS. Although it's not easy, working on your weaker points can help you break new ground in your learning. For example, if you're a verbal person in a math- and logic-oriented class, increase your focus and concentration during class so that you get as much as you can from the presentation. Then you can spend extra study time on the material, ask others from your class to help you, and search for additional supplemental materials and exercises that might reinforce your knowledge.

YOU CAN ASK YOUR INSTRUCTOR FOR ADDITIONAL HELP. For example, a visual person might ask an instructor to recommend visuals that would help to illustrate the points made in class. If the class breaks into smaller groups, you might ask the instructor to divide those groups roughly according to learning style, so that students with similar strengths can help each other.

YOU CAN "CONVERT" CLASS MATERIAL DURING STUDY TIME.   For example, an interpersonal learner takes a class with an instructor who presents big-picture information in lecture format. This student might organize study groups and, in those groups, focus on filling in the factual gaps using reading materials assigned for that class. Likewise, a visual student might rewrite notes in different colors to add a visual element—for example, assigning a different color to each main point or topic, or using one color for central ideas, another for supporting examples.

Instructors are as individual as students. Taking time to focus on their teaching styles, and on how to adjust, will help you learn more effectively and avoid frustration. Don't forget to take advantage of your instructor's office hours when you have a learning style issue that is causing you difficulty.

Now that you know you have something to gain, look at some ways you can explore your particular learning style.

How Can You Discover Your Learning Style?

Many different kinds of assessments give people a method of self-discovery, providing different means of exploring strengths and weaknesses, abilities and limitations. This chapter contains one each of two particular types—learning-style assessments and personality assessments.

Learning-style assessments focus on the process by which you take in, retain, and use information. Students may use learning-style assessment results to maximize study efficiency and to choose courses that suit their styles. Personality assessments indicate how you respond to both internal and external situations—in other words, how you react to thoughts and feelings as well as to people and events. Employers may give such assessments to employees and use the results to set up and evaluate teams.

The learning-style assessment in this chapter is called *Pathways to Learning* and is based on the Multiple Intelligences Theory. It can help you determine how you best take in information as well as how you can improve the areas where you have trouble learning. Immediately following *Pathways to Learning*, you will find the *Personality Spectrum*, a personality assessment that helps you evaluate how you react to people and situations in your life. *Pathways to Learning* and the *Personality Spectrum* provide two different perspectives that together give you a more complete picture of how you interact with everything you encounter—information, people, and your own inner thoughts.

MULTIPLE INTELLIGENCES THEORY

There is a saying "It is not how smart you are, but how you are smart." In 1983, Howard Gardner, a Harvard University professor, changed the way people perceive intelligence and learning with his theory of Multiple Intelligences. Gardner believes there are at least eight distinct intelligences possessed by all people, and that every person has developed some intelligences more fully than others. An intelligence, according to Gardner, is an ability to solve problems or fashion products that are useful in a particular cultural setting or community. Most people have at one time learned something quickly and comfortably. Most have also had the opposite experience: no matter how hard they try, something they want to learn just won't sink in. According to the Multiple Intelligences Theory, when you find a task or subject easy, you are probably using a more fully developed intelligence; when you have more trouble, you may be using a less developed intelligence.[1]

Table 2.1 has brief descriptions of the focus of each of the intelligences. You will find information on related skills and study techniques on page 33. The *Pathways to Learning* assessment helps you determine the levels to which your intelligences are developed.

TABLE 2.1 *Multiple intelligences.*

INTELLIGENCE	DESCRIPTION
Verbal–Linguistic	Ability to communicate through language (listening, reading, writing, speaking)
Logical–Mathematical	Ability to understand logical reasoning and problem solving (math, science, patterns, sequences)
Bodily–Kinesthetic	Ability to use the physical body skillfully and to take in knowledge through bodily sensation (coordination, working with hands)
Visual–Spatial	Ability to understand spatial relations and to perceive and create images (visual art, graphic design, charts and maps)
Interpersonal	Ability to relate to others, noticing their moods, motivations, and feelings (social activity, cooperative learning, teamwork)
Intrapersonal	Ability to understand one's own behavior and feelings (self-awareness, independence, time spent alone)
Musical	Ability to comprehend and create meaningful sound (music, sensitivity to sound, understanding patterns)
Naturalistic	Ability to understand features of the environment (interest in nature, environmental balance, ecosystem, stress relief brought by natural environments)

PERSONALITY SPECTRUM

One of the first instruments to measure psychological types, the Myers-Briggs Type Indicator® (MBTI), was designed by Katharine Briggs and her daughter, Isabel Briggs Myers. Later, David Keirsey and Marilyn Bates combined the 16 Myers-Briggs types into four temperaments and developed an assessment, based on those temperaments, called the Keirsey Sorter. These assessments are two of the most widely used personality tests, both in psychology and in the business world.

The *Personality Spectrum* assessment in this chapter can help you better understand yourself and those around you. Based on the Myers-Briggs and Keirsey theories, the assessment adapts and simplifies their material into four personality types—Thinker, Organizer, Giver, and Adventurer—and was developed by Joyce Bishop (1997).[2] The *Personality Spectrum* gives you a personality perspective on how you can maximize your functioning at school and at work. Each personality type has its own abilities that improve work and school performance, suitable learning techniques, and ways of relating in interpersonal relationships. Page 35 gives you more details about each type.

USING THE ASSESSMENTS

The two assessments follow this section of text. After each assessment, you will find a page that details the traits of each dimension and offers strategies to help students make the most of that dimension's tendencies.

Complete both assessments, trying to answer the questions objectively—in other words, mark the answers that best indicate who you are, not who you want to be. The closer you can see yourself today, the more effectively you can set goals for where you want to go from here. Then, enter your scores on p. 36, where you will see a brain diagram on which to plot *Personality Spectrum* scores and boxes in which to enter your *Pathways to Learning* scores. This page is organized so that you can see your scores for both assessments at a glance, giving you an opportunity to examine how they relate to one another. Don't be concerned if some of your scores are low—that is true for most everyone. For *Pathways to Learning*, 21–24 indicates a high level of development, 15–20 a moderate level, and below 15 an underdeveloped intelligence. For the *Personality Spectrum*, 26–36 indicates a strong tendency in that dimension, 14–25 a moderate tendency, and below 14 a minimal tendency.

Knowing how you learn will help you to improve your understanding of yourself—how you may function at school, in the workplace, and in your personal life. Keep in mind that these or any other assessments are intended not to label you, but to be *indicators* of who you are. Your thinking skills—your ability to evaluate sources of information—will best enable you to see yourself as a whole, including both gifts and areas for growth. Your job is to verify and sift each piece of information and arrive at the most accurate portrait of yourself at this point in time.

Developed by Joyce Bishop, Ph.D., and based upon Howard Gardner's *Frames of Mind: The Theory of Multiple Intelligences.*

Directions: Rate each statement as follows:
Write the number of your response (1–4) on the line
next to the statement and total each set of six questions.

rarely   sometimes   usually   always
1   2   3   4

1. _____ I enjoy physical activities.
2. _____ I am uncomfortable sitting still.
3. _____ I prefer to learn through doing.
4. _____ When sitting I move my legs or hands.
5. _____ I enjoy working with my hands.
6. _____ I like to pace when I'm thinking or studying.
_____ **TOTAL for Bodily–Kinesthetic**

7. _____ I enjoy telling stories.
8. _____ I like to write.
9. _____ I like to read.
10. _____ I express myself clearly.
11. _____ I am good at negotiating.
12. _____ I like to discuss topics that interest me.
_____ **TOTAL for Verbal–Linguistic**

13. _____ I use maps easily.
14. _____ I draw pictures/diagrams when explaining ideas.
15. _____ I can assemble items easily from diagrams.
16. _____ I enjoy drawing or photography.
17. _____ I do not like to read long paragraphs.
18. _____ I prefer a drawn map over written directions.
_____ **TOTAL for Visual–Spatial**

19. _____ I like math in school.
20. _____ I like science.
21. _____ I problem solve well.
22. _____ I question how things work.
23. _____ I enjoy planning or designing something new.
24. _____ I am able to fix things.
_____ **TOTAL for Logical–Mathematical**

25. _____ I listen to music.
26. _____ I move my fingers or feet when I hear music.
27. _____ I have good rhythm.
28. _____ I like to sing along with music.
29. _____ People have said I have musical talent.
30. _____ I like to express my ideas through music.
_____ **TOTAL for Musical**

31. _____ I need quiet time to think.
32. _____ I think about issues before I want to talk.
33. _____ I am interested in self-improvement.
34. _____ I understand my thoughts and feelings.
35. _____ I know what I want out of life.
36. _____ I prefer to work on projects alone.
_____ **TOTAL for Intrapersonal**

37. _____ I like doing a project with other people.
38. _____ People come to me to help settle conflicts.
39. _____ I like to spend time with friends.
40. _____ I am good at understanding people.
41. _____ I am good at making people feel comfortable.
42. _____ I enjoy helping others.
_____ **TOTAL for Interpersonal**

43. _____ I enjoy nature whenever possible.
44. _____ I think about having a career involving nature.
45. _____ I enjoy studying plants, animals, or oceans.
46. _____ I avoid being indoors except when I sleep.
47. _____ As a child I played with bugs and leaves.
48. _____ When I feel stressed I want to be out in nature.
_____ **TOTAL for Naturalistic**

Adapted by Joyce Bishop, Ph.D., from *Seven Pathways of Learning*, David Lazear, © 1994.

SKILLS	STUDY TECHNIQUES
Verbal–Linguistic • Analyzing own use of language • Remembering terms easily • Explaining, teaching, learning, using humor • Understanding syntax and meaning of words • Convincing someone to do something	**Verbal–Linguistic** • Read text and highlight no more than 10 percent • Rewrite notes • Outline chapters • Teach someone else • Recite information or write scripts/debates
Musical–Rhythmic • Sensing tonal qualities • Creating or enjoying melodies and rhythms • Being sensitive to sounds and rhythms • Using "schemas" to hear music • Understanding the structure of music	**Musical–Rhythmic** • Create rhythms out of words • Beat out rhythms with hand or stick • Play instrumental music/write raps • Put new material to songs you already know • Take music breaks
Logical–Mathematical • Recognizing abstract patterns • Reasoning inductively and deductively • Discerning relationships and connections • Performing complex calculations • Reasoning scientifically	**Logical–Mathematical** • Organize material logically • Explain material sequentially to someone • Develop systems and find patterns • Write outlines and develop charts and graphs • Analyze information
Visual–Spatial • Perceiving and forming objects accurately • Recognizing relation between objects • Representing something graphically • Manipulating images • Finding one's way in space	**Visual–Spatial** • Develop graphic organizers for new material • Draw mind maps • Develop charts and graphs • Use color in notes to organize • Visualize material (method of loci)
Bodily–Kinesthetic • Connecting mind and body • Controlling movement • Improving body functions • Expanding body awareness to all senses • Coordinating body movement	**Bodily–Kinesthetic** • Move or rap while you learn; pace and recite • Use "method of loci" or manipulatives • Move fingers under words while reading • Create "living sculptures" • Act out scripts of material, design games
Intrapersonal • Evaluating own thinking • Being aware of and expressing feelings • Understanding self in relationship to others • Thinking and reasoning on higher levels	**Intrapersonal** • Reflect on personal meaning of information • Visualize information/keep a journal • Study in quiet settings • Imagine experiments
Interpersonal • Seeing things from others' perspectives • Cooperating within a group • Communicating verbally and nonverbally • Creating and maintaining relationships	**Interpersonal** • Study in a group • Discuss information • Use flash cards with others • Teach someone else
Naturalist • Deep understanding of nature • Appreciation of the delicate balance in nature	**Naturalistic** • Connect with nature whenever possible • Form study groups of people with like interests

STEP 1. Rank order all 4 responses to each question from most like you (4) to least like you (1). Place a 1, 2, 3, or 4 in each box next to the responses.

1. I like instructors who
   - a. ☐ tell me exactly what is expected of me.
   - b. ☐ make learning active and exciting.
   - c. ☐ maintain a safe and supportive classroom.
   - d. ☐ challenge me to think at higher levels.

2. I learn best when the material is
   - a. ☐ well organized.
   - b. ☐ something I can do hands-on.
   - c. ☐ about understanding and improving the human condition.
   - d. ☐ intellectually challenging.

3. A high priority in my life is to
   - a. ☐ keep my commitments.
   - b. ☐ experience as much of life as possible.
   - c. ☐ make a difference in the lives of others.
   - d. ☐ understand how things work.

4. Other people think of me as
   - a. ☐ dependable and loyal.
   - b. ☐ dynamic and creative.
   - c. ☐ caring and honest.
   - d. ☐ intelligent and inventive.

5. When I experience stress I would most likely
   - a. ☐ do something to help me feel more in control of my life.
   - b. ☐ do something physical and daring.
   - c. ☐ talk with a friend.
   - d. ☐ go off by myself and think about my situation.

6. I would probably not be close friends with someone who is
   - a. ☐ irresponsible.
   - b. ☐ unwilling to try new things.
   - c. ☐ selfish and unkind to others.
   - d. ☐ an illogical thinker.

7. My vacations could be described as
   - a. ☐ traditional.
   - b. ☐ adventuresome.
   - c. ☐ pleasing to others.
   - d. ☐ a new learning experience.

8. One word that best describes me is
   - a. ☐ sensible.
   - b. ☐ spontaneous.
   - c. ☐ giving.
   - d. ☐ analytical.

STEP 2. Add up the total points for each letter.

TOTAL for a. ☐ Organizer　TOTAL for c. ☐ Giver

TOTAL for b. ☐ Adventurer　TOTAL for d. ☐ Thinker

STEP 3. Plot these numbers on the brain diagram on page 36.

THINKER

Personal strengths—You enjoy solving problems and love to develop models and systems. You have an abstract and analytical way of thinking. You love to explore ideas. You dislike unfairness and wastefulness. You are global by nature, always seeking universal truth.

Work/school—You work best when assigned projects which require analytical thinking and problem solving. You are inspired by futuristic ideas and potentials. You need the freedom to go beyond the established rules. You feel appreciated when praised for your ingenuity. You dislike repetitive tasks.

Relationships—You thrive in relationships that recognize your need for independence and private time to think and read. Stress can come from the fear of appearing foolish. You want others to accept that you feel deeply even though you may not often express it.

Learning—You like quiet time to reflect on new information. Learning through problem solving and designing new ways of approaching issues is most interesting to you. You may find it effective to convert material you need to learn into logical charts and graphs.

ORGANIZER

Personal strengths—You value the traditions of family and support social structures. You never take responsibility lightly. You have a strong sense of history, culture, and dignity. You value order and predictability. You dislike disobedience or nonconformity. You value loyalty and obligation.

Work/school—You enjoy work that requires detailed planning and follow-through. You prefer to have tasks defined in clear and concrete terms. You need a well-structured, stable environment, free from abrupt changes. You feel appreciated when you are praised for neatness, organization, and efficiency. You like frequent feedback so you know you are on the right track.

Relationships—You do best in relationships that provide for your need of security, stability, and structure. You appreciate it when dates that are important to you are remembered by others.

Learning—You must have organization to the material and know the overall plan and what will be required of you. Depending on your most developed Multiple Intelligences, organizing the material could include any of the following: highlighting key terms in text, rewriting and organizing notes from class or text, making flash cards.

GIVER

Personal strengths—You value honesty and authenticity above all else. You enjoy close relationships with those you love and there is a strong spirituality in your nature. Making a difference in the world is important to you, and you enjoy cultivating potential in yourself and others. You are a person of peace. You are a natural romantic. You dislike hypocrisy and deception.

Work/school—You function best in a warm, harmonious working environment with the possibility of interacting with openness and honesty. You prefer to avoid conflict and hostility. You thrive when your creative approach to your work is appreciated and praised.

Relationships—You thrive in relationships that include warm, intimate talks. You feel closer to people when they express their feelings and are open and responsive. You think romance, touch, and appreciation are necessary for survival. You blossom when others express a loving commitment to you and you are able to contribute to the relationship.

Learning—You enjoy studying with others and also helping them learn. Study groups are very effective for you to remember difficult information.

ADVENTURER

Personal strengths—Your strength is skillfulness. You take pride in being highly skilled in a variety of fields. Adventure is your middle name. A hands-on approach to problem solving is important to you. You need variety, and waiting is like "emotional death." You live in the here and now. It is your impulsiveness that drives everything you do. You dislike rigidity and authority.

Work/school—You function best in a work environment that is action-packed with a hands-on approach. You appreciate the opportunity to be skillful and adventurous, and to use your natural ability as a negotiator. You like freedom on the job so you can perform in nontraditional ways and in your own style. Keeping a good sense of humor and avoiding boredom on the job is important to you. You feel appreciated when your performance and skills are acknowledged.

Relationships—You function best in relationships that recognize your need for freedom. You thrive on spontaneous playfulness and excitement.

Learning—You learn exciting and stimulating information easiest, so pick classes and instructors carefully. Study with fun people in a variety of ways and places. Keep on the move. Develop games and puzzles to help memorize terminology.

THINKER
Technical
Scientific
Mathematical
Dispassionate
Rational
Analytical
Logical
Problem Solving
Theoretical
Intellectual
Objective
Quantitative
Explicit
Realistic
Literal
Precise
Formal

ORGANIZER
Tactical
Planning
Detailed
Practical
Confident
Predictable
Controlled
Dependable
Systematic
Sequential
Structured
Administrative
Procedural
Organized
Conservative
Safekeeping
Disciplined

Directions: Place a dot on the appropriate number line for each of your four scores, connect the dots, and color the polygon. Write your scores in the four shaded boxes.

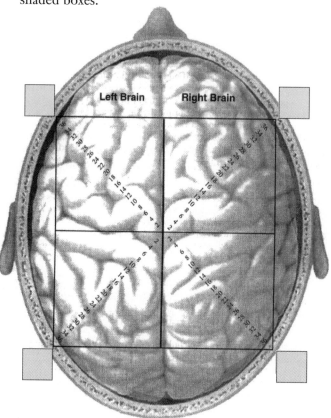

Left Brain   Right Brain

Source: *Understanding Psychology*, 3/e, by Morris, © 1996. Adapted by permission of Prentice-Hall, Inc., Upper Saddle River, NJ.

GIVER
Interpersonal
Emotional
Caring
Sociable
Giving
Spiritual
Musical
Romantic
Feeling
Peacemaker
Trusting
Adaptable
Passionate
Harmonious
Idealistic
Talkative
Honest

ADVENTURER
Active
Visual
Risking
Original
Artistic
Spatial
Skillful
Impulsive
Metaphoric
Experimental
Divergent
Fast-paced
Spontaneous
Competitive
Imaginative
Open-minded
Adventuresome

Pathways to Learning

From page 32, write your eight intelligences in the boxes, according to your total scores.

Scores: 21–24 = Highly Developed	15–20 = Moderately Developed	below 15 = Underdeveloped

PERSPECTIVE ON LEARNING STYLE

Both of the assessments provide you with self-knowledge that can help you manage yourself in school, at work, and at home in the most effective way possible. However, no one assessment can give you the final word on who you are and what you can and cannot do. It's human to want an easy answer—a one-page printout of the secret to your identity—but this kind of quick fix does not exist. You are a complex person who cannot be summed up by a test or evaluation.

Use Assessments for Reference

The most reasonable way to approach any assessment is as a reference point rather than as a label. There are no "right" answers, no "best" set of scores. Instead of boxing yourself into one or more categories, which limits you, approach any assessment as a tool with which you can expand your idea of yourself. Think of it as a new set of eyeglasses for a person with somewhat blurred vision. The glasses will not create new paths and possibilities for you, but they will make your view of the paths and possibilities that already exist clearer and give you the power to explore, choose, and act with confidence.

You continually learn, change, and grow throughout your life. Any evaluation is simply a snapshot, a look at who you are in a given moment. The answers can, and will, change as you change and as circumstances change. They provide an opportunity for you to identify a moment and learn from it by asking questions: Who am I right now? How does this compare to who I want to be?

Use Assessments for Understanding

Understanding your tendencies will help you understand yourself. Avoid narrowly labeling yourself by using one intelligence or personality type, such as saying, "I'm no good in math" or "I'm never a thinker." Anyone can learn math; however, some people learn math more efficiently through intelligences other than logical–mathematical. For example, a visual–spatial learner may want to draw diagrams of as much of a math problem as possible. Everyone is a thinker; however, some people tend to approach life situations more analytically than others.

People are a blend of all the intelligences and personality types, in proportions unique to them. Most often one or two intelligences or types are dominant. When material is very difficult or when you are feeling insecure about learning something new, use your most dominant areas. When something is easy for you, however, this is an opportunity for you to improve your less developed areas. All of your abilities will continue to develop throughout your lifetime.

In addition, you may change which abilities you emphasize, depending on the situation. For example, an organizer-dominant student might find it easy to take notes in outline style when the instructor lectures in an organized way. However, if another instructor jumps from topic to topic, the same student might choose to use a think link. The more you know yourself, the more you will be able to assess any situation and set appropriate goals.

Elsewhere in the text you will see how your personality types and intelligences influence other skills and life areas. As you read, try to examine how your tendencies affect you in different areas—study techniques, time management, personal wellness, communication, and so on. Knowing your style can help you improve how you function in every area of your life.

Avoid Overreacting to Challenges

The assessments you complete show areas of challenge as well as ability. If you assume that your limitations are set in stone or let them dominate your self-image, you may deny yourself growth. Rather than dwelling on limitations (which often results in a negative self-image) or ignoring them (which often leads to unproductive choices), use what you know from the assessments to face your limitations and work to improve them.

In any area of challenge, look at where you are and set goals that will help you reach where you want to be. If a class is difficult, examine what improvements you need to make in order to succeed. If a work situation requires you to perform in an area that causes trouble for you, face your limitations head-on and ask for help. Exploring what you will gain from working on a limitation helps you gain the motivation you need to move ahead.

EXPERT INSIGHT

Broaden Your Perspective on Learning Styles

I didn't have a good experience through many of my school years because of struggling in certain classes. School is based very strongly on verbal–linguistic learning, which is my weakest intelligence. Lectures, especially, were a real struggle. Students who have strong verbal–linguistic and logical–mathematical intelligences are usually successful in school, while those of us who are strong in the other six intelligence areas have a harder time. What's important to learn is that there are tools that can help us work around our learning-style problems and that having another type of intelligence defines us as an individual in the most positive way.

JOYCE BISHOP, PROFESSOR OF PSYCHOLOGY,
GOLDEN STATE COLLEGE

If you are interested in more assessments and additional information about Myers-Briggs, check your career planning and placement center—you might find additional assessments and information through your school's career counselors. Also, try looking online.

All of the self-knowledge you are building will be very important for your life decisions. Take what you know into account when thinking about your career.

How Will Knowing Your Learning Style Help You in Your Career?

Different careers require different abilities; there is no one "best" learning style for all careers. Develop self-knowledge through honest analysis and then match what you do best with a career that makes the most of your strengths. This exploration will prepare you for choosing the right career path. It will also help you relate to the following reasons why knowing your learning style may help in your career.

YOU WILL PERFORM MORE SUCCESSFULLY.   Your learning style is essentially your working style. If you know how you learn, you will be able to look for an environment that suits you best. You will perform at the top of your ability if you work at a job in which you feel competent and happy. Even when you are working at a job that isn't your ideal, knowing yourself can lead you to on-the-job choices that make your situation as agreeable as possible.

Knowing your learning style will also give you strategies to complete your day-to-day tasks. For example, if you are a visual learner, you may want to summarize documents in the form of a think link or a chart or table. Using these devices will help you remember important information and use critical thinking to see relationships.

YOU WILL BE ABLE TO FUNCTION WELL IN TEAMS.   Teamwork is a primary feature of the modern workplace. The better your awareness of your abilities, the easier it is to identify what tasks you will perform best in a team situation. The better your awareness of personality traits—your own as well as those of others—the more skillful you will be at communicating with and relating to your coworkers.

YOU WILL BE ABLE TO TARGET AREAS THAT NEED IMPROVEMENT.   The more you know about your learning styles, the easier it is to pinpoint the areas that are difficult for you. That has two advantages: One, you can begin to work on difficult areas, step-by-step. Two, when a task requires a skill that is tough for you, you can either take special care with it or suggest someone else whose style may be better suited to it.

In college, self-knowledge starts with your choice of major because many majors emphasize particular learning styles. For example, science and math curricula demand strength in analytical thinking, and education courses often involve extensive interpersonal interaction. Look at your stronger and weaker areas and see what majors are likely to make the most of what you do well. If you are drawn to a major that requires ability in one of your weaker areas, explore the major to see where you would need extra help and where your strengths would benefit you.

Sabiduría

In Spanish, the term *sabiduría* represents the two sides of learning, knowledge and wisdom. Knowledge—building what you know about how the world works—is the first part. Wisdom—deriving meaning and significance from knowledge and deciding how to use it—is the second. As you continually learn and experience new things, the *sabiduría* you build will help you make knowledgeable and wise choices about how to lead your life.

Think of this concept as you discover more about how you learn and receive knowledge in all aspects of your life—in school, work, and personal situations. As you learn how your unique mind works and how to use it, you can confidently assert yourself. As you expand your ability to use your mind in different ways, you can create lifelong advantages for yourself.

CHAPTER 2

Study Skills in Action

Test Competence

MEASURING WHAT YOU'VE LEARNED

MULTIPLE CHOICE. *Circle or highlight the answer that seems to fit best.*

1. A *learning style* is
   - A. the best way to learn when attending classes.
   - B. a particular way of being intelligent.
   - C. an affinity for a particular job choice or career area.
   - D. a way in which the mind receives and processes information.

2. If your learning style does not match your instructor's teaching style, options for handling the situation include all of the following **except**
   - A. focusing on your weaker areas if they correspond with the class emphasis.
   - B. using study time to convert class material to a format that makes more sense to you.
   - C. finding an instructor who better matches your style.
   - D. asking your instructor for additional help.

3. "An ability to solve problems or fashion products that are useful in a particular setting or community," according to Howard Gardner, is
   - A. bodily–kinesthetic intelligence.
   - B. a learning style.
   - C. an intelligence.
   - D. a personality profile.

4. *Intrapersonal* intelligence is the ability to
   - A. relate to others.
   - B. understand one's own behavior and feelings.
   - C. understand spatial relationships.
   - D. use the physical body skillfully.

5. The ability to communicate through language refers to
   A. visual intelligence.
   B. visual–spatial intelligence.
   C. interpersonal intelligence.
   D. verbal–linguistic intelligence.

6. The *Personality Spectrum* personality types are
   A. Myers-Briggs, Keirsey, Gardner, and Bishop.
   B. Visual, Verbal, Interpersonal, and Intrapersonal.
   C. Thinker, Visionary, Organizer, and Verbal.
   D. Thinker, Organizer, Giver, and Adventurer.

7. Explaining material sequentially and finding patterns in information would best suit
   A. a visual–spatial learner.
   B. a logical–mathematical learner.
   C. a bodily–kinesthetic learner.
   D. a naturalistic learner.

8. Working in study groups and interacting with honesty bring out the best in
   A. an organizer.
   B. an adventurer.
   C. a thinker.
   D. a giver.

9. An adventurer's strengths include
   A. skillfulness and a hands-on approach to learning.
   B. loyalty and obligation.
   C. exploring ideas and solving problems.
   D. honesty and cultivating potential.

10. The best way to use learning-style assessments is to see them as
    A. a reference point rather than a label; a tool with which to see yourself more clearly.
    B. a road map for your life; a message that shows the paths you must take in order to be successful.
    C. a lesson about group learning; a way to find the group of learners with whom you work best.
    D. a definitive label for your working style; a clear-cut category where you fit.

TRUE/FALSE. *Place a T or an F beside each statement to indicate whether you think it is true or false.*

1. _____ There is one best way to learn any academic subject.

2. _____ Teamwork is going out of style in today's workplace.

3. _____ Learning-style assessments are intended to be indicators of who you are, not concrete labels.

4. _____ In an area of limitation, your best bet is to look at where you are and set goals that will help you reach where you want to be.

5. _____ Only logical–mathematical learners can succeed in math courses.

Brain Power

BUILDING VOCABULARY FITNESS

The paragraphs below are taken from the current media. Read the paragraph, noting the context of the vocabulary words shown in bold type. Next, for each vocabulary word (reprinted in the left-hand column), highlight the word or phrase in column A, B, or C that is the most similar in meaning. Finally, on a separate sheet of paper, solidify your understanding of these words by using each in a sentence of your own.

> But on one point I was correct. This club did one really smart thing that the rest of us could—and should—**emulate.** Before they dived into the markets, they decided they needed an education. So they placed a call to Marlene Jupiter, the author of *Savvy Investing for Women*, and hired her to teach them. Jupiter started her course at the beginning: with an explanation of stocks and the market. Then she plowed through lessons on reading financial statements and, finally, into technical analysis.
>
> She also brought in guest speakers. I sat in on the group's session on Wednesday, April 12, a **dismal** day in the markets, with the Dow off 162 and the Nasdaq down 286. And Prudential Securities technical **guru** Ralph Acampora was there to explain it all. He did it in the group's language. "I'm a market psychologist," he began. "One thing that bothered me about today and about yesterday in the market was that I didn't see fear. I didn't see **capitulation,** where investors throw the good stocks out with the bad. That is when the market will turn."
>
> From "Group Therapy: Taking a Few Lessons from an Investment Club of Psychologists," by Jean Sherman Chatzky, *Money*, July 2000, p. 168.

Vocabulary Words	A	B	C
1. **emulate**	attempt	admire	imitate
2. **savvy**	wise	modern	successful
3. **dismal**	uncomfortable	dreadful	foreboding
4. **guru**	expert	teacher	enthusiast
5. **capitulation**	surrender	victory	battle

Strategic Thinking

GETTING THE BIG PICTURE

Answer the following questions on a separate piece of paper or in a journal.

Describe your learning-style profile. What are your strong areas? Where are you less proficient? Describe how you think your profile of stronger and weaker areas will affect your studies and eventually your career. What study techniques or courses seem to make sense for your learning style? What careers might suit your strengths?

NOTES

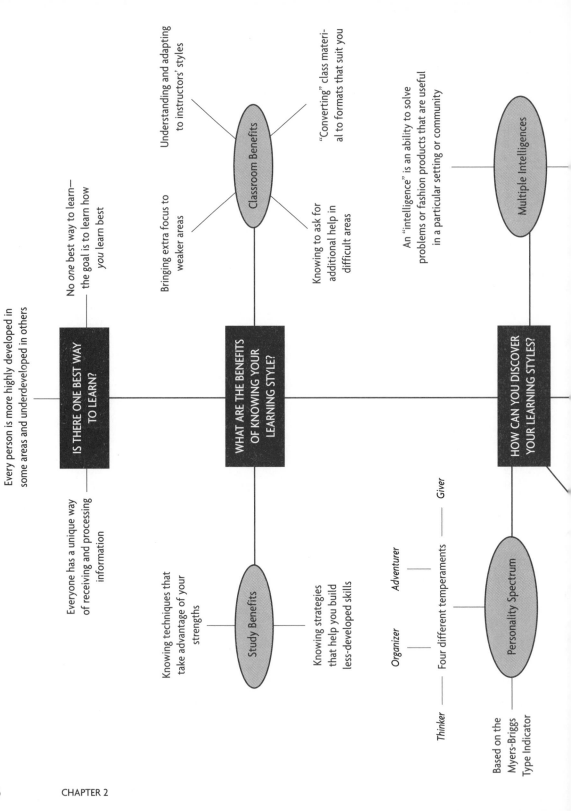

Every person is more highly developed in some areas and underdeveloped in others

No *one* best way to learn—the goal is to learn how *you* learn best

IS THERE ONE BEST WAY TO LEARN?

Everyone has a unique way of receiving and processing information

Understanding and adapting to instructors' styles

"Converting" class material to formats that suit you

Classroom Benefits

Bringing extra focus to weaker areas

Knowing to ask for additional help in difficult areas

WHAT ARE THE BENEFITS OF KNOWING YOUR LEARNING STYLE?

Knowing techniques that take advantage of your strengths

Study Benefits

Knowing strategies that help you build less-developed skills

An "intelligence" is an ability to solve problems or fashion products that are useful in a particular setting or community

Multiple Intelligences

HOW CAN YOU DISCOVER YOUR LEARNING STYLES?

Thinker —— Four different temperaments —— *Giver*

Organizer .... *Adventurer*

Personality Spectrum

Based on the Myers-Briggs Type Indicator

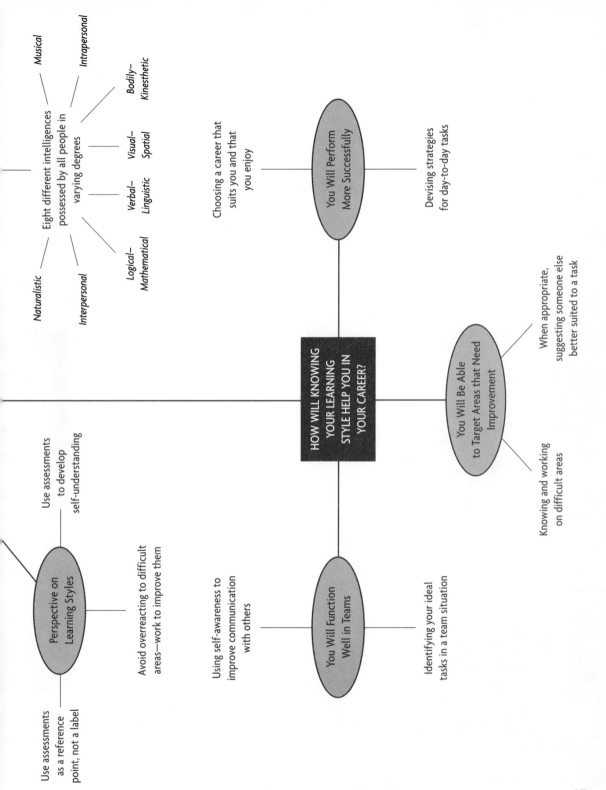

Naturalistic

Interpersonal

Eight different intelligences possessed by all people in varying degrees

Musical

Intrapersonal

Bodily–Kinesthetic

Visual–Spatial

Verbal–Linguistic

Logical–Mathematical

HOW WILL KNOWING YOUR LEARNING STYLE HELP YOU IN YOUR CAREER?

You Will Perform More Successfully

Choosing a career that suits you and that you enjoy

Devising strategies for day-to-day tasks

You Will Be Able to Target Areas that Need Improvement

When appropriate, suggesting someone else better suited to a task

Knowing and working on difficult areas

Perspective on Learning Styles

Use assessments to develop self-understanding

Avoid overreacting to difficult areas—work to improve them

Use assessments as a reference point, not a label

You Will Function Well in Teams

Using self-awareness to improve communication with others

Identifying your ideal tasks in a team situation

ASPIRE

MONDAY, APRIL 1
TUESDAY, APRIL 2
WEDNESDAY, APRIL 3
PASSOVER begins at sundown

Achieving the kind of success you dream of in your studies and
your career may often seem difficult or even
impossible. When you set goals, prioritize, and
manage your time effectively, however, you can
develop the kind of focus that will help you achieve
what you dream. Managing time successfully means
being able to translate your goals into daily, weekly,
monthly, and yearly steps, as you avoid the self-defeating
trap of procrastination. Effective time management and goal
setting will also help you reduce the stress you experience
when you have too much to do in too little time. Similarly,
staying healthy and knowing where to turn when you have a
problem will lessen stress and provide a sense of calm, control,
and well-being.

This chapter explains how taking specific steps toward
goals can help you turn your dreams into reality. At the end of
the chapter, you will be able to answer these questions:

- How do you set and achieve goals?
- What are your priorities?
- How can you manage your time?
- Why is procrastination a problem?
- How can you reduce stress?

GOAL SETTING AND TIME MANAGEMENT

MAPPING YOUR COURSE AND REDUCING STRESS

How Do You Set and Achieve Goals?

A goal can be something as concrete as passing a midterm exam or as abstract as working to control your temper. From major life decisions to the tiniest day-to-day activities, setting goals will help you define how you want to live and what you want to achieve.

Paul Timm, an expert in self-management, feels that focus is a key ingredient in setting and achieving goals: "Focus adds power to our actions. If somebody threw a bucket of water on you, you'd get wet. . . . But if water was shot at you through a high-pressure nozzle, you might get injured. The only difference is focus."[1] Focus your goal-setting energy by placing your goals in long-term and short-term time frames, evaluating goals in terms of your values, and exploring the different types of goals.

PLACING GOALS IN TIME

Everyone has the same 24 hours in a day, but it often doesn't feel like enough. Your commitments can overwhelm you unless you decide how to use time to plan your steps toward goal achievement. Planning your progress step-by-step will help you maintain your efforts over the extended time period often needed to accomplish a goal.

Setting Long-Term Goals

Establish the goals that have the largest scope first, the long-term goals that you aim to attain over a lengthy period of time, up to a few years or more. As a student, you know what long-term goals are all about. You have set yourself a goal to attend school and earn a degree or certificate. Becoming educated is an admirable goal that often takes years to reach.

Some long-term goals are lifelong, such as a goal to continually learn more in your career area. Others have a more definite end, such as a goal to complete a course successfully. To determine your long-term goals, think about what you want out of your professional, educational, and personal life.

For example, you may establish long-term goals such as these:

- I will graduate from school and know that I have learned all that I could, whether my grade point average shows it or not.
- I will use my current and future job experience to develop practical skills that will help me get a satisfying, well-paying job.

Long-term goals don't have to be lifelong goals. Think about your long-term goals for the coming year. Considering what you want to accomplish in a year's time will give you clarity, focus, and a sense of what needs to take place right away. Continuing the example above, you might adopt these goals for the coming year:

- I will look for a part-time job with a local newspaper or newsroom.
- I will learn to navigate the Internet and research topics online.

Setting Short-Term Goals

When you divide your long-term goals into smaller, manageable goals that you hope to accomplish within a relatively short time, you are setting short-term goals. Short-term goals narrow your focus, helping you to maintain your progress toward your long-term goals. They are the steps that take you where you want to go. Say you have set the long-term goals you just read in the previous section. To stay on track toward those goals, you may want to accomplish these short-term goals in the next six months:

- I will make an effort to ask my coworkers for advice on how to get into the news business.
- I will use Yahoo.com and Askjeeves.com to conduct research.

These same goals can be broken down into even smaller parts, such as one month:

- I will have lunch with my office mate at work so that I can talk with him about his work experience.
- I will learn to use the most effective keyword language choices in my Internet searches.

In addition to monthly goals, you may have short-term goals that extend for a week, a day, or even a few hours in a given day. Take as an example an article you plan to write for the school paper on effective Internet searches. Such short-term goals may include the following:

- By 3 P.M. today: Brainstorm ideas for the article (more on brainstorming and freewriting in Chapter 11).
- By the end of today: Freewrite about the subject of the article, and narrow down to a specific topic.
- One week from now: First draft ready. Ask my writing instructor if he will review it.

- Two weeks from now: Second draft ready. Give it to one more person to review.
- Three weeks from now: Final draft ready. Submit it to the editor.

As you consider your long-term and short-term goals, notice how all of your goals are linked to one another. As Figure 3.1 shows, your long-term goals establish a context for the short-term goals. In turn, your short-term goals make the long-term goals seem clearer and easier to reach. The whole system works to keep you on track.

LINKING GOALS WITH VALUES

If you are not sure how to start defining your goals, look to your *values* to guide you. Your personal values are the principles or qualities that you consider important, right, or good. Values—for example, family togetherness, education, caring for others, worthwhile employment—are the beliefs that guide your choices. Set your goals based on what is important to you.

FIGURE 3.1 *Linking goals together.*

LONG-TERM		Earn a degree	
YEAR LONG	Declare major	Pass classes	
SEMESTER	Explore career areas	Work with study group	Be in class and on time
ONE MONTH	Meet with academic advisor	Plan group meetings	Cut down on late-night socializing
THIS WEEK	Call advisor to set up appointment	Call friends from class about getting a group together	Study weeknights and go out on Friday night

Understanding your values will help you set goals because any goal can help you achieve what you value. If you value physical fitness, your long-term goal might be to run a marathon, while your short-term goals might involve your weekly exercise and eating plan. Similarly, if you value teamwork, your study goals might emphasize study groups and peer review of schoolwork.

Goals enable you to put values into practice. When you set and pursue goals that are based on values, you demonstrate and reinforce values by taking action. The strength of those values, in turn, reinforces your goals. You will experience a stronger drive to achieve if you build goals around what is most important to you. When you use your values as a compass for your goals, make sure the compass is pointed in the direction of your real feelings. Be careful not to set goals that reflect past values that have changed, or other people's values that you don't necessarily share. Keep in touch with your life's changes so your goals can reflect who you are.

DIFFERENT KINDS OF GOALS

People have many different goals, involving different parts of life and different values. Because school is currently a focus in your life, examine your educational goals.

Identifying Educational Goals

People have many reasons for attending college. You may be here in order to build marketable skills in a particular career area, get a degree that will help you move up in the workplace, or pursue studies in a subject that has always interested you. Whatever they are, your reasons for being here will define a context for your study goals. For example, if you need a particu-

Effective goals are specific, moderately difficult, but not impossible. Say, for example, you're taking a chemistry course, and there are exercises at the end of every chapter. An effective goal would be to work and understand all the exercises—not at the end of each chapter, but at the end of THIS chapter. That's a much better goal than "I'm going to get a B in this class," or "I'm going to study harder," or even "I'm going to study for four hours a day." The goal of solving and understanding the problems at the end of "this" chapter is specific, near-term, and easily monitored. And it is psychologically powerful because it puts you in total control.

PAUL EGGEN, PROFESSOR OF EDUCATION,
UNIVERSITY OF NORTH FLORIDA

EXPERT INSIGHT

**Set Goals that
Put You in Control**

lar major, your study goals will include earning satisfactory grades in the courses required for that major. If you are focusing on a skill, your study goals will include doing the work that makes you competent in that skill.

To get more specific about your education, identify goals in the following areas:

- class selection, schedule selection, instructor selection
- selection of the degree or certificate you are pursuing
- any honors or awards that are important to you and for your career goals
- what subjects you want to learn about
- connections you want to make with others at school

The more specific you are, the easier it is to focus your time and energy on the achievement of these goals.

Identifying Career Goals

Establish the long-term and short-term goals for your career path as well as for your educational path. Remember that all of your goals are interconnected. A school goal is often a step toward a career goal. Think of career goals in terms of job, finances, and lifestyle.

- *First, consider the job you want after you graduate.* What are the requirements, job duties, hours, coworkers, salary, transportation, and company size, style, and location? How much responsibility do you want? Do you want to become a manager, a supervisor, an independent contractor, a business owner? Think about the field you want to enter—whether it is health, education, finances, publishing, construction, computer technology, or any other.
- *Then, consider financial goals.* How much money do you need to pay your bills, live comfortably, and save for the future? Do you need to borrow money for school or a major purchase such as a car? Do you need to reduce your bills? Compare your current financial picture to how you want to live, and set goals that will help you bridge the gap.
- *Finally, consider your ideal lifestyle.* Where do you want to live, in what kind of space, and with whom? How do you want to participate in your community? Do you want to be able to support a family? Consider career goals that allow you to live the way you want to live.

Setting and working toward goals takes a lot of practice and repeated efforts. As long as you do all that you can to achieve a goal, you haven't failed, even if you don't achieve it completely or in the time frame you had planned. Even one step in the right direction is an achievement. For example, if you wanted to raise your course grade to a B from a D, and you ended up with a C, you have still accomplished something important.

Achieving goals becomes easier when you are realistic about what is possible. Setting priorities will help you make that distinction.

What Are Your Priorities?

A priority is an action or intention that takes precedence in time, attention, or position. When you set a priority, you identify what's important at any given moment. Prioritizing helps you focus on your most important goals, especially when the important ones are the most difficult. Human nature often leads people to tackle easy goals first and leave the tough ones for later. The risk is that you might never reach for goals that are crucial to your success.

To explore your priorities, think about your personal mission and look at your school, career, and personal goals. Do one or two of these paths take priority for you right now? In any path, which goals take priority? Which goals take priority over all? You are a unique individual, and your priorities are yours alone. What may be top priority to someone else may not mean that much to you, and vice versa.

First and foremost, your priorities should reflect your goals. In addition, they should reflect your relationships with others. For example, if you are a parent, your children's needs will be high on the priority list. You may be in school so you can get a better job and give them a better life. If you are in a committed relationship, you may schedule your classes so that you and your partner are home together as often as possible. Even as you consider the needs of others, though, be true to your own goals and priorities so that you can make the most of who you are.

Setting priorities moves you closer to accomplishing specific goals. It also helps you begin planning to achieve your goals within specific time frames. Being able to achieve your goals is directly linked to effective time management.

How Can You Manage Your Time?

Time is one of your most valuable and precious resources. Everyone has the same 24 hours in a day, every day. Your responsibility and your potential for success lie in how you use yours. You cannot change how time passes, but you can spend it wisely by taking steps to achieve your goals. Efficient time management helps you achieve your goals in a steady, step-by-step process.

People have a variety of approaches to time management. Your learning style (see Chapter 2) can help you understand how you use time. For example, students with strong logical–mathematical intelligence and thinker types tend to organize activities within a framework of time. Because they stay aware of how long it takes them to do something or travel somewhere, they are usually prompt. By contrast, adventurer types and less logical learners with perhaps stronger visual or interpersonal intelligences may neglect details such as how much time they have to complete a task. They can often be late without meaning to be.

Time management, like physical fitness, is a lifelong pursuit. Throughout your life, your ability to manage your time will vary with your stress level, how busy you are, and other factors. Don't expect perfection— just do your best and keep working at it. Time management involves building a schedule, taking responsibility for how you spend your time, planning strategically, and being flexible.

BUILDING A SCHEDULE

Just as a road map helps you travel from place to place, a schedule is a time-and-activity map that helps you get from the beginning of the day (or week or month) to the end as smoothly as possible. Schedules help you gain control of your life in two ways: They allocate segments of time for the fulfillment of your daily, weekly, monthly, and long-term goals, and they serve as a concrete reminder of tasks, events, due dates, responsibilities, and deadlines. Few moments are more stressful than suddenly realizing you have forgotten to take a test or be on duty at work. Scheduling can help you avoid events like these.

Keep a Date Book

A date book, or planner, is indispensable for keeping track of your time. Paul Timm says, "Most time management experts agree that rule number one in a thoughtful planning process is: Use some form of a planner where you can write things down."[2]

There are two major types of date books. The day-at-a-glance version devotes a page to each day. Although it gives you ample space to write the day's activities, it's harder to see what's ahead. The week-at-a-glance book gives you a view of the week's plans but has less room to write per day. If you write detailed daily plans, you might like the day-at-a-glance version. If you prefer to remind yourself of plans ahead of time, try the book that shows a week's schedule all at once.

Another option is an electronic planner—a compact minicomputer that can hold a large amount of information. You can use it to schedule your days and weeks, make to-do lists, and create and store an address book. You can also do this on your computer, using a program such as Microsoft Outlook.

Set Weekly and Daily Goals

The most ideal time management starts with the smallest tasks and builds to bigger ones. Setting short-term goals that tie in to your long-term goals lends the following benefits:

- Increased meaning for your daily activities
- Shaping your path toward the achievement of your long-term goals
- A sense of order and progress

For college students as well as working people, the week is often the easiest unit of time to consider at one shot. Weekly goal setting and planning allows you to keep track of day-to-day activities while giving you the larger perspective of what is coming up during the week. Take some time before each week starts to remind yourself of your long-term goals. Keeping long-term goals in mind will help you determine related short-term goals you can accomplish during the week to come.

Figure 3.2 shows parts of a daily schedule and a weekly schedule.

Daily and weekly schedule. **FIGURE 3.2**

Monday, March 20

Time	Tasks	Priority
7:00 AM		
8:00	Up at 8am — finish homework	*
9:00	Class	
10:00		
11:00	Class	
12:00 PM	Renew driver's license @ DMV	*
1:00	Lunch	
2:00	Writing Seminar (peer editing today)	*
3:00	↓	
4:00	check on Ms. Schwartz's office hrs.	
5:00	5:30 work out	
6:00	↳6:30	
7:00	Dinner	
8:00	Read two chapters	
9:00	for Chemistry	
10:00		
11:00		

Monday, March 20

8		Call: Mike Blair	1
9	BIO 212	Financial Aid Office	2
10		EMS 262 *Paramedic	3
11	CHEM 203	role-play*	4
12			5
Evening	6pm yoga class		

Tuesday, March 21

8	Finish reading assignment!	Work @ library	1
9			2
10	ENG 112	(study for quiz)	3
11	↓		4
12			5
Evening		↓ until 7pm	

Wednesday, March 22

8		Meet w/advisor	1
9	BIO 212		2
10		EMS 262	3
11	CHEM 203 *Quiz		4
12		Pick up photos	5
Evening	6pm Aerobics		

Link Daily and Weekly Goals with Long-Term Goals

After you evaluate what you need to accomplish in the coming year, semester, month, week, and day to reach long-term goals, use your schedule to record those steps. Write down the short-term goals that will enable you to stay on track. Here is how a student might map out two different goals over a year's time.

This year:	Complete enough courses to graduate.
	Win a summer internship in publishing.
This semester:	Complete my accounting class with a B average or higher.
	Meet with representatives from publishing companies.
This month:	Set up study-group schedule to coincide with quizzes.
	Send query letters to publishing companies.
This week:	Meet with study group; go over material for Friday's quiz.
	Research internship possibilities online.
Today:	Go over Chapter 3 in accounting text.
	Locate a list of publishers in the area.

Prioritize Goals

Prioritizing enables you to use your date book with maximum efficiency. On any given day, your goals will have varying degrees of importance. Record your goals first, and then label them according to their level of importance, using these categories: Priority 1, Priority 2, and Priority 3. Identify these categories by using any code that makes sense to you. Some people use numbers (1, 2, 3), and some use letters (A, B, C). Some write activities in different colors according to priority level. Some use symbols (*, +, −).

- *Priority 1* activities are the most important things in your life. They may include attending class, picking up a child from day care, and paying bills.

- *Priority 2* activities are part of your routine. Examples include grocery shopping, working out, participating in a school organization, or cleaning. Priority 2 tasks are important but more flexible than Priority 1 tasks.

- *Priority 3* activities are those you would like to do but can reschedule without much sacrifice. Examples might be a trip to the mall, a visit to a friend, a social phone call, or a sports event. As much as you would like to accomplish them, you don't consider them urgent. Many people don't enter Priority 3 tasks in their date books until they are sure they have time to get them done.

Prioritizing your activities is essential because some activities are more important than others, and effective time management requires that you

When I begin to feel as though I have too much to do, I literally stop and make a list of everything that I have to do, down to buying a birthday card for Aunt Mary. Once it's all in front of me, I star the items that absolutely must be done as soon as possible. Then I try to find the time to do them. When I think that I can't fit anything more in, I look at my schedule to see if I'm spending my time on lower priority tasks.

At the end of the day, I can look back and see what I accomplished. Even if I didn't get everything done, I still feel that I did my best. I freed up as much time as I could and I allocated it efficiently to the most important things. If I didn't finish them all, I don't feel guilty. I did everything I could conceivably do in the time I had.

CHARLES G. MORRIS, PROFESSOR OF PSYCHOLOGY, UNIVERSITY OF MICHIGAN

EXPERT INSIGHT

Make a List, Then Prioritize

focus most of your energy on Priority 1 items. In addition, looking at all your priorities helps you plan when you can get things done. Often, it's not possible to get all of your Priority 1 activities done early in the day, especially if they involve scheduled classes or meetings. Prioritizing helps you set Priority 1 items and then schedule Priority 2 and 3 items around them as they fit.

Keep Track of Events

Your date book also enables you to schedule events. Think of events in terms of how they tie in with your long-term goals, just as you would your other tasks. For example, being aware of quiz dates, due dates for assignments, and meeting dates will aid your goals to achieve in school and become involved.

Note events in your date book so that you can stay aware of them ahead of time. Write them in daily, weekly, monthly, or even yearly sections, where a quick look will remind you that they are approaching. Writing them down will also help you see where they fit in the context of all your other activities. For example, if you have three big tests and a presentation all in one week, you'll want to take time in the weeks before to prepare for them.

The following are some kinds of events worth noting in your date book:

- Due dates for papers, projects, presentations, and tests

- Important meetings, medical appointments, or due dates for bill payments
- Birthdays, anniversaries, social events, holidays, and other special occasions
- Benchmarks for steps toward a goal, such as due dates for sections of a project

As the least important tasks, Priority 3 tasks often get pushed off from one day to the next. One solution is to keep a list of Priority 3 tasks in a separate place in your date book. That way, when you have an unexpected pocket of free time, you can consult your list and see what you have time to accomplish.

TAKING RESPONSIBILITY FOR HOW YOU SPEND YOUR TIME

When you plan your activities with an eye toward achieving your most important goals, you are taking responsibility for how you live. The following strategies will help you stay in charge of your choices.

PLAN YOUR SCHEDULE EACH WEEK. Before each week starts, note events, goals, and priorities. Decide where to fit activities like studying and Priority 3 items. For example, if you have a test on Thursday, you can plan study sessions on the preceding days. If you have more free time on Tuesday and Friday than on other days, you can plan workouts or Priority 3 activities at those times. Looking at the whole week will help you avoid being surprised by something you had forgotten was coming up.

MAKE AND USE TO-DO LISTS. Use a to-do list to record the things you want to accomplish. If you generate a daily or weekly to-do list on a separate piece of paper, you can look at all tasks and goals at once. This will help you consider time frames and priorities. You might want to prioritize your tasks and transfer them to appropriate places in your date book. You can tailor a to-do list to an important event such as exam week or an especially busy day when you have a family gathering or a presentation to make. This kind of specific to-do list can help you prioritize and accomplish an unusually large task load.

POST MONTHLY AND YEARLY CALENDARS AT HOME. Keeping a calendar on the wall will help you stay aware of important events. Use a yearly or a monthly version (Figure 3.3 shows a monthly calendar), and keep it where you can refer to it often. If you live with family or friends, make the calendar a group project so that you stay aware of each other's plans. Knowing each other's schedules can also help you avoid problems such as two people needing the car at the same time.

FIGURE

3.3

OCTOBER 2000

SUNDAY	MONDAY	TUESDAY	WEDNESDAY	THURSDAY	FRIDAY	SATURDAY
1	2 WORK	3 Turn in English paper topic	4	5 Chem test	6 Yoga 6 pm	7
8 Frank's Birthday	9 9 am Psych test WORK	10 6:30 pm meeting at student ctr.	11	12 History study group	13 WORK	14 WORK
15	16 English paper due WORK	17	18 WORK	19 Dentist 2 pm	20 Yoga 6 pm	21 Dinner @ Ann's
22	23 WORK	24 Statistics test	25	26 History study group	27 WORK	28 WORK
29	30 WORK	31	* Register to vote this month.			

SCHEDULE DOWN TIME.   When you're wiped out from too much activity, you don't have the energy to accomplish as much. A little down time will refresh you and improve your attitude. Even half an hour a day will help. Fill the time with whatever relaxes you—reading, watching television, chatting online, playing a game or sport, walking, writing, or just doing nothing. Make down time a priority.

PLANNING STRATEGICALLY

Strategy is the plan of action, the method, the "how" behind any goal you want to achieve. As a student, you have planned strategically by deciding that the effort of school is a legitimate price to pay for the skills and opportunities you will receive. Chapter 1 of this text also helped you develop the mindset of a strategic learner.

Strategic planning means looking at the next week, month, year, or 10 years and examining the positive and negative effects that current choices or actions may have. It means asking questions such as:

GOAL SETTING AND TIME MANAGEMENT   **61**

- If you aim for a certain goal, what actions may help you to achieve that goal?
- What are the potential effects, positive or negative, of different actions or choices?
- What can you learn from previous experiences that may inspire similar or different actions?
- Which set of effects would be most helpful or desirable to you?

For any situation that would benefit from strategic planning, from getting ready for a study session to aiming for a career, these steps will help you make choices that bring about the most positive effects.

1. *Establish a goal.* What do you want to achieve? When do you want to achieve it?

2. *Brainstorm possible plans.* What are some ways that you can get where you want to go? What steps toward your goal will you need to take one year, five years, 10 years, or 20 years from now?

3. *Anticipate all possible effects of each plan.* What positive and negative effects may occur, both soon and in the long-term? What approach may best help you achieve your goal?

4. *Put your plan into action.* Act on the decision you have made.

5. *Evaluate continually.* Your strategies might not have the effects you predicted. If you discover that things are not going the way you planned, for any reason, reevaluate and change your strategy.

Here's how you might use these steps to develop a strategic plan for going into the field of medicine.

1. *Establish your goal.* What corner of the medical field interests you? Do you want to be a researcher, nurse, doctor, professor, technician, pharmacist? When do you want to be able to begin your career?

2. *Brainstorm possible plans.* Come up with ideas about how you could receive your training and how you could fulfill any other requirements (certificates, board exams, internships).

3. *Anticipate possible effects.* Think through each plan and evaluate the positive and negative effects it would have on you and those close to you—look at the effects of the jobs themselves, the education and training they require, the money it costs to receive the proper degree and training, and so on. Evaluate which plan would be best to pursue.

4. *Put your plan into action.* Move ahead toward your goal.

5. *Evaluate continually.* As you go, periodically "check in" with yourself to see how it's going. Do you still want the position you thought you wanted? Are you succeeding in the classes required for the major you need to have? Does the material still interest you?

The most important critical-thinking question for successful strategic planning is the question "how." *How* do you remember what you learn?

How do you develop a productive idea at work? The process of strategic planning, in a nutshell, helps you find the best answer to "how."

Strategic planning has many important positive effects. For example, a student who wants to do well in a course must plan study sessions. A lawyer needs to anticipate how to respond to points raised in court. Strategic planning creates a vision into the future that allows the planner to anticipate possibilities—and being flexible will help at those times when the unanticipated happens.

BEING FLEXIBLE

No matter how well you plan your time, the changes that life brings can make you feel out of control. One minute you seem to be on track, and the next minute chaos hits—in forms as minor as a room change for a class or as major as a medical emergency. Coping with changes can cause stress. As your stress level rises, your sense of control dwindles.

Although you cannot always choose your circumstances, you may have some control over how you *handle* them. Use the following ideas to cope with changes large and small.

Day-to-Day Changes

Anytime, small changes can result in priority shifts that jumble your schedule. On Monday, a homework assignment due in a week might be Priority 2; then if you haven't gotten to it by Saturday, it has become Priority 1. Sometimes a class may be canceled, and you will have extra time on your hands. Perhaps your baby-sitter doesn't show up, and you need to figure out how to provide care for your child.

Think of change as part of life and you will be able to effectively solve the dilemmas that come up. For some changes that occur frequently, you can think through a backup plan ahead of time (such as having a friend on call for emergency child care). For unexpected extra time on your hands, you could keep some work or reading with you. The best you can do is to keep an open mind about possibilities and to remember to call on your resources in a pinch.

Life Changes

Sometimes changes are more serious than a class schedule shift. Your car breaks down, your relationship falls apart, you fail a class, you or a close family member develops a medical problem, or you get laid off at work. Such changes call for more extensive problem solving. They also require an ability to look at the big picture. Although a class change affects your schedule for a day, a medical problem may affect your schedule for much longer.

When life hands you a major curve ball, first remember that you still have some choices about how to handle the situation. Then sit down and figure them out, ideally with people who can help you think everything through. Explore all of your options before choosing a solution (the problem-solving skills in Chapter 4 will serve you well here). Finally, make full use of your school resources. Your academic advisor, counselor, dean, financial aid advisor, or instructors may have ideas and assistance to offer you—but they can only help if you let them know what you need.

No matter how well you schedule your time, you will have moments when it's hard to stay in control. Knowing how to identify and avoid procrastination and other time traps will help you get back on track.

Why Is Procrastination a Problem?

Procrastination is postponing a task until a later date. Having trouble with goal setting is one reason why people procrastinate. People may project goals too far into the future, set unrealistic goals that are too frustrating to reach, or have no goals at all. Procrastination is human; if taken to the extreme, however, it can develop into a habit that will cause problems at school, on the job, and at home.

Jane B. Burka and Lenora M. Yuen, authors of *Procrastination: Why You Do It and What To Do About It*, say that habitual procrastinators are often perfectionists who create problems by using their ability to achieve as the only measure of their self-worth: "The performance becomes the only measure of the person; nothing else is taken into account. An outstanding performance means an outstanding person; a mediocre performance means a mediocre person. . . . As long as you procrastinate, you never have to confront the real limits of your ability, whatever those limits are."[3] For the procrastinator, the fear of failure inhibits the risk-taking that could bring success.

Some ways to fight your tendencies to procrastinate include:

- *Weigh the benefits (to you and others) of completing the task versus the effects of procrastinating.* What rewards lie ahead if you get it done? What will be the effects if you continue to put it off? Which situation has better effects? Chances are you will benefit more in the long-term from facing the task head-on.

- *Set reasonable goals.* Plan your goals carefully, allowing enough time to complete them. Unreasonable goals can be so intimidating that you do nothing at all. "Get an 'A' in every course" could throw you. However, "earn passing grades in my courses this semester" might inspire you to take action.

- *Break the task into smaller parts.* Look at the task in terms of its parts. How can you approach it step-by-step? If you can concentrate on achieving one small goal at a time, the task may become less of a burden. In addition, setting concrete time limits for each task may help you feel in control.

- *Get started whether or not you "feel like it."* Going from doing nothing to doing something is often the hardest part of avoiding procrastination. The motivation techniques from Chapter 1 might help you take the first step. Once you start, you may find it easier to continue.

- *Ask for help with tasks and projects at school, work, and home.* You don't always have to go it alone. For example, if you have put off an assignment, ask your instructor for guidance. If you need accommodations because of a disability, don't assume that others know about it. Once you identify what's holding you up, see who can help you face the task.

- *Don't expect perfection.* No one is perfect. Most people learn by starting at the beginning and wading through plenty of mistakes and confusion. It's better to try your best than to do nothing at all.

Of course no one is going to be able to avoid procrastination all of the time. Do the best that you can. The first step is awareness of your particular tendencies. Once you know how you tend to waste time, you can take steps to change your habits.

Avoiding procrastination will help you to reduce the stress in your life. The following section explains some other strategies that can help as well.

How Can You Reduce Stress?

When you hear the word *stress*, you may think of tension, anger, and other negative thoughts and emotions. However, stress can have good results as well as bad. Stress is an effect of life change. It refers not to the change itself, but to how you react to the change. For this reason, even positive events can cause stress. Graduating or starting a new and better job can cause as much stress as can trouble with an instructor or a problem at work.

Today's college students are under high levels of stress. In fact, the *New York Times* reported that a national survey by researchers at the University of California at Los Angeles found that students are experiencing the highest levels of stress in a generation. In 1985, 16 percent of students said that they were frequently overwhelmed; this jumped to 30.2 percent in 1999. These stress levels are due in part to financial difficulties (many students need to work to pay all or part of their tuition) and the pressure to secure a good job after graduation (increased job competition has led to a need to perform well academically plus be active in diverse activities).[4]

Almost any change in your life can create some level of stress. Goal setting and time management, however, are key tools in handling stress because they help you make the most of your resources—time, energy, and outside help. Use your skills to set goals and to plan your time so that you can achieve those goals successfully.

GOAL: STRESS MANAGEMENT AND MENTAL HEALTH

Despite the popular belief that all stress is bad, some stress is actually good for your mental and physical health. When you are under stress, the increased energy and edginess you feel can motivate you to achieve peak performance. Studies have shown that moderate levels of stress can improve efficiency, while too little stress may result in boredom or inactivity. Only when your stress level is too high do you experience unproductive anxiety levels that can weaken performance and even immobilize you. Figure 3.4, based on research by Drs. Robert M. Yerkes and John D. Dodson, illustrates this concept.

Negative reactions to stress are a problem at school, especially as students try to adjust to the demands of college life. Thousands of students drop out each year and even more perform poorly because they are overwhelmed with the workload or the environment. Their anxiety level robs them of the ability to manage their time effectively and find solutions. Stress levels are also high in the workplace. According to a report issued by the American Institute of Stress and the American Psychological Association, job stress costs companies an estimated $200 billion a year.[5]

FIGURE

3.4

Yerkes-Dodson Law.

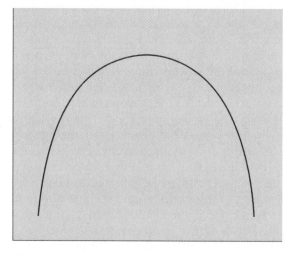

How can you manage stress? Here is where your goal-setting and time-management skills come in. These, and a few other helpful strategies, can help you successfully handle any stressful situation.

- *Set reasonable, manageable goals.* Trying to achieve something that is out of your reach will cause more stress than success.
- *Break big goals into smaller, short-term pieces.* Goals will appear more manageable when approached as a series of smaller steps. Perform a smaller task well rather than a larger one not so well.
- *Avoid procrastination.* However distasteful the task, it will be much worse when time runs short and the expectations of others hang over your head.
- *Limit your responsibilities and learn to say "no."* Stop stress before it starts by evaluating your time available and delegating what can be or should be taken care of by someone else.
- *Think positively.* Perceiving stress as good encourages you to push the boundaries of your abilities. For example, students who respond positively to the expectations of college instructors might be encouraged to improve their study and time-management skills in order to make the best use of their study time. In contrast, students who respond negatively to the same expectations may become overwhelmed.

GOAL: PHYSICAL HEALTH

Although your daily schedule may leave you little time to take care of yourself, you need to eat right, exercise, and get enough sleep in order to maintain a healthy body and minimize stress. The healthier you are, the more energy you'll have to pursue your studies and accomplish work tasks successfully.

Eating Right

The foods you eat help build and maintain your body. If you eat well, you are more likely to be strong and healthy. Learning to make healthier choices about what you eat on a daily basis can lead to more energy, better general health, reduced stress, and an enriched quality of life.

The U. S. Departments of Agriculture and Health and Human Services have developed a publication called *Dietary Guidelines for Americans* that lists seven important rules of healthy eating.

1. Eat a variety of foods.
2. Maintain a healthy weight.
3. Choose a diet low in fat and cholesterol.
4. Eat plenty of vegetables, fruits, and grain products.
5. Use sugars in moderation.
6. Use salt and sodium only in moderation.

7. If you drink alcoholic beverages, do so in moderation.

Maintaining balance and eating in moderation can help you maintain a healthy diet.

MAINTAINING BALANCE. If you vary your diet, you are more likely to take in the different nutrients that your body needs. A good balance will ensure that you get adequate amounts of fruits and vegetables, breads and cereals, and proteins, while minimizing substances that, in large quantities (e.g., sugars, fats, salt, caffeine), can damage your health.

EATING IN MODERATION. College, with its late-night study sessions, cafeterias, and fast-food availability, doesn't always make moderation easy. Eating moderate amounts of food, however, will help you avoid storing extra food as fat. Try not to eat more than your body can use. Eating too much of even the healthiest food still means more calories than one body needs. Unfortunately, eating disorders are fairly common in college student populations. If you feel that you have a problem controlling your eating or your feelings about food, speak with a counselor or nurse.

Exercising

Good physical fitness increases your energy efficiency. An efficient body system has more energy and more ability to direct that energy toward problem solving and the fulfillment of goals. A fit body also helps the mind handle stress. During physical activity, the brain releases endorphins, chemical compounds that have a positive and calming effect on the body.

Like a car, your body's physical power can decrease unless you put it to work. Staying in shape requires discipline. For maximum benefit, make regular exercise a way of life. If you haven't been exercising regularly, start slowly. Always check with a physician before beginning any exercise program, and adjust your program to your physical type and fitness level.

The type of exercise you choose depends on factors such as time available, physical limitations, preferences, available facilities, cost, and level of fitness. Types of exercise fall into three main categories.

- *Cardiovascular training* is exercise that strengthens your heart muscle and lung capacity. Examples include running, swimming, in-line skating, aerobic dancing, and biking.

- *Strength training* is exercise that strengthens many different muscle groups. Examples include using weight machines and free weights, or doing pushups and abdominal crunches.

- *Flexibility training* is exercise that maintains and increases muscle flexibility. Examples include various stretches and forms of yoga.

Student life, both in school and out, is crammed with responsibilities. You can't always make a nice, neat plan that gets you to the gym three days a week for two hours each time. You also may not have the money for an expensive health club. Check into your school's fitness opportunities—they may be low-cost or even included in your tuition. Use your time-management skills to fit exercise into your day. For example, you could walk to classes and meetings, take an exercise class at a campus fitness center nearby, or use exercise tapes at home.

Exercise is a key component of a healthy mind and body, as is adequate rest.

Getting Enough Sleep

No one can function well without adequate sleep. A lack of sleep, or poor sleep, causes poor concentration and irritability, which can mean a less-than-ideal performance at school and at work. Gauge your needs by evaluating how you feel. If you aren't fatigued or irritable during the day, you may have slept adequately. On the other hand, if you are groggy in the morning or doze off at various times, you may be sleep deprived.

College students often don't sleep enough. Worrying about exams, quizzes, or projects coming due may make you restless. Long study sessions may keep you up late, and early classes may get you up early. Assignments pile up and start to seem more important than a good night's sleep. Socializing, eating, and drinking may make it hard to settle down. Sleep expert Gregg D. Jacobs, Ph.D. recommends the following steps to better sleep.[6]

- *Reduce consumption of alcohol and caffeine.* Caffeine may keep you awake. Alcohol causes you to sleep lighter, making you feel less rested and refreshed when you awaken.
- *Exercise regularly.* Studies show that regular exercise, especially in late afternoon or early evening, promotes good sleep because it raises body temperature and then allows it to fall.
- *Complete tasks an hour or more before you sleep.* Getting things done some time before you turn in gives you a chance to wind down and calm your brain activity.

At times you may have trouble managing all the stresses in your life alone. That's when you should consider turning to others who are part of your school's resource network.

GOAL: USE YOUR SCHOOL'S RESOURCE NETWORK TO REDUCE STRESS

Whether you complete your studies over the course of six months or 60 years, your school's resource network can help you get where you want to go. Most schools offer a student orientation near the beginning of your first semester that explains the help that is available to you, including people, student services, organizations, and literature.

People

Your school has an array of people who can help you make the most of your educational experience. They are there to help you. Take the opportunity to get to know them and to let them get to know you. Together you can explore ways in which they can help you achieve your goals.

INSTRUCTORS. Your instructors can clarify course material or homework and advise you on course selection in their departments. An instructor who knows you well may even introduce you to prospective employers or give you a positive job reference. Instructors are busy; however, most keep office hours and will tell you the location and times. You are responsible for seeking out your instructor during office hours. If your schedule makes this impossible, let your instructor know, and perhaps you can schedule another time to meet or can communicate via e-mail.

TEACHING ASSISTANTS. Teaching assistants help an instructor with a course. You may or may not have teaching assistants in your courses. Sometimes they teach the small discussion or lab sections that accompany a large group lecture. They can be a great resource for help and advice, and are often available if your instructor is too swamped to talk to you.

ADMINISTRATORS. Members of your school's administrative staff have the responsibility to deliver to you—the student consumer—a first-rate product (i.e., your education, comprised of facilities, instructors, materials, and courses). Although students don't often have regular interaction with administrators, it is the business of administrative personnel to know how the school is serving you. If you have an issue you haven't been able to resolve on your own, schedule a meeting with your dean or department chair.

ADVISORS AND COUNSELORS. These individuals can help with both the educational and personal sides of being a student. They provide information, advice, a listening ear, and referrals. Generally, students are assigned academic advisors with whom they meet at least once a semester. Your academic advisor will help you find out about classes, choose a schedule, and select a major. Personal counselors, although not usually assigned, are available through student services or student health. These counselors can help you work through problems so you can refocus on your studies.

Student Services

Your school has a variety of services aimed at helping students. Basic services may include student health, career placement, and tutoring. Depending on your school, you may also find other services such as housing and transportation, adult education services, and academic centers.

Organizations

No matter your needs or interests, your school probably has an organization that will satisfy them. Organizations may be school sponsored (academic clubs), independent (government ROTC programs), or student run (Latino Student Association). Some focus on courses of study (Nursing Club), some are social (fraternities and sororities), some are artistic (Chamber Orchestra), and some are geared toward a hobby or activity (Runner's Club). Some you join to help others (Big Brothers or Big Sisters), and some offer to help you (Overeaters Anonymous). To find out about organizations, ask friends and instructors, consult your student handbook, or check the activities office if your school has one.

Helpful Literature

The college catalog and the student handbook can help you find your way. The *college catalog* is your school's academic directory, listing every department and course available at the school. The catalog groups courses according to subject matter and lists them from the lowest-level courses to the most advanced (see Figure 3.5 for a segment of an actual college catalog from Baltimore City Community College[7]). Catalogs may also contain school policies, instructional programs, and more.

College catalog page. **FIGURE 3.5**

Course Descriptions

BIO 112: Anatomy and Physiology II (4 credits)

45 lecture hours; 45 lab hours
Fall, Spring - day, eve

Prerequisites: MAT 81; ENG 80 and RDG 82 or appropriate ACCUPLACER scores

Lab fee

This course provides a continuation of BIO 111 designed to provide up-to-date principles of the cardiovascular, lymphatic, respiratory, digestive, excretory (urinary), and reproductive (male and female) systems. Embryology, genetics and immunology are included. A consideration of the effects of stress on normal anatomy and physiology is interwoven throughout the course.

BIO 115: Principles of Ecology (3 credits)

45 lecture hours

The science of ecology is introduced with the major components of an ecosystem examined. Energy, biogeochemical cycles, and ecosystem structures and relationships are studied in both lecture and field components. Current environmental issues are also considered.

BIO 199: Individual Study in Biology (3 credits)

See IS -Individual Study.

This course is mainly offered to students in the

BIO 212: Microbiology (4 credits)

45 lecture hours; 45 lab hours
Fall, Spring - day, eve

Prerequisite: 6-8 credits in biology and/or chemistry

Lab fee

This course includes topics in morphology, physiology, genetics, control, culture and identification of microorganisms, along with a separate unit focusing on immunology. Emphasis is placed on the role of microorganisms in health and diseases.

BIOTECHNOLOGY—BTC

BTC 101: Special Topics in Biotechnology I (2 credits)

30 lecture hours
Fall, Spring - day

Students are introduced to the field of biotechnology with a preview of basic research and development techniques, laboratory safety, and career awareness. Field trips, computer simulations, lectures, and guest speakers are used in this course.

BTC 102: Special Topics in Biotechnology II (2 credits)

30 lecture hours
Fall - day

Your *student handbook* looks beyond specific courses to the big picture, helping you to navigate student life. In it you will find some or all of the following, and maybe more: information on available housing (for on-campus residents) and on parking and driving (for commuters); overviews of the support offices for students, such as academic advising and financial aid; descriptions of special-interest clubs; and details about library and computer services. It may also list hours, locations, phone numbers, and addresses for offices, clubs, and organizations.

Keep both the catalog and handbook handy. They can save you a lot of time and trouble when you need to find information about a resource or service.

In Hebrew, the word *chai* means "life," representing all aspects of life—spiritual, emotional, family, educational, and career. Individual Hebrew characters have number values. Because the characters in the word *chai* add up to 18, the number 18 has come to be associated with good luck. As you plan your goals, think about your view of luck. Many people feel that a person can create his or her own luck by pursuing goals persistently and staying open to possibilities and opportunities.

Consider that your vision of life may largely determine how you live. You can prepare the way for luck by establishing goals, educational and otherwise, and forging ahead toward them. If you believe that the life you want awaits you, you will be able to recognize and make the most of luck when it comes around. L'Chaim—to life, and good luck.

Study Skills in Action

CHAPTER 3

Test Competence

MEASURING WHAT YOU'VE LEARNED

MULTIPLE CHOICE. *Circle or highlight the answer that seems to fit best.*

1. Long-term goals can be defined as
   A. goals that you think about for a long time before setting them.
   B. only those goals that focus on career and family decisions.
   C. the goals that you will only be able to reach when you are much older.
   D. the broad goals that you want to accomplish over a long period of time.

2. Short-term goals can be defined as
   A. goals with a narrower focus that are often steps toward a long-term goal.
   B. goals that are not as important as other long-term goals.
   C. goals that you can almost always accomplish in less than a day.
   D. goals that are independent of your long-term educational and career goals.

3. By identifying your educational goals, you will be able to do all of the following **except**
   A. select the subjects and courses related to your educational and career goals.
   B. connect with others who share your interests.
   C. identify the skills you must master while you are still in college.
   D. decide where you want to live after you graduate.

4. The purpose of time management is
   A. to make sure you have no down time that interferes with your study schedule.
   B. to effectively build and manage your schedule so you can accomplish your goals.
   C. to make you conscious of time and how you use it from day to day.
   D. to make your schedule rather than your goals your central focus.

5. It is important to link daily and weekly goals with long-term goals because
    A. the process will help you focus on the things that are most important to you.
    B. short-term goals have no meaning if they are not placed in a longer time frame.
    C. the process will help you eliminate frivolous activities.
    D. others expect you to know how everything you do relates to what you want to accomplish in life.

6. Strategic planning to achieve your goals will enable you to
    A. learn to react to whatever happens to you as you pursue your goals.
    B. accept the course of action toward your goals suggested by your college advisor.
    C. become more competitive.
    D. explore the possible positive and negative effects of your current decisions.

7. When you schedule, two ways you gain control of your life are
    A. allocating time for goals and reminding yourself of tasks and events.
    B. taking time to write in your date book and finding the best way to plan.
    C. discovering your priorities and acting on them.
    D. managing time and fighting procrastination.

8. According to Burka and Yuen, procrastination is a problem for all of the following reasons **except**
    A. it promotes the measuring of the person solely according to the performance.
    B. it promotes a fear of failure that prevents risk-taking.
    C. it prevents you from adjusting your goals.
    D. it is based on the expectation of perfection.

9. Stress is most accurately defined as
    A. always negative and problematic.
    B. endured only by people with poor coping skills.
    C. an effect of both positive and negative life change.
    D. unrelated to time management or personal goals.

10. Your school's resource network includes

    A. your parents, friends, and the college catalog.

    B. your study-group members and social organizations.

    C. your employer and the college-career center.

    D. your instructors and the student handbook.

TRUE/FALSE. *Place a T or an F beside each statement to indicate whether you think it is true or false.*

1. _____ Your goals are not connected to your values.

2. _____ Financial and lifestyle goals should be considered when you are choosing a career path.

3. _____ A priority is an action or intention that takes precedence in time, attention, or position.

4. _____ Always using a date book to help manage your time will limit your flexibility.

5. _____ Once you set a long-term goal, you shouldn't adjust it.

Brain Power

BUILDING VOCABULARY FITNESS

The paragraphs below are taken from the current media. Read the paragraph, noting the context of the vocabulary words shown in bold type. Next, for each vocabulary word (reprinted in the left-hand column), highlight the word or phrase in column A, B, or C that is the most similar in meaning. Finally, on a separate sheet of paper, solidify your understanding of these words by using each in a sentence of your own.

> "What is happening is an enormous backlash by the public," said Dr. Bernard Lown, a Nobel prize laureate and a leader of the Massachusetts initiative drive.
>
> A push to **overhaul** the health care system, he said, "has to come from below, from the state level; you're closer to the people, you're closer to their pain, and they're more readily **mobilized.**"
>
> He and other campaigners say they believe a **convergence** of several factors is at work in their favor. They point to the swelling numbers of uninsured people, the trouble that many patients have paying for their prescription drugs, the **spiraling** costs of medical care and the widespread complaints from doctors and nurses that new **constraints** are keeping them from offering the best care to their patients.
>
> From "State Initiatives Seek Overhaul of Health Care," by Carey Goldberg, *The New York Times*, Sunday, June 11, 2000.

Vocabulary Words	A	B	C
1. **overhaul**	repair	evaluate	replace
2. **mobilized**	concerned	energized	marshalled
3. **convergence**	meeting	force	hiding
4. **spiraling**	fast-falling	fast-rising	steady
5. **constraints**	annoyances	problems	restrictions

Strategic Thinking

GETTING THE BIG PICTURE

Answer the following questions on a separate piece of paper or in a journal.

Try to name five time-management strategies that you think would help you to reduce stress at school and at your job. Choose two that you believe are most helpful to you, given your particular needs and learning style, and describe how you plan to use them. If you are or have been in the workplace, tell a brief story about how any one particular strategy saved you time and trouble (or, if you want, how not using one made life difficult for you).

NOTES

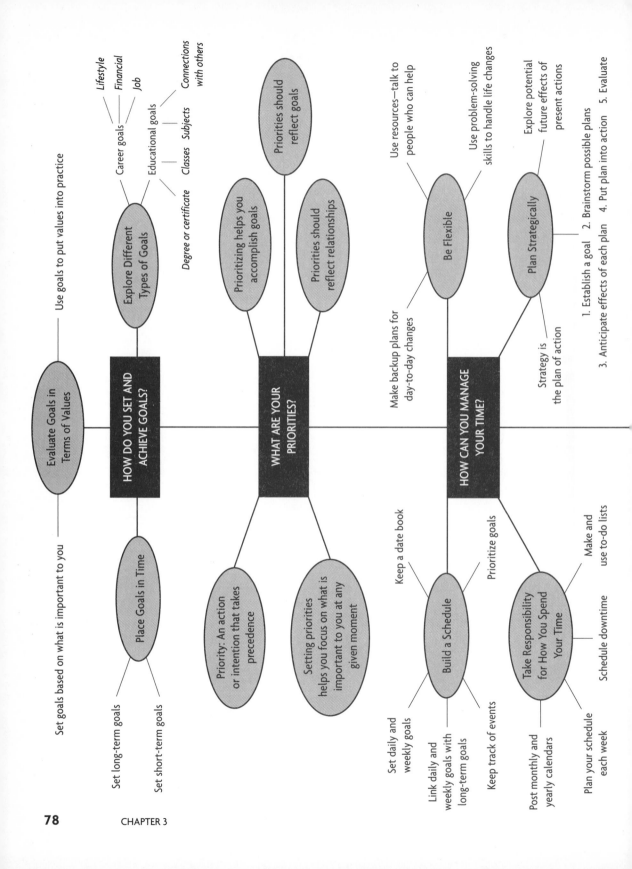

Set goals based on what is important to you — Use goals to put values into practice

Evaluate Goals in Terms of Values

HOW DO YOU SET AND ACHIEVE GOALS?

Explore Different Types of Goals

Lifestyle
Financial
Job

Career goals

Educational goals — Classes Subjects

Connections with others

Degree or certificate

Place Goals in Time

Set long-term goals

Set short-term goals

WHAT ARE YOUR PRIORITIES?

Priorities should reflect goals

Prioritizing helps you accomplish goals

Priorities should reflect relationships

Priority: An action or intention that takes precedence

Setting priorities helps you focus on what is important to you at any given moment

HOW CAN YOU MANAGE YOUR TIME?

Use resources—talk to people who can help

Be Flexible

Use problem-solving skills to handle life changes

Make backup plans for day-to-day changes

Explore potential future effects of present actions

Plan Strategically

Strategy is the plan of action

1. Establish a goal   2. Brainstorm possible plans
3. Anticipate effects of each plan   4. Put plan into action   5. Evaluate

Keep a date book

Build a Schedule

Prioritize goals

Set daily and weekly goals

Link daily and weekly goals with long-term goals

Keep track of events

Take Responsibility for How You Spend Your Time

Make and use to-do lists

Post monthly and yearly calendars

Schedule downtime

Plan your schedule each week

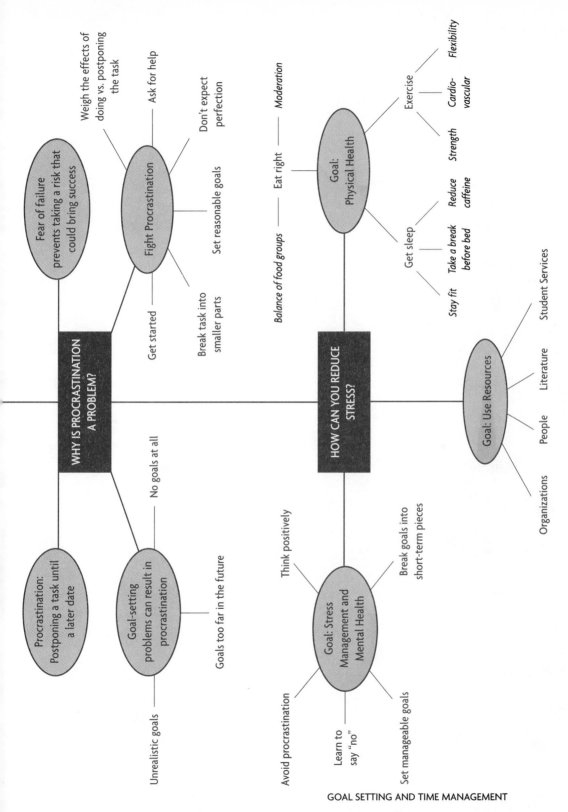

Fear of failure prevents taking a risk that could bring success

Weigh the effects of doing vs. postponing the task

Ask for help

Fight Procrastination

Don't expect perfection

Set reasonable goals

Get started

Break task into smaller parts

WHY IS PROCRASTINATION A PROBLEM?

Procrastination: Postponing a task until a later date

No goals at all

Goal-setting problems can result in procrastination

Goals too far in the future

Unrealistic goals

Balance of food groups — Eat right — *Moderation*

Exercise

Flexibility

Cardio-vascular

Strength

Goal: Physical Health

Reduce caffeine

Get sleep

Take a break before bed

Stay fit

HOW CAN YOU REDUCE STRESS?

Think positively

Break goals into short-term pieces

Goal: Stress Management and Mental Health

Avoid procrastination

Learn to say "no"

Set manageable goals

Goal: Use Resources

Student Services

Literature

People

Organizations

CREATE

4

Your mind's powers show in everything you do, from the smallest chores to the most complex situations. Critical thinking enables your mind to process, store, and create with the facts and ideas it encounters. Understanding how your mind works is the first step toward critical thinking. When you have that understanding, you can perform the essential critical-thinking task: asking important questions about ideas, information, and media. Such questions are as important in your course work as they are on the job. As you work to accumulate new knowledge, consider it in light of what you already know, and put what you know to work deriving new ideas and solutions to problems.

This chapter will show you both the mind's basic actions and the strategies and thought processes that incorporate them. You will explore how being an open-minded critical thinker will promote your success in college, career, and life. At the end of the chapter, you will be able to answer these questions:

- What is critical thinking?
- How does critical thinking help you solve problems?
- How do you construct and evaluate arguments?
- How do you think logically?
- What is media literacy?

CRITICAL THINKING

TAPPING THE POWER OF YOUR MIND

> *"We do not live to think, but, on the contrary, we think in order that we may succeed in surviving."*
>
> **José Ortega y Gasset**

What Is Critical Thinking?

Although you might figure that the word "critical" implies something difficult and negative, critical thinking is "critical" mainly in the sense of one particular dictionary definition of *critical:* "indispensable" and "important." You think critically every day, though you may not realize it.

DEFINING CRITICAL THINKING

The following is one way to define critical thinking:

> Critical thinking is thinking that *goes beyond the basic recall of information* but depends on the information recalled. It focuses on the *important, or critical, aspects* of the information. Critical thinking means *asking questions.* Critical thinking means that you *take in information, question it, and then use it* to create new ideas, solve problems, make decisions, construct arguments, make plans, and refine your view of the world.

Think about responses you or others have had to different situations. Consider when you have seen critical thinking take place, and when you haven't, and what resulted from each way of responding. This will help you begin to see what kind of an effect critical thinking can have on the way you live.

THE PATH OF CRITICAL THINKING

Look at Figure 4.1 to see a visual representation of critical thinking. The path involves taking in information, questioning information, and then using information.

Taking In Information

Although most of this chapter focuses on questioning and using information, the first step of the process is just as crucial. The information you

The critical-thinking path.

FIGURE

4.1

What you hear   What you experience   What you say   What you do

Take in information   ASK QUESTIONS   Use information

What you see   What you read   What you write   What you create

receive is the raw material that you will examine and mold into something new. If you take in information accurately and without judgment, you will have the best material with which to work as you think. Once you have the clearest, most complete information possible, then you can begin to examine its important aspects through questioning.

Questioning Information

A critical thinker asks many kinds of questions about a given piece of information, such as: *Where did it come from? What could explain it? In what ways is it true or false? How do I feel about it, and why? How is this information similar to or different from what I already know? Is it good or bad? What caused it, and what effects does it have?* Critical thinkers also try to transform information into something they can use. They ask whether information can help them solve a problem, make a decision, learn or create something new, or anticipate the future.

As an example of the questioning process, consider the following as your "information in": You encounter a number of situations—financial strain, parenting on your own, and being an older student—that seem to be getting in the way of your success at school. Whereas nonquestioning thinkers may assume defeat, critical thinkers will examine the situation with questions. Here are some you might ask:

- *What exactly are my obstacles?* Examples of my obstacles are a heavy work schedule, single parenting, being in debt, and returning to school after 10 years out. **(recall)**

- *Are there other cases different from mine?* I do have one friend who is going through problems worse than mine, and she's getting by. I also know another guy who doesn't have too much to deal with that I can tell, and he's struggling just like I am. **(difference)**

- *Who has problems similar to mine?* Well, if I consider my obstacles specifically, my statement might mean that single parents and returning adult students will all have trouble in school. That is not necessarily true. People who have obstacles may still become successful. **(similarity)**

- *What is an example of someone who has had success despite obstacles?* What about Oseola McCarty, the cleaning woman who saved money all her life and raised $150,000 to create a scholarship at the University of Southern Mississippi? She didn't have what anyone would call advantages, such as a high-paying job or a college education. **(idea to example)**

- *What conclusion can I draw from my questions?* From thinking about my friend and about Oseola McCarty, I conclude that people can successfully overcome their obstacles by working hard, focusing on their abilities, and concentrating on their goals. **(example to idea)**

- *Why am I worried about this?* Maybe I am scared of returning to school. Maybe I am afraid to challenge myself. Whatever the cause, the effect is that I feel bad about myself and don't work to the best of my abilities, and that can hurt me and others who depend on me. **(cause and effect)**

- *How do I evaluate the effects of my worries?* I think they're harmful. When we say that obstacles equal difficulty, we can damage our desire to try to overcome them. When we say that successful people don't have obstacles, we might overlook that some very successful people have to deal with hidden disadvantages such as learning disabilities or abusive families. **(evaluation)**

Remember these types of questions. When you explore the seven mind actions (building blocks of thought) later in the chapter, refer to these questions to see how they illustrate the different actions your mind performs.

Using Information

After taking in and examining information, critical thinkers try to transform it into something they can use. They use information to help them solve a problem, make a decision, learn or create something new, or anticipate what will happen in the future. This part of the critical-thinking path is where you benefit from the hard work of asking questions. This is where inventions happen, new processes are born, theories are created, and information interacts with your own thoughts to create something new.

THE VALUE OF CRITICAL THINKING

Critical thinking has many positive effects, or benefits, including the following:

YOU WILL INCREASE YOUR ABILITY TO PERFORM THINKING PROCESSES. Critical thinking is a learned skill, just like shooting a basketball or using a word-processing program. As with any other skill, the more you use it, the better you become. The more you ask questions, the better you think. The better you think, the more effective you will be in school, work, and life situations.

YOU CAN PRODUCE KNOWLEDGE, RATHER THAN JUST REPRODUCE IT. The interaction of newly learned information with what you already know creates new knowledge. Its usefulness can be judged by your ability to apply it. For instance, it won't mean much for education students to quote the stages of child development on an exam unless they can evaluate children's needs when they begin working as teachers.

YOU CAN BE A MORE VALUABLE EMPLOYEE. You won't be a failure if you follow directions. However, you will be even more valuable if you ask strategic questions—ranging from "Is there a better way to deliver messages?" to "How can we increase enrollment?"—that will improve productivity. Employees who think critically are more likely to progress in their careers than those who simply do what they are told.

Your mind has some basic moves, or actions, that it performs in order to understand the relation between ideas and concepts. Sometimes it uses one action by itself, but most often it uses two or more in combination. These actions are the blocks you will use to build the critical-thinking processes you will explore later in the chapter.

LEARNING HOW YOUR MIND WORKS

Identify your mind's actions using a system originally conceived by educators Frank Lyman, Arlene Mindus, and Charlene Lopez[1] and developed by numerous other instructors. Based on their studies of how students think, they named seven basic building blocks of thought. These actions are not new to you, although some of their names may be. They represent the ways in which you think all the time.

Through exploring these actions, you can go beyond just thinking and learn how you think. This will help you take charge of your own thinking. The more you know about how your mind works, the more control you will have over thinking processes such as problem solving and decision making.

Following are explanations of each of the mind actions, including examples. As you read, write your examples in the blank spaces. Icons representing each action will help you visualize and remember them.

RECALL. *Facts, sequence,* and *description.* This is the simplest action. When you **recall** you name or describe facts, objects, or events, or put them into sequence. *Examples:*

- Naming the steps of a geometry proof, in order.
- Remembering your best friends' phone numbers.

Your example. Recall two important school-related events this month.

_____

_____

The icon. Capital R stands for recall or remembering.

SIMILARITY. *Analogy,* *likeness,* and *comparison.* This action examines what is **similar** about one or more things. You might compare situations, ideas, people, stories, events, or objects. *Examples:*

- Comparing notes with another student to see what facts and ideas you both consider important.
- Analyzing the arguments you've had with your partner this month and seeing how they all seem to be about the same problem.

Your example. Tell what is similar about two of your best friends.

_____

_____

The icon. The Venn diagram illustrates the idea of similarity. The two circles represent the things being compared, and the shaded area of the intersection indicates that they have some degree or element of similarity.

DIFFERENCE. *Distinction* and *contrast.* This action examines what is **different** about one or more situations, ideas, people, stories, events, or objects, contrasting them with one another. *Examples:*

- Seeing how two instructors differ—one divides the class into small groups for discussions; the other keeps desks in place and delivers lectures.
- Contrasting a day when you combine work and school with a day when you only attend class.

Your example. Explain how your response to a course you like differs from how you respond to a course you don't like as much.

_____

_____

The icon. Here the Venn diagram is used again, to show difference. The nonintersecting parts of the circles are shaded, indicating that the focus is on what is not in common.

CAUSE AND EFFECT. *Reasons,* *consequences,* and *prediction.* Using this action, you look at what has **caused** a fact, situation, or event and what **effects,** or consequences, come from it. In other words, you examine what led up to something and what will follow because of it. *Examples:*

- Staying up late causes you to oversleep, which causes you to be late to class. This causes you to miss some material, which has the further effect of your having problems on the test.
- When you pay your phone and utility bills on time, you create effects such as a better credit rating, uninterrupted service, and a better relationship with your service providers.

Your example. Name what causes you to like your favorite class and the effects the class has on you.

_____

_____

The icon. The arrows, pointing toward one another in a circular pattern, show how a cause leads to an effect.

EXAMPLE TO IDEA.   *Generalization, classification,* and *conceptualization.* From one or more **examples** (facts or events), you develop a general **idea** or ideas. Grouping facts or events into patterns may allow you to make a general statement about several of them at once. Classifying a fact or event helps you build knowledge. This mind action moves from the specific to the general. *Examples:*

- You have had trouble finding a baby-sitter. A classmate even brought her child to class once. Your brother drops his daughter at day care and doesn't like not seeing her all day. From these examples, you derive the idea that your school needs an on-campus day-care program.
- You see a movie and you decide it is mostly about pride.

Your example. Name activities you enjoy. From them, derive an idea of a class you want to take.

_____

_____

The icon. The arrow and "Ex" pointing to a light bulb on the right indicate how an example or examples lead to the idea (the light bulb, lit up).

IDEA TO EXAMPLE.   *Categorization, substantiation,* and *proof.* In a reverse of the previous action, you take an **idea** or ideas and think of **examples** (events or facts) that support or prove that idea. This mind action moves from the general to the specific. *Examples:*

- For a paper, you start with this thesis statement: "Computer knowledge is a must for the modern worker." To support that idea, you gather examples, such as the number of industries that use computers, the kinds of training employers are requiring, and so on.

- You talk to your instructor about changing your major, giving examples that support your idea, such as the fact that you have worked in the field you want to change to and you have fulfilled some of the requirements for that major already.

Your example. Name an admirable person. Give examples that show how that person is admirable.

_____

_____

The icon. In a reverse of the previous icon, this one starts with the light bulb and has an arrow pointing to "Ex." This indicates that you start with the idea and then move to the supporting examples.

EVALUATION. *Value, judgment,* and *rating.* Here you **evaluate** whether something is useful or not useful, important or unimportant, good or bad, or right or wrong by identifying and weighing its positive and negative effects (pros and cons). Be sure to consider the specific situation at hand (a cold drink might be good on the beach in August, not so good in the snowdrifts in January). With the facts you have gathered, you determine the value of something in terms of both predicted effects and your own needs. Cause-and-effect analysis always accompanies evaluation. *Examples:*

- For one semester, you schedule classes in the afternoons and spend nights working. You find that you tend to sleep late and lose your only study time. From this harmful effect, you evaluate that it doesn't work for you. You decide to schedule earlier classes next time.

- Someone offers you a chance to cheat on a test. You evaluate the potential effects if you are caught. You also evaluate the long-term effects of not actually learning the material and of doing something ethically wrong. You decide that it isn't right or worthwhile to cheat.

Your example. Evaluate your mode of transportation to school.

_____

_____

The icon. A set of scales out of balance indicates how you weigh positive and negative effects to arrive at an evaluation.

You may want to use a *mnemonic device*—a memory tool, as explained in Chapter 8—to remember the seven mind actions. You can make a sentence of words that each start with a mind action's first letter, such as "Really Smart Dogs Cook Eggs In Enchiladas."

Understanding the seven mind actions puts you in control of your mind and your life. You are privy to the mechanics and language of thinking in a way that you wouldn't be if you didn't have this understanding. For example, this knowledge can help you focus immediately on what a professor wants when he asks an *inferential* question. Knowing that he or she is asking you to draw a cause-and-effect connection will help you feel in control. From a broader perspective, the teacher is no longer the high priest of the mind. You now play an equal and active part in the faith of cognition.

FRANK LYMAN, EDUCATIONAL CONSULTANT,
UNIVERSITY OF MARYLAND

EXPERT INSIGHT

**Learn the Mind
Actions and Take Control**

HOW MIND ACTIONS BUILD THINKING PROCESSES

The seven mind actions are the fundamental building blocks that indicate the relations between ideas and concepts. You will rarely use one at a time in the step-by-step process, as presented here. You will usually combine them, overlap them, and repeat them, using different actions for different situations. For example, when a test question asks you to explain prejudice, you might give *examples*, *different* from one another, that show your *idea* of prejudice (combining "difference" with "example to idea").

When you combine mind actions in working toward a goal, you are performing a thinking process. The next sections discuss three of the most important critical-thinking processes: solving problems, constructing and evaluating arguments, and thinking logically. Each thinking process helps to direct your critical thinking toward the achievement of your goals. Figure 4.6, appearing later in the chapter, reminds you that the mind actions form the core of the thinking processes.

How Does Critical Thinking
Help You Solve Problems?

Problem solving is probably the most crucial and common thinking process, and requires various mind actions. Although it has multiple steps, you will not always have to work through each step. As you become more comfortable with solving problems, your mind will automatically click through the steps. Also, you will become more adept at evaluating which problems need serious consideration and which can be taken care of quickly and simply.

Life constantly presents problems to be solved, ranging from average daily problems (how to manage study time) to life-altering situations (how to design a child-custody plan during a divorce). Choosing a solution without thinking critically may have negative effects. If you use the steps of the following problem-solving process, however, you have the best chance of coming up with a favorable solution.

You can apply this problem-solving plan to any problem. Taking the steps maximizes the number of possible solutions you generate and allows you to explore each one as fully as possible.

STEP 1. *Identify the problem accurately.* What are the facts? *Recall* the details of the situation. To define a problem correctly, focus on its causes rather than its effects. Consider the Chinese saying, "Give a man a fish, and he will eat for a day. Teach a man to fish, and he will eat for a lifetime." If you state the problem as "The man is hungry," giving him a fish seems like a good solution. Unfortunately, the problem returns—because hunger is an effect. Focusing on the cause brings a new problem statement: "The man does not know how to find food." Given that his lack of knowledge is the true cause, teaching him to fish will truly solve the problem.

Sample problem. A student is not understanding course material.

STEP 2. *Analyze the problem.* Analyze, or break down into understandable pieces, what surrounds the problem. What *effects* of the situation concern you? What *causes* these effects? Are there hidden causes? Look at the causes and effects that surround the problem.

Sample problem. If some effects of not understanding include poor grades and lack of interest, some causes may include poor study habits, not listening in class, or lack of sleep.

STEP 3. *Brainstorm possible solutions.* Brainstorming means freeing your mind to come up with as many possible ideas as you can without immediately deciding that they are good or bad. Evaluate ideas later, after you have had a chance to think about them. Remember that to get to the heart of a problem you must base possible solutions on the most significant causes instead of putting a bandage on the effects.

Sample problem. Looking at his study habits, the student comes up with ideas like seeking help from his instructor or working with a study group.

STEP 4. *Explore each solution.* Why might your solution work, or not? Might a solution work partially, or in a particular situation? *Evaluate* ahead of time the pros and cons (positive and negative effects) of each plan.

Create a chain of causes and effects in your head, as far into the future as you can, to see where this solution might lead.

Sample problem. The student considers the effects of improved study habits, more sleep, tutoring, or dropping the class.

STEP 5. *Choose and execute the solution you decide is best.* Decide how you will put your solution to work. Then, execute your solution.

Sample problem. The student decides on a combination of improved study habits and tutoring.

STEP 6. *Evaluate the solution that you acted upon, looking at its effects.* What are the positive and negative *effects* of what you did? In terms of your needs, was it a useful solution or not? Could the solution use any adjustments to be more useful? Would you do the same again or not? In evaluating, you are collecting data.

Sample problem. Evaluating his choice, the student may decide that the effects are good but that his fatigue still causes a problem.

STEP 7. *Continue to evaluate and refine the solution.* Problem solving is a process. You may have opportunities to apply the same solution again. Evaluate repeatedly, making changes that you decide make the solution better (i.e., more reflective of the causes of the problem).

Sample problem. The student may decide to continue to study more regularly but, after a few weeks of tutoring, could opt to trade in the tutoring time for some extra sleep. He may decide to take what he has learned from the tutor so far and apply it to his increased study efforts.

Using this process will enable you to solve school, work, and personal problems in a thoughtful, comprehensive way. The think link in Figure 4.2 demonstrates a way to visualize the flow of problem solving. Figure 4.3 shows how one person used this plan to solve a problem. It represents the same plan as Figure 4.2 but gives room to write so that it can be used in the problem-solving process.

Decision making is similar to problem solving. You can apply the problem-solving model to a decision, although it makes more sense to use it for decisions that require that you solve a problem (e.g., not many people would say that deciding what to order for lunch is a problem). Decisions are choices. Making a choice, or decision, requires thinking critically through the possible choices and evaluating which will work best for you and for the situation.

Solving problems can take time. Think through any situation thoroughly, considering your own ideas as well as those of others you trust, but don't hesitate to act once you have your plan. You cannot benefit from your chosen solution until you act upon it and follow through.

FIGURE

4.2

Problem-solving plan.

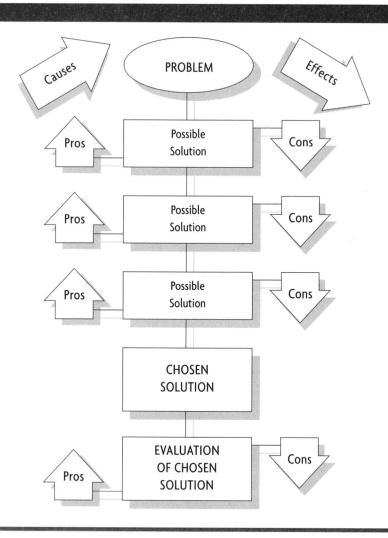

How Do You Construct and Evaluate Arguments?

In this case, "argument" refers to a persuasive case that you make to prove or disprove a point. It is a set of connected ideas supported by examples. Any time a statement is presented and supported—such as in textbook reading, newspaper articles, or lectures—an argument is taking place.

LIST CAUSES OF PROBLEM:

Must go to school to take classes

Can't have child with me in class

No one else at home to watch
  child

STATE PROBLEM HERE:

Need some way to
provide child-care
while I'm at school

LIST EFFECTS OF PROBLEM:

Missed exams and classes sometimes

Logistics take extra time, transport

Stress created for me and child

Lack of routine & comfort

*Use boxes below to list
possible solutions:*

List potential **POSITIVE**
effects for each solution:

Care is consistent

Reliable and familiar setting

Doesn't matter if child is sick

SOLUTION #1

Have a nanny at home

List potential **NEGATIVE**
effects for each solution:

Expensive

Hard to find someone to trust

Person must follow my schedule

SOLUTION #2

Join child-care co-op

Meet parents like myself

Child has playmates

Inexpensive

Must trust other parents

Sick child might get others sick

SOLUTION #3

Get school to provide
child care on campus

Close by to classes

Reliable care

No extra transport time

Costs school money

Need to find space and create facility

Restrictions & waiting lists

*Now choose the solution
you think is best—and try it.*

CHOSEN SOLUTION

Join child-care co-op

List the actual **POSITIVE**
effects for each solution:

Met some helpful people who understand me

My child likes the other three children

Low cost helps my budget

List the actual **NEGATIVE**
effects for each solution:

When it's my turn, I have to care for four children

Sometimes our schedules clash

Can't let a sick child participate

FINAL EVALUATION: Was it a good or bad choice?

All in all, I think this is the best I could do on my budget. There are times when I have to
stay home with a sick child, buy I'm mostly able to stay committed to both parenting and school.

CONSTRUCTING AN ARGUMENT

You will often encounter situations in which your success depends on your ability to persuade someone, either verbally or in writing, to agree with you. You may need to write a paper persuading the reader that a particular historical event changed the world, for example, or you may need to persuade a prospective employer that you are the one for the job.

An argument is based on a particular topic and issue. It starts with an idea or *premise*, gives examples to support that premise, and finally asserts a conclusion. See Figure 4.4 for an example of an argument.

To construct an argument, follow these steps:

1. *Establish the premise.* Define what you want to argue. Establish the topic of your argument (the subject) and the issue at hand (the question that your argument will answer in a certain way).

2. *Gather examples in support.* Gather evidence that supports your premise, then put it into logical order. You might want to use "chain support"—a set of reasons that build on one another.

3. *Anticipate questions and points against you.* What might you be asked to explain? What could someone say that argues against you? Decide what you will say to address issues and opposing points.

4. *Draw a conclusion.* Formulate a conclusion that summarizes how this evidence supports your initial premise. Keep your goal in mind and make sure that your conclusion reflects that goal.

FIGURE 4.4   *A sample argument.*

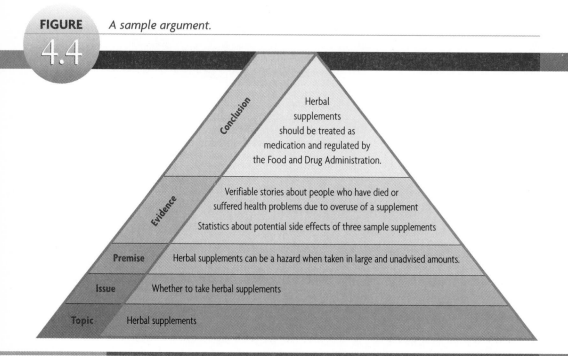

Conclusion: Herbal supplements should be treated as medication and regulated by the Food and Drug Administration.

Evidence: Verifiable stories about people who have died or suffered health problems due to overuse of a supplement
Statistics about potential side effects of three sample supplements

Premise: Herbal supplements can be a hazard when taken in large and unadvised amounts.

Issue: Whether to take herbal supplements

Topic: Herbal supplements

As an example, here is one way to present an argument for a raise and promotion at work.

- *Your topic:* Job status
- *Your issue:* What role you should have at this point in your career
- *Your premise:* You deserve a raise and promotion
- *Your audience:* Your supervisor (who may or may not be receptive, depending on your relationship)
- *Your evidence, or examples, that support your idea:* You are a solid, creative performer. You feel that your experience and high level of motivation will have positive effects for the company.

   Questions you anticipate: "What have you achieved in your current position?" "What do you know about the position you want to take?" "What new and creative ideas do you have?"

   Potential counter-arguments: Your supervisor might say that you may not be able to handle the new position's hours because of your school schedule. In preparation, you could look into what it would take to reschedule classes and make adjustments in your other commitments.

- *Your conclusion:* Promoting you would have positive effects for both you and the company.

Above all, always work to remain flexible. You never know what turn a conversation will take, or how a written argument will be interpreted. Keep your mind active and ready to address any surprises that come your way, and watch out for errors in thinking—on your part or on the part of your audience.

EVALUATING AN ARGUMENT

It's easy—and common—to accept or reject an argument outright, according to whether it fits with one's own opinions and views. If you ask questions about an argument, however, you will be able to determine its validity and will learn more from it. Furthermore, critical thinking will help you avoid accepting opinions and assumptions that are not supported by evidence.

Thinking critically about an argument involves a two-part evaluation:

- Evaluating the quality of the evidence itself
- Evaluating whether the evidence adequately supports the premise

These two considerations will give you a pretty good idea of whether the argument works. If good quality evidence (true input) combines with good quality use of evidence (valid reasoning), you get a solid argument (true output).

Evidence Quality

Ask the following questions in order to see whether the evidence itself is valid.

- What type of evidence is it—fact or opinion?
- How is the evidence similar to, or different from, what I already believe to be true?
- Where is the evidence from? Are those sources reliable and free of bias? (Examples of sources include intuition, authorities, personal experience, and observation.)

Support Quality

Ask these questions to determine whether you think the evidence successfully makes the argument.

- Do examples logically follow from ideas, and ideas logically lead to given examples?
- Does the evidence show similarity to what I consider common sense?
- Are there enough pieces of evidence to support the conclusion well?
- Do I know of any competing views or pieces of evidence that differ from this evidence?
- Has the argument evaluated all of the positive and negative effects involved? Is there any unconsidered negative effect to what the conclusion is arguing? For whom, and why?

The more you read and listen to arguments, the more adept you will become at evaluating them. Read a newspaper and listen to public radio. Pay attention to the views of people around you. Make an effort not to take anything as true or false without spending some time asking questions about it first.

How Do You Think Logically?

Logical thinking involves questioning the truth and accuracy of information in order to find out whether it is true or reliable. Logical thinking includes these two primary tasks: distinguishing fact from opinion and identifying and evaluating assumptions.

DISTINGUISHING FACT FROM OPINION

Fact, according to the dictionary, is information presented as objectively real and verifiable. *Opinion* is defined as a belief, conclusion, or judgment and is inherently difficult, if not impossible, to verify. Being able to distin-

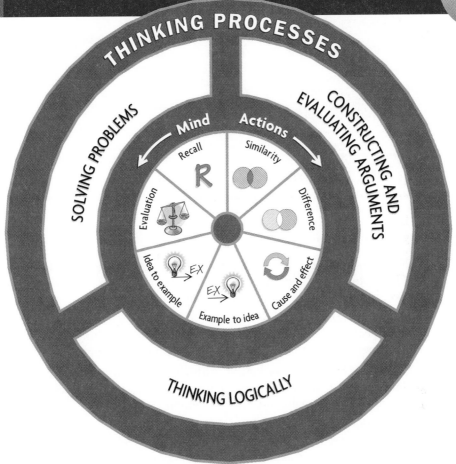

guish fact from opinion is crucial to your understanding of reading material and your ability to decide what information to believe and put to use. See Table 4.1 for some more examples of factual statements versus statements of opinion. From the information in the table, observe that facts refer to the observable or measurable, while opinions involve cause-and-effect exploration.

Characteristics of Facts and Opinions

Following are some indicators that will help you determine what is fact and what is opinion.[2]

TABLE

4.1

Examples of facts and opinions.

TOPIC	FACTUAL STATEMENT	STATEMENT OF OPINION
Stock market	In 1999 the Dow Jones Industrial average rose above 10,000 for the first time.	The Dow Jones Industrial average will continue to grow throughout the first decade of the twenty-first century.
Weather	It's raining outside.	This is the worst rainstorm I've ever seen.
History	Franklin Roosevelt and his administration developed a plan, entitled The New Deal, to address the problems of the Great Depression.	The problems of the Social Security system are a direct result of Roosevelt's New Deal legislation.

Indicators of opinion are:

- *Statements that show evaluation.* Any statement of value—such as "Television is bad for children"—indicates an opinion. Words such as *bad, good, pointless,* and *beneficial* indicate value judgments.

- *Statements that predict future events.* Nothing that will happen in the future can be definitively proven in the present. Anything that discusses something that will happen in the future is an opinion.

- *Statements that use abstract words.* Although "one gallon" can be defined, "love" has no specific definition. Abstract words—*strength, misery, success*—usually indicate an opinion.

- *Statements that use emotional words.* Emotions are by nature unverifiable. Chances are that statements using words such as *delightful, nasty, miserable,* or *wonderful* will present an opinion.

- *Statements that use qualifiers.* Absolute qualifiers such as *all, none, never,* and *always* can point to an opinion. For example, "All students need to work while in school" is an opinion.

Indicators of fact are:

- *Statements that deal with actual people, places, objects, or events.* If the existence of the elements involved can be verified through observation, chances are that the statement itself can also be proven true or false. "Jimmy Carter was a peanut farmer in Georgia" is an example of this principle.

- *Statements that use concrete words or measurable statistics.* Any statement that uses concrete, measurable terms and avoids the abstract is likely to be a fact. Examples include "Thirty-six inches constitute a yard" and "There are 2,512 full-time students enrolled this semester."

It is important to separate the concepts of "fact" and "opinion" from those of "true" and "false." Neither a fact nor an opinion is automatically true or false. Actually, a fact can be false and an opinion can be true. The status of any statement as fact or opinion has to do with how it is presented, not the inherent truth or falsehood of what it says. Consider the following:

FACTS CAN BE WRONG. A fact is a statement presented as objectively real. Whether it is actually true is up to individual evaluation and investigation. For example, if someone tells you class is at 10:00, and you discover upon checking the course catalog that it is actually at 11:00, that person has given you an incorrect statement of fact.

OPINIONS CAN SEEM LIKE FACTS. A statement of opinion can masquerade as fact. For example, an article may state, "Twenty to thirty minutes of vigorous exercise three to five times a week is essential for good health." That may sound like a fact. Upon examination, however, you realize that it is impossible to determine whether the same frequency and level of exercise would have the same effect on all people. To be safe, consider all statements opinions until proven otherwise.

When you find yourself feeling that an opinion is fact, it may be because you agree strongly with the opinion. Don't discount your feelings; "not verifiable" is not the same as "inaccurate." Opinions are not necessarily wrong even if you cannot prove them.

Using Questions to Investigate Truth and Accuracy

Once you label a statement as a fact or opinion, explore its degree of truth. Both facts and opinions require investigation through questioning. Critical-thinking experts Sylvan Barnet and Hugo Bedau state that when you test for the truth of a statement, you "determine whether what it asserts corresponds with reality; if it does, then it is true, and if it doesn't, then it is false."[3] In order to determine to what degree a statement "corresponds with reality," ask questions such as the following:

- What facts or examples provide evidence of truth?
- How does the maker of the statement know this to be true?
- Is there another fact that disproves this statement or information, or shows it to be an opinion?
- How reliable are the sources of information?
- What about this statement is similar to or different from other information I consider fact?

Another crucial step in determining the truth is to question the assumptions that you and others hold and that are the underlying force in shaping opinions.

IDENTIFYING AND EVALUATING ASSUMPTIONS

"If it's more expensive, it's better." "You should study in a library." These statements reveal assumptions—evaluations or generalizations influenced by values and based on observing cause and effect—that can often hide within seemingly truthful statements. An assumption can influence choices—you may assume that you should earn a certain degree or own a car. Many people don't question whether their assumptions make sense, nor do they challenge the assumptions of others.

Assumptions come from sources such as parents or relatives, television and other media, friends, and personal experiences. As much as you think such assumptions work for you, it's just as possible that they can close your mind to opportunities and even cause harm. Investigate each assumption as you would any statement of fact or opinion, analyzing its causes and effects.

The first step in uncovering the assumptions that underlie a statement is to look at the cause-and-effect pattern of the statement, seeing if the way reasons move to conclusions is supported by evidence or involves a hidden assumption. See Figure 4.6 for questions you can ask to evaluate an assumption.

For example, here's how you might use these questions to investigate the following statement: "The most productive schedule involves getting

FIGURE 4.6   *Questioning an assumption.*

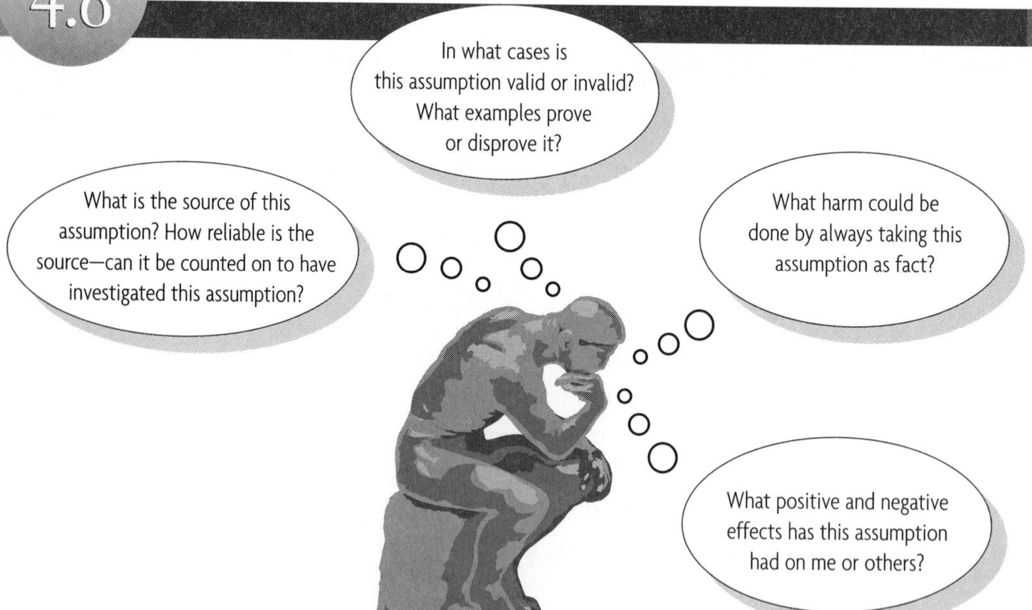

In what cases is this assumption valid or invalid? What examples prove or disprove it?

What is the source of this assumption? How reliable is the source—can it be counted on to have investigated this assumption?

What harm could be done by always taking this assumption as fact?

What positive and negative effects has this assumption had on me or others?

started early in the day." First of all, a cause-and-effect evaluation shows that this statement reveals the following assumption: "The morning is when people have the most energy and are most able to get things done." Here's how you might question the assumption:

- This assumption may be true for people who have good energy in the morning hours. But the assumption may be not true for people who work best in the afternoon or evening hours.

- Society's standard of daytime classes and 8:00 A.M. to 5:00 P.M. working hours supports this assumption. Therefore, the assumption may work for people who have early jobs and classes. It may not work, however, for people who work shifts or who teach or take evening classes.

- Maybe people who believe this assumption were raised to start their days early. Or, perhaps they just go along with what seems to be the standard. Still, there are plenty of people who operate on a different schedule and yet enjoy successful, productive lives.

- Taking this assumption as fact could hurt people who don't operate at their peak in the earlier hours. For example, if a "night owl" tries to take early classes, he may experience concentration problems that would not necessarily occur later in the day. In situations that favor their particular characteristics—night classes or late shift jobs, for example—such people have just as much potential to succeed as anyone else.

Be careful to question all assumptions, not just those that seem problematic from the start. Form your opinion after investigating the positive and negative effects of any situation.

One particularly important area in which you will benefit from thinking critically is in how you approach the media that you encounter on a daily basis.

To me as a toy inventor, critical thinking is an absolute necessity. It gives us the tools to find not just the next step, but also the step after the next step. By looking at all the things around us—the fads, the movies, the Internet—and mixing it together with what we know about how kids play and such diverse factors as the impact of gender roles and where they live, we begin to develop new and better ideas that no one ever thought of before. Critical thinking accomplishes this.

WAYNE KUNA, INVENTOR AND ENTREPRENEUR

EXPERT INSIGHT

Do Business with Critical Thinking

What Is Media Literacy?

Do you believe everything you read, see on television, or find on the Internet? Think about it for a moment. If you trusted every advertisement, you would believe that at least four fast-food restaurants serve "the best burger available." If you agreed with every magazine article, you would know that Elvis passed away many years ago and yet still believe that he was shopping for peanut butter last week in Oklahoma. It is impossible to believe it all without becoming completely confused about what is real.

If literacy refers to the ability to read, media literacy can be seen as the ability to read the media. Media literacy—the ability to respond with critical thinking to the media that you encounter—is essential for a realistic understanding of the information that bombards you daily. It means that instead of accepting anything a newspaper article, TV commercial, or Internet site says is fact, you take time to question the information, using your mind actions and critical-thinking processes.

The founders of the Center for Media Literacy work to encourage others to think critically about the media. They have put forth what they call the "Five Core Concepts of Media Literacy."[4]

ALL MEDIA ARE CONSTRUCTIONS. Any TV show or advertisement, for example, is not a view of actual life or fact but rather a carefully constructed presentation that is designed to have a particular effect on the viewer—to encourage you to feel a certain emotion, develop a particular opinion, or buy the product advertised. For example, an article that wants the reader to feel good about the President will focus on his strengths rather than his shortcomings.

MEDIA USE UNIQUE "LANGUAGES." The people who produce media carefully choose wording, background music, colors, images, timing, and other factors to produce a desired effect. When watching a movie, listen to the music that plays behind an emotional scene or a high-speed chase.

DIFFERENT AUDIENCES UNDERSTAND THE SAME MEDIA MESSAGE DIFFERENTLY. Individual people understand media in the context of their own unique experiences. For this reason people may often interpret media quite differently. A child who has not experienced violence in her life but who watches it on TV may not understand that violence brings pain and suffering. In contrast, a child who has witnessed or experienced violence first-hand may react to TV violence with fear for her personal safety.

MEDIA HAVE COMMERCIAL INTERESTS. Rather than being driven by the need to tell the truth, media are driven by the intent to sell you something.

Television programs, newspapers, magazines, and commercial Internet sites make sure that the advertisers who support them get a chance to convey a message to the consumer. Advertising is chosen so that it most appeals to those most likely to be reading or seeing that particular kind of media; for example, ads for beer and cars dominate the airwaves during major sports events.

MEDIA HAVE EMBEDDED VALUES AND POINTS OF VIEW. Any media product carries the values of the people who created it. For example, even by choosing the topics on which to write articles, a magazine's editor conveys an opinion that those topics are important. *Runner's World* thinks that knowing how to stay warm on a winter run is important, for example.

The whole point of media literacy is to approach what you see, hear, and read with thought and consideration. Use your critical-thinking processes to analyze the media and develop an informed opinion.

- *Ask questions based on the mind actions.* Is what you read in a newspaper similar to something you already know to be true? Do you evaluate a magazine article to be useful or not? Do you agree with the causes or effects that are cited?

- *Evaluate the truth of the argument.* If a TV ad argues that a certain kind of car is the best on the road, evaluate this information the way that you would any argument. With what facts do they back up their claims? Are the claims opinion? Does assuming their claims to be true cause any harm? What strategies are they using to persuade you to adopt their idea?

- *Recognize perspective.* It is just as important to avoid rejecting the media automatically as it is to avoid accepting them automatically. Any media offering has its own particular perspective, coming from the person or people who created it. Explore this perspective, asking what positive and negative effects it might have. For example, if a website encourages you to adopt the perspective that you should dislike a particular ethnic group, this may have harmful effects.

Becoming media literate will help you become a smart consumer of the media who ultimately is responsible for your actions. Don't let a TV ad or a Web banner tell you what to think or do. Evaluate messages critically and make your own decisions. Media literacy is a key to a responsible, self-powered life and is vital to your academic and career success.

Κρινειν

The word "critical" is derived from the Greek word *krinein*, which means to separate in order to choose or select. To be a mindful, aware critical thinker, you need to be able to separate, evaluate, and select ideas, facts, and thoughts.

Think of this concept as you apply critical thinking to your reading, writing, and interaction with others. Be aware of the information you take in and of your thoughts, and be selective as you process them. Critical thinking gives you the power to make sense of life by deliberately selecting how to respond to the information, people, and events that you encounter.

Study Skills in Action

CHAPTER 4

Test Competence

MEASURING WHAT YOU'VE LEARNED

MULTIPLE CHOICE. *Circle or highlight the answer that seems to fit best.*

1. The definition of critical thinking includes all of the following elements **except**
   A. focusing on key points.
   B. asking questions related to the information.
   C. using the information to create new ideas and solve problems.
   D. repeating information exactly as you heard or read it.

2. The questioning process is central to critical thinking because
   A. it requires that you reword new information in question form.
   B. shows others your willingness to ask questions.
   C. it helps you transform unfiltered information into information you can use to solve a problem, make a decision, innovate, or anticipate.
   D. none of the above.

3. Critical thinking will help make you a valued employee for all of the following reasons **except**
   A. it will encourage you to examine the status quo.
   B. it will encourage you to seek creative solutions to common problems.
   C. it will encourage you to spend a lot of time talking with your coworkers.
   D. it will help improve your productivity.

4. Mind actions include
   A. recall, similarity, difference, cause and effect, example to idea, idea to example, evaluation.
   B. recall, similarity, difference, innovation, example to idea, idea to example, evaluation.
   C. recall, vocabulary building, difference, cause and effect, example to idea, idea to example, evaluation.
   D. recall, similarity, difference, cause and effect, risk-taking, idea to example, evaluation.

5. The problem-solving process is complete after you have
   A. identified the problem.
   B. brainstormed possible solutions.
   C. evaluated and refined your chosen solution.
   D. chosen and executed the solution you think is best.

6. The steps in the process to construct an argument include
   A. establishing a premise, gathering supporting examples, anticipating questions, reworking your premise.
   B. establishing a premise, gathering supporting examples, anticipating questions, drawing a conclusion.
   C. establishing a premise, gathering allies, anticipating questions, drawing a conclusion.
   D. brainstorming, gathering supporting examples, anticipating questions, drawing a conclusion.

7. Logical thinking includes which two primary tasks?
   A. writing a thesis statement and acknowledging biases
   B. crediting expert sources and distinguishing fact from opinion
   C. distinguishing fact from opinion and identifying and evaluating assumptions
   D. identifying and evaluating assumptions and using figures of speech

8. Assumptions are
   A. your direct observations of how people relate to one another.
   B. value-based evaluations or generalizations.
   C. value-free evaluations or generalizations that are linked to observations of cause and effect.
   D. attitudes that only prejudiced people hold.

9. Opinions can be identified because they often
   A. use abstract words, show evaluations, and predict future events.
   B. include statistics.
   C. include precise, specific facts that are hard to dispute.
   D. the result of thorough, exhaustive research.

10. Media literacy requires critical thinking for all of the following reasons **except**
    A. it involves recognizing the values of the media source.
    B. it requires that you evaluate the truth of ads and programming.
    C. it requires that you identify and understand the power of media manipulation.
    D. it helps you decide which computer or television to buy.

1. _____ Example-to-idea thinking can also be described as *generalization*, *classification*, and *conceptualization*.

2. _____ Cause and effect rarely involves evaluation.

3. _____ When brainstorming solutions, evaluate each solution as you go and stop when you hit on the best one.

4. _____ If something is a fact, it is correct.

5. _____ Media literacy will help you intelligently navigate the Internet.

Brain Power

BUILDING VOCABULARY FITNESS

The paragraphs below are taken from the current media. Read the paragraph, noting the context of the vocabulary words shown in bold type. Next, for each vocabulary word (reprinted in the left-hand column), highlight the word or phrase in column A, B, or C that is the most similar in meaning. Finally, on a separate sheet of paper, solidify your understanding of these words by using each in a sentence of your own.

Last year, the National **Aeronautics** and Space Administration was the gang that couldn't shoot straight. It had a string of well-publicized flops, one of which occurred because engineers confused miles with kilometers. But the **embattled** agency got a shot in the arm from last week's announcement that one of its spacecraft had uncovered evidence that liquid water may have flowed "recently"—thousands of years ago—on the surface of Mars. The **cynic** may be suspicious about the **fortuitous** timing of this announcement—coming as it does while Congress is **scrutinizing** NASA's budget—but there is real science behind this story. . . .

The new photographs from the Mars Global **Surveyor,** with a resolution 20 times better than previous probes, show the remarkable signs of grooves and channels inside the walls of meteor craters created by flowing water. This indirectly hints at the presence of volcanic activity that melts the ice, allowing liquid water to flow on the forbidding surface of Mars. Not only does this mean that underground hot springs may exist on Mars, but the **permafrost** may be just a few feet below the surface. In other words, this literally may be just the tip of the iceberg.

From: "Mars' Water May Be Just the Tip of the Iceberg," by Michio Kaku, *The Wall Street Journal*, June 26, 2000, p. A46.

(continued on p. 110)

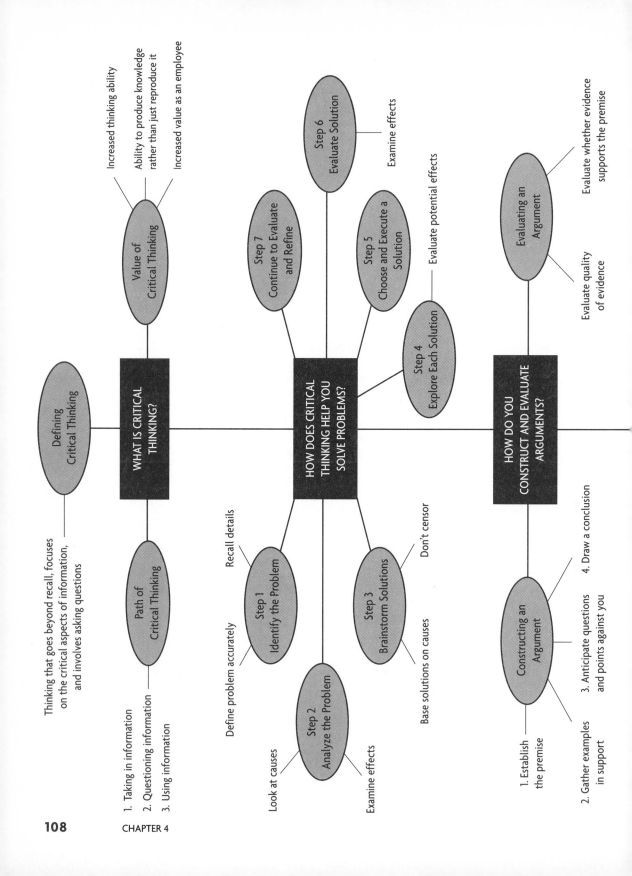

Thinking that goes beyond recall, focuses on the critical aspects of information, and involves asking questions

Defining Critical Thinking

Path of Critical Thinking

1. Taking in information
2. Questioning information
3. Using information

Value of Critical Thinking

Increased thinking ability

Ability to produce knowledge rather than just reproduce it

Increased value as an employee

WHAT IS CRITICAL THINKING?

HOW DOES CRITICAL THINKING HELP YOU SOLVE PROBLEMS?

Step 6 Evaluate Solution

Examine effects

Step 7 Continue to Evaluate and Refine

Step 5 Choose and Execute a Solution

Step 4 Explore Each Solution

Evaluate potential effects

Step 1 Identify the Problem

Recall details

Define problem accurately

Step 2 Analyze the Problem

Look at causes

Examine effects

Step 3 Brainstorm Solutions

Don't censor

Base solutions on causes

HOW DO YOU CONSTRUCT AND EVALUATE ARGUMENTS?

Evaluating an Argument

Evaluate whether evidence supports the premise

Evaluate quality of evidence

Constructing an Argument

1. Establish the premise

2. Gather examples in support

3. Anticipate questions and points against you

4. Draw a conclusion

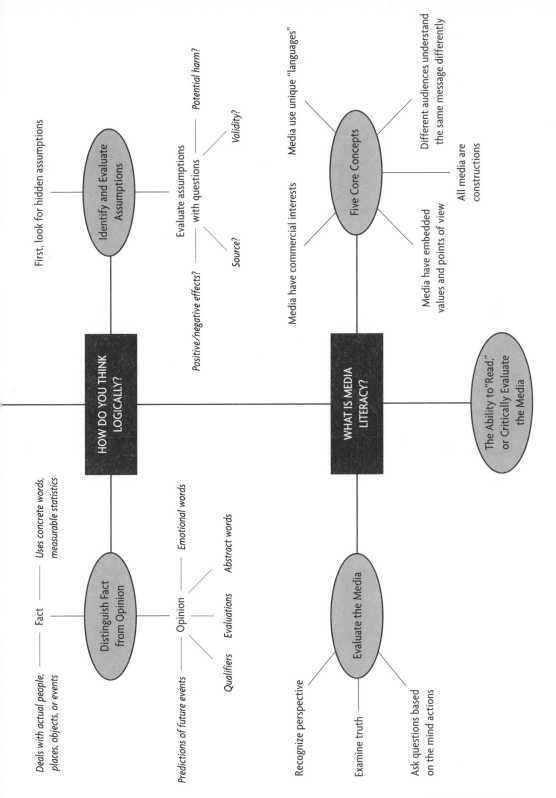

First, look for hidden assumptions

Identify and Evaluate Assumptions

Evaluate assumptions with questions — Potential harm?

Validity?

Source?

Positive/negative effects?

HOW DO YOU THINK LOGICALLY?

Deals with actual people, places, objects, or events

Uses concrete words, measurable statistics

Fact

Distinguish Fact from Opinion

Opinion — Emotional words

Abstract words

Evaluations

Qualifiers

Predictions of future events

Media use unique "languages"

Different audiences understand the same message differently

Five Core Concepts

All media are constructions

Media have commercial interests

Media have embedded values and points of view

WHAT IS MEDIA LITERACY?

The Ability to "Read," or Critically Evaluate the Media

Evaluate the Media

Recognize perspective

Examine truth

Ask questions based on the mind actions

Vocabulary Words	A	B	C
1. **aeronautics**	relating to aircraft	relating to boats	relating to cars
2. **embattled**	embarrassed	beleaguered	powerless
3. **cynic**	skeptic	optimist	advocate
4. **fortuitous**	formal	accidental	poor
5. **scrutinizing**	ignoring	watching	inspecting
6. **surveyor**	inspector	reader	communicator
7. **permafrost**	warmth	permanent frost	water

Strategic Thinking

GETTING THE BIG PICTURE

Answer the following questions on a separate piece of paper or in a journal.

Problem solving is a skill that you will need again and again, in every aspect of your life. Think about a problem you are experiencing right now, at school or at work. Work your way through the problem-solving steps in writing by describing the problem, its causes and effects, potential solutions and their potential positive and negative effects. Finally, indicate the solution you will select and implement, and describe why you think it is the best solution.

Making Connections

The following multiple-choice, true/false, fill-in-the-blank, matching, and essay questions will reinforce the concepts you learned in the four chapters that make up Part I, *Knowledge, Skills, and Preparation: Where the Future Begins*, and will build critical-thinking skills as well. Whereas the end-of-chapter objective quizzes focus mainly on material from that particular chapter, many of the following questions encourage you to compare material from different chapters and find ways that different ideas connect. Recognizing the key relations between ideas will help you master and use knowledge in the most effective way.

MULTIPLE CHOICE.   *Circle or highlight the answer that seems to fit best.*

1. It is important to recognize your learning style to maximize learning while still in school for all of the following reasons **except**

   A. it will prepare you to be part of a learning organization, a company that emphasizes lifelong learning.

   B. understanding your learning style will help you make the right career choices.

   C. learning-style awareness will help you adapt rapidly and readily to change.

   D. your employer expects you to be able to name and describe your learning style on your employment application.

2. The *primary* reason critical-thinking skills will help you adapt to changing technologies is

   A. they enable you to analyze how to use new technologies to increase your productivity and problem-solving ability.

   B. they give you the skill to assemble and learn to use new computer systems.

   C. if you change jobs, you will have little trouble learning new systems.

   D. critical thinking is the basis for understanding which computer system to buy for your company.

3. If as futurist Daniel Burns said in Chapter 1, "the future belongs to those who are capable of being retrained again and again," basic time-management skills are more important today then ever before because

A. looking for a different job while working requires the ability to prioritize tasks and responsibilities.

B. retraining while you are working requires the ability to meet your job commitments and learn new information and skills.

C. needing retraining is often the result of not being able to manage your time effectively.

D. time management is the basis for all future success in every career area you enter.

4. It is important to learn to manage stress while you are still in school for all of the following reasons **except**

A. adapting to the many changes you will inevitably face in your career is likely to create stress reactions.

B. when you are overwhelmed by stress and pressure, you are less likely to be able to effectively use your critical-thinking skills to solve problems.

C. by learning to manage stress now, you will be stress-free after you graduate.

D. effective stress management is important to lifelong physical and mental health.

5. Learning to set goals, manage your time, and become aware of your personal learning style are the basis for effective studying because

A. studying is a process that forces you to examine your personal style.

B. studying is related to future goals.

C. studying is often done in groups, and this knowledge will help you adapt to the styles of other group members.

D. effective studying depends on effective work habits as well as an understanding of how best to accomplish your goals.

TRUE/FALSE. *Place a T or an F beside each statement to indicate whether you think it is true or false.*

1. _____ The questioning process that is at the heart of critical thinking is incompatible with effective time management.

2. _____ When your work environment changes rapidly, it doesn't make sense to set specific goals.

3. _____ Study skills are the most important factor in becoming a strategic learner.

4. _____ Once you understand the mind actions that are part of critical thinking, you are less likely to procrastinate.

5. _____ Self-awareness implies a self-centered approach that will most likely interfere with teamwork.

FILL-IN-THE-BLANK. *Complete the following sentences with the appropriate word(s) or phrase(s) that best reflect what you learned in Part I. Choose from the items that follow each sentence.*

1. Lifelong learning requires a flexibility that _____ change. (embraces, rejects, ignores)

2. As the primary guide to your own journey of lifelong learning, you must welcome the challenge to become a _____ learner. (fast, self-directed, careful)

3. Solid study stills will help you achieve success at work in a _____ organization. (technological, profitable, learning)

4. Howard Gardner's theory of multiple intelligences recognizes _____ distinctive forms of intelligence. (8, 6, 2)

5. Teamwork depends on an understanding of personal _____ and interpersonal dynamics. (backgrounds, learning styles, career goals)

6. It is important to set short- and long-term _____ goals while you are in school and _____ goals while at work. (recreational/financial, interpersonal/lifestyle, educational/career)

7. Keeping your personal schedule in a date book will help you effectively manage your _____. (career options, time, money)

8. Critical thinking enables you to apply the information you now have to new situations through the process of _____. (accepting the status quo, memorization, questioning)

9. Constructing an effective argument involves the ability to _____ others to accept your point of view by presenting _____ in support of your position. (persuade/examples, bribe/conclusions, entice/a thesis statement)

10. _____ literacy involves the ability to use _____ thinking to evaluate information you acquire through the various media. (Reading/good, Basic/clear, Media/critical)

MATCHING. *Match each item in the left-hand column to an item in the right-hand column by writing the letter from the right that corresponds best to the number on the left.*

1. _____ flexibility

2. _____ learning organization

3. _____ strategic learners

4. _____ bodily–kinesthetic learners

5. _____ naturalistic intelligence

6. _____ priorities

7. _____ procrastination

8. _____ similarity

9. _____ cause and effect

10. _____ example to idea

A. people who have the ability to learn through bodily sensations

B. postponing a task until later

C. a mind action that involves classification and conceptualization

D. an attitude that embraces change

E. ability to understand environmental features

F. work environment that expects employees to continue to learn

G. a mind action that focuses on reasons and consequences

H. learners who acquire the attitudes, skills, and self-monitoring they need to succeed as critical thinkers

I. personal decisions and actions that define what is important to you and how you will spend your time

J. a mind action that focuses on likeness and comparisons

Essay Question

Carefully read the following excerpt from Psychology, *3rd ed., by Saul Kassin, a college textbook published by Prentice Hall, and then answer the essay question that follows. This exercise will help you focus on the meaning of the selection, apply your personal knowledge and experiences to the reading, organize your ideas, and communicate your thoughts effectively in writing.*

Before you begin writing your essay, it is a good idea to spend a few minutes planning. Try brainstorming possible approaches, writing a thesis statement, and jotting down your main thoughts in the form of an outline or think link. Because most essay tests are timed, limit the time you take to write your response to no more than one-half hour. This will force you to write quickly and effectively as it prepares you for actual test conditions.

WHAT PEOPLE DREAM ABOUT

In *Our Dreaming Mind*, Robert Van de Castle (1994) notes that dreams have always fascinated people. More than eight thousand years ago, the Assyrians believed that dreams were messages sent from evil spirits. Later, Egyptians believed they were messages sent by the gods. The Inuits of Hudson Bay and the Pantani of Malaysia believe that one's soul leaves the body during sleep and enters another world. Among the Kurds and Zulus, dreaming of an adulterous affair is considered an offense, and if you dream of receiving a gift, you must compensate the gift giver in waking life. In Western cultures, people assume that dreams, if properly analyzed, tell us something about the dreamer's past, present, or future. To some extent, then, dreams reflect a culture's beliefs, values, and concerns (Shulman & Stroumsa, 1999).

Over the years, psychologists and anthropologists have looked for common themes in what people from different cultures tend to dream about. Summarizing this research, G. William Domhoff (1996) notes that certain aspects of the dreams found in Western cultures are found elsewhere as well. For example, it appears that people everywhere dream more about acts of aggression than about friendship and kindness, and in these dreams, we are more likely to dream of being victims of aggression than the perpetrators. Certain gender differences in dream content also seem to be universal. For example, men dream more about aggression, while women dream more about acquaintances, friends, and family members.

Although there are cultural similarities in dream reports, Domhoff (1996) notes that there are also some striking differences that uniquely reflect each culture's beliefs, values, and social structures. In India, devout Hindus who live gender-segregated lives report having precious few sex characters in their dreams. In Japan, a "collective" society that places family and group interests ahead of those of the individual, people's dreams contain more human characters than are found in American dreams—and these characters are more likely to be familiar. Among the Yir Yomont hunters of Australia, men dream often of killing animals—and of sharing meat with familiar female characters and others. Clearly, what we dream about is shaped by our waking lives, which, in turn, is shaped by the invisible hand of culture.

Source: Excerpted from Saul Kassin, *Psychology*, 3rd ed., Upper Saddle River, NJ: Prentice Hall, 2001, p. 149. Reprinted with permission.

ESSAY QUESTION. Describe a recent dream you remember or a dream you have had many times in the past. Discuss how your dream is consistent with or different from the ethnic or religious culture in your family and how it is consistent with or divergent from the general American culture. Based on your response, explain why you agree or disagree with the author's statement that "dreams reflect a culture's beliefs, values, and concerns."

Teamwork

PERSONALITY TYPES AND STUDY HABITS. Divide into groups according to the four types of the Personality Spectrum: Thinker-dominant students in one group, organizer-dominant students in another, giver-dominant students in a third, and adventurer-dominant students in the fourth. If you have scored the same in more than one of these types, join whichever group is smaller. With your group, brainstorm four lists for your type:

1. The study *strengths* of this type (the courses, study strategies, and situations that bring out the best in you).
2. The *struggles* it brings in school (the courses, situations, and assignments that are almost always problematic).
3. The study situations that cause particular *stress* for your type (courses or scenarios that mentally psyche you out).
4. The *careers* that tend to suit this type (career areas or jobs that seem to make the most of your strengths and avoid your problem areas).

Take a look at your list of struggles and stresses. With your group, brainstorm strategies for dealing with them.

If there is time, each group can present the information they have compiled to the entire class through a presentation or even by photocopying it and distributing it to the other students. This will have two positive effects: One, it will enable everyone to have a better understanding and acceptance of one another's intelligences, and two, students with strengths in areas other than their group will benefit from the information.

READING, REMEMBERING, AND UNDERSTANDING

MAKING MEANING FROM WHAT YOU LEARN

PART

II

117

UNDERSTAND

Your reading background— your past as a reader—may not necessarily prepare you for the new challenges of college reading. In the past, you may have had more time to read less material, with less necessity for deep-level understanding. In college, however, your reading will often be complex, and you may experience an overload of assignments. You may encounter similar pressures at work. Many careers will require you to read articles, books, reports, and memos—materials that you will need to digest and use within a relatively short span of time.

The reading you do in college and throughout your life requires you to grasp content and meaning as rapidly as possible. The material in this chapter will present techniques to increase your reading comprehension and build your vocabulary while boosting your speed. At the end of the chapter, you will be able to answer these questions:

- What will help you understand what you read?
- How can you set the stage for reading?
- How do you build a better vocabulary?
- How can you become more comfortable reading American English?
- How can you increase your reading speed?

READING COMPREHENSION, VOCABULARY, AND SPEED
READING FASTER AND UNDERSTANDING MORE

> *"A book is a garden carried in the pocket."*
>
> **Arabian proverb**

What Will Help You Understand What You Read?

More than anything else, reading is a process that requires you, the reader, to *make meaning* from written words. This involves far more than interpreting the alphabet symbols on the page. When you make meaning, you connect yourself to the concepts being communicated. Your prior knowledge or familiarity with a subject, culture and home environment, life experiences, and even personal interpretation of words and phrases affect your understanding.

Because these factors are different for every person, your reading experiences are uniquely your own. For example, say your family owns a hardware store where you have worked from time to time. Although you may read a retailing chapter in a business textbook in the context of what you observed while working, most of your classmates probably have no first-hand knowledge of how a retail business operates. Your reading includes comparing text concepts to the methods your family used to run the store, but your classmates are reading for basic vocabulary and concepts.

Reading *comprehension* refers to your ability to understand what you read. True comprehension goes beyond just knowing facts and figures—a student can parrot back a pile of economics statistics on a test, for example, without understanding what they mean. Only when you thoroughly comprehend the information you read can you make the most effective use of that information. In the previous example, your comprehension of retailing is on a higher level than that of others, and it will be easier for you to use what you have learned.

All reading strategies have the ultimate purpose of helping you to achieve greater understanding of what you read. Therefore, every section in this chapter will in some way help you maximize your comprehension. Some general comprehension boosters to keep in mind as you work through the chapter and as you tackle individual reading assignments include:

- *Build knowledge through reading and studying.* More than any other factor, what you already know before you read a passage will influence your ability to understand and remember important ideas. Previous knowledge gives you a context for what you read.

- *Think positively.* Instead of telling yourself that you cannot understand, think positively. Tell yourself: *I can learn this material. I am a good reader.*

- *Think critically.* Ask yourself questions. Do you understand the sentence, paragraph, or chapter you just read? Are ideas and supporting examples clear? Could you explain the material to someone else? Chapter 6 presents strategies for responding critically to what you read.

- *Build vocabulary.* Lifelong learners consider their vocabulary a work in progress because they never finish learning new words. The more you know, the more material you can understand without stopping to wonder what new words mean.

Reading expert Kathryn Redway sums it up: "Comprehension is subjective, and the quality or level of your comprehension will vary according to what you read and your purpose in reading it."[1] This puts you in charge of deciding how you approach everything you read. Give yourself the best chance at comprehension by setting the stage effectively.

How Can You Set the Stage for Reading?

On any given day during your college career, you may be faced with reading assignments like this:

- A textbook chapter on the history of South African apartheid (world history)

- An original research study on the relation between sleep deprivation and the development of memory problems (psychology)

- Chapters 4–6 in John Steinbeck's classic novel, *The Grapes of Wrath* (American literature)

- A technical manual on the design of computer antivirus programs (computer science, software design)

- A current trade magazine or report from your boss on changes in your industry (if you are a working student)

This material is rigorous by anyone's standards. To get through it—and master its contents—you'll need a systematic approach to reading.

The material in this chapter will help you to set the stage in a way that gives you the greatest chance at reading success. Later, the information in Chapter 6 will help you to develop strategies that will improve your ability to remember and apply key concepts from all kinds of materials, today and in the future.

Note that if you have a reading disability, if English is not your primary language, or if you have limited reading skills, you may need additional support. Most colleges provide services for students through a reading center or tutoring program. Take the initiative to seek help if you need it. Many accomplished learners have benefited from help in specific areas. Remember that the ability to be successful corresponds in large part to the ability to ask for and receive help.

TAKE AN ACTIVE APPROACH TO DIFFICULT TEXTS

Because texts are often written to challenge the intellect, even well-written, useful texts may be difficult to read. Some textbooks may be written by experts who may not explain information in the friendliest manner for nonexperts. A few textbooks may be poorly written and organized.

Generally, the further you advance in your education and your career, the more complex your required reading is likely to be. You may encounter new concepts, words, and terms that feel like a foreign language. Assignments can also be difficult when the required reading is from *primary sources*—original documents rather than another writer's interpretation of the documents—or from academic journal articles and scientific studies that don't define basic terms or supply a wealth of examples. Among the primary sources you may encounter are:

- historical documents
- works of literature (novels, poems, and plays)
- scientific studies, including lab reports and accounts of experiments
- journal articles

The following strategies may help you approach difficult material actively and positively:

- Approach reading assignments with an open mind. Be careful not to prejudge them as impossible or boring before you even start to read.
- Know that some texts may require extra work and concentration. Set a goal to make your way through the material, whatever it takes. If you want to learn, you will.
- Define concepts that your material does not explain. Consult resources—instructors, students, reference materials—for help.

To help with your make-meaning-of-textbooks mission, you may want to create your own minilibrary at home. Collect reference materials that you use often, such as a dictionary, a thesaurus, a writer's style handbook, and maybe an atlas or computer manual (many of these are available as computer software or CD-ROMs). You may also benefit from owning reference materials in your particular areas of study. "If you find yourself going to the library to look up the same reference again and again, consider purchasing that book for your personal or office library," advises library expert Sherwood Harris.[2]

CHOOSE THE RIGHT SETTING

Finding a place and time that minimize outside distractions will help you achieve the focus and discipline that your reading requires. Here are some suggestions.

SELECT THE RIGHT COMPANY. If you prefer to read alone, establish a relatively interruption-proof place and time, such as an out-of-the-way spot at the library or an after-class hour in an empty classroom. Even if you don't mind activity nearby, try to minimize distraction.

SELECT THE RIGHT LOCATION. Many students study at a library desk. Others prefer an easy chair at the library or at home, or even the floor. Choose a spot that's comfortable but not so cushy that you fall asleep. Make sure that you have adequate lighting and aren't too hot or cold. At home, you may want to avoid the distraction of studying in a room where a television is on.

SELECT THE RIGHT TIME. Choose a time when you feel alert and focused. Try reading just before or after the class for which the reading is assigned, if you can. Eventually, you will associate preferred places and times with focused reading.

Students with families have an additional factor involved in their decisions about when, where, and how to read. Figure 5.1 explores some ways that parents or other people caring for children may be able to maximize their study efforts. These techniques will also help after college if you choose to telecommute—work from home through an Internet-linked computer—while your children are still at home under your care.

DEFINE YOUR PURPOSE FOR READING

When you define your purpose, you ask yourself *why* you are reading a particular piece of material. One way to do this is by completing this sentence: "In reading this material, I intend to define/learn/answer/achieve. . . ." With a clear purpose in mind, you can decide how much time and effort to expend on various reading assignments. Nearly 375 years ago, Francis

FIGURE

5.1

Exploring options and solutions for students who are parents.

MANAGING CHILDREN WHILE STUDYING

Keep them up-to-date on your schedule.

Let them know when you have a big test or project due and when you are under less pressure, and what they can expect of you in each case.

Explain what your education entails.

Tell them how it will improve your life and theirs. This applies, of course, to older children who can understand the situation and compare it to their own schooling.

Find help.

Ask a relative or friend to watch your children or arrange for a child to visit a friend's house. Consider trading baby-sitting hours with another parent, hiring a sitter to come to your home, or using a day-care center that is private or school-sponsored.

Keep them active while you study.

Give them games, books, or toys to occupy them. If there are special activities that you like to limit, such as watching videos on TV, same them for your study time.

Study on the phone.

You might be able to have a study session with a fellow student over the phone while your child is sleeping or playing quietly.

Offset study time with family time and rewards.

Children may let you get your work done if they have something to look forward to, such as a movie night, a trip for ice cream, or something else they like.

SPECIAL NOTES FOR INFANTS

Study at night if your baby goes to sleep early, or in the morning if your baby sleeps late.

Study during nap times if you aren't too tired yourself.

Lay your notes out and recite information to the baby. The baby will appreciate the attention, and you will get work done.

Put baby in a safe and fun place while you study, such as a playpen, motorized swing, or jumping seat.

Bacon, the great English philosopher, recognized that "some books are to be tasted, others to be swallowed, and some few to be chewed and digested; that is, some books are to be read only in parts, others to be read but not curiously; and some few to be read wholly, and with diligence and attention."

Achieving your reading purpose requires adapting to different types of reading materials. Being a flexible reader—adjusting reading strategies and pace—will help you adapt successfully.

Purpose Determines Reading Strategy

With purpose comes direction; with direction comes a strategy for reading. The following are four reading purposes, examined briefly. You may have one or more for any "reading event."

PURPOSE 1: READ FOR UNDERSTANDING. In college, studying involves reading for the purpose of comprehending the material. The two main components of comprehension are *general ideas* and *specific facts or examples*. These components depend on each other. Facts and examples help to explain or support ideas, and ideas provide a framework that helps the reader to remember facts and examples.

General ideas. General-idea reading is rapid reading that seeks an overview of the material. You search for general ideas by focusing on headings, subheadings, and summary statements.

Specific facts or examples. At times, readers may focus on locating specific pieces of information—for example, the stages of intellectual development in young children. Often, a reader may search for examples that support or explain more general ideas—for example, the causes of economic recession. Because you know exactly what you are looking for, you can skim the material quickly.

PURPOSE 2: READ TO EVALUATE CRITICALLY. Critical evaluation involves understanding. It means approaching the material with an open mind, examining causes and effects, evaluating ideas, and asking questions that test the writer's argument and search for assumptions. Critical reading brings an understanding of material that goes beyond basic information recall (see Chapter 6 for more on critical reading). A student evaluating a fellow student's essay, or an employee reading a draft of a press release, will read critically.

PURPOSE 3: READ FOR PRACTICAL APPLICATION. A third purpose for reading is to gather usable information that you can apply toward a specific goal. When you read a textbook preface or an instruction booklet for a new software package, your goal is to learn how to do something. Reading and action usually go hand in hand. Remembering the specifics requires a certain degree of general comprehension.

PURPOSE 4: READ FOR PLEASURE. Some materials you read for entertainment, such as *Sports Illustrated* magazine or the latest John Grisham courtroom thriller. Entertaining reading may also go beyond materials that seem obviously designed to entertain. Whereas some people may read a Jane Austen novel for a class assignment, others may read her books for pleasure.

As Yale professor Harold Bloom points out, reading for pleasure gives you the opportunity to enlarge your life and to enter into "alternate realities." "Why read?" he asks. "Because you can know, intimately, only a very few people, and perhaps you never know them at all. After reading [the Thomas Mann masterpiece] *The Magic Mountain* you know Hans Castorp thoroughly, and he is greatly worth knowing."[3]

Purpose Determines Pace

George M. Usova, senior education specialist and graduate professor at Johns Hopkins University, explains: "Good readers are flexible readers. They read at a variety of rates and adapt them to the reading purpose at hand, the difficulty of the material, and their familiarity with the subject area."[4] For example, you may need to read academic and/or unfamiliar materials more slowly, whereas you will increase your reading speed for journalism, magazines, and online publications. As Table 5.1 shows, good readers link the pace of reading to their reading purpose.

A strong vocabulary increases reading speed and comprehension—when you understand words you are reading, you don't have to stop to think about what they mean. The next section will help you learn strategies to expand your vocabulary.

EXPERT INSIGHT

What you have to do with learning materials is to get yourself actively involved in the process. You can't just passively wait for it to come in. I recommend that students stop before they read a text chapter, look at the outline, and ask themselves questions about the chapter. What does this mean, why is this being done this way? If there's no outline, go through the chapter and make one. Then read the summary at the end of the chapter to see if some of your questions were answered.

When you begin to actually read the chapter, read it actively in chunks. I tell students to read a chunk and then stop and ask themselves, what have I learned? How does that relate to my life? Can I think of examples? You need active involvement before going on.

CHARLES G. MORRIS, PROFESSOR OF PSYCHOLOGY, UNIVERSITY OF MICHIGAN

Get Involved with Reading

TYPE OF MATERIAL	READING PURPOSE	PACE
Academic readings • Textbooks • Original sources • Articles from scholarly journals • Online publications for academic readers • Lab reports • Required fiction	• Critical analysis • Overall mastery • Preparation for tests	Slow, especially if the material is new and unfamiliar
Manuals • Instructions • Recipes	Practical application	Slow to medium
Journalism and nonfiction for the general reader • Nonfiction books • Newspapers • Magazines • Online publications for the general public	Understanding of general ideas, key concepts, and specific facts for personal understanding or practical application	Medium to fast
Nonrequired fiction	Understanding of general ideas, key concepts, and specific facts for enjoyment	Variable, but tending toward the faster speed

Source: Adapted from Nicholas Reid Schaffzin, *The Princeton Review Reading Smart,* New York: Random House, 1996, p. 15.

How Do You Build a Better Vocabulary?

As your reading materials at school and at work become more complex, how much you comprehend—and how readily you do it—will depend on your vocabulary. Is your word power minimal, general, and static? Or is it large, specialized, and ever-expanding?

The best way to build your vocabulary is to commit yourself to learning new and unfamiliar words as you encounter them. Building your vocabulary in the context of work is at the heart of the meaning-making process you learned about earlier. This involves using the four steps described next.

ANALYZE WORD PARTS

Often, if you understand part of a word, you will be able to figure out what the entire word means. This is true because many English words are made up of a combination of Greek and Latin prefixes, roots, and suffixes. *Prefixes* are word parts that are added to the beginning of a root. The *root* is the central part or basis of a word around which prefixes and suffixes are added to produce different words. *Suffixes* are added to the end of the root. Table 5.2 contains just a few of the prefixes, roots, and suffixes you will encounter as you read. There are literally thousands more. Taking the time to memorize these verbal building blocks will dramatically increase your vocabulary because you will encounter them over and over again in different words.

Figure 5.2 shows how one root can be the stem of many different words.

TABLE 5.2 *Common prefixes, roots, and suffixes.*

PREFIX	PRIMARY MEANING	EXAMPLE
a, ab	from	abstain, avert
ad, af, at	to	adhere, affix, attain
con, cor, com	with, together	convene, correlate, compare
di	apart	divert, divorce
il	not	illegal, illegible
ir	not	irresponsible
post	after	postpone, postpartum
sub, sup	under	subordinate, suppose

ROOT	PRIMARY MEANING	EXAMPLE
com	fill	incomplete
strict	bind	restriction
cept	take	receptacle
chron	time	synchronize
ann	year	biannual
sper	hope	desperate
clam	cry out	proclamation
voc	speak, talk	convocation

SUFFIX	PRIMARY MEANING	EXAMPLE
able	able	recyclable
arium	place for	aquarium, solarium
cule	very small	molecule
ist	one who	pianist
meter	measure	thermometer
ness	state of	carelessness
sis	condition of	hypnosis
y	inclined to	sleepy

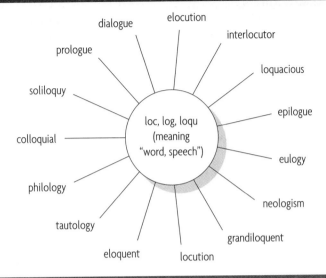

Using prefixes, roots, and suffixes, you can piece together the meaning of many of the new words you encounter. To use a simple example, the word *prologue* is made up of the prefix *pro* (before) and the root *logue* (to speak). Thus, *prologue* refers to words spoken or written before the main text.

USE A DICTIONARY

When reading a textbook, the first "dictionary" to search is the glossary. Textbooks often include an end-of-book glossary that explains technical words and concepts. The definitions there are usually limited to the meaning of the term as it is used in the text.

Standard dictionaries provide broader information such as word origin, pronunciation, part of speech, synonyms (words that are similar), antonyms (words with opposite meanings), and multiple meanings. Using a dictionary whenever you read will increase your comprehension. Buy a standard dictionary, keep it nearby, and consult it for help in understanding passages that contain unfamiliar words.

You may not always have time for the following suggestions, but when you can use them, they will help you make the most of your dictionary.

- *Read every meaning of a word, not just the first.* Think critically about which meaning suits the context of the word in question, and choose the one that makes the most sense to you.

- *Say the word out loud—then write it down to make sure you can spell it.* Check your pronunciation against the dictionary symbols as you say each word. Speaking and writing new words as you use them will boost your recall.

- *Substitute a word or phrase from the definition for the word.* Use the definition you have chosen. Imagine, for example, that you encounter the following sentence and do not know what the word *indoctrinated* means:

  The cult indoctrinated its members to reject society's values.

  In the dictionary, you find several definitions, including *brainwashed* and *instructed.* You decide that the one closest to the correct meaning is *brainwashed.* With this term, the sentence reads as follows:

  The cult brainwashed its members to reject society's values.

- *Restate the definition in your own words.* To make sure you really know what a word means, define it again in your own words. When you can do this with ease, you know that you understand the meaning and are not merely parroting a dictionary definition.

- *Keep a journal of every new word you learn, including definitions.* Review the journal on a regular basis and watch your vocabulary grow.

LEARN COMMON FOREIGN WORDS AND PHRASES

Many non-English words and phrases have become part of our American vocabulary, including words in French, Italian, Spanish, German, and Latin. Because they are used so frequently, it is a good idea to familiarize yourself with them so that you can add them to your own vocabulary. Table 5.3 includes some of the words and phrases you may encounter in your school and career-related reading.

USE MEMORY AIDS TO ENSURE RECALL

Your next task is to memorize your new vocabulary—to learn new words permanently so that you can use them at will in writing and speaking and understand them when you hear or read them.

You'll need tools to help you memorize, including mnemonic devices and flash cards. These are discussed in detail in Chapter 8. Most students find that their most important vocabulary-building tool is the flash card. Your efforts will be painless if you study several cards a day and push yourself to use your new words in conversation and writing. You may also want to work together with another student to review the cards both of you have made. A buddy system may give you the motivation to master your new vocabulary as it exposes you to the vocabulary your partner has identified.

Foreign words and phrases commonly used in English.   TABLE

5.3

FOREIGN WORD OR PHRASE PRONUNCIATION AND PART OF SPEECH	MEANING AND DERIVATION	EXAMPLE
ad hoc (ad HAHK)—adjective	For a particular purpose. (Latin)	An ad hoc committee is dealing with the production problems associated with the company-wide flu outbreak, which is keeping three out of ten employees out of work.
carte blanche (kahrt blanch) —noun	A blank card, the power to take any action. (French)	The chief executive gave his operation's director carte blanche to streamline the human resources department.
de rigueur (duh ri GUR) —adjective	Indispensable, obligatory. (French)	Until recently, the suit was de rigueur for business dress.
faux pas (foh PAH)—noun	An embarrassing social mistake. (French)	The job candidate committed a faux pas at lunch when she ordered a two-pound lobster, the most expensive item on the menu.
laissez-faire (les ay FER) —adjective	A doctrine of government noninterference in the economy; any approach that is seen as noninterference. (French)	The Federal Reserve has taken a laissez-faire attitude toward interest rates, and has not raised rates for over a year.
non sequitur (nahn SEK wi tur) —noun	A statement that does not follow logically from what went before it. (Latin)	The customer's request for a credit line extension was a non sequitur after the discussion of the company's delinquent payments.
quid pro quo (kwid proh KWOH) —noun	Something that is given or done in direct return for something else. (Latin)	When the purchasing agent asked for money as a quid pro quo for giving the printer business, he was asking for a bribe.
zeitgeist (TSYTE gyste) —noun	The spirit of the times. (German)	In the first decade of the millennium, risk-taking and flexibility are the zeitgeist of business.

LEARN SPECIALIZED VOCABULARY

When you focus on one academic subject by working toward a major, or when you begin working, you may encounter a very specialized vocabulary that few outsiders know. Most of these words, phrases, and initials may be unfamiliar to you even if you were born and raised in the United States. To learn them, take the same approach you used to improving your basic vocabulary. Even if you feel like you are diving into a foreign language, you can take comfort in knowing that you will quickly learn this new language because you are being exposed to it every day.

For example, if you are studying or working in banking and finance, here are just a few of the new terms you will encounter:

bear market	book value
bull market	common stocks
compound interest	yield
price/earnings ratio	IPO
prime rate	leveraged buy-out
warrant	

Similarly, if you are pursuing work in the medical field, you may encounter the following terms:

HMO (health maintenance orgaization)	EKG
PPO (preferred provider organization)	ER
Medicare	resident
Medicaid	intern
CAT Scan	specialist
stress test	co-payment

Finally, if you specialize in computers, you will need to know these terms, among others:

DOS	hard drive
RAM	floppy drive
ROM	antivirus program
video card	sound card

Much of acquiring the vocabulary specific to any discipline or career field involves learning as you go. Don't rush through materials that have unfamiliar words or concepts—look them up, ask other students or coworkers about them, and relate them to concepts you already know. Only on a solid knowledge base can you build additional learning; give yourself that base by taking the time to understand the vocabulary of what you study and what you do.

If you are not a native English speaker, you may find that particular words and phrases in American English are as unfamiliar to you as the vocabulary specific to your field. You can approach this problem much as you would learning any specific vocabulary.

How Can You Become Comfortable Reading American English?

You may be one of the millions of students in the United States who speak English as a second language or who are unfamiliar with American English because you came from an English-speaking country other than the United States, such as Jamaica, Ireland, or South Africa. Although you are comfortable enough with the basics of American English to pursue a college degree, you may have trouble understanding the idiosyncrasies of American English—the slang and initials that are often used in written materials and in speech.

These can be learned in the same way as you learn new vocabulary. Try to define them in the context of the sentence. Look them up in a dictionary or in a specialized reference book. (An excellent volume is Robert L. Chapman, *American Slang: The Abridged Edition of the Dictionary of American Slang*, New York: HarperPerennial, 1998.) Fix them in your memory with mnemonics and flash cards.

UNDERSTANDING AMERICAN SLANG

Slang is nonstandard English that has accepted usage among all or part of the population and that expresses thoughts in an informal way. Often, the words and phrases of slang seem to have little direct relation to their meaning, yet our culture accepts the meaning. Word experts, known as lexicographers, have successfully traced the meanings of many slang expressions back to their origin. For example, the phrase, *to toe the mark* means *to behave properly* and derives from runners placing their toes at the mark that indicates the starting point of a race. Table 5.4 includes a number of common slang expressions you may encounter as you read.

UNDERSTANDING COMMONLY USED INITIALS

As a nonnative speaker, you may also encounter commonly used initials that you are expected to recognize. Table 5.5 includes just a few initials that you may encounter as you read.

TABLE
5.4

Common slang you may encounter in writing and speech.

EXPRESSION AND PART OF SPEECH	MEANING	DERIVATION
also-ran (noun)	A loser; a person, product, etc. that does not succeed.	From the term for a racehorse who runs fourth or worse.
bite the bullet (verb)	To do something painful but necessary; to accept the cost of a course of action.	From the early surgical practice of having the patient bite hard on a bullet to divert the mind from pain and prevent screaming.
catch-22 (noun)	A condition or requirement very hard to fulfill, especially one that flatly contradicts others.	From the title of a 1961 satirical war novel by Joseph Heller.
dot com (noun)	A virtual business with a presence on the Internet.	From the .com suffix for commercial enterprises on the World Wide Web.
ego trip	Something done primarily to build one's self-esteem or display superior qualities.	Based on drug-induced psychedelic narcotic experiences, or trips.
freewheeling (noun)	Independence of action.	From the feature of certain 1930s cars permitting them to coast freely without being slowed by the engine.
go for the gold	To strive for the highest reward.	From the gold medal awarded to the first place finisher in Olympic competitions.
hit pay dirt (verb)	To find what one is looking for or needs; to earn a profit.	From the efforts of workers to drill through dirt until they hit oil, a saleable commodity.
in the red (noun)	In debt, losing money.	From the color of the ink traditionally used by bookkeepers to record financial losses.
off the charts (adjective phrase)	Too large to be measured.	From the published charts that show top-selling musical albums.

Source: Examples from Robert L. Chapman and Barbara Ann Kipfer, *American Slang,* 2nd Ed., New York: HarperPerennial, 1998.

TABLE

5.5

INITIALS	MEANING	INITIALS	MEANING
ASAP	As soon as possible	MVP	Most valuable player
AWOL	Absent without leave	SRO	Standing room only
FBI	Federal Bureau of Investigation	VCR	Video cassette recorder
FYI	For your information	VIP	Very important person
IRA	Individual Retirement Account		

With so much to read now and in your future career, it is important to set a goal to improve your reading speed along with your comprehension. You will learn techniques to become a faster reader next.

How Can You Increase Your Reading Speed?

Most students lead busy lives, carrying heavy academic loads while perhaps working or even caring for a family. It's difficult to make time to study at all, let alone handle the reading assignments for your different classes. In the workplace, many jobs have such a fast pace and so many tasks to be done that very little time is available for the reading that needs to be done. When physicians need to read medical journals to keep up with the latest research, for example, teachers need to read updated curriculum guides, or public servants need to read the latest news reports, they often have to do so on their own time outside of the workplace. Increasing your reading comprehension and speed will save you valuable time and effort.

Rapid reading won't do you any good if you can't remember the material or answer questions about it. However, reading too slowly can eat up valuable time and give your mind space to wander. Your goal is to read for maximum speed *and* comprehension. Because greater comprehension is the primary goal and actually promotes faster reading, make comprehension your priority over speed.

TEST YOUR SPEED AND COMPREHENSION

To make your own reading-speed assessment, time how rapidly you read the following 500-word selection from start to finish without stopping.

This excerpt, entitled "Back to School at Middle Age," is adapted from the seventh edition of Grace J. Craig's college text *Human Development*.[5]

Although today's college campuses are filled with 18- to 22-year-olds, they are also filled with older, nontraditional students who are returning to school. Nearly 1.5 million women and more than 700,000 men over the age of 35 are attending college—as 4-year students, in 2-year degree programs, and as graduate students. While there has been a dramatic increase in this segment of the college population, the percentage of typical college students—men and women between the ages of 18 and 22—has actually declined since 1980.

This dramatic demographic shift coincides with the recognition that humans are lifelong learners with cognitive abilities that adapt to life demands. Despite societal stereotypes that the primary period for learning is over after adolescence, we now know that it is during middle age that adults acquire the information and skills they need to meet the changing demands of their jobs. This is as true for bankers as it is for computer scientists, both of whom work in fields that have changed radically in recent years as a result of an explosion in technology.

In large part, middle-aged students are returning to school because they have to. Many are unemployed—the victims of corporate downsizing. Others are moving into the job market after spending time at home as full-time parents. A financial planner who stopped working for 5 years to raise her daughter may need recertification before any firm will hire her. Even adults who worked part-time during their child-rearing years may have to return to school to acquire the knowledge they need to qualify for a full-time job. This is especially true in fields with a high degree of professional obsolescence.

Whatever the reason for their return, studies show that the majority of middle-aged students are conscientious about their work. They attend classes regularly and get better grades, on average, than other segments of the student population.

The decision to return to school involves personal introspection and assessment of one's skills and abilities. The student role is generally different from the other roles middle-aged adults assume, and it requires considerable adaptation. A student is in a subordinate position as a learner. Also, mature adults may find themselves among a large number of students who are considerably younger than they are, and the faculty may also be younger. Initially, the age difference may be a source of discomfort.

Family members must often take on new responsibilities when a middle-aged member assumes the role of college student. A husband may have to do more household chores, while a wife may have to return to work to supplement the family income. In addition, the student may need emotional support. Sometimes this involves awkward role reversals and the disruption of familiar interaction patterns.

With the realization that middle-aged students are here to stay, community colleges and universities are making substantial adjustments to meet their needs. In addition, many students receive the training they need at work. Many large corporations run training departments designed to maintain a competent work force.

Source: Human Development, 7th Ed., Craig, © 1994. Adapted by permission of Prentice-Hall, Inc., Upper Saddle River, NJ.

Use the following formula to calculate how quickly you read this material:

- Note the time it took you in minutes to read the passage. Use decimals for fractions of a minute. That is, if it took you 1 minute and 45 seconds, then write 1.75 minutes.
- Divide the number of words in the passage by your reading time.

The number you come up with is your reading speed in words per minute. If you spent 1.75 minutes reading this 500-word selection, you would divide 500 by 1.75 to come up with a reading speed of approximately 286 words per minute.

Now answer the following questions without looking back at the text:

1. How many men and women over the age of 35 are now enrolled in various college programs?
   A. approximately 1.5 million women and 700,000 men
   B. 5 million men and women
   C. approximately 1.5 million men and 700,000 women

2. How has the enrollment of 18- to 22-year-old college students changed since 1980 in relation to the total college population?
   A. The percentage of students in this age group has increased.
   B. The percentage of students in this age group has remained the same.
   C. The percentage of students in this age group has decreased.

3. According to the passage, which one of the following reasons does **not** describe why older adults return to school?
   A. Unemployed adults return to school to acquire new work-related skills.
   B. After spending time at home raising children, many adults are moving onto another stage of life, which involves returning to work.
   C. Adults with discretionary income are choosing to invest money in themselves.

4. According to the text, why is the student role different from the other roles middle-aged adults assume?
   A. As learners, students are in a subordinate position, which can be uncomfortable for mature adults.
   B. Adults are not used to studying.
   C. Middle-aged adults often find it difficult to talk to young adults.

Here are the correct answers: 1A, 2C, 3C, 4A. You should have gotten at least three of the four questions correct. In general, your comprehension percentage, as judged by the number of questions like these that you answer correctly, should be above 70 percent. Lower scores mean that you are missing or forgetting important information.

PROBLEMS AND SOLUTIONS FOR SLOWER READERS

The average American adult reads between 150 and 350 words-per-minute. Slow readers fall below this range while faster readers are capable of speeds of 500 to 1,000 words-per-minute and sometimes faster.[6] Researchers point to a number of specific causes for slow reading. Identifying these patterns in your own reading style is your first step to correcting them. You are then ready to apply proven solutions.[7]

WORD-BY-WORD READING. When you first learned to read, as a young child, your teachers may have told you to read one word at a time as you moved systematically from one line to the next. This technique limits your reading speed. As a speed reader, you must train your eyes to "capture" and read groups of words at a time. Try swinging your eyes from side to side as you read a passage instead of stopping at various points to read individual words. When reading narrow columns, focus your eyes in the middle of the column and read down the page. With practice, you'll be able to read the entire column width.

LACK OF CONCENTRATION. Word-by-word reading inevitably leads to poor concentration. That is, you may be reading too slowly to keep your mind occupied, and soon your thoughts begin to wander. As a result, you may find reading boring, and even find it a sure-fire method to put yourself to sleep. Reading groups of words, instead of single words, will help counteract this effect as you provide your mind with the stimulation it needs to remain engaged.

VOCALIZATION AND SUBVOCALIZATION. Vocalizers tend to speak words as they read them or move their lips while reading. In contrast, subvocalizers pronounce inwardly every word they read. Both habits will slow your reading speed. Your first step to changing this behavior is awareness. Monitor your reading; if you notice either habit cropping up, make a conscious effort to stop what you're doing. A self-adhesive note in the margin with the reminder DON'T VOCALIZE may help your efforts in the early stages.

LIMITED VOCABULARY. If your vocabulary is small, you may be continually puzzled by the meanings of words. As you try to figure out meaning from context or consult a dictionary, your reading speed will slow. Follow the suggestions from the vocabulary-building section earlier in the chapter to build your vocabulary. Try to learn as many prefixes, roots, and suffixes as you can with the help of memory aids and flash cards.

UNCONSCIOUS REGRESSION. This involves rereading words that you've already read because your eyes stay on the same line instead of moving ahead. If you find yourself doing this, use your index finger as a visual guide. Reading expert Steve Moidel explains the technique:

> When you finish a line, bring your index finger to the beginning of the next line with a motion as fast and smooth as you can make it. It is important that the return be fluid. If you jerk your finger back, it may become a distraction and ultimately hurt your comprehension. Pretend that your finger is gliding, skiing, or ice skating back to the beginning of the next line: fast yet smooth.[8]

SLOW RECOVERY TIME. The time it takes your eye to move from the end of one line to the beginning of the next is known as *recovery time*. Slow readers spend far too long searching for the next line. Using your finger as a guide will also help speed your recovery time.

The key to building reading speed is practice and more practice, says reading expert Steve Moidel. To achieve your goal of reading between 500 and 1,000 words-per-minute, Moidel suggests that you start practicing at three times the rate you want to achieve, a rate that is much faster than you can comprehend. For example, if your goal is 500 words-per-minute, speed up to 1,500 words-per-minute. Reading at such an accelerated rate will push your eyes and mind to adjust to the faster pace. When you slow down to 500 words-per-minute—the pace at which you can read and comprehend—your reading rate will feel comfortable even though it is much faster than your original speed.

Atii

Inuktitut is the traditional language of the Inuit, formerly known as the Eskimo people, who live in the eastern arctic region in Canada and Alaska. The Inuit have at least 40 different words that describe different forms of snow and ice. Over the centuries, they have adapted their language and their lifestyle to suit the resources available to them. They make the most of their world, living successfully in a climate that many others might find forbidding.

Atii is an Inuktitut word that means "let's go." Think of the Inuit when you consider the value of skillful reading. Take the initiative to improve your speed and build your comprehension. Your efforts will help you take in information quickly and comprehensively so that you can spend more time and energy making use of that information. *Atii!*

Test Competence

MEASURING WHAT YOU'VE LEARNED

MULTIPLE CHOICE. *Circle or highlight the answer that seems to fit best.*

1. Making meaning from written words is a personal process because
   A. everyone has a different vocabulary level.
   B. you connect yourself to the concepts on the page.
   C. reading comprehension is always objective.
   D. it is unrelated to your reading purpose.

2. *Primary sources* are defined as
   A. periodicals.
   B. original documents.
   C. expert opinions of experimental results.
   D. resource materials.

3. The most important goals in choosing a particular setting for reading are to
   A. minimize distractions and maximize focus and discipline.
   B. find the best people with whom to read and work with them.
   C. learn how to concentrate in a library and study there regularly.
   D. learn how to read with children around and decide how to distract them.

4. A *reading purpose* can be described as
   A. the list of required texts you receive from your instructors.
   B. what you intend to learn or gain from your reading material.
   C. how quickly you intend to complete an assigned work.
   D. not related to any specific goals.

5. Primary purposes for reading academic materials include all of the following **except**
   A. practical application.
   B. critical analysis.
   C. overall mastery.
   D. preparing for writing assignments.

6. Your reading pace should be fairly slow when you are reading
   A. manuals and instruction books.
   B. newspapers and general online publications.
   C. original sources and scholarly journal articles.
   D. fiction novels and nonfiction books.

7. You can build a better vocabulary by focusing on all of the following elements **except**
   A. prefixes.
   B. word roots.
   C. spelling.
   D. suffixes.

8. For maximum comprehension when you use a dictionary, you should
   A. read only the first meaning of a word.
   B. memorize the exact wording of the dictionary definition.
   C. list all the new words you learn in a journal, without including their definitions.
   D. restate the definition in your own words and use it in a sentence.

9. Slow readers tend to do all of the following **except**
   A. believe that slow reading is better reading.
   B. read words one at a time.
   C. vocalize and subvocalize.
   D. lose their place as they read and read the same line more than once.

10. At work your vocabulary is likely to do all of the following **except**
    A. grow as you are exposed to specialized words, phrases, and initials linked to your field.
    B. remain static because your vocabulary building years are now behind you.
    C. give your coworkers information about your educational background.
    D. affect your career advancement.

TRUE/FALSE. *Place a T or an F beside each statement to indicate whether you think it is true or false.*

1. _____ Critical reading involves asking questions based on the mind actions.

2. _____ If you find yourself going back to a particular reference book again and again, you might want to own a copy.

3. _____ Reading comprehension is influenced by the knowledge you have gained through previous reading and studying.

4. _____ Foreign words and phrases are rarely used in any of the reading materials you are likely to see.

5. _____ Although *regression* and *slow recovery time* can slow your reading speed, one solution is to use your index finger as a visual guide on the page.

Brain Power

BUILDING VOCABULARY FITNESS

The paragraphs below are taken from the current media. Read the paragraph, noting the context of the vocabulary words shown in bold type. Next, for each vocabulary word (reprinted in the left-hand column), highlight the word or phrase in column A, B, or C that is the most similar in meaning. Finally, on a separate sheet of paper, solidify your understanding of these words by using each in a sentence of your own.

> After decades of **intensive** lobbying, deaf Americans have gained a place in the national consciousness. American Sign Language interpreters seem to be everywhere, from the State of the Union address to the Miss America **pageant.** Many universities and high schools now offer sign language as a foreign language course.
>
> But some **advocates** for the deaf say that a **fervent** devotion to the exclusive use of sign language by many of the deaf has helped **foster** a little known and surprising problem: The average 18-year-old deaf American reads at a fourth-grade level.
>
> Whether the problem is because of **reliance** on sign language, as they say, or stems from other causes, these advocates are seeking to lead a revolution in deaf education through a 34-year-old method called cued speech. The supporters of cued speech say the overreliance on sign language fosters a kind of false pride in deaf separatism.

From: "Among the Deaf, Ubiquitous Sign Language Faces a Challenge," by Lynette Holloway, *The New York Times*, June 22, 2000, p. A1.

Vocabulary Words	A	B	C
1. **intensive**	exhaustive	sketchy	irregular
2. **pageant**	contest	procession	campaign
3. **advocates**	opponents	mediators	supporters
4. **fervent**	impassioned	indifferent	excessive
5. **foster**	discourage	ignore	promote
6. **reliance**	dependence	control	contempt for

Strategic Thinking

GETTING THE BIG PICTURE

Answer the following questions on a separate piece of paper or in a journal.

In most jobs you are constantly faced with material you need to read and understand. Think about, and describe, your greatest challenge in reading. Discuss the effects that the struggle you experience with this challenge might have on your performance in the workplace. Finally, describe your plan for addressing this challenge, using any of the strategies in this chapter that you think will help you improve.

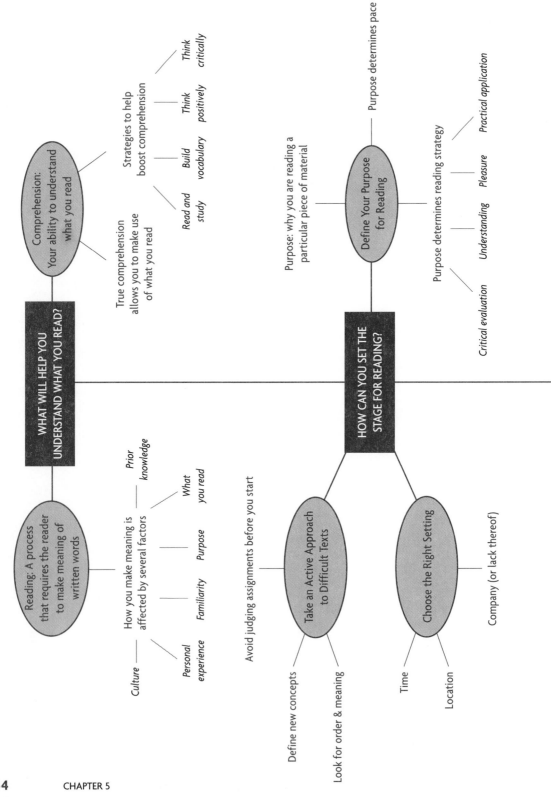

Comprehension:
Your ability to understand
what you read

Strategies to help
boost comprehension

Read and *Build* *Think* *Think*
study *vocabulary* *positively* *critically*

True comprehension
allows you to make use
of what you read

**WHAT WILL HELP YOU
UNDERSTAND WHAT YOU READ?**

Reading: A process
that requires the reader
to make meaning of
written words

How you make meaning is
affected by several factors

Prior
knowledge

What
you read

Culture

Familiarity *Purpose*

Personal
experience

Purpose: why you are reading a
particular piece of material

Define Your Purpose
for Reading

Purpose determines pace

Practical application

Pleasure

Understanding

Purpose determines reading strategy

Critical evaluation

**HOW CAN YOU SET THE
STAGE FOR READING?**

Avoid judging assignments before you start

Take an Active Approach
to Difficult Texts

Choose the Right Setting

Define new concepts

Look for order & meaning

Time

Location

Company (or lack thereof)

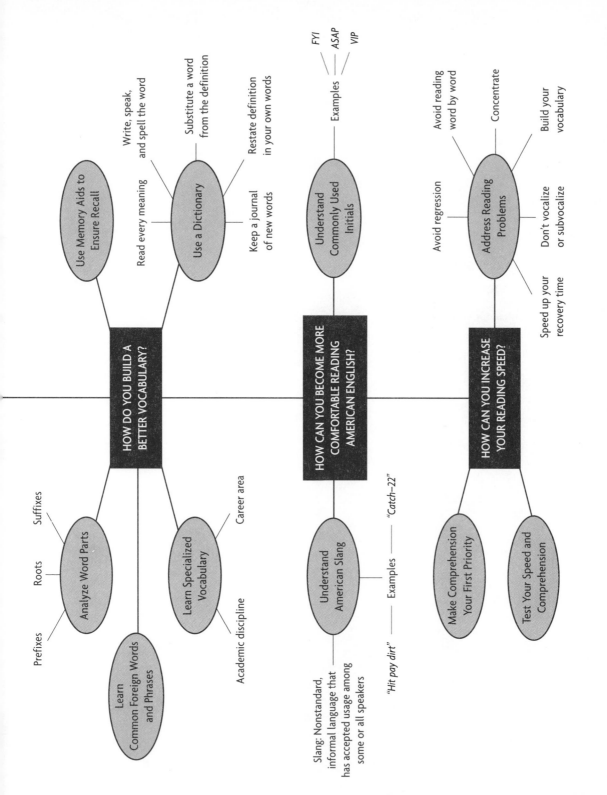

HOW DO YOU BUILD A BETTER VOCABULARY?

- Use Memory Aids to Ensure Recall
- Use a Dictionary
  - Write, speak, and spell the word
  - Substitute a word from the definition
  - Read every meaning
  - Restate definition in your own words
  - Keep a journal of new words
- Analyze Word Parts
  - Prefixes
  - Roots
  - Suffixes
- Learn Common Foreign Words and Phrases
- Learn Specialized Vocabulary
  - Career area
  - Academic discipline

HOW CAN YOU BECOME MORE COMFORTABLE READING AMERICAN ENGLISH?

- Understand Commonly Used Initials
  - Examples
    - FYI
    - ASAP
    - VIP
- Understand American Slang
  - Examples
    - "Hit pay dirt"
    - "Catch–22"
  - Slang: Nonstandard, informal language that has accepted usage among some or all speakers

HOW CAN YOU INCREASE YOUR READING SPEED?

- Address Reading Problems
  - Avoid reading word by word
  - Concentrate
  - Avoid regression
  - Build your vocabulary
  - Don't vocalize or subvocalize
  - Speed up your recovery time
- Make Comprehension Your First Priority
- Test Your Speed and Comprehension

ANALYZE

Your ability to take in, understand, retain, and interpret the written word is the foundation for your learning and accomplishment, now and in the future. For example, although today you may need to master a technical manual in order to pass an exam in a software design course, in a few years your understanding of computer antivirus programs may help you choose the right protection for a computer network at your job. A strategic approach to studying new material is an invaluable tool whether you are focusing on a biology text or a business proposal.

Now that you have set the stage for reading success with Chapter 5, this chapter will help you hone your reading strategies so that you can master any kind of content. At the end of the chapter, you will be able to answer these questions:

- How can SQ3R help you own what you read?
- How can you respond critically to what you read?
- What special approaches should you take to reading literature?
- How will reading skills help you in your career?

MASTERING CONTENT
STUDYING TEXTBOOKS, TECHNICAL DOCUMENTS, AND LITERATURE

How Can SQ3R Help You Own What You Read?

When you study, you take ownership of the material you read. "Owning" what you read means that you learn it well enough to apply it to what you do. For example, by the time students studying to be computer-hardware technicians complete their course work, they should be able to analyze hardware problems that lead to malfunctions. On-the-job computer technicians use the same study technique to keep up with changing technology. Studying to understand and learn also gives you mastery over concepts. For example, a dental hygiene student learns the causes of gum disease, and a journalism student learns about reporting and rhetoric.

SQ3R is a technique that will help you grasp ideas quickly, remember more, and review effectively for tests. The symbols S–Q–3–R stand for *survey, question, read, recite,* and *review*—all steps in the studying process. Developed more than 55 years ago by Francis Robinson, the technique is still being used today because it works.[1] It is particularly helpful for studying all kinds of textbooks.

Moving through the stages of SQ3R requires that you know how to skim and scan. *Skimming* involves rapid reading of chapter elements, including introductions, conclusions, and summaries; the first and last lines of paragraphs; boldface or italicized terms; pictures, charts, and diagrams. The goal of skimming is a quick construction of the main ideas. In contrast, *scanning* involves the careful search for specific facts and examples. You might use scanning during the review phase of SQ3R, when you need to locate particular information (such as a chemistry formula).

As you explore the steps of SQ3R, approach the system as a framework on which you build your particular house, not as a tower of stone. In other words, instead of following each step by rote, bring your personal learning styles and study preferences to SQ3R. For example, you and another classmate may focus on elements in a different order when you survey, write different types of questions, read at a different pace, prefer different ways of reciting, and favor different sets of review strategies. Take in all of the information about the system, explore the strategies, evaluate what works and what doesn't, and then use the system in a way that makes it your own.

SURVEY

When reading textbooks, surveying can help you learn and is encouraged. *Surveying* refers to the process of previewing, or pre-reading, a book before you study it. Compare it to looking at a map before you drive somewhere—those few minutes spent taking a look at your surroundings and where you intend to go will save you a lot of time and trouble once you are on the road.

Most textbooks include devices that give students an overview of the whole text as well as of the contents of individual chapters. When you survey, pay attention to the following elements.

THE FRONTMATTER.   Before you even get to page 1, most textbooks have a table of contents, a preface, and other materials. The table of contents gives you an important overview. Seeing what the book covers, which topics are emphasized, in what order the topics are placed, and the special features each chapter contains can give you valuable preliminary clues about a book. The preface, in particular, can point out the book's unique approach. For example, the preface for the American history text *Out of Many* states that it "offers a distinctive and timely approach to American history, highlighting the experiences of diverse communities of Americans in the unfolding story of our country."[2] This tells you right away that the text looks at American history through the eyes of the different people who settled the North American continent, and informs you that cultural diversity will be a central theme.

THE CHAPTER ELEMENTS.   Generally, each chapter has numerous devices that help you make meaning out of the bulk of its text. Among these are:

- The chapter title, which establishes the topic and often the author's perspective toward the topic
- The chapter introduction, outline, list of objectives, or list of key topics, designed to give you a helpful overview
- Within the chapter, headings large and small, tables and figures, quotes, marginal notes, and photographs and captions that help you perceive the structure of the material, isolate main ideas, and pull out important concepts
- Special chapter features, often presented in boxes set off from the main text, that point you to ideas connected to themes that run through the text
- Particular styles or arrangements of type (**boldface,** *italics,* <u>underline,</u> larger fonts, bulletpoints, text with adjusted margins, boxed text) that

call your attention to new words, words that are defined in the glossary, or important concepts

At the end of a chapter, a summary may help you tie concepts together. Review questions and exercises help you review and think critically about the material.

THE BACKMATTER.   Many textbooks have a text-specific "dictionary" called a *glossary* that defines terms found in the text. You will also find an index to help you locate individual topics and a bibliography that lists additional reading on particular topics covered in the text.

Figure 6.1 shows the many devices that books employ. Think about how many of these devices you already use, and which you can start using now to boost your comprehension.

QUESTION

Your next step is to examine the chapter headings and, on your own paper, write *questions* linked to them. If your reading material has no headings, develop questions as you read. These questions focus your attention and increase your interest, helping you build comprehension and relate new ideas to what you already know. You can take questions from the textbook

FIGURE
6.1   *Text and chapter previewing devices.*

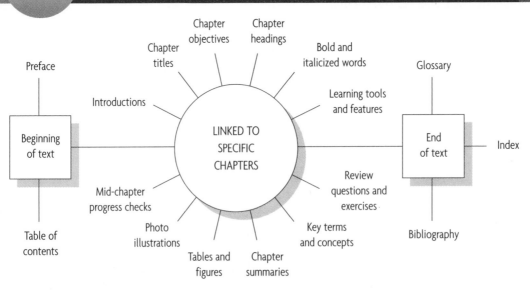

or from your lecture notes, or come up with them on your own when you survey, based on what ideas you think are most important.

Here is how this technique works. The column on the left contains primary- and secondary-level headings from a section of *Out of Many*. The column on the right rephrases these headings in question form.

THE MEANING OF FREEDOM	WHAT DID FREEDOM MEAN FOR BOTH SLAVES AND CITIZENS IN THE UNITED STATES?
Moving About	Where did African Americans go after they were freed from slavery?
The African American Family	How did freedom change the structure of the African American family?
African American Churches and Schools	What effect did freedom have on the formation of African American churches and schools?
Land and Labor after Slavery	How was land farmed and maintained after slaves were freed?
The Origins of African American Politics	How did the end of slavery bring about the beginning of African American political life?

There is no "correct" set of questions. Given the same headings, you could create your own particular set of questions. The more useful kinds of questions engage the critical-thinking mind actions and processes found in Chapter 4.

READ

Your questions give you a starting point for *reading*, the first R in SQ3R. Learning from textbooks requires that you read *actively*. *Passive* reading—reading the material without interacting with it by questioning, writing, noting, or highlighting—is a trap many students fall into out of fatigue, boredom, or simply not knowing how else to approach a text. When you read passively, you receive very little learning and retention for your efforts.

Active reading means engaging with the material through questioning, writing, note taking, and other activities. If you spend your time and energy wisely, engaged in active reading, you will receive enormous benefits. As you can see in Figure 6.2, the activities of SQ3R promote active reading. The following are some specific strategies that will keep you active when you read.

FOCUS ON YOUR Q STAGE QUESTIONS. Read the material with the purpose of answering each question you raised. As you come upon ideas and examples that relate to your question, write them down or note them in the text.

FIGURE
6.2

Use SQ3R to become an active reader.

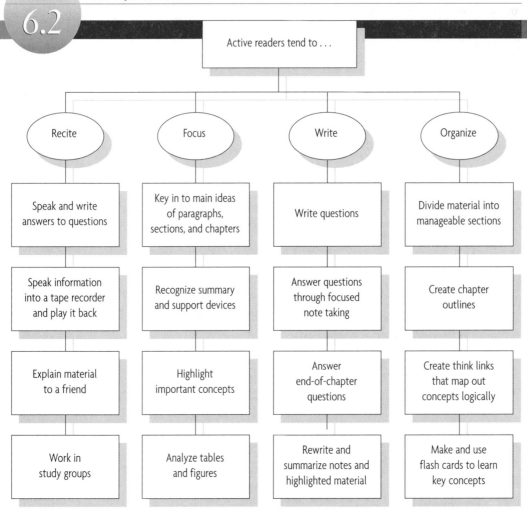

LOOK FOR CENTRAL IDEAS.   Pay special attention to the first and last lines of every paragraph to learn what the paragraph is about. As you read, record key words, phrases, and concepts in your notebook. Some students divide the notebook into two columns, writing questions on the left and answers on the right. This method is called the Cornell note-taking system (see Chapter 9).

MARK UP YOUR TEXTBOOK.   Being able to make notations will help you to make sense of the material; for this reason, owning your textbooks is an enormous advantage. You may want to write notes in the margins, circle key ideas, or highlight key points. Some people prefer to underline, although underlining adds more ink to the lines of text and may overwhelm your eye. Bracketing an entire key passage is a good alternative to underlining. Selective highlighting may help you pinpoint material to review before an exam, although excessive highlighting may actually interfere with comprehension. Here are some tips on how to strike a balance.

- *Mark the text after you read the material through once.* If you do it on the first reading, you may mark less important passages.
- *Highlight key terms and concepts.* Mark the examples that explain and support important ideas.
- *Avoid overmarking.* A phrase or two in any paragraph is usually enough. Set off long passages with brackets rather than marking every line.
- *Don't mistake highlighting for learning.* You will not learn what you highlight unless you interact with it through careful review—questioning, writing, and reciting.

One critical step in this phase is to divide your reading into digestible segments. Pace your reading so that you understand as you go. If you find you are losing the thread of the ideas you are reading, you may want to try smaller segments, or you may need to take a break and come back to it later. Try to avoid reading in mere sets of time—such as, "I'll read for 30 minutes and then quit"—or you may destroy the meaning by stopping in the middle of a key explanation.

RECITE

Once you finish reading a topic, stop and answer the questions you raised in the Q stage of SQ3R. You may decide to *recite* each answer aloud, silently speak the answers to yourself, tell the answers to another person as though you were teaching her, or write your ideas and answers in brief notes. Writing is often the most effective way to solidify what you have read because writing from memory checks your understanding.

Don't discount the value of reciting aloud from the text. Although it may seem silly or embarrassing, speaking greatly increases your chance of remembering and learning because it engages three body processes at the same time: One, your eyes take in the information as you read it. Two, speaking the information engages your physical muscle memory. Three, hearing yourself speak engages your ears to further solidify the memory of the information.

Keep your learning styles (Chapter 2) in mind when you explore different strategies. For example, an intrapersonal learner may prefer writing, while an interpersonal learner might want to recite answers aloud to a classmate. A logical–mathematical learner may benefit from organizing material into detailed outlines, while a musical learner might want to chant information aloud to a rhythm.

After you finish one section, read the next. Repeat the question-read-recite cycle until you complete the entire chapter. If during this process you find yourself fumbling for thoughts, you may not yet "own" the ideas. Reread the section that's giving you trouble until you master its contents. Understanding each section as you go is crucial because the material in one section often forms a foundation for the next.

REVIEW

Review soon after you finish a chapter. Reviewing, both immediately and periodically in the days and weeks after you read, is a crucial step of the process. Chances are good that if you close the book after you read, much of your focused reading work will slip away from memory. See review as an opportunity to clarify the main ideas, solidify your understanding, and enable you to move into a more critical evaluation of the material. Reviewing makes learning possible. Here are some techniques for reviewing—try many and use what seems to work best for you.

- Skim and reread your notes. Then try summarizing them from memory.
- Answer the text's end-of-chapter review, discussion, and application questions.
- Quiz yourself using the questions you raised in the Q stage. If you can't answer one of your own or one of the text's questions, go back and scan the material for answers.
- Review and summarize in writing the material you have highlighted or bracketed.
- Create a chapter outline in standard outline form or think-link form.
- Reread the preface, headings, tables, and summary.
- Recite important concepts to yourself, or record important information on a cassette tape and play it on your car's tape deck or your portable cassette player.
- Make flash cards that have an idea or word on one side and examples, a definition, or other related information on the other. Test yourself.
- Think critically: Break ideas down into examples, consider similar or different concepts, recall important terms, evaluate ideas, and explore causes and effects (see the next section, "How Can You Respond Critically to What You Read?").
- Discuss the concepts with a classmate or in a study group. Trying to teach study partners what you learned will pinpoint the material you know and what still needs work.
- Make think links that show how important concepts relate to one another.

If you need help clarifying your reading material, ask your instructor. Pinpoint the material you want to discuss, schedule a meeting during office hours, and bring a list of questions.

Speaking of review, see Table 6.1 for a review of the steps of SQ3R.

STAGE OF THE PROCESS	DESCRIPTION
Survey	Pre-reading a book before studying it: Involves skimming, scanning, and examining book elements such as the table of contents, chapter objectives, headers within the text, and study questions.
Question	Involves developing questions linked to chapter headings or to ideas that popped out during the S stage. Questions can be inspired by lecture notes as well, and help to engage critical thinking while reading.
Read	Involves reading the material with the purpose of answering the questions formulated in the Q stage. May also involve taking notes on the reading and marking the text to identify key ideas and information.
Recite	Involves answering the questions from the Q stage, either recited aloud, spoken silently to yourself, told to a study partner, or written down in brief notes.
Review	Involves using various techniques—skimming and summarizing notes, answering study questions, writing outlines or think links, reciting concepts, using flash cards, thinking critically, and so on—to renew and solidify your knowledge.

Refreshing your knowledge is easier and faster than learning it the first time. Set up regular review sessions, for example, once a week. Reviewing in as many different ways as possible increases the likelihood of retention. Critical reading may be the most important of these ways.

How Can You Respond Critically to What You Read?

You've surveyed, questioned, read, recited, and reviewed. You've taken in new information and developed a solid basic understanding of what you've read. Now comes the real learning, the work that takes your understanding to a deeper and more productive level.

Critical reading is both making meaning of the original text and adding your personal response to it. It goes beyond rote memorization (taking in and regurgitating material) because it involves analyzing the material in light of what you already know. Critical reading enables you to develop a thorough understanding of reading material through evaluation and analysis.

Think of critical reading as an extension of the Q stage, one that comes after you have completed the initial steps of SQ3R. In the Q stage you raised questions based on chapter headers—when you read critically, you develop new questions and relate answers to other information. Your answers to Q-stage questions help you identify key ideas—when you read critically, you can explore whether those ideas are true or accurate, and you can also synthesize those ideas to come up with the central idea of the material. A critical reader can also compare one piece of information or material to another and evaluate which makes more sense, which proves its thesis more successfully, or which is more useful for the reader's purposes.

Engage your critical-thinking processes by using the following suggestions.

USE SQ3R TO "TASTE" READING MATERIAL

Sylvan Barnet and Hugo Bedau, authors of *Critical Thinking, Reading, and Writing—A Brief Guide to Argument*, suggest that the active reading of SQ3R will help you form an initial idea of what a piece of reading material is all about. Through surveying, skimming for ideas and examples, highlighting and writing comments and questions in the margins, and reviewing, you can develop a basic understanding of its central ideas and contents.[3] This understanding is the "raw material" that you then begin to examine critically.

Summarizing, part of the SQ3R review process, is one of the best ways to develop an understanding of a piece of reading material. To construct a *summary*, focus on the central ideas of the piece and the main examples that support them. A summary does not contain any of your own ideas or your evaluation of the material. It simply condenses the material, making it easier to focus on the structure and central ideas of the piece when you go back to read more critically. At that point, you can begin to ask questions, evaluating the piece and introducing your own ideas. Using the mind actions will help you.

ASK QUESTIONS BASED ON THE MIND ACTIONS

Instead of simply accepting what you read, seek a more thorough understanding by questioning the material as you go along. Using the mind actions to formulate your questions will help you understand the material.

What parts of the material you focus on will depend on your purpose for reading. For example, if you are writing a paper on the causes of World War II, you might look at how certain causes fit your thesis. If you are comparing two pieces of writing that contain opposing arguments, you may focus on picking out the central ideas and evaluating how well the writers use examples to support them. You can question components such as:

- The central idea of the entire piece
- A particular idea, statement, or supposed fact
- The examples that support an idea, statement, or fact

The following are some ways to critically question reading material, based on the mind actions. Apply them to any component you want to question by substituting the component for the words *it* and *this*.

Similarity:	What does this remind me of, or how is it similar to something else I know?
Difference:	What different conclusions are possible? How is this different from my experience?
Cause and Effect:	Why did this happen, or what caused this? What are the effects or consequences of this? What effect does the author intend, or what is the purpose of this material? What effects support a stated cause?
Example to Idea:	How would I classify this, or, what is the best idea to fit this example? How would I summarize this, or what are the key ideas? What is the thesis or central idea?
Idea to Example:	What evidence supports this, or what examples fit this idea?
Evaluation:	How would I evaluate this? Is it useful or well constructed? Does this example support my thesis or central idea? Is this information or point of view important to my work? If so, why?

ENGAGE CRITICAL-THINKING PROCESSES

Certain thinking processes from Chapter 4 can help to deepen your analysis and evaluation of what you read. These processes are establishing truth and constructing an argument. Within these processes you will ask questions that use the mind actions.

Thinking Logically

With what you know about logical thinking, you can evaluate any statement in your reading material, identifying it as fact, opinion, or assumption and challenging how it is supported. Evaluate statements, ideas, or entire pieces of material, using questions such as the following:

- Is this fact? Is the factual statement true? How does the writer know?

- Is this opinion? How could I test its validity?
- What assumptions underlie this?
- What else do I know that is similar to or different from this?
- What information that I already know supports or disproves this?
- What examples disprove this as fact or do not fit this assumption?

For example, imagine that a piece of writing states, "The dissolving of the family unit is the main cause of society's ills." You may question this statement by looking at what facts and examples support it or by comparing it to other materials. You may question the writer's sources of information. You could find hidden assumptions underneath this statement, such as an assumed definition of what a family is or of what constitutes "society's ills." You could also find examples that do not fit this assumption, such as successful families that don't fit the traditional definition of "family" used by the writer.

Evaluating an Argument

As you read in Chapter 4, an argument is a persuasive case that seeks to prove or disprove a point. When reading material contains one or more arguments, use what you know about arguments to evaluate whether the writer has constructed his argument effectively. Ask questions like:

- Do I believe this argument? How is the writer trying to persuade me?
- If the author uses cause-and-effect reasoning, does it seem logical?
- Do the examples adequately support the central idea of the argument?
- Is the evidence fact or opinion? Is it true or verifiable?
- What different and perhaps opposing arguments seem just as valid?
- If I'm not sure whether I believe this, how could I construct an opposing argument?

For example, say you are reading an article in support of one flat income tax rate for all citizens. You might start by examining whether you believe the argument right off the bat. Then, look at the examples that the writer uses to support this position. First of all, are they fact or opinion, and how do you know? Secondly, do they support the idea effectively? Then consider what other arguments may be valid, and why—you could consider arguments favoring the current tax system. This may involve additional research if you are uncertain of other points of view or if your information is out-of-date. Finally, if you are not convinced, you might devise an argument against the flat tax, supporting it with adequate examples.

Don't rule out the possibility that you may agree completely with an argument. However, use critical thinking to make an informed decision, rather than accepting the argument outright.

BE MEDIA LITERATE

Even seemingly objective textbooks are written by a person or persons who have particular points of view, which may influence the information they include or how they include it. For instance, the growing awareness of the multicultural heritage of the United States has prompted revisions of history texts that previously ignored or shortchanged topics such as Native American history; *Out of Many* is a prime example. In all of your reading, especially primary sources, remember the following:

- Authors may use particular wording or tone to create an effect on a reader.
- Different readers may have different interpretations of a piece of reading material, depending on individual perspective and experience.
- Any written material carries the values of the people who created it and is influenced, to varying degrees, by the perspectives and intents of the authors.

To analyze perspective as you read, seek to unearth the ideas that influence the material by questioning its perspective. Consider what the author or authors want you to believe, and why. Evaluate how they support their perspective, and decide if you think the examples they use are valid. As a media-literate reader, you have the ability to stay aware of these realities and to sift through your materials critically so that you gain from them what is most useful to you.

SEEK UNDERSTANDING

The fundamental purpose of all college reading is comprehension. Reading critically allows you to reach the highest possible level of understanding. Think of your reading process as an archaeological dig. The first step is to excavate a site and uncover the artifacts, which corresponds to

Students do critical reading, not only in college, but their whole lives. My best advice for critical reading is to probe into the material, dive into it, question everything that you can. And always have a purpose for reading. When you have a purpose, you get involved in what you are reading; you are an active reader. Critical readers challenge assumptions as they read, question ideas, and reject ideas. There is nothing passive in this process.

KIM FLACHMANN, PROFESSOR OF ENGLISH,
CALIFORNIA STATE UNIVERSITY AT BAKERSFIELD

EXPERT INSIGHT

Be a Critical Reader and an Active Reader

your initial survey and reading of the material. As important as the excavation is, the process would be incomplete if you took home a bunch of dirt-covered items and stopped there. The second half of the process is to investigate each item, evaluate what each one means, and derive new knowledge and ideas from what you discover. Critical reading allows you to complete that crucial second half of the process.

Critical reading is the process of making order and meaning out of what might often be seemingly chaotic materials. Finding order within chaos is an important skill, not just in the mastery of reading, but also in life. This skill can give you power by helping you "read" (think through) work dilemmas, personal problems, and educational situations.

Remember that critical reading takes time and focus. Give yourself a chance to be a successful critical reader by finding a time, place, and purpose for your reading. Take advantage of the opportunity to learn from others by working in pairs or groups whenever you can.

What you now know about reading can apply in large part to literature as well as textbooks. Although reading literature may seem to involve less fact-finding and memorization, being able to comprehend the various layers and elements of a story requires strong active-reading skills.

What Special Approaches Should You Take to Reading Literature?

When you pick up a novel, poem, play, or other piece of literature, you can read it on many different levels. You can devour the James Bond thriller *On Her Majesty's Secret Service* by Ian Fleming just for the fun of it, or you can approach the classic Toni Morrison novels, *Beloved* and *The Bluest Eye*, as serious literature.

In your literature courses, your instructors will help you learn to critically analyze what you read. This involves looking at a work in terms of its literary elements in order to find meaning and understanding on different levels. Don't resist the process or believe that too much analysis will spoil your reading enjoyment. On the contrary, it may help you see things that you never knew were there and appreciate the author's message in all its depth. These skills add immeasurably to your understanding of the book, in the short run, and your life, in the long run.

UNDERSTANDING LITERARY ELEMENTS

Novels and short stories are works of literature that tell a story through twists and turns in plots and subplots, the actions of characters, writing style, imagery, setting, and more. The following elements will help you analyze and critically evaluate a work.

SETTING.   *Setting* is where and when the action occurs; it includes such elements as the country (or supernatural world) in which the author centers the plot, the climate, and the season. Setting also includes the economic and social environment. Is there war or peace, prosperity or economic hardship, famine or plenty, a political democracy or dictatorship? Finally, setting includes historical context. For example, does the work describe a time before women had equal rights, when children were considered property, when people of color were slaves? Or does it reflect a society and time that embraced equal rights and opportunities for all?

In Pearl S. Buck's Pulitzer Prize winning novel *The Good Earth*, the setting is northern China, during a time of revolution in the early twentieth century that transformed the country. It was a time in which slavery was condoned and women submitted to the wishes of their fathers and husbands. It was also a time when peasants lived desperate lives if their crops failed and when law and order were controlled by the strongest and most powerful. Finally, it was a time when parents expected unquestioning respect and obedience from their children.

The setting reflects the inequality that existed in Chinese society. As you read books about different historical contexts, remember that authors are writing about conditions and attitudes that may or may not still exist. Know too that authors do not necessarily agree with the cultural standards they depict. Try to understand the text from both the author's and the narrator's perspectives. Examine their motives and prejudices.

STRUCTURE.   The term *structure* describes how the work is organized and how the parts are linked to each other and the whole. The following structural sequence is common: an introduction or exposition, a complication, rising action, the climax, falling action, and the conclusion.

PLOT.   The *plot* tells the story; it is the events and actions that take place. In *The Good Earth*, the plot centers on the life cycle of a Chinese peasant, Wang Lung. The author takes the reader through the events of Wang Lung's life, including his marriage, the birth of healthy sons, plentiful harvests, near starvation conditions, the birth of a feeble-minded daughter, the death of another child, and more. The reader watches as Wang Lung overcomes obstacles to become a wealthy farmer. At the end of the book, he learns that his sons have no intention of farming his land after he dies because they have no respect for their father's ties to the good earth.

CHARACTERS.   These are the personalities, thoughts, and actions of the people moving the plot forward. As you examine the characters in a literary work, think about whether they remain essentially the same or grow in response to changing circumstances, whether they are stereotypes who serve a function but are not unique individuals, or whether they have complex motivations and actions. As you analyze the actors in a novel or short story, you will see that some play major and others minor roles. Among the major characters, you will often discover a *protagonist*—a person who struggles toward someone or something—and an *antagonist*, one who struggles against someone or something. The struggle may be internal or external. It may involve a character's attempt to achieve hopes and goals, to overcome emotional problems that limit life, to defeat others who stand in the way of a goal, to change society, to deal with the forces of nature, and more.

In *The Good Earth*, the central character and protagonist, Wang Lung, has built his entire life around farming. He is ambitious and determined to succeed against obstacles that include drought, flood, and robbers. His wife, O-lan, a slave bought by Wang Lung's father to marry Wang Lung, is devoted and obedient and is willing to loot the homes of the rich during a civil war in order to get the money the family needs to buy land. However, O-lan is not a stereotype. Her obedience ends when Wang Lung wants to bring his concubine, Lotus, into the family home. O-lan refuses Wang Lung's wishes, and he is forced to find her a home elsewhere.

THEME.   The *theme* is the work's central message as revealed through the interplay of character and plot. A central theme of *The Good Earth* is a peasant's rise from poverty, hardship, and obscurity into a position of importance and wealth. Wang Lung spends his life trying to provide security for his family through his work on the land. The link between security and the earth is important in the novel, and, in fact, the earth theme appears throughout the book. Wang Lung's greatest satisfaction is to look at his land, hold it in his hand, and work it for food and security.

Another theme is the struggle against natural elements, forces, and cycles. The opening paragraphs of *The Good Earth* are filled with naturalistic references, such as *air, sky, wind, rain, water, sunshine, dawn,* and *spring.*

POINT OF VIEW.   The author's perspective on the material he is presenting is described as the *point of view.* Point of view is often revealed through the voice of a third-person narrator, an objective observer presenting information without comment, praise, or criticism. When authors use a first-person narrator, information is presented through the filter of one of the story's main characters. Using a first-person narrator gives the author the opportunity to present a point of view to which readers may have a strong reaction. Remember that the author may not necessarily agree with the views of his narrator. In *The Good Earth*, Pearl S. Buck tells her story through the eyes of the main character, Wang Lung.

STYLE.   The term *style* describes how the author's words, sentences, and paragraphs communicate thoughts and feelings. Is the style sparse and bare, like that used by Ernest Hemingway in *For Whom the Bell Tolls*? Is it richly descriptive, as in *Great Expectations* by Charles Dickens? Is it romantic with a focus on the intensity of feelings, as in *Wuthering Heights* by Emily Brontë?

Pearl S. Buck's style in *The Good Earth* is one of a straightforward narrative in which she relates the main story line without the use of complicated literary techniques such as *foreshadowing* (presenting an indication or suggestion of something that will occur later in the work) or *flashbacks* (the interruption of a story in order to portray or recount an incident or scene from the past). The author's style is to present a series of dramatic episodes through the experiences of her characters. She continually focuses on her story and avoids subplots that divert the reader's attention.

IMAGERY. *Imagery* describes the figures of speech the author uses to create pictures in the reader's mind. As mentioned earlier, the most important literary image throughout *The Good Earth* is the earth itself.

Table 6.2 describes some forms of figurative language that are at the heart of literary imagery. The examples are from the works of the great American humorist Mark Twain, who lived between 1835 and 1910.

Figures of speech. **TABLE 6.2**

FIGURE OF SPEECH	DEFINITION	EXAMPLE
Metaphor	A comparison between two or more things that are not similar, without using the words *like* or *as* in the comparison.	"Put all your eggs in the one basket and—WATCH THAT BASKET."
Simile	A direct, explicit comparison between two things that lack similarity. The word *like* or *as* structures the comparison.	"Soap and education are not as sudden as a massacre, but they are more deadly in the long run."
Hyperbole	A gross, deliberate exaggeration for emphasis.	"Tomorrow night I appear for the first time before a Boston audience—4,000 critics."
Understatement	A statement presented with restraint for effect.	"Good breeding consists of concealing how much we think of ourselves and how little we think of the other person."
Personification	When a distinctly human trait is given to an inanimate object, animal, or idea.	"Habit is habit, and not to be flung out of the window by any man, but coaxed downstairs a step at a time."
Analogy	A comparison of similar traits between dissimilar things.	"The fact that man knows right from wrong proves his *intellectual* superiority to the other creatures; but the fact that he can *do* wrong proves his *moral* inferiority to any creature that *cannot*."
Irony	The use of words in the opposite way than their intended meaning.	"An experienced, industrious, ambitious, and often quite picturesque liar."

When reading and analyzing fiction or non-fiction, it is important to keep in mind the idea of a "continuum of language" from the purely scientific to the purely poetic. Figures 6.3 and 6.4 below are based on descriptions and illustrations of the idea by Norma B. Kahn, an expert on helpful ways of reading and studying.

No matter how scientific or poetic the language of your material, critical thinking will allow you to plumb the depths of its meaning. You need critical-reading skills in order to select important ideas, identify examples that support them, and ask questions about the material, especially when it is a primary source or literary work that does not have clearly marked features.

FIGURE 6.3

A continuum of language.

PURELY SCIENTIFIC	PURELY POETIC
One word: One meaning	**One word: Many meanings**
1. states	1. suggests
2. denotes	2. connotes
3. appeals to intellect primarily	3. appeals to senses, emotions, intellect, imagination

Source: Norma B. Kahn, *More Learning in Less Time: A Guide for Students, Professionals, Career-Changers, and Lifelong Learners,* 5th Ed., Gwynedd Valley, PA: Ways-to Books, Inc., 1998, p. 68.

FIGURE 6.4

Examples of scientific and poetic language.

SCIENTIFIC LANGUAGE

Thirst is the sensation of dryness in the mouth related to a need or desire to drink.

POETIC LANGUAGE—FROM A POEM BY LORD BYRON (1788–1824)

"Fame is the thirst of youth."

POETIC LANGUAGE—FROM A WORK BY JEROME KLAPKA JEROME (1859–1927)

"Let your boat of life be light, packed with only what you need—a homely home and simple pleasures, one or two friends, worth the name, someone to love and someone to love you, a cat, a dog, and a pipe or two, enough to eat and enough to wear, and a little more than enough to drink; for thirst is a dangerous thing."

Source: Adapted from Norma B. Kahn, *More Learning in Less Time: A Guide for Students, Professionals, Career-Changers, and Lifelong Learners,* 5th Ed., Gwynedd Valley, PA: Ways-to Books, Inc., 1998, p. 67.

USING CRITICAL THINKING TO EVALUATE LITERATURE

You can also use critical thinking to analyze works of literature. It's a good idea to start with overview questions that help you define your personal reactions. For example:

- What is the work trying to accomplish? What are its themes? What do they mean to you?
- Is this an "important" work? Why or why not? Would you recommend that others read it?
- Did you enjoy reading the work? Do you think the work will change your life? In what ways? Has the work changed your thoughts, attitudes, or feelings in any way?
- Did you personally identify with any of the characters? Did you see part of yourself in any of them?
- Did the work give you greater understanding of a different time or culture? Did you see the characters as products of their culture?

Now get more specific by raising critical-thinking questions that focus on the various literary elements described earlier in the chapter. For example:

CHARACTER. How do the characters reveal their true nature? *(Example to Idea)* What are the major similarities between the main characters? *(Similarity)* How do a character's actions change the course of the story? *(Cause and Effect)*

PLOT. How would you evaluate the power of the story? Did it hold your interest? *(Evaluation)*

SETTING. What relationship does the setting have to the actions of the major and minor characters? *(Cause and Effect)*

POINT OF VIEW. How is the author's point of view expressed through the actions of a minor character? *(Example to Idea)*

STYLE. Did the author's style add to or detract from your enjoyment of the work? *(Evaluation)*

IMAGERY. The author is trying to communicate a particular mood through the use of language. What specific metaphors and similes helped achieve this feeling? *(Idea to Example)*

This analysis will help you appreciate literature on many levels. Every time you analyze a work, you peel away layers of meaning to reveal artistry you may not see in a superficial reading. For example, on one level, *The Good Earth* relates Wang Lung's struggles to raise and support his family, battle the elements and his social environment, and pass a legacy onto his sons. On another level, it is a universal tale of the destiny of man. It is one of the joys of life to get to the core of a literary work and apply your new insights to your own life.

How Will Reading Skills Help You in Your Career?

Keeping up and *moving ahead* are the challenges you face after you graduate. In an environment where change and innovation are constants in business—and where a company's survival may depend on finding new solutions—your employer expects you to be on top of the current knowledge in your field. Thinking, "I learned everything I need to know from my college instructors and courses. Now I can coast," will leave you far behind soon after you graduate.

It's in your best interest to focus on learning throughout your career. If you make it a point to keep up with new information in your field and related fields, you will be better at your job. In addition, you will probably stay more interested in your job, and more excited by it. In many career fields, examples to learn from include publications, seminars, conferences, and other situations—all requiring focused, effective reading skills. Whether you take the time to attend an education seminar on the latest strategies for retaining students, spend a week at an annual sales meeting for the computer hardware company for which you work, or receive in the mail a monthly journal on strategies for running a not-for-profit company, you want your efforts to result in learning for the long-term.

In our era of advanced technology, much of your on-the-job reading will be as demanding—or even more demanding—than your college texts. However, you will have an important advantage when you approach this material. It focuses on your chosen field, a field in which you have interest and strength as well as a solid background in the basics. You learned the concepts and the vocabulary that were "state of the art" during your college years. Now you need to build on this foundation to remain personally competitive in an ever-changing job market.

Put yourself on the road to lifelong self-improvement with career advancement and personal achievement as your goals. Then develop a reading strategy that will help you master your career-related readings efficiently and effectively.

STRATEGIES FOR EFFECTIVE READING AT WORK

Here are some suggestions for applying the reading and study skills you learned in Chapters 5 and 6 to the reading challenges you will face at work:

DEFINE YOUR PURPOSE FOR READING EACH DOCUMENT. Then decide how you will read it. Will you scan it for an overview or read in detail? Your decision will depend, in part, on how relevant the material is to your job. Say, for example, you are an employee-relations representative in a large corporation in charge of making sure your company complies with Federal employment standards. Every time the Federal Equal Employment Opportunity Commission issues new guidelines, you have to study and learn them in the same way you learned information in your college texts. You won't be tested on your reading, but your ability to do your job and advance will depend on your ability to apply key concepts to the workplace.

APPLY SPEED-READING TECHNIQUES. These skills will be invaluable in handling the hundreds of work-related documents that many employees must deal with on a regular basis.

BUILD CAREER-RELATED VOCABULARY CONTINUOUSLY. Every field has a specialized vocabulary. Make flash cards to help you remember new terms, and cement them into memory by using them in conversation with your colleagues.

USE SQ3R TO STUDY AND LEARN IMPORTANT DOCUMENTS. This technique will help you identify and learn important job-related concepts in ways that will maximize recall.

READ CRITICALLY, ASKING QUESTIONS BASED ON THE MIND ACTIONS. The best employees use new information as the basis for creative thinking and innovation. Use your critical-thinking skills to help your company or organization succeed in a competitive marketplace.

REVIEW IMPORTANT DOCUMENTS WITH COLLEAGUES. As with college study groups, informal on-the-job study sessions will help every participant understand complex materials and envision their impact on the working environment.

MANAGE DISTRACTIONS. Encourage coworkers to respect the privacy of your space, especially if you work in an office with cubicles instead of closed-in rooms. You may also want to save important reading material for quiet times or for your commute. If you work at home, it is important to define your workspace and time. Include family members, partners, and friends in your thinking so they will understand what you are trying to accomplish.

FINDING SOURCES OF WORK-RELATED INFORMATION

Unlike college, where professors assign material for study, you will have to locate many of your career-related readings on your own. This is not difficult if you develop a strategy to uncover current sources:

- *Exchange information with coworkers.* Observe the publications and specific articles others are reading.
- *Join professional organizations.* If you are an accountant, for example, become a member of the American Institute of Certified Public Accountants. If you are a travel agent, join the American Society of Travel Agents. Attend meetings, listen to lectures, and study suggested readings that apply to what you do. Scan monthly newsletters for sources related to your field.
- *Do research.* Browse through libraries and bookstores for books, magazines, and journals with the latest information in your field. Go online for bibliographies, and then order the materials on the Web. Collect and read career-related publications. Set up a filing system to keep work-related newspaper, magazine, and journal articles organized and accessible.
- *Visit websites that focus on your career interests.* Think of them as information sources and leads to additional sites. Print the material you want to study in depth. Bookmark career-related websites so you can make easy return visits.

Most importantly, consider all of your efforts as a commitment to personal responsibility and improvement. You are on the road to lifelong learning.

читать

This word may look completely unfamiliar to you, but anyone who can read the Russian language and alphabet will know that it means "read." People who read languages that use different kinds of characters, such as Russian, Japanese, or Greek, learn to process those characters as easily as you process the letters of your native alphabet. Your mind learns to process individually each letter or character you see. This ability enables you to move to the next level of understanding—making sense of those letters or characters when they are grouped to form words, phrases, and sentences.

Think of this concept when you read. Remember that your mind processes immeasurable amounts of information so that you can understand the concepts on the page. Give it the best opportunity to succeed by reading often and by focusing on all of the elements that help you read to the best of your ability.

Study Skills in Action

Test Competence

MEASURING WHAT YOU'VE LEARNED

MULTIPLE CHOICE. *Circle or highlight the answer that seems to fit best.*

1. *SQ3R* helps you take ownership of what you read by helping you to
   A. learn how to skim and scan material so that you find the most important information.
   B. read textbooks quickly and comprehensively.
   C. understand ideas and remember them for tests.
   D. learn the material well enough to apply it to what you do.

2. *Scanning* involves
   A. a careful search for specific facts and examples.
   B. rapid reading of chapter elements.
   C. a quick construction of the main ideas.
   D. coming up with questions.

3. Selective highlighting does **not** include
   A. marking the text after reading it once through.
   B. highlighting key terms and concepts.
   C. marking important paragraphs in their entirety.
   D. setting off long passages with brackets.

4. *Structure* and *plot* are
   A. literary elements.
   B. part of every literary work.
   C. opposite to each other.
   D. indicative of the economic and social environment.

5. When a passage suggests something that will occur later in the work, this is called
   A. flashback.
   B. foreshadowing.
   C. theme.
   D. perspective.

6. *Simile* differs from *metaphor* in that
   A. simile uses the word "like" or "as"; metaphor does not.
   B. metaphor makes a comparison in the present; simile uses a future comparison.
   C. metaphor compares similar things; simile compares different things.
   D. simile compares concepts; metaphor compares objects.

7. Being able to identify what in a piece of reading material is true or accurate is part of
   A. reviewing.
   B. hyperbole.
   C. cause and effect.
   D. critical reading.

8. Evaluating the logic of the information in your reading material would **not** include
   A. investigating the credentials of the author.
   B. considering whether the information is fact or opinion.
   C. looking at whether examples fit ideas.
   D. examining the material for assumptions.

9. An author creates pictures in the reader's mind primarily through the use of
   A. setting.
   B. plot.
   C. imagery.
   D. personification.

10. The most important workplace goal that your reading skills will help you achieve is
   A. staying on top of the latest technology advancements.
   B. attending seminars and workshops at a professional conference.
   C. meeting with more advanced workers in your field.
   D. keeping current on the latest knowledge in your career area.

TRUE/FALSE. *Place a T or an F beside each statement to indicate whether you think it is true or false.*

1. _____ SQ3R refers to Survey, Query, Read, Reread, Review.

2. _____ *Reciting* means reading an entire section of text aloud to another person.

3. _____ A *protagonist* is a character who struggles toward someone or something.

4. _____ An author who uses a third-person narrator presents information through the perspective of one of the main characters.

5. _____ Any written material carries the values of the person who created it and is influenced by the author's perspectives.

Brain Power

BUILDING VOCABULARY FITNESS

The paragraphs below are taken from the current media. Read the paragraph, noting the context of the vocabulary words shown in bold type. Next, for each vocabulary word (reprinted in the left-hand column), highlight the word or phrase in column A, B, or C that is the most similar in meaning. Finally, on a separate sheet of paper, solidify your understanding of these words by using each in a sentence of your own.

I suppose we should be gloating a bit right now, those of us who don't drive sport utility vehicles. What with the rising cost of gasoline putting the squeeze on folks who tool about town in the **reputedly** bigger-is-better tanks, the current gas crunch is merely a case of "what goes around, comes around," right? But whenever I think about how truly wasteful those behemoths are, I feel **despondent,** not **smug,** because I know that their gross fuel inefficiency affects us all.

I admit it. I have never liked SUVs, and I'm as tired of their **overblown proportions** as anyone else. I'm frustrated when I have to strain to see through or around them while I'm driving in traffic. And I'm fed up with having to squeeze into my parked car because an SUV driver has wedged his or her vehicle too close to mine. I'm pretty sure I could learn to cope with these minor inconveniences, if there wasn't the much broader issue of how SUVs hurt our environment.

Many of us are old enough to remember the gasoline shortage of the '70s, when car owners waited to refuel on the day of the week that corresponded with their odd- or even-numbered license plates. We vividly remember when there were so many cars lined up at the pumps that they overflowed out of the service-station driveways. We can recall when terms such as "Earth Day" and "recycling" came into our **collective** consciousness. And while a subject such as ozone **depletion** may have initially seemed too remote to concern us, all we've needed to do lately is look at our changing weather patterns to realize that hey, our actions do affect our environment.

From "SUVs: Fuel-Wasting Garbage Trucks?" by Tito Morales, *Newsweek,* June 26, 2000, p. 12. Reprinted by permission.

Vocabulary Words

	A	B	C
1. **reputedly**	enormously	disgustingly	supposedly
2. **despondent**	curious	angry	hopeless
3. **smug**	suspicious	self-satisfied	cheerful
4. **overblown**	inflated	reasonable	important
5. **proportions**	reputations	dimensions	proposal
6. **collective**	shared	gathered	single
7. **depletion**	disappearance	regulation	reduction

Strategic Thinking

GETTING THE BIG PICTURE

Answer the following questions on a separate piece of paper or in a journal.

Consider a career area you are in or plan to be in. What reading skills from this chapter, in particular, will serve you on the job? Describe specifically how these skills will be useful. Make some plans for improvement: First, name one particular reading skill you intend to improve and describe why this improvement will help you. Second, name one piece of reading material you intend to read that will help you improve your career-related knowledge and explain why it will help.

NOTES

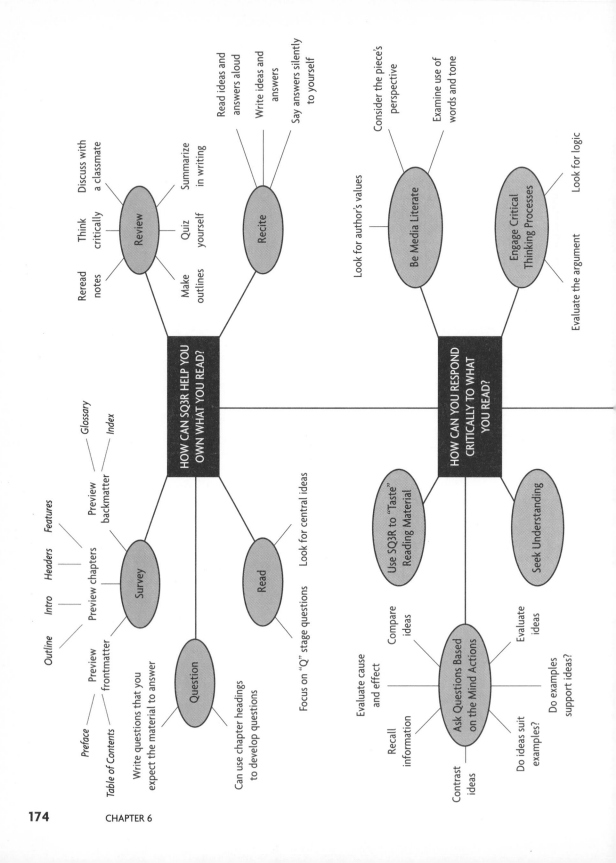

HOW CAN SQ3R HELP YOU OWN WHAT YOU READ?

Review
- Reread notes
- Think critically
- Discuss with a classmate
- Quiz yourself
- Make outlines
- Summarize in writing

Recite
- Read ideas and answers aloud
- Write ideas and answers
- Say answers silently to yourself

Survey
- Outline
- Intro
- Headers
- Features
- Preface
- Preview frontmatter
- Preview chapters
- Preview backmatter
- Glossary
- Index
- Table of Contents

Question
- Write questions that you expect the material to answer
- Can use chapter headings to develop questions

Read
- Focus on "Q" stage questions
- Look for central ideas

HOW CAN YOU RESPOND CRITICALLY TO WHAT YOU READ?

Be Media Literate
- Look for author's values
- Consider the piece's perspective
- Examine use of words and tone

Engage Critical Thinking Processes
- Look for logic
- Evaluate the argument

Use SQ3R to "Taste" Reading Material

Seek Understanding

Ask Questions Based on the Mind Actions
- Evaluate cause and effect
- Compare ideas
- Evaluate ideas
- Recall information
- Do examples support ideas?
- Contrast ideas
- Do ideas suit examples?

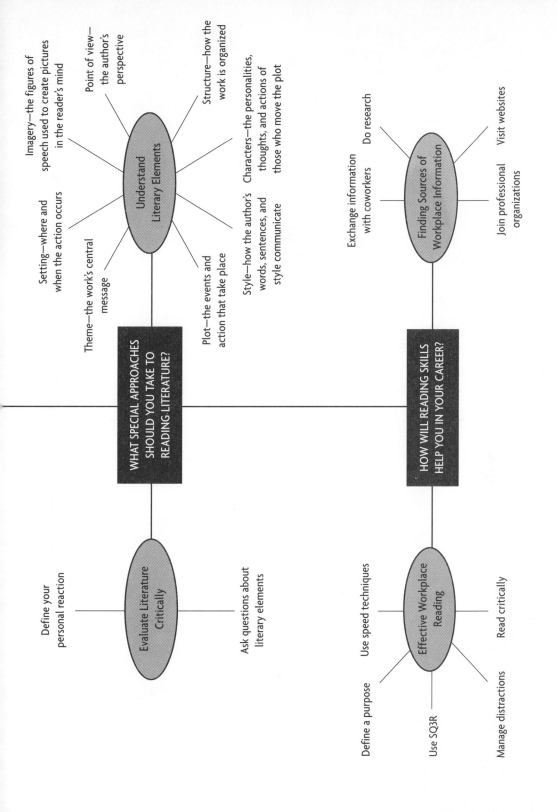

Understand Literary Elements

- Imagery—the figures of speech used to create pictures in the reader's mind
- Point of view—the author's perspective
- Structure—how the work is organized
- Characters—the personalities, thoughts, and actions of those who move the plot
- Style—how the author's words, sentences, and style communicate
- Plot—the events and action that take place
- Theme—the work's central message
- Setting—where and when the action occurs

WHAT SPECIAL APPROACHES SHOULD YOU TAKE TO READING LITERATURE?

Evaluate Literature Critically
- Define your personal reaction
- Ask questions about literary elements

Finding Sources of Workplace Information
- Do research
- Visit websites
- Join professional organizations
- Exchange information with coworkers

HOW WILL READING SKILLS HELP YOU IN YOUR CAREER?

Effective Workplace Reading
- Use speed techniques
- Read critically
- Manage distractions
- Use SQ3R
- Define a purpose

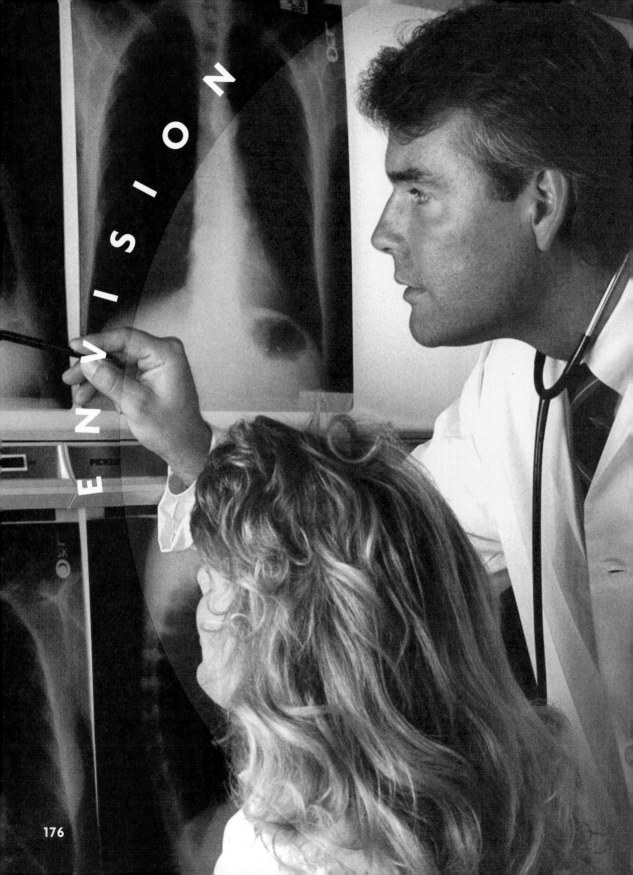

ENVISION

We live in a visual age. Motion pictures, television, and computers have made us comfortable receiving information in visual form and, as a result, we are rapidly becoming skilled at "capturing" information at a glance. Being visually oriented prepares you to understand and interpret the information you find in the visual aids that are in your textbooks and that are common in newspapers, magazines, books, journals, and a variety of business documents. Visuals provide you with just one of many ways to experience the world and learn from what you experience.

This chapter will help you interpret what you see with the goal of extracting the data you need for your academic studies and your work. At the end of the chapter, you will be able to answer these questions:

- What are visual aids and how are they used?
- How do you read a table?
- What do charts show?
- What are other types of visual aids?
- How do you use critical thinking to evaluate visual aids?

READING VISUAL AIDS
OBTAINING DATA THROUGH VISUAL SOURCES

> *"Learning means keeping the mind open and active to receive all kinds of experience."*
>
> **Gilbert Highet**

What Are Visual Aids and How Are They Used?

Visual aids present data in tables, charts, illustrations, maps, and photographs. Their purpose is to present, clarify, or summarize information in a form that shows comparisons and that is easy to read and understand. Visual aids save space and speed up the reading process. A table or chart can present information more concisely than if the information were presented in paragraph form. Math is often heavily involved in the creation and reading of visual aids because so many visual aids focus on statistics (see Chapter 14 for extensive ideas about how to become more comfortable with quantitative learning).

Look through nearly any textbook on your bookshelf and you will find a variety of visual aids. They are there to present new information and to help you study. When your sociology text presents a pie chart showing the percentage of families in different income categories, you can quickly see the numerical relations between the rich, poor, and middle class. Similarly, when your health text presents a table summarizing and comparing different methods of birth control, their effectiveness in preventing conception, and their effectiveness in preventing sexually transmitted diseases, you can use the table as a review and study tool.

Visual aids are now a staple of business reports and proposals in all kinds of career areas and are even included in e-mail messages. Examples you might see include:

- A statistical graph showing how many freshmen continued on as sophomores at a college
- A bar chart showing monthly earnings for a clothing company
- A colored map showing how each state's constituents voted on a particular political issue
- A line chart showing the progression of HIV infection in a particular country over a span of 10 years

Many students want to avoid math. When they finish their last course, they believe that they will never again have to deal with anything mathematical. The reality is quite different. Most careers involve mathematics in one form or another. For example, sales representatives use math when they process customer orders or submit their expense accounts. At a higher level, a manager may be in charge of a half-million-dollar budget. So try not to think of math as a separate entity that you can take in college and never deal with again for the rest of your life. I promise you, as you move through your career, mathematics will be part of it.

ELAYN MARTIN-GAY, UNIVERSITY OF NEW ORLEANS

EXPERT INSIGHT

Embrace Math

The popularity of visual aids in the workplace is related to their ability to present, compare, and contrast financial data, inventories, enrollments, customer preferences, sales, employee benefits, social or economic trends relevant to the organization, and thousands of other variables that affect day-to-day operations. The fact that so many people are now comfortable with visual presentations is linked to the ease with which they can now be created, using computer software programs such as PowerPoint and Excel.

What you learn about visual aids in this chapter will give you some of the basic information you need to create visuals for your own use as study aids. For example, in a botany course, you can create a table as a summary tool to help you learn the parts and functions of plant cells. The orientation toward and comfort with visual presentations that you develop during your college years will prove invaluable to you in your career.

How Do You Read a Table?

Tables arrange data or words systematically in rows and columns in order to provide information and facilitate comparisons. Table 7.1 is a model of a typical table, including the individual parts and their arrangement on the page.

The table is arranged in columns and rows and has the following elements:

- The *table number* identifies the table and is usually referred to in the text.

TABLE

7.1

The parts and arrangements of a table.

TABLE NUMBER	TITLE OF TABLE			
STUB HEAD	CAPTION		CAPTION	
	SUBCAPTION	SUBCAPTION	SUBCAPTION	SUBCAPTION
Stub	XXXX	XXXX	XXXX	XXXX
Stub	XXXX	XXXX[a]	XXXX	XXXX
Stub	XXXX	XXXX	XXXX	XXXX
Stub	XXXX	XXXX	XXXX	XXXX
Stub	XXXX	XXXX	XXXX	XXXX
Total	XXXX	XXXX	XXXX[b]	XXXX

[a]Footnote
[b]Footnote
Source:

Source: "The Parts and Arrangements of a Table" from *Business Writing,* 2/e, by J. Harold Janis and Howard R. Dresner. Copyright © 1956, 1972 by J. Harold Janis. Reprinted by permission of HarperCollins Publishers, Inc.

- The *table title* helps readers focus on the table's message.
- The *captions*, also known as column titles, identify the material that falls below.
- The *subcaptions* divide the columns into smaller sections.
- The *stubs* refer to the captions running along the horizontal rows. The nature of the stubs is identified by the stub head.
- The *footnotes* are used to explain specific details found in the table.
- The *source* acknowledges where the information comes from.

Some tables have all of these elements while others include only a few. Keep in mind that the person who creates a visual aid determines its design and elements, so you are likely to encounter a variety of styles. The best advice is to be prepared for many variations.

The two basic types of tables are data tables and word tables. *Data tables* present numerical information—for example, the number of schools with Internet connections in all fifty states. As you examine Table 7.2, which compares complex statistical data on health problems by weight category and gender, you can see how easy it is to compare and contrast vital information.

Word tables summarize and consolidate complex information, making it easier to study and evaluate. By definition, they are wordier than data tables, which focus on numbers and especially financial data. Table 7.3 is an example of a word table you might encounter in a personal finance text. Keep in mind that a table like this highlights key points, but does not present the complete picture. Go back to the text or another source for greater detail.

TABLE 7.2

PERCENTAGE OF U.S. POPULATION WITH SELECTED HEALTH PROBLEMS, BY WEIGHT CATEGORY[1] AND GENDER

	UNDER-WEIGHT		NORMAL WEIGHT		OVER-WEIGHT		OBESE CLASS 1		OBESE CLASS 2		OBESE CLASS 3	
	M	W	M	W	M	W	M	W	M	W	M	W
Coronary Heart Disease	12.5%	12.1%	8.9%	6.9%	9.6%	11.1%	16.0%	12.6%	10.2%	12.3%	14.0%	10.2%
High Cholesterol[2]	6.7	13.4	26.7	26.9	35.7	45.6	39.2	40.4	34.0	41.0	35.7	36.4
High Blood Pressure[3]	23.4	19.8	23.5	23.3	34.2	38.8	49.0	48.0	65.5	54.5	64.5	63.2
Adult-Onset Diabetes	4.7	4.8	2.0	2.4	4.9	7.1	10.1	7.2	12.3	13.2	10.6	19.9

[1]Underweight: body mass index below 18.5; normal weight: 18.5 to 24.9; overweight 25.0 to 29.9; obese class 1: 30.0 to 34.9; obese class 2: 35.0 to 39.9; obese class 3: greater than 40.0. To calculate body mass index, divide your weight in kilograms by the square of your height in meters. Height in meters is inches times 0.0254; weight in kilograms is pounds times 0.45.

[2]Total cholesterol greater than 240   [3]Blood pressure greater than 140/90   M=Men W=Women

Source: Centers for Disease Control and Prevention.

TABLE 7.3

COMPARING FIXED AND ADJUSTABLE RATE MORTGAGE AGREEMENTS

Type	Description	Considerations
Fixed rate	Fixed interest rate; usually long term; equal monthly payments of principal and interest until debt is paid in full.	Offers stability and long-term tax advantages; interest rates may be higher than other types of financing; new fixed rates are rarely assumable.
Adjustable rate	Interest rate changes over life of the loan; possible changes in monthly payments, loan term, and/or principal; some plans have rate or interest caps.	Starting interest rate is slightly below market, but payments can increase sharply and frequently if index increases; payment caps prevent wide fluctuations in payment but may cause negative amortization; rate caps limit the total amount that the debt can expand.

Source: The Federal Trade Commission, *The Mortgage Money Guide* (Washington, D.C.: U.S. Government Printing Office, n.d.).

Although charts may be used to present some of the same information as tables, they also make visual comparisons that tables cannot make. You will learn what charts are and how to read them next.

What Do Charts Show?

Charts, also known as graphs, show statistical comparisons in visual form. They present *variables*, which are numbers that can change, often along a *vertical*—top to bottom—and *horizontal*—side to side—axis. Common comparisons include:

- *trends over time* (e.g., the number of computers with Internet connections per household in 2001 as compared to the number in 1997)
- *relative rankings* (e.g., the size of the advertising budgets of four major consumer-products companies)
- *distributions* (e.g., student performance on standardized tests by geographic area)
- *cycles* (e.g., the regular upward and downward movement of the nation's economy as defined by periods of prosperity and recession)

These comparisons are presented in different forms including pie charts, bar and column charts, and line charts.

UNDERSTANDING PIE CHARTS

The *pie chart* is one of the most common and easy-to-understand visual aids. It presents data as wedge-shaped sections of a circle in order to show the relative size of each item as a percentage of the whole. If you look at a pie chart as representing 100 percent of a whole, each wedge is a portion of the whole, with the combined wedges equaling the entirety. Figure 7.1 is an example of a pie chart that shows the percentage of Americans who exercise as defined by four exercise categories.

UNDERSTANDING BAR AND COLUMN CHARTS

Bar charts, also known as bar graphs, consist of horizontal bars of varying length, with each bar symbolizing a different item. Unlike pie charts, which compare the components of a single whole, bar charts compare different items. To be effective and meaningful, a bar chart must always compare items in the same category.

Figure 7.2, an example of a bar chart, compares the top Internet job sites, as measured by the number of visits to the site, during one month. With the length of the bars arranged in descending order from most to least popular, readers can quickly get the information they need.

FIGURE

7.1

PERCENTAGE OF AMERICANS WHO EXERCISE AS DEFINED BY FOUR EXERCISE CATEGORIES

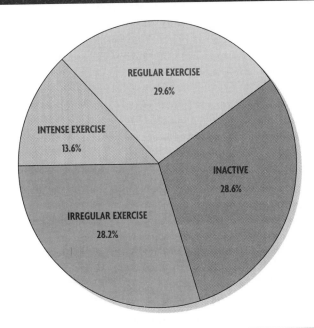

NOTE:
Regular exercise is defined as at least 20 minutes three times per week. Intense exercise is defined as at least 30 minutes five times per week.

Source: Center for Disease Control and Prevention, 1998 data.

A sample bar chart.

FIGURE

7.2

TOP INTERNET JOB SITES AS MEASURED BY THE NUMBER OF VISITS TO EACH SITE

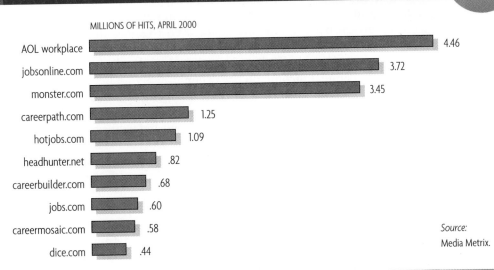

MILLIONS OF HITS, APRIL 2000

Site	Hits
AOL workplace	4.46
jobsonline.com	3.72
monster.com	3.45
careerpath.com	1.25
hotjobs.com	1.09
headhunter.net	.82
careerbuilder.com	.68
jobs.com	.60
careermosaic.com	.58
dice.com	.44

Source:
Media Metrix.

FIGURE

7.3

A sample column chart.

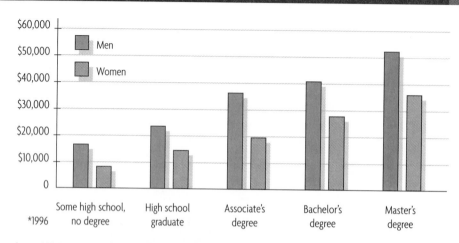

MEDIAN ANNUAL INCOME OF PERSONS WITH INCOME 25 YEARS OLD AND OVER, BY HIGHEST DEGREE ATTAINED AND GENDER.*

Source: U.S. Department of Commerce, Bureau of the Census, *Current Population Reports,* Series P-60, "Money Income of Households, Families, and Persons in the United States: 1996."

Bar charts often show subdivisions within each category or bar. For example, a bar chart in a sociology text, comparing the population size of different racial groups in the United States may break each group into the percentage of males and females. Similarly, it may show the percentage that has completed at least two years of college versus the percentage that has not.

When bar charts are arranged vertically, they are known as *column charts.* Instead of using horizontal bars, column charts are comprised of a series of vertical bars. These charts are used to show changes that take place over time as well as other comparisons. For example, the chart in Figure 7.3 shows the relation between educational level and gender, on the one hand, and annual income on the other.

Figure 7.4 is a grouped column chart that compares two items for each category. Each grouping compares recommended servings in a food group with average servings actually consumed by men and women. The chart also shows the percentage of recommended servings consumed in each category.

Bar charts and column charts are also sometimes more complex, with segmented bars or columns used to present additional data. For example, Figure 7.5 is of a chart showing the statistics on students following less traditional educational paths. The bar showing how many students are working while in school is subdivided. To visually differentiate the information, the percentage of working students with part-time jobs is shown in one shade, while the percentage of working students with full-time jobs is shown in another.

USDA RECOMMENDATIONS FOR CONSUMPTION OF FOODS IN PRIMARY FOOD CATEGORIES*

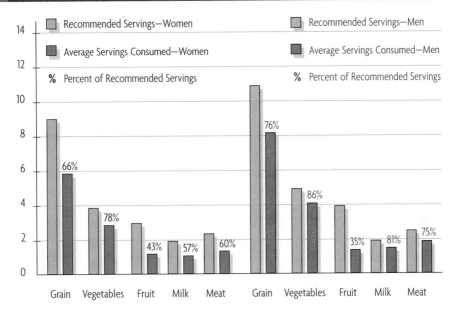

*For men and women ages 25–50
Source: Department of Agriculture.

PERCENTAGE OF UNDERGRADUATE STUDENT BODY FOLLOWING LESS TRADITIONAL EDUCATIONAL PATHS*

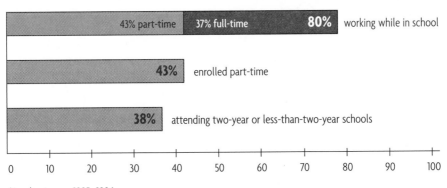

*Academic year 1995–1996
Source: U.S. Department of Education, National Center for Education Statistics.

FIGURE

7.6

A sample line chart.

NUMBER OF MEN AND WOMEN EARNING BACHELOR'S DEGREES

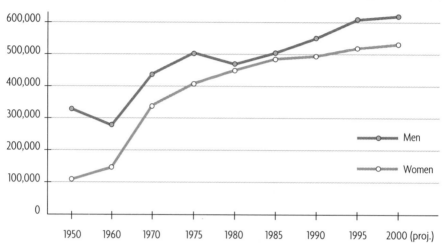

Source: *Psychology*, 2/e, by Davis and Palladino. © 1997. Reprinted by permission of Prentice Hall, Inc., Upper Saddle River, NJ.

UNDERSTANDING LINE CHARTS

Finally, *line charts* show continuous trends over time. The horizontal axis shows a span of time, while the vertical axis represents a specific measurement such as dollars or units of various kinds. The line chart in Figure 7.6 shows how the number of men and women earning bachelor's degrees has increased in the past 50 years.

What Are Other Types of Visual Aids?

You may also encounter other types of visual aids as you read. These include maps, illustrations, and photographs.

Maps show data comparisons by geographic areas. For example, a map may show the unit sales of computers in different regions of the country for a recent month. Maps generally do not include great detail because of the difficulty in reading a cluttered presentation. Because of this, they are often accompanied by a table or chart. Figure 7.7 shows how a map is used to illustrate influenza outbreaks across the United States.

Illustrations often focus on a particular detail of a mechanical system. For example, an illustration in your biology text may highlight the parts of

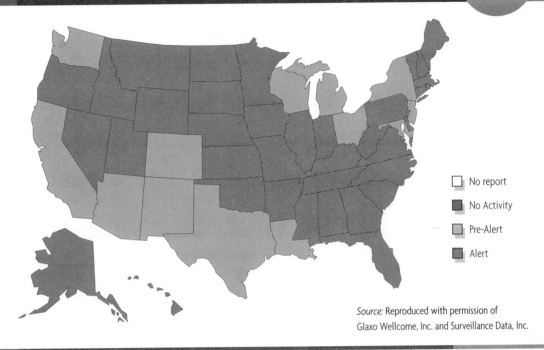

INFLUENZA ACTIVITY ESTIMATES REPORTED BY ALL 50 STATES FOR THE WEEK OF DECEMBER 20, 1999

☐ No report

■ No Activity

■ Pre-Alert

■ Alert

Source: Reproduced with permission of Glaxo Wellcome, Inc. and Surveillance Data, Inc.

the human brain. The artist eliminates extraneous detail in order to help you see and learn specific material.

Photographs also provide valuable information as they present accurate factual representations. However, photos generally are not as focused as illustrations on communicating specific information. Instead, they provide a sense of reality as they show anything from historical situations to the actual appearance of a medical problem, such as the rash caused by Lyme's Disease or how rheumatoid arthritis can deform the hands.

How Do You Use Critical Thinking to Evaluate Visual Aids?

Although most charts accurately show important relations and comparisons, it is important to look at every chart with a critical mind.[1] This careful analysis is important because charts, especially line charts, may actually distort the facts they are trying to show. This often happens when the person presenting the data wants to convince you to accept his point of view.

FIGURE

7.8

An example of a distorted line chart.

HOW CHARTS CAN MISLEAD

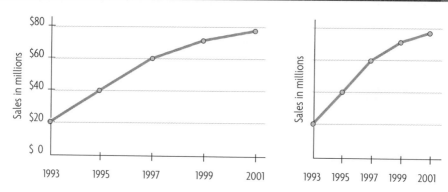

Source: Adapted from *How to Lie with Statistics,* by Darrell Huff and illustrated by Irving Geis. © 1954, 1982 by Huff and Geis. Used by permission of W. W. Norton & Company, Inc.

For example, if it is improperly drawn, a line chart can indicate more growth or fewer problems than actually occurred. Look at the charts in Figure 7.8 to see how this distortion can occur. Although the charts are based on the same statistical data, the sales-trend line in the chart on the left indicates a slower growth than the line in the chart on the right. This occurs because the horizontal scale on the right is shortened in comparison to the scale on the left. As a result, if you were shown just the chart on the right, you might be more impressed with the sales increase than if you were shown the chart on the left.

Critical-thinking questions will help you avoid statistical manipulations that distort accuracy. Among the questions you should ask when you look at a chart are:

- Do the charts include all relevant data?
- Are the charts complete or has an important variable been omitted?
- Have the proportions between the vertical and horizontal axes been changed to produce a desired effect?
- Have the axes been extended or shortened to change the trend line?
- Does the author have an agenda that would give him or her reason to manipulate the data or to draw the chart in a way that unfairly supports a specific point of view?

Charts that distort information in order to manipulate the reader's response are generally not found in textbooks or in other college study materials. Textbook authors try their best to present accurate data without distortion and without reflecting their own personal bias. You are more likely to find misleading charts in business where it is in a company's best interest to present their products, services, and financial picture in a favorable light.

Fortunately, government regulations help protect the public against statistical manipulation of business data. For example, public companies are required to present their financial data according to Security and Exchange Commission guidelines, to submit their financial statements to independent auditors, and to use generally accepted accounting practices. Even with these safeguards, it makes good sense to use your critical-thinking skills to analyze the accuracy of charts and to protect yourself from misleading presentations.

Je ne sais quoi

The French have a phrase that has become commonly used in the English language as well: *je ne sais quoi*, which literally means "I don't know what." The phrase refers to that which cannot be adequately described in words, and often is used to describe a unique quality possessed by a person, as in, "She has a certain *je ne sais quoi*."

Think of visual aids as adding that certain *je ne sais quoi* to your textbooks by providing that which goes beyond verbal description. There is certainly more to the world than what can be described in words. Any kind of visual image, graph, drawing, or other kind of representation can add an important nonverbal dimension, deepening your comprehension and introducing you to new and different perspectives. Let yourself experience knowledge on many different levels, even when you cannot always describe that knowledge in words.

Study Skills in Action

Test Competence

MEASURING WHAT YOU'VE LEARNED

MULTIPLE CHOICE. *Circle or highlight the answer that seems to fit best.*

1. The primary reasons visual aids are used so extensively in business include all of the following **except**
   A. they are relatively easy to generate.
   B. they allow readers to compare and contrast data at a glance.
   C. they save paper by condensing presentations.
   D. they are easy to understand.

2. Parts of a table include
   A. charts, graphs, and columns.
   B. number, title, and statistics.
   C. captions, subcaptions, and graphs.
   D. title, number, and captions.

3. The two basic types of tables are
   A. data tables and word tables.
   B. summary tables and word tables.
   C. bar tables and column tables.
   D. data tables and chart tables.

4. Common comparisons shown by charts include
   A. trends over time, relative rankings, distributions, cycles.
   B. goals and priorities, relative rankings, distributions, cycles.
   C. trends over time, values and beliefs, distributions, cycles.
   D. stereotypes, critical reviews, relative rankings, cycles.

5. A pie chart shows
   A. comparisons between different, unrelated items.
   B. wedge-shaped sections of a circle, which are percentages of a single whole.
   C. information that summarizes the central facts in an article or chapter.
   D. the changes in particular economic cycles over a set period of time.

6. Bar charts compare
    A. different items in the same category.
    B. the components of a single whole.
    C. quantitative and qualitative data.
    D. different items in different categories.

7. Subdivided column charts show
    A. complex data within a specific category.
    B. the relation between seemingly unrelated events.
    C. summary information.
    D. time-sensitive data.

8. Maps are used when a presenter wants to
    A. be sure to have an updated and comprehensive presentation.
    B. make as general a presentation as possible.
    C. clarify the geography of a particular area of the country or globe.
    D. show data comparisons by geographic areas.

9. Critical thinking is important during your analysis of visual aids because
    A. charts may be too small or too detailed to understand accurately on a first reading.
    B. you should always assume that visual aids distort information for the purposes of those who created the visuals.
    C. there is no way to compare the data presented in different visuals without critical thinking.
    D. it may be in the best interest of the person or group presenting the data to mislead you by distorting chart presentation.

10. Misleading data on corporate financial charts is monitored by the
    A. Federal Communication Commission.
    B. Federal Bureau of Investigation.
    C. Justice Department.
    D. Securities and Exchange Commission.

TRUE/FALSE. *Place a T or an F beside each statement to indicate whether you think it is true or false.*

1. _____ Visual aids help clarify and summarize data.

2. _____ A table should never contain footnotes.

3. _____ The horizontal axis on a line chart shows a specific measurement such as dollars while the vertical axis shows a span of time.

4. _____ Photographs are often included as visuals in textbooks because they present accurate factual representations.

5. _____ The most commonly manipulated chart is the pie chart.

Brain Power

BUILDING VOCABULARY FITNESS

The paragraphs below are taken from the current media. Read the paragraph, noting the context of the vocabulary words shown in bold type. Next, for each vocabulary word (reprinted in the left-hand column), highlight the word or phrase in column A, B, or C that is the most similar in meaning. Finally, on a separate sheet of paper, solidify your understanding of these words by using each in a sentence of your own.

In this, the information age, there is no shortage of data about public companies available to investors. The **phalanx** of newspapers and magazines devoted to financial matters has **ballooned** in recent years, as have cable television programs and Internet chat rooms focused on investing. And Wall Street research, once shared only with a **privileged** few, has become widely available to investors on the Web.

But as Edward Kerschner, chief investment strategist at PaineWebber, points out, there is a big difference between information and knowledge. He believes that the instant **dissemination** of information today carries a **substantial** cost: the tendency among investors to act first and think second. That behavior, he said, may account for the recent jump in stock market **volatility.**

From "Flying Blind in a Fog of Data," by Gretchen Morgenson, *The New York Times*, Sunday, June 18, 2000, p. BU–1.

Vocabulary Words	A	B	C
1. **phalanx**	style	group	category
2. **ballooned**	risen	expanded	popped
3. **privileged**	selected	private	intelligent
4. **dissemination**	gathering	dispersion	negativity
5. **substantial**	subpar	solid	considerable
6. **volatility**	worth	anger	changeability

Strategic Thinking

GETTING THE BIG PICTURE

Answer the following question on a separate piece of paper or in a journal.

Visual cues are everywhere in the information age. Think back to your learning-style exploration in Chapter 2: Are you a visual learner? If so, describe what educational and career choices you are making, or plan to make, in order to make the most of that strength. If you are not, describe what strategies from this chapter will help you make the most of visual data when you encounter it, and how you plan to use them.

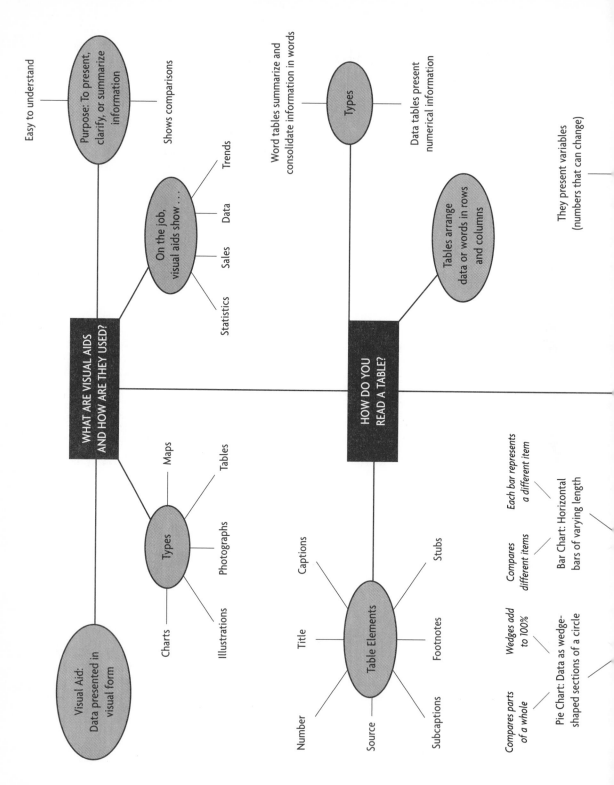

WHAT ARE VISUAL AIDS AND HOW ARE THEY USED?

Easy to understand

Purpose: To present, clarify, or summarize information

Shows comparisons

On the job, visual aids show . . .

Statistics

Sales

Data

Trends

Visual Aid: Data presented in visual form

Types

Charts

Illustrations

Photographs

Tables

Maps

HOW DO YOU READ A TABLE?

Word tables summarize and consolidate information in words

Types

Data tables present numerical information

They present variables (numbers that can change)

Tables arrange data or words in rows and columns

Table Elements

Number

Title

Captions

Source

Footnotes

Subcaptions

Stubs

Compares parts of a whole

Wedges add to 100%

Compares different items

Each bar represents a different item

Pie Chart: Data as wedge-shaped sections of a circle

Bar Chart: Horizontal bars of varying length

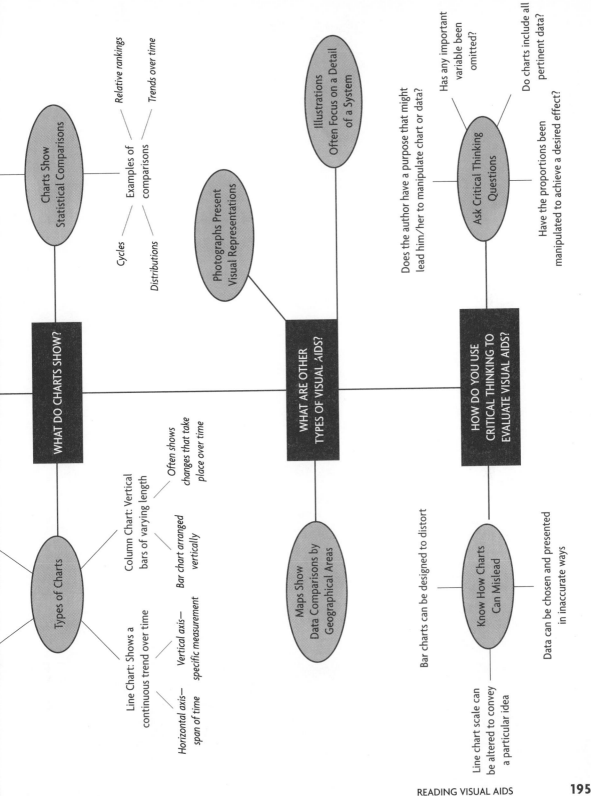

Charts Show
Statistical Comparisons

Examples of
comparisons

Relative rankings

Trends over time

Cycles

Distributions

WHAT DO CHARTS SHOW?

Types of Charts

Column Chart: Vertical
bars of varying length

Often shows
changes that take
place over time

Bar chart arranged
vertically

Line Chart: Shows a
continuous trend over time

Vertical axis—
specific measurement

Horizontal axis—
span of time

Photographs Present
Visual Representations

Illustrations
Often Focus on a Detail
of a System

WHAT ARE OTHER
TYPES OF VISUAL AIDS?

Maps Show
Data Comparisons by
Geographical Areas

Does the author have a purpose that might
lead him/her to manipulate chart or data?

Has any important
variable been
omitted?

Do charts include all
pertinent data?

Ask Critical Thinking
Questions

Have the proportions been
manipulated to achieve a desired effect?

HOW DO YOU USE
CRITICAL THINKING TO
EVALUATE VISUAL AIDS?

Bar charts can be designed to distort

Know How Charts
Can Mislead

Data can be chosen and presented
in inaccurate ways

Line chart scale can
be altered to convey
a particular idea

FOCUS

L istening is a vital skill that will help you to know and understand the world around you. You take in countless bits of information as you listen to instructors, students, study partners, and others. In your working life, listening is just as crucial—you need to rely on your ability to listen to supervisors, coworkers, suppliers, and customers. Compare your listening ability to a camera. Even when you see an image through the viewfinder, you may not be able to tell what it is until you carefully focus the lens. Similarly, careful listening allows you to clarify what you have heard.

Once you've listened to the facts, opinions, and ideas to which college exposes you daily, you need to be able to remember them and build knowledge that you can use throughout your life. This chapter will explore specific techniques to boost your ability to take in and remember what you learn. At the end of the chapter, you will be able to answer these questions:

- How can you become a better listener?
- How does memory work?
- How can you improve your memory?
- How can you use mnemonic devices to boost memory power?

LISTENING AND MEMORY
TAKING IN AND REMEMBERING INFORMATION

> *"The true art of memory is the art of attention."*
>
> **Samuel Johnson**

How Can You Become a Better Listener?

The act of hearing isn't quite the same as the act of listening. Although *hearing* refers to sensing spoken messages from their source, *listening* involves a complex process of communication. Successful listening occurs when the speaker's intended message reaches the listener. In school and at home, poor listening may cause communication breakdowns and mistakes. Skilled listening, however, promotes progress and success. Listening is a teachable—and learnable—skill.

Listening is also one of the most important skills in the workplace. The way in which employees and managers listen to customers and to one another affects their efficiency and effectiveness. If you don't accurately hear what others tell you, the quality of your work can be undermined, no matter how many hours you have spent completing an assignment. For example, if you fail to act on a coworker's request for immediate action on an important project and the project falls apart because of your failure, claiming that you never heard the request will get little sympathy and may even cost you your job. Accurate listening is an important key to your personal career success and the success of your organization.

To see how complex listening can be, look at Figure 8.1. The left-hand column contains an excerpt from a typical classroom lecture on peer-group influence during adolescence, and the right-hand column records some examples of what an eighteen- or nineteen-year-old student might be thinking while the instructor is speaking. In many ways, the column on the right is more interesting than the one on the left because it reveals the complexity of listening, as well as some of the barriers that block communication.

During the act of listening to a typical classroom lecture, this student doesn't focus consistently on the information presented. Instead, he reacts to specific parts of the message and gets caught up in evaluating and judging what he hears. Internal and external distractions, in the form of hunger and whispering, also affect his concentration.

The example in Figure 8.1 represents the kinds of thoughts, or barriers, that can interfere with effective listening. Understanding the listening process and why people may have trouble listening well can help you overcome these barriers.

The complexity of listening. **FIGURE 8.1**

A peer group is a social group made up of members with a lot in common. During adolescence, common interests often center on dating, popular music, clothing, and sports.

"Peer groups!" I've heard that term before. I'd better take notes; it'll probably be on the test.

The appeal of the group often comes from the fact that adults would not approve of what group members are doing. As a result, illicit activities—such as car racing, alcohol abuse, and drugs— are often the most popular.

What's this guy saying? That my friends and I do things just because our parents would object? Yeah, I guess I want to be different, but gimme a break! I don't drink and drive. I don't do drugs. I don't ignore my school work. Anyway, I'd better remember the connection between peer group popularity and adult disapproval. What were his exact words? I wish I remembered . . . on second thought maybe he has a point. I know kids who do things just to get a rise out of their parents.

Peer groups exert such a strong influence during adolescence because they give students the opportunity to form social relationships that are separate and apart from the one they have with their families. This is a time of rebellion and breaking away: a rough time for both adolescents and their parents.

Is it lunchtime yet? I'm really hungry! Stop thinking of food and start listening . . . back to work! Yeah, he's right, social relationships that have nothing to do with my family are important to me. I'd better write this down.

The good news for parents is that peer group pressure is generally strongest during adolescence. Teens achieve a greater balance between the influence of family and friends as the years pass. This doesn't make it any easier for parents trying to persuade their sons and daughters not to dye their hair green or pierce their eyebrows, but at least it tells them that the rebellion is temporary.

Why is he talking down to us? Why is he reassuring parents instead of focusing on how hard it is for teens to deal with life? He must be a parent himself . . . I wish those guys behind me would stop talking! I can't hear the lecture . . . there's a generation gap coming from the front of the room that's the size of the Grand Canyon! What's wrong with green hair and pierced eyebrows? He sounds like he knows all the answers and that we'll eventually see the light. I'm going to ask him how teens are supposed to act when they believe that their parents' values are wrong. Now, how should I word my question . . .

KNOW THE STAGES OF LISTENING

Listening is made up of four stages that build on one another: sensing, interpreting, evaluating, and reacting. These stages take the message from the speaker to the listener and back to the speaker (see Figure 8.2).

- During the *sensation* stage (also known as hearing), your ears pick up sound waves and transmit them to the brain. For example, you are sitting in class and hear your instructor say, "The only opportunity to make up last week's test is Tuesday at 5:00 P.M."

- During the *interpretation* stage, listeners attach meaning to a message. This involves understanding what is being said and relating it to what you already know. You relate this message to your knowledge of the test, whether you need a make-up, and what you are doing on Tuesday at 5:00 P.M.

- During the *evaluation* stage of listening, you decide how you feel about the message—whether, for example, you like it or agree with it. This involves evaluating the message as it relates to your needs and values. If the message goes against your values or does not fulfill your needs, you may reject it, stop listening, or argue in your mind with the speaker. In this example, if you do need to make up the test but have to work Tuesday at 5:00 P.M., you may evaluate the message as less than satisfactory. As you saw in Figure 8.1, what happens during the evaluation phase can interfere with listening.

- During the final stage of listening, there occurs a *reaction* to the message in the form of direct feedback. In a classroom, direct feedback

FIGURE

8.2

Stages of listening.

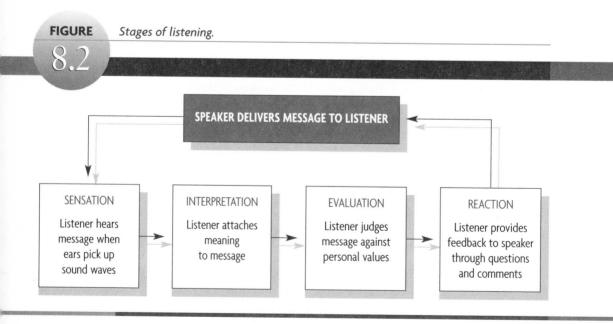

SPEAKER DELIVERS MESSAGE TO LISTENER

SENSATION	INTERPRETATION	EVALUATION	REACTION
Listener hears message when ears pick up sound waves	Listener attaches meaning to message	Listener judges message against personal values	Listener provides feedback to speaker through questions and comments

often comes in the form of questions and comments. Your reaction, in this case, may be to ask the instructor if he can schedule another test time. If the student in Figure 8.1 actually asks a question, he will give the instructor the opportunity to clarify the lecture or, perhaps, to add information.

According to psychologist Beatrice Harris, "People can be trained to listen to content and tone. But learning takes persistence and motivation."[1] Improving your listening skills involves two primary actions: managing listening challenges and becoming an active listener. Although becoming a better listener will help in every class, it is especially important in subjects that are challenging for you. For example, if your natural strength is in English, your ability to listen in physics class may affect how much you learn and whether you pass the course. Similarly, a copywriter for an ad agency may have trouble listening to a budget presentation, but that does not lessen his responsibility to understand and apply the budget to all of his work projects.

MANAGE LISTENING CHALLENGES

Communication barriers can interfere with listening at every stage. In fact, classic studies have shown that immediately after listening, students are likely to recall only half of what was said. This is partly due to particular listening challenges, such as divided attention and distractions, the tendency to shut out the message, the inclination to rush to judgment, and partial hearing loss or learning disabilities.[2]

To help create a positive listening environment in both your mind and your surroundings, explore how to manage these challenges.

Divided Attention and Distractions

Imagine yourself at a noisy end-of-year party, talking with a friend about plans for the summer, when you hear your name mentioned across the room. Your name was not shouted, and you weren't consciously listening to anything outside your own conversation. However, once you hear your name, you strain to hear more as you now listen with only half an ear to what your friend is saying. Chances are you hear neither person very well.

Situations like this happen all the time at school and on the job, and they demonstrate the consequences of divided attention. Although you are capable of listening to more than one message at the same time, you may not completely hear or understand any of them. Learning to focus your attention—even as it is being pulled in different directions—is one of your most important listening challenges.

Internal and external distractions often divide your attention. *Internal distractions* include anything from hunger to headache to personal worries. Something the speaker says may also trigger a recollection that may cause

Research suggests that a poor attitude can undermine the listening process. So if you wake up late one morning and get a speeding ticket on your way to the lecture hall, you'll certainly be in a bad mood when you get there. You have to be able to put that aside, improve your attitude, and concentrate on getting the key points from the lecture.

KATHY YORK, COMMUNICATIONS CONSULTANT

your mind to drift. In contrast, *external distractions* include noises (whispering, police sirens, the loud hum of an air conditioner) and excessive heat or cold. It can be hard to listen in an overheated room that is putting you to sleep.

Your goal is to reduce distractions so that you can focus on what you're hearing. Sitting where you can see clearly and hear will help. You may even be more willing to listen because knowing that instructors can see you may encourage you to receive their messages more actively. To avoid distracting activity, you may want to avoid sitting near or with people who might chat or make noise.

Make sure you are as relaxed and alert as possible. Work to concentrate on the present situation—class, a meeting at work—when you are there and save worrying about personal problems for later. Try to avoid being hungry or thirsty. Dress comfortably. Bring a sweater or sweatshirt if you anticipate that the classroom or workplace will be cold. If there's a chance that it will be overheated, wear a removable layer of clothing.

Shutting Out the Message

Instead of paying attention to everything the speaker says, many students fall into the trap of focusing on specific points and shutting out the rest of the message. If you perceive that a subject is too difficult or uninteresting, you may tune out. Shutting out the message makes it tough to listen well from that point on because the information you miss may be the foundation for what goes on in future classes—or may be crucial for you to move further ahead in your career.

Creating a positive listening environment includes accepting responsibility for listening. Although instructors and other speakers are responsible for communicating information to you, they cannot force you to listen. You are responsible for taking in the information that comes your way during class or at work.

One important motivation is believing that what speakers say is valuable. For example, some students might assume that anything not covered in the textbook isn't really important. During class, however, instructors often cover material from outside the textbook and then test on that material. If you work to take in the whole message in class, you will be able to read over your notes later and think critically about what is most important.

The Rush to Judgment

As the student's thoughts in Figure 8.1 show, people may tend to stop listening during the evaluation stage when they hear something they don't like. If you rush to judge what you've heard, your focus turns to your personal reaction rather than the content of the speaker's message. Students who disagree during a lecture often spend a lot of their thinking time figuring out exactly how they want to word a question or comment in response. Employees who react negatively to a comment from a coworker or supervisor may focus on formulating a comeback instead of listening to the whole message.

Judgments also involve reactions to the speakers themselves. If you do not like your instructors or coworkers or if you have preconceived notions about their ideas or cultural background, you may decide that their words have little value. Anyone whose words have ever been ignored because of race, ethnic background, gender, or disability understands how prejudice can interfere with listening.

Understanding how your emotions and opinions can interfere with listening will help you recognize and control your judgments. Being aware of what you tend to judge will help you avoid putting up a barrier against messages that clash with your opinions or feelings. Consider education as a continuing search for evidence, regardless of whether that evidence supports or negates your point of view.

Partial Hearing Loss and Learning Disabilities

Good listening techniques don't solve every listening problem. Students who have a partial hearing loss have a physical explanation for why listening is difficult. If you have some level of hearing loss, seek out special services that can help you listen in class. You may require special equipment or you might benefit from tutoring. You may be able to meet with your instructor outside of class to clarify your notes.

Other disabilities, such as attention deficit disorder (ADD) or problems with processing spoken language, can add to listening difficulties. People with these problems may have trouble paying attention or understanding what they hear. Although some may find ways to compensate for their listening problems, others may continue to struggle. If you have a disability that creates a listening challenge, don't blame yourself. Instead, seek help through your counseling or student health center, an advisor, or an instructor.

BECOME AN ACTIVE LISTENER

On the surface, listening seems like a passive activity; you sit back and listen as someone else speaks. Effective listening, however, is really an active process that involves setting a purpose for listening, asking questions, putting listening "spaces" to good use, paying attention to verbal signposts, and knowing what helps and hinders listening.

Set Purposes for Listening

Active listening is only possible if you know (and care) why you are listening. In any situation, establish what you want to achieve through listening, such as greater understanding of the material, staying awake in class, or better note taking. Having a purpose gives you a goal that motivates you to listen.

Ask Questions

Asking questions is not a sign of a lack of intelligence. In fact, a willingness to ask questions shows a desire to learn and is the mark of an active listener and critical thinker. Some questions are *informational*—seeking information—such as any question beginning with the phrase "I don't understand. . . ." *Clarifying* questions state your understanding of what you have just heard and ask if that understanding is correct. Some clarifying questions focus on a key concept or theme ("So, some learning disorders can be improved with treatment?"), others highlight specific facts ("Is it true that dyslexia can cause people to reverse letters and words?"). For the role questions play in critical thinking, see Chapter 4.

Although your questions and comments make you an active participant in the listening process, you might spend so much time thinking about what to ask that you miss some of the message. One way to avoid this is to quickly jot down your questions and come back to them during a discussion period or when you can talk to the instructor or a coworker alone. When you know that your question is on paper, you can relax and listen.

Pay Attention to Verbal Signposts

You can identify important facts and ideas and predict test questions by paying attention to the speaker's specific choice of words. For example, an idea described as "new and exciting" or "classic" is more likely to be on a test than one described as "interesting" or as "another approach." Verbal signposts often involve transition words and phrases that help organize information, connect ideas, and indicate what is important and what is not. Let phrases like those in Table 8.1 direct your attention to the material that follows them. These words will help you focus on key points in school and in the workplace.

TABLE

8.1

SIGNALS POINTING TO KEY CONCEPTS	SIGNALS OF SUPPORT
There are two reasons for this . . .	For example, . . .
A critical point in the process involves . . .	Specifically, . . .
Most importantly, . . .	For instance, . . .
The result is . . .	Similarly, . . .
SIGNALS POINTING TO DIFFERENCES	**SIGNALS THAT SUMMARIZE**
On the contrary, . . .	Finally, . . .
On the other hand, . . .	Recapping this idea, . . .
In contrast, . . .	In conclusion, . . .
However, . . .	As a result, . . .

Source: Adapted from George M. Usova, *Efficient study strategies: Skills for successful learning,* Pacific Grove, CA: Brooks/Cole, 1989, p. 69.

Know What Helps and Hinders Listening

Ralph G. Nichols, a pioneer in listening research, wanted to define the characteristics of successful and unsuccessful listeners. To do so, he studied 200 students in the freshman class at the University of Minnesota over a nine-month period. His findings, summarized in Table 8.2, demonstrate that effective listening depends as much on a positive attitude as on specific skills.[3]

MAKE STRATEGIC USE OF TAPE RECORDERS

The selective use of a tape recorder can provide helpful backup to your listening skills. If you want to use a tape recorder, here are some guidelines:

- *Use a tape recorder in class only when permitted by the instructor.* Ask your instructor whether you may use one.
- *Participate actively in class.* Don't let the tape recorder act as a substitute for your participation. Take notes just as you would if the tape recorder were not there.
- *Use the tapes effectively when studying.* Listen to important sections of the lecture again, or clarify sections that confused you.

Although effective listening will enable you to acquire knowledge, retaining that knowledge demands that you remember what you've heard. A good memory is made up of skills that improve with practice.

TABLE

8.2

What helps and hinders listening.

LISTENING IS HELPED BY . . .	LISTENING IS HINDERED BY . . .
. . . making a conscious decision to work at listening; viewing difficult material as a listening challenge.	. . . caring little about the listening process; tuning out difficult material.
. . . fighting distractions through intense concentration.	. . . refusing to listen at the first distraction.
. . . continuing to listen when a subject is difficult or dry, in the hope that one might learn something interesting.	. . . giving up as soon as one loses interest.
. . . withholding judgment until hearing everything.	. . . becoming preoccupied with a response as soon as a speaker makes a controversial statement.
. . . focusing on the speaker's theme by recognizing organizational patterns, transitional language, and summary statements.	. . . getting sidetracked by unimportant details.
. . . adapting note-taking style to the unique style and organization of the speaker.	. . . always taking notes in outline form, even when a speaker is poorly organized, leading to frustration.
. . . pushing past negative emotional responses and forcing oneself to continue to listen.	. . . letting an initial emotional response shut off continued listening.
. . . using any spare moments to evaluate, summarize, and question what one just heard and anticipating what will come next.	. . . thinking about other things and, as a result, missing much of the message.

How Does Memory Work?

Human memory works like a computer. Both have essentially the same purpose: to encode, store, and retrieve information.

- During the *encoding stage*, information is changed into usable form. On a computer, this occurs when keyboard entries are transformed into electronic symbols and stored on a disk. In the brain, sensory information becomes impulses that the central nervous system reads and codes. You are encoding, for example, when you study a list of chemistry formulas.

- During the *storage stage* information is held in memory (the mind's version of a computer's hard drive) so it can be used later. In this example, after you complete your studying of the formulas, your mind stores them until you need to use them.

- During the *retrieval stage*, memories are recovered from storage by recall, just as a saved computer program is called up by name and used again. In this example, your mind would retrieve the chemistry formulas when you had to take a test or solve a problem.

Memories are stored in three different storage banks. The first, called *sensory memory*, is an exact copy of what you see and hear and lasts for a second or less. Certain information is then selected from sensory memory and moves into *short-term memory*, a temporary information storehouse that lasts no more than 10 to 20 seconds. You are consciously aware of material in your short-term memory. Unimportant information is quickly dumped, and important information is transferred to *long-term memory*—the mind's more permanent information storehouse.

Suppose your history instructor lists five major causes of the Civil War. As you listen to the causes, the incoming information immediately becomes part of sensory memory, and because you are paying attention, it is quickly transferred to short-term memory. Nearby whispering may never get past the stage of sensory memory because your mind selectively pays attention to some things while ignoring others. Realizing that you will probably be tested on this information, you consciously decide that it is important enough to remember. It then becomes part of long-term memory.

Having information in long-term memory does not necessarily mean that you will be able to recall it when needed. Particular techniques can help you improve your recall.

How Can You Improve Your Memory?

Your accounting instructor is giving a test tomorrow on bookkeeping programs. You feel confident because you spent hours last week memorizing the material. Unfortunately, by the time you take the test, you may remember very little—most forgetting occurs within minutes after memorization.

In a classic study conducted in 1885, researcher Herman Ebbinghaus memorized a list of meaningless three-letter words such as CEF and LAZ. He then examined how quickly he forgot them. It happened in a surprisingly short time: Within one hour he had forgotten more than 50 percent of what he had learned; after two days, he knew fewer than 30 percent of the memorized words. Although Ebbinghaus's recall of the nonsense syllables remained fairly stable after that, his experiment shows how fragile memory can be—even when you take the time and expend the energy to memorize information.[4]

If forgetting is so common, why do some people have better memories than others? Some may have an inborn talent for remembering. More often, though, they succeed because they have practiced and mastered techniques for improving recall. Remember that techniques aren't a cure-all for memory difficulties, especially for those with learning disabilities. If you have a disability, the following strategies may help but might not be enough. Seek specific assistance if you consistently have trouble remembering.

USE SPECIFIC MEMORY STRATEGIES

In school and in your career, your job is to understand, learn, and remember information—everything from general concepts to specific details. Remembering involves two kinds of memory processes: general remembering and verbatim memorization.

- *General remembering,* the most common type of memory task, involves remembering ideas but not the exact words in which the ideas are expressed.
- *Verbatim memorization* involves learning a mathematical formula, an unfamiliar language, the sequence of operating a machine, and so on.

The following suggestions will help improve your recall in both memory processes.

Have Purpose and Intention

Why can you remember the lyrics to dozens of popular songs but not the functions of the pancreas? Perhaps this is because you want to remember the lyrics, you connect them to a visual image, or you have an emotional tie to them. To achieve the same results at school or on the job, make sure you have a purpose for what you are trying to remember. When you know why it is important, you will be able to strengthen your intention to remember it.

One particular experiment demonstrates what developing the will to remember can do for you. Think for a moment about the common, ordinary U. S. penny. Although it is easy to remember that Abraham Lincoln's picture is engraved on the penny's head, it is hard to recall anything else. Try it yourself. What are the phrases on the coin? Where are they located? What image is on the reverse side?

Most people have trouble describing a penny accurately because it was never important for them to focus on the details of the coin's design. Thus, they "forget" because they never created the memory in the first place.

Understand What You Memorize

Make sure that everything you want to remember makes sense to you. Something that has meaning is easier to recall than something that is gibberish. This basic principle applies to everything you study—from biology and astronomy to changes in the accounting practice you use at work to learning the intricacies of new computer software. If something you need to memorize makes no sense, consult textbooks or technical manuals, fellow students or coworkers, or an instructor or supervisor for an explanation.

Determine any logical connections in the information you are trying to remember, and use them. For example, in a plant biology course, memorize plants by grouping them according to family or a particular trait; in a history course, memorize events by linking them chronologically or in a cause-and-effect chain.

Finally, use organizational tools such as a formal or informal outline or a think link to record the material you want to recall and the logical connections between the elements. These tools will expose gaps in your understanding as they help you study and learn.

Recite, Rehearse, and Write

When you *recite* material, you repeat key concepts aloud, in your own words, to remember them. *Rehearsing* is similar to reciting but is done silently. It is the process of mentally repeating, summarizing, and associating information with other information. *Writing* is reciting on paper.

All three processes actively involve you in learning and memorizing the material. When you recite, using your voice to speak concepts and using your ears to hear what you say helps solidly plant the concepts in memory. Rehearsing encourages you to think about concepts and relate them to other information as you read. Writing further imprints concepts through the experience of physically writing them and visually seeing them again as you write.

You get the greatest benefit if you separate your learning into the following steps:

- Focus as you read on the key points you want to remember. These are usually found in the topic sentences of paragraphs. Then recite, rehearse, or write the ideas down.
- Convert each main idea into a keyword or phrase—something that is easy to recall and that will set off a chain of memories that will bring you back to the original information. Write each keyword or phrase on an index card.
- One by one, look at the keywords on your cards and recite, rehearse, or write all the associated information you can recall. Check your recall against your original material.

Reciting, rehearsing, and writing involve much more than simply rereading material—parroting words out loud, in your head, or on paper. You can reread without thinking or learning because there is no involvement. However, you cannot help but think and learn as you convert text concepts into key points, key points into keywords and phrases, and judge your learning by assessing and evaluating what you know and what you still need to learn.

Separate Main Points from Unimportant Details

As you just learned, one of your most important tasks is to use your critical-thinking skills to select and focus on the most important information so that you can avoid overloading your memory with extra clutter. To focus on key points, highlight only the most important information in your texts and workplace materials and write notes in the margins about central ideas. When you review notes, highlight or rewrite the most important information to remember. Figure 8.3 shows how this is done on a section of text that introduces the concept of markets. This excerpt is from the fourth edition of *Marketing: An Introduction*, a Prentice Hall textbook written by professors Philip Kotler and Gary Armstrong.[5]

FIGURE

8.3

Effective highlighting and marginal notes aid memory.

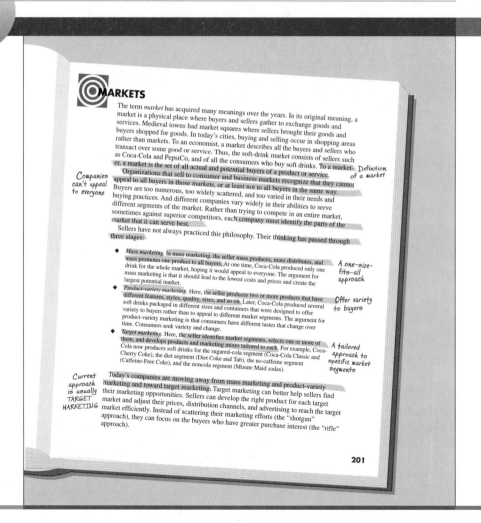

Study During Short but Frequent Sessions

Research has shown that you can improve your chances of remembering material if you learn it more than once. To get the most out of your study sessions, spread them over time. A pattern of short sessions followed by brief periods of rest is more effective than continual studying with little or no rest. Even though you may feel as though you accomplish a lot by studying for an hour without a break, you'll probably remember more from three 20-minute sessions. With this in mind, try studying during breaks in your schedule. Although studying between classes isn't for everyone, you may find that it can help you remember more of what you study.

Sleep can actually aid memory because it reduces the interference that new memories can create. Because you can't always go to sleep immediately after studying for an exam, try postponing the study of other subjects until your exam is over. When studying for several tests at a time, avoid studying two similar subjects back to back. You'll be less confused when you study history right after biology rather than, for example, chemistry after biology.

Separate Material Into Manageable Sections

Generally, when material is short and easy to understand, studying it from start to finish improves recall. With longer material, however, you may benefit from dividing it into logical sections, mastering each section, putting all the sections together, and then testing your memory of all the material. Actors take this approach when learning the lines of a play, and it can work just as well for students and employees trying to learn new concepts.

Practice the Middle

When you are trying to learn something, you usually study some material first, attack other material in the middle of the session, and approach still other topics at the end. The weak link in your recall is likely to be the material you study midway. It pays to give this material special attention in the form of extra practice.

Create Groupings

When items do not have to be remembered in any particular order, the act of grouping can help you recall them better. Say, for example, that you have to memorize these five 10-digit numbers:

9806875087   9876535703   7636983561   6724472879   5312895312

It may look impossible. If you group the numbers to form telephone numbers, however, the job may become more manageable:

(980) 687–5087   (987) 653–5703   (763) 698–3561
(672) 447–2879   (531) 289–5312

In general, try to keep groups to around 10 items or fewer. It's hard to memorize more at one time.

Use Visual Aids

Any kind of visual representation of study material can help you remember. Try converting material into a think link or outline. Use any visual that helps you recall it and link it to other information.

Flash cards are a great memory tool. They give you short, repeated review sessions that provide immediate feedback. Make your cards from 3-by-5-inch index cards. Use the front of the card to write a word, idea, or phrase you want to remember. Use the back side for a definition, explanation, and other key facts. Figure 8.4 shows two flash cards used to study for a psychology exam. You can also use this technique at work.

Here are some suggestions for making the most of your flash cards:

- *Use the cards as a self-test.* Divide them into two piles—the material you know and the material you are learning. You may want to use rubber bands to separate the piles.

FIGURE

8.4

Sample flash cards.

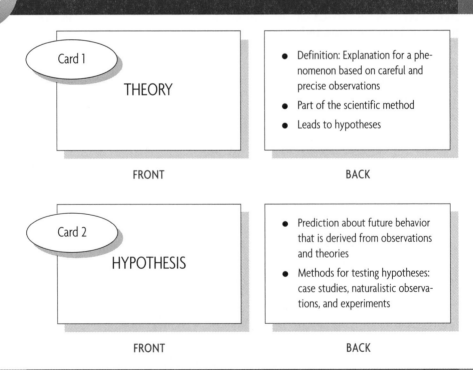

Card 1

THEORY

FRONT

- Definition: Explanation for a phenomenon based on careful and precise observations
- Part of the scientific method
- Leads to hypotheses

BACK

Card 2

HYPOTHESIS

FRONT

- Prediction about future behavior that is derived from observations and theories
- Methods for testing hypotheses: case studies, naturalistic observations, and experiments

BACK

- *Carry the cards with you and review them frequently.* You'll learn the most if you start using cards early in the course, well ahead of exam time.
- *Shuffle the cards and learn the information in various orders.* This will help you avoid putting too much focus on some information and not enough on others.
- *Test yourself in both directions.* First, look at the terms and provide the definitions or explanations. Then, turn the cards over and reverse the process.

Use Tape-Recorded Material

Questions on tape can work like audio flash cards. One way to do it is to record study questions, leaving 10 to 15 seconds between questions for you to answer out loud. Recording the correct answer after the pause will give you immediate feedback. For example, part of a recording for a writing class might say, "The three elements of effective writing are . . . . (10–15 seconds) . . . . topic, audience, and purpose."

USE CRITICAL THINKING

Your knowledge of the critical-thinking mind actions can help you remember information. Many of the mind actions use the principle of *association*—considering new information in relation to information you already know. The more you can associate a piece of new information with your current knowledge, the more likely you are to remember it.

EXPERT INSIGHT

Successful students are constantly looking for links between what they are learning and other information. Less successful students tend to learn information in isolation through cramming. In most cases, this information will stay with them for a short time because it isn't linked to anything else.

When you listen to a lecture, ask yourself questions: What is this part of? What's the bigger idea? How is it similar to the topic we dealt with in the last class? How is it different? By identifying similarities and differences, you're associating the ideas you are trying to learn with other memories and making it more likely that you will remember.

PAUL EGGEN, PROFESSOR OF EDUCATION,
UNIVERSITY OF NORTH FLORIDA

**Look for Links
Between What You Know
and What You Are Learning**

Imagine that you have to remember information about a specific historical event—for example, the signing of the Treaty of Versailles, the agreement that ended World War II. You might put the mind actions to work in the following ways:

- *Recall* everything that you know about the topic.
- Think about how this event is *similar* to other events in history, recent or long ago.
- Consider what is *different* and unique about this treaty in comparison to other treaties.
- Explore the *causes* that led up to this event, and look at the event's *effects*.
- From the general *idea* of treaties that ended wars, explore other *examples* of such treaties.
- Think about *examples* of what happened during the treaty signing, and from those examples come up with *ideas* about the tone of the event.
- Looking at the facts of the event, *evaluate* how successful you think the treaty was.

Working through every mind action might take time; you don't always have to use every one in every memory situation. Choose the ones that will help you most. The more information and ideas you can associate with the new item you're trying to remember, the more successful you will be.

How Can You Use Mnemonic Devices to Boost Memory Power?

Certain performers entertain their audiences by remembering the names of 100 strangers or flawlessly repeating 30 ten-digit phone numbers. These performers probably have superior memories, but genetics alone can't produce these results. They also rely on memory techniques, known as *mnemonic devices* (pronounced neh MAHN ick), for assistance.

Mnemonic devices work by connecting information you are trying to learn with simpler information or information that is familiar. Instead of learning new facts by rote (repetitive practice), associations give you a hook on which to hang these facts and later retrieve them. Mnemonic devices make information familiar and meaningful through unusual, unforgettable mental associations and visual pictures.

There are different kinds of mnemonic devices, including visual images and associations and acronyms. Study how these devices work; then apply them to your own memory challenges at school and in your career.

CREATE VISUAL IMAGES AND ASSOCIATIONS

Visual images are easier to remember than images that rely on words alone. In fact, communication through visual images goes back to the prehistoric era, when people made drawings on cave walls. It is no accident that the phrase "a picture is worth a thousand words" is so familiar. The best mental images often involve bright colors, three dimensions, action scenes, inanimate objects with human traits, ridiculousness, and humor.

Turning information into mental pictures helps improve memory, especially for visual learners. To remember that the Spanish artist Picasso painted *The Three Women*, you might imagine the women in a circle dancing to a Spanish song with a pig and a donkey (pig-asso). Don't reject outlandish images—as long as they help you. Often the strongest, oddest, most vivid images are the most effective.

Here is another example: Say you are trying to learn some basic Spanish vocabulary, including the words *carta*, *río*, and *dinero*. Instead of trying to learn these words by rote, you might come up with mental images such as those in Table 8.3.

Using Visual Images to Remember Items in a List

Two mental imagery techniques will help you remember items in a list: taking a mental walk in a familiar place and forming an idea chain.

A *mental walk* is a memory strategy in which you imagine that you store new ideas in familiar locations. Think, for example, of the route you take to and from the library. You pass the college theater, the science center, the bookstore, the cafeteria, the athletic center, and the social science building before reaching the library. At each spot along the route, you "place" an idea or concept you want to learn. Say, for example, that in biology you have been assigned the task of remembering the major

Visual images aid recall.

TABLE 8.3

SPANISH VOCABULARY	DEFINITION	MENTAL PICTURE
carta	letter	A person pushing a shopping cart filled with letters into a post office.
río	river	A school of sharks rioting in the river. One of the sharks is pulling a banner inscribed with the word *riot*. A killer shark bites off the t in riot as he takes charge of the group.
dinero	money	A man eating lasagna at a diner. The lasagna is made of layers of money.

FIGURE

8.5

A mental walk.

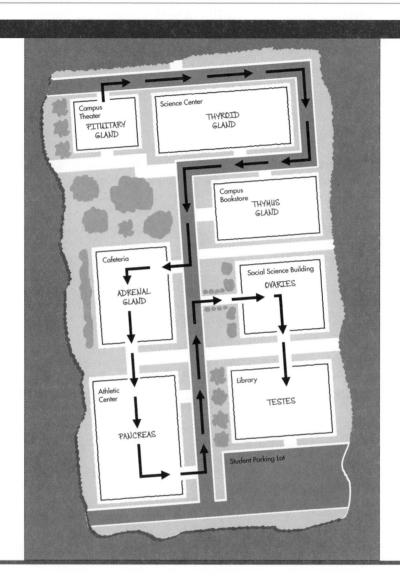

endocrine glands, starting in the brain and working downward through the body. Using the mental walk technique, here is how you would do this (see Figure 8.5 for a visual representation of this technique):

> At the college theater, you would place the pituitary gland; at the science center, the thyroid gland; at the college bookstore, the thymus gland; at the cafeteria, the adrenal gland; at the athletic center, the pancreas; at the social science building the ovaries (female); and at the library, the testes (male).

An *idea chain* is a memory strategy that involves forming exaggerated mental images of 20 or more items. The first image is connected to the second image, which is connected to the third image, and so on. Imagine, for example, that you want to remember the seven mind actions that appear in the critical-thinking chapter: recall, similarity, difference, cause and effect, example to idea, idea to example, and evaluation. You can use the visual icons to form an idea chain that goes like this:

The letter R rolls down a hill (recall) and bumps into two similar intersecting circles (similarity) that start rolling and bump into two different intersecting circles (difference). Everything rolls past a sign with two circling arrows on it telling them to keep rolling (cause and effect). It then bumps into an EX at the bottom of the hill that turns on a light bulb (example to idea). That light bulb shines on another EX (idea to example). The two EXs are sitting on either side of a set of scales (evaluation).

CREATE ACRONYMS

Another helpful association method involves the use of the *acronym*—a word formed from the first letters of a series of words, created in order to help you remember the series. In history, you can remember the big-three Allies during World War II—Britain, America, and Russia—with the acronym BAR. This is referred to as a *word acronym* because the first letters of the items you want to remember spell a word. The word (or words) spelled don't necessarily have to be real words.

One commonly used acronym, "Roy G. Biv," helps people remember the actual colors of the spectrum: red, orange, yellow, green, blue, indigo, and violet. In this case the first letter of each color combines to form one name, which is easier to remember than the individual colors. Other acronyms take the form of an entire sentence in which the first letter of each word in each sentence stands for the first letter of the memorized term. This is also called a *list order acronym*. For example, when science students want to remember the list of planets in order of their distance from the sun (Mercury, Venus, Earth, Mars, Jupiter, Saturn, Uranus, Neptune, and Pluto), they learn this sentence:

My very elegant mother just served us nine pickles.

Here's another example, from music. Use this phrase to remember the notes that correspond to the lines on the treble clef (E, G, B, D, and F):

Every Good Boy Does Fine.

You can create your own acronyms. Suppose you want to remember the names of the first six presidents of the United States. You notice that the first letters of their last names—Washington, Adams, Jefferson, Madison, Monroe, and Adams—together read W A J M M A. To remember them, first you might add an e after the J and create a short nonsense word: *wajemma*. Then, to make sure you don't forget the nonsense word, you might picture the six presidents sitting in a row and wearing pajamas.

USE SONGS OR RHYMES

Some of the most classic mnemonic devices are rhyming poems that tend to stick in your mind effectively. One you may have heard is the rule about the order of "i" and "e" in spelling:

> I before E, except after C, or when sounded like "A" as in "neighbor" and "weigh." Four exceptions if you please: either, neither, seizure, seize.

Make up your own poems or songs, linking tunes or rhymes that are familiar to you with information you want to remember. Thinking back to the "wajemma" example from the previous section, imagine that you want to remember the presidents' first names as well. You might set those first names—George, John, Thomas, James, James, and John—to the tune of "Happy Birthday." Or, to maintain the history theme, you might use the first musical phrase of the National Anthem.

Improving your memory requires energy, time, and work. In school, it also helps to master SQ3R, the textbook study technique that was introduced in Chapter 6. By going through the steps in SQ3R and using the specific memory techniques described in this chapter, you will be able to learn more in less time—and remember what you learn long after exams are over.

In Sanskrit, the written language of India and other Hindu countries, the characters above read *sem ma yeng chik*, meaning "do not be distracted." This advice can refer to the focus for a task or job at hand, the concentration required to critically think and talk through a problem, the mental discipline of meditation, or many other situations.

Think of this concept as you strive to improve your listening and memory techniques. Focus on the task, the person, or the idea at hand. Try not to be distracted by other thoughts, other people's notions of what you should be doing, or any negative messages. Be present in the moment to truly hear and remember what is happening around you. Do not be distracted.

Study Skills in Action

Test Competence

MEASURING WHAT YOU'VE LEARNED

MULTIPLE CHOICE. *Circle the answer that seems to fit best.*

1. When listening, you decide how you feel about a message in the
   A. interpretation stage.
   B. sensation stage.
   C. evaluation stage.
   D. reaction stage.

2. *Listening challenges* do **not** include
   A. rushing to judgment.
   B. divided attention and distractions.
   C. learning disabilities.
   D. slow recovery time.

3. Verbal signposts
   A. indicate what is important.
   B. involve transition words and phrases.
   C. help identify facts and ideas.
   D. all of the above.

4. *Short-term memory* is a memory storage bank that
   A. lasts no more than 10 to 20 seconds.
   B. is an exact copy of what you see and hear.
   C. stores information you are not aware of.
   D. stores information for a set period of time.

5. *Reciting* does **not** involve
   A. writing.
   B. oral presentations.
   C. summarizing information.
   D. mentally repeating information.

6. You can improve your memory of particular material by
   A. spreading your study sessions over time.
   B. studying for an hour or two without a break.
   C. studying during class.
   D. studying in the evenings.

7. Strategies for using flash cards to help memory do **not** include
   A. testing yourself on one side of the cards only.
   B. using the cards as a self-test.
   C. shuffling the cards and learning the information in various orders.
   D. carrying cards with you and reviewing them frequently.

8. *Association* means
   A. considering how information is updated.
   B. finding the differences between two sets of information.
   C. considering new information on its own terms.
   D. considering new information in relation to information you already know.

9. A *mental walk* and an *idea chain* are
   A. mnemonic devices that use visual images.
   B. ways to build paths through the brain.
   C. memory strategies that use aural sensation.
   D. storage banks for memory.

10. A word formed from the first letters of a series of words, created in order to help you remember the series, is
    A. an acronym.
    B. a mnemonic device.
    C. a signpost.
    D. a visual image.

TRUE/FALSE. *Place a T or an F beside each statement to indicate whether you think it is true or false.*

1. _____ Fatigue is an external distraction.

2. _____ Clarifying questions determine whether your understanding of a fact or idea is correct.

3. _____ Verbatim memorization involves remembering ideas but not the exact details or words of the ideas.

4. _____ To get the most out of your study sessions, minimize study breaks.

5. _____ Material you study midway through a study session tends to be a weak link in your recall.

Brain Power

BUILDING VOCABULARY FITNESS

The paragraphs below are taken from the current media. Read the paragraph, noting the context of the vocabulary words shown in bold type. Next, for each vocabulary word (reprinted in the left-hand column), highlight the word or phrase in column A, B, or C that is the most similar in meaning. Finally, on a separate sheet of paper, solidify your understanding of these words by using each in a sentence of your own.

Long before Jim Carrey became a Hollywood superstar, he wrote himself a check for $10 million, with the notation *For Services **Rendered**.*

Prior to creating the Dilbert cartoon, Scott Adams wrote at least 15 times a day, *I will become a syndicated cartoonist.*

These stories dramatically demonstrate how writing is such a powerful tool for achieving goals—from getting the perfect job . . . to meeting someone special . . . to feeling content.

Writing down goals is better than just thinking about them. It **stimulates** the "filtering" part of the brain, called the Reticular **Activating** System (RAS). . . . When you write your goals, the RAS begins collecting **pertinent** information and **routes** it to the conscious part of your mind. You become aware of opportunities you would never have noticed otherwise.

From "There's a Very Simple Way To Achieve Your Goals . . . Just Write Them Out," by Henriette Anne Klauser, *Bottom Line Personal*, June 1, 2000, p. 13. Reprinted with permission of *Bottom Line Personal*, 55 Railroad Ave., Greenwich, CT 06830, www.BottomLineSecrets.com.

Vocabulary Words	A	B	C
1. **rendered**	fixed	performed	expressed
2. **stimulates**	rouses	numbs	views
3. **activating**	beginning	triggering	exercising
4. **pertinent**	irrelevant	applicable	time-sensitive
5. **routes**	segments	unifies	directs

(continued on p. 224)

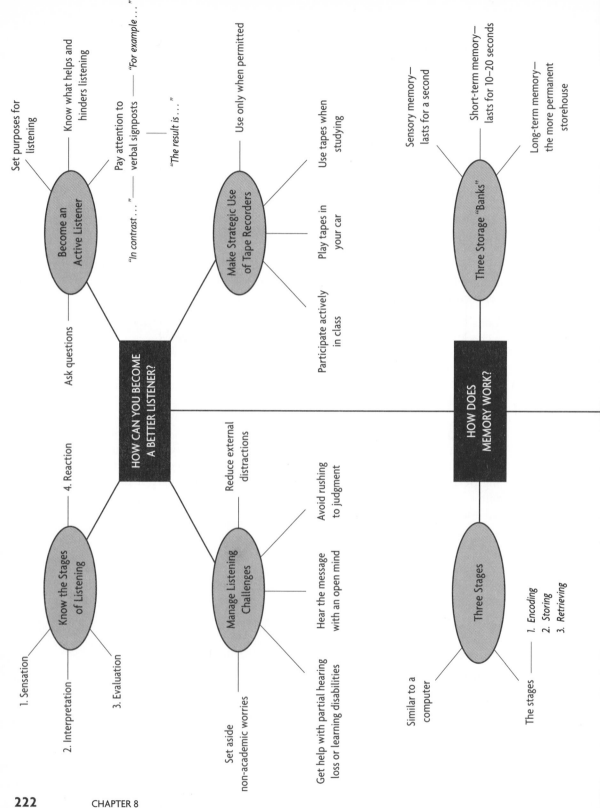

HOW CAN YOU BECOME A BETTER LISTENER?

Become an Active Listener
- Set purposes for listening
- Know what helps and hinders listening
- Pay attention to verbal signposts — "For example . . ." — "In contrast . . ." — "The result is . . ."
- Ask questions

Make Strategic Use of Tape Recorders
- Use only when permitted
- Use tapes when studying
- Play tapes in your car
- Participate actively in class

Know the Stages of Listening
- 1. Sensation
- 2. Interpretation
- 3. Evaluation
- 4. Reaction

Manage Listening Challenges
- Reduce external distractions
- Avoid rushing to judgment
- Hear the message with an open mind
- Set aside non-academic worries
- Get help with partial hearing loss or learning disabilities

HOW DOES MEMORY WORK?

Three Storage "Banks"
- Sensory memory—lasts for a second
- Short-term memory—lasts for 10–20 seconds
- Long-term memory—the more permanent storehouse

Three Stages
- Similar to a computer
- The stages — 1. Encoding
  2. Storing
  3. Retrieving

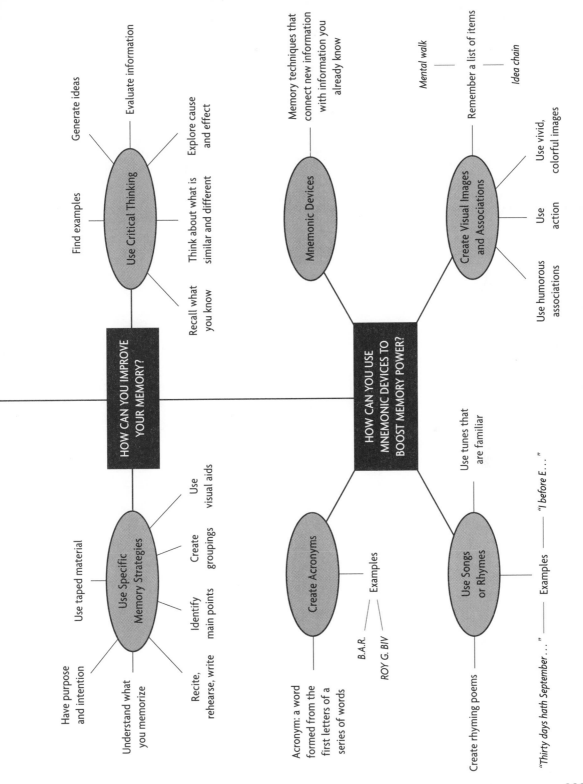

HOW CAN YOU IMPROVE YOUR MEMORY?

Use Critical Thinking
- Evaluate information
- Generate ideas
- Find examples
- Explore cause and effect
- Think about what is similar and different
- Recall what you know

Use Specific Memory Strategies
- Use visual aids
- Create groupings
- Use taped material
- Identify main points
- Have purpose and intention
- Understand what you memorize
- Recite, rehearse, write

HOW CAN YOU USE MNEMONIC DEVICES TO BOOST MEMORY POWER?

Mnemonic Devices
- Memory techniques that connect new information with information you already know

Create Visual Images and Associations
- Remember a list of items
  - *Mental walk*
  - *Idea chain*
- Use vivid, colorful images
- Use action
- Use humorous associations

Create Acronyms
- Acronym: a word formed from the first letters of a series of words
- Examples
  - *B.A.R.*
  - *ROY G. BIV*

Use Songs or Rhymes
- Use tunes that are familiar
- Create rhyming poems
- Examples
  - *"I before E . . . "*
  - *"Thirty days hath September . . . "*

Strategic Thinking

GETTING THE BIG PICTURE

Answer the following questions on a separate piece of paper or in a journal.

Consider one course you are taking currently. What is the biggest memory challenge in this course? What listening and memory techniques would best help you overcome this challenge? Briefly describe what you could do to increase your retention of what you are learning in this particular course. Be specific about what techniques you plan to use and how.

Making Connections

The following multiple-choice, true/false, fill-in-the-blank, matching, and essay questions will reinforce the concepts you learned in the four chapters that make up Part II, *Reading, Remembering, and Understanding: Making Meaning From What You Learn*, and will build critical-thinking skills as well. Whereas the end-of-chapter objective quizzes focus mainly on material from that particular chapter, many of the following questions encourage you to compare material from different chapters and find ways that different ideas connect. Recognizing the key relations between ideas will help you master and use knowledge in the most effective way.

MULTIPLE CHOICE. *Circle or highlight the answer that seems to fit best.*

1. Improving your comprehension is important for text reading for all of the following reasons **except**
   A. you are likely to be tested on what you read in the textbooks and handouts you receive in class.
   B. understanding what you read the first time you read it will help you handle your workload and manage your time.
   C. comprehension is the basis for all of the most important critical-thinking processes.
   D. if your comprehension is good, you will be able to resell your text immediately after the course is over.

2. Being able to recognize the meaning of prefixes, roots, and suffixes will help you
   A. do well when you study a foreign language.
   B. understand the meaning of words and remember information.
   C. create visual aids.
   D. identify your purpose for reading.

3. SQ3R is a textbook study method that depends, in part, on

    A. goal setting.

    B. time management.

    C. critical thinking.

    D. listening.

4. Purely poetic language is often a greater challenge than purely scientific language because the former

    A. requires a flexible approach to learning.

    B. uses more difficult vocabulary.

    C. suggests, rather than states, meaning.

    D. requires greater memorization.

5. It is important to improve your comprehension of tables and charts for all of the following reasons **except**

    A. learning to read and understand visual aids will help you study more effectively.

    B. information is often more readily recalled when it is presented in visual form.

    C. visual aids are more interesting than straight text.

    D. textbooks often present critical information in visual form.

TRUE/FALSE. *Place a T or an F beside each statement to indicate whether you think it is true or false.*

1. _____ The modern emphasis on visual images in the media means that many people are more likely to remember comparisons presented in charts than straight text.

2. _____ Using critical thinking to analyze data will help you spot a chart that presents misleading information.

3. _____ Listening is an intellectual skill as well as an interpersonal skill.

4. _____ As you use SQ3R to question text concepts, it is important to add questions that occurred to you during class lectures.

5. _____ Visual aids are not a factor in helping you to remember data and information.

FILL-IN-THE-BLANK. *Complete the following sentences with the appropriate word(s) or phrase(s) that best reflect what you learned in Part II. Choose from the items that follow each sentence.*

1. As you set your study schedule, you should define your purpose for reading because purpose determines _____. (pace, interest, motivation)

2. Vocabulary building depends on memory aids including _____ and _____. (rote memorization/motivation, effective listening/ time management, mnemonic devices/flash cards)

3. Mastering American English involves understanding idiosyncratic _____. (visual aids, alphabet symbols, slang)

4. _____ and _____ tend to be slow readers who have a hard time keeping up with their reading assignments and managing their time. (Procrastinators/critical thinkers, Vocalizers/subvocalizers, Flexible learners/foreign-born students)

5. SQ3R will encourage you to read _____. (critically, quickly, slowly)

6. When you read critically, you will ask questions that enable you to evaluate the author's _____ and _____. (style/language, education/family background, argument/perspective)

7. The fastest way to find the latest career-related information is through _____ research. (popular magazines, Internet, text)

8. Listening problems may be associated with _____ and _____. (vision problems/back problems, handwriting problems/poor time management, partial hearing loss/learning disabilities)

9. Active listeners pay attention to the instructor's _____ to identify important information before it is presented. (verbal signposts, body language, tone of voice)

10. Mnemonic devices include visual images, associations, and _____. (word prefixes, acronyms, word roots)

MATCHING. *Match each item in the left-hand column to an item in the right-hand column by writing the letter from the right that corresponds best to the number on the left.*

1. _____ word root

   A. charts with horizontal bars, each representing a different item

2. _____ specialized work vocabulary

   B. where and when the action takes place in a nonfiction work

3. _____ SQ3R

   C. tables that present numerical information

4. _____ literary setting

   D. central part of a word around which prefixes and suffixes are added

5. _____ characters

   E. survey, question, read, recite, review

6. _____ imagery

   F. a memory strategy that involves forming exaggerated mental images of numerous related items

7. _____ data tables

   G. words, phrases, and initials that convey meaning to people doing similar jobs

8. _____ bar charts

   H. a memory strategy in which you imagine that you store new ideas in familiar locations

9. _____ idea chain

   I. the personalities, thoughts, and actions of the people moving the plot forward

10. _____ mental walk

   J. figures of speech that create pictures in the reader's mind

Essay Question

Carefully read the following excerpt from Business Essentials, *3rd Ed., by Ronald J. Ebert and Ricky W. Griffin, a college textbook published by Prentice Hall, and then answer the essay question that follows. This exercise will help you focus on the meaning of the selection, apply your personal knowledge and experiences to the reading, organize your ideas, and communicate your thoughts effectively in writing.*

Before you begin writing your essay, it is a good idea to spend a few minutes planning. Try brainstorming possible approaches, writing a thesis statement, and jotting down your main thoughts in the form of an outline or think link. Because most essay tests are timed, limit the time you take to write your response to no more than one-half hour. This will force you to write quickly and effectively as it prepares you for actual test conditions.

MANAGERIAL STYLES

Early theories of leadership tried to identify specific traits associated with strong leaders. For example, physical appearance, intelligence, and public speaking skills were once thought to be "leadership traits." Indeed, it was once believed that taller people made better leaders than shorter people. The trait approach, however, proved to be a poor predictor of leadership potential. Ultimately, attention shifted from managers' traits to their behaviors, or **managerial styles**—patterns of behavior that a manager exhibits in dealing with subordinates. Managerial styles run the gamut from autocratic to democratic to free rein. Naturally, most managers do not conform to any one style, but these three major types of styles involve very different kinds of responses to human relations problems. Under different circumstances, any given style or combination of styles may prove appropriate.

- Managers who adopt an **autocratic style** generally issue orders and expect them to be obeyed without question. The military commander prefers and usually needs the autocratic style on the battlefield. Because no one else is consulted, the autocratic style allows for rapid decision making. It may, therefore, be useful in situations testing a firm's effectiveness as a time-based competitor.
- Managers who adopt a **democratic style** generally ask for input from subordinates before making decisions but retain final decision-making power. For example, the manager of a technical group may ask other group members to interview and offer opinions about job applicants. The manager, however, will ultimately make the hiring decision.
- Managers who adopt a **free-rein style** typically serve as advisors to subordinates who are allowed to make decisions. The chairperson of a volunteer committee to raise funds for a new library may find a free-rein style most effective.

According to many observers, the free-rein style of leadership is currently giving rise to an approach that emphasizes broad-based employee input into decision making and the fostering of workplace environments in which employees increasingly determine what needs to be done and how.

Regardless of theories about the ways in which leaders ought to lead, the relative effectiveness of any leadership style depends largely on the desire of subordinates to share input or to exercise creativity. Whereas some people, for example, are frustrated, others prefer autocratic managers because they do not want a voice in making decisions. The democratic approach, meanwhile, can be disconcerting both to people who want decision-making responsibility and to those who do not. A free-rein style lends itself to employee creativity, and thus to creative solutions to pressing problems. This style also appeals to employees who like to plan their own work. Not all subordinates, however, have the necessary background or skills to make creative decisions. Others are not sufficiently self-motivated to work without supervision.

Source: Excerpted from Ronald J. Ebert and Ricky W. Griffin, *Business Essentials*, 3rd Ed., Upper Saddle River, NJ: Prentice Hall, 2000, pp. 197–198.

ESSAY QUESTION.   If you are currently working or have worked for different employers in permanent, short-term, or part-time jobs, categorize your supervisors' managerial style. Provide specific examples that show why your supervisors fit into the categories you chose. Then, describe how you responded to each style: Did it motivate you to work harder or to slack off? Based on this analysis, evaluate which managerial style you would be likely to use if you were a department head.

Teamwork

READING AND GROUP DISCUSSION.   Divide into small groups of three or four. Take a few minutes to preview an article or other short section of reading material assigned to you for this class (other than your textbook). Then, write down the questions that came up during your preview. Each person should select one question to focus on while reading (no two people should select the same question). Group members should then read the material on their own, using critical-thinking skills to explore their particular questions as they read, and finally they should write down answers to their questions.

When you answer your question, focus on finding ideas that help to answer the question and examples that support them. Consider other information you know, relevant to your question, that may be similar to or different from the material in the passage. If your questions look for causes or effects, scan for them in the passage. Be sure to make notes as you read.

When you have finished reading critically, gather as a group. Each person should take a turn presenting the question, the answer that was derived through critical reading, and any other ideas that came up while reading. The group then has an opportunity to present any other ideas to add to the discussion. Continue until each person has had a chance to present what they worked on.

NOTES, RESEARCH, AND WRITING

INTERPRETING & EXPRESSING IDEAS

PART

III

EMPOWER

9

During class, you may encounter worlds of ideas and information. Although listening well allows you to take in what you hear in class lectures and discussions, not much will stay with you unless you record it somehow. The next crucial step, therefore, is to be able to take notes that will help you remember what you have heard. The quality of your learning depends on the quality of your notes because what you write down is what you study. The quality of your work also will depend on recording information—you will often need to note carefully what you hear in a presentation, discuss over the phone, develop in a planning session, or take in when meeting with a supervisor.

This chapter will show you note-taking skills that can help you successfully record and organize all kinds of information. At the end of the chapter, you will be able to answer these questions:

- How does taking notes help you?
- How can you make the most of class notes?
- What note-taking system should you use?
- How can you write faster when taking notes?

TAKING LECTURE NOTES
RECORDING THE IDEAS OF OTHERS

"The wise person learns from everyone."

Ethics of the Fathers

How Does Taking Notes Help You?

Note taking isn't always easy to do. You might feel that it prevents you from watching your instructor, or that you can't write fast enough, or that you seem to remember enough material even when you don't take notes. The act of note taking, however, is an important part of the learning process both in class and during study time. If you weigh whatever you feel are the negative effects of note taking against the possible benefits, you may see why good note taking can be a useful habit. Benefits include the following:

- Your notes provide material that helps you study information and prepare for tests.
- When you take notes, you listen better and become more involved in class.
- Notes help you organize ideas.
- The information you learn in class may not appear in any text; you will have no way to study it without writing it down.
- If it is difficult for you to process information while in class, having notes to read and make sense of later can help you learn.
- Note taking is a skill for life that you will use in almost any kind of career.

Note taking depends on, and builds, critical-thinking skills. Because it is virtually impossible to take notes on everything you hear or read, the act of note taking encourages you to evaluate what is worth remembering. Asking yourself questions like the following will help you judge what is important enough to write down:

- Do I need this information?
- Is the information important to the lecture or reading or is it just an interesting comment?
- Is the information fact or opinion? If it is opinion, is it worth remembering? (To explore this question, see How Do You Think Logically? in Chapter 4.)

Your responses will guide your note taking in class and help you decide what to study before an exam. With practice, you will know how to use notes to your advantage. Furthermore, these skills will be indispensable in the workplace. You will use them over and over again to record what goes on at job-related meetings, lectures, and conferences.

How Can You Make the Most of Class Notes?

Class notes—the notes you take while listening to an instructor—may contain key terms and definitions (e.g., Marketing research is . . .), explanations of concepts and processes (what happens during photosynthesis), or narratives of who did what to whom and when (The events that led to the Persian Gulf War were . . .). If lectures include material that is not in your text or if your instructor talks about specific test questions, your class notes become even more important as a study tool.

PREPARE TO TAKE CLASS NOTES

Your class notes have two purposes: First, they should reflect what you heard in class, and second, they should be a resource for studying, writing, or comparing with your text material. Taking good class notes depends on good preparation.

PREVIEW YOUR READING MATERIAL. Survey the text (or any other assigned reading material) to become familiar with the topic and any new concepts that it introduces. Visual familiarity helps note taking during lectures.

GATHER YOUR SUPPLIES. Start a new piece of 8.5-by-11-inch paper for each class meeting. If you use a three-ring binder, punch holes in handouts and insert them immediately following your notes for that day. Make sure your pencils are sharp and your pens aren't about to run out of ink.

LOCATION, LOCATION, LOCATION. Find a comfortable seat where you can easily see and hear—sitting near the front, where you minimize distraction and maximize access to the lecture or discussion, might be your best bet. Be ready to write as soon as the instructor begins speaking.

CHOOSE THE BEST NOTE-TAKING SYSTEM. Select a system that is most appropriate for the situation. Later in the chapter, you will learn about different note-taking systems.

Take the following factors into account when choosing the system to use in any class:

- *The instructor's style* (you'll be able to determine this style after a few classes). Whereas one instructor may deliver organized lectures at a normal speaking rate, another may jump from topic to topic or talk very quickly.

- *The course material.* You may decide that an informal outline works best for a highly structured philosophy course, but that a think link is the right choice for a looser sociology course. Try working with the note-taking system you choose for a few classes, then make whatever adjustments are necessary.

- *Your learning style.* Choose strategies that seem to make the most of your strong points and help boost your weaker areas. A visual–spatial learner might prefer think links or the Cornell system, a thinker type might stick to outlines, an interpersonal learner might use the Cornell system and fill in the cue column in a study group setting. You might even find that one system is best in class and another works best for review sessions.

GATHER SUPPORT.   For each class, set up a support system with two students. That way, when you are absent, you can get the notes you missed. (It's smart to have two "buddies" instead of one in case one is absent.)

RECORD INFORMATION DURING CLASS

Because no one has time to write down everything he or she hears, the following strategies will help you choose and record what you feel is important, in a format that you can read and understand later. This is not a list of "musts." Rather, it is a source list of ideas to try, as you work to find the note-taking system that works best for you. Keep an open mind and experiment with these strategies until you feel that you have found a successful combination.

Remember that the first step in note taking is to listen actively; you can't write down something that you don't hear. Use the listening strategies in Chapter 8 to make sure you are prepared to take in the information that comes your way during class.

- Date and identify each page. When you take several pages of notes during a lecture, add an identifying letter or number to the date on each page: 11/27A, 11/27B, 11/27C, for example, or 11/27—1 of 3, 11/27—2 of 3, 11/27—3 of 3. This will help you keep track of the order of your pages.

- Add the specific topic of the lecture at the top of the page. For example: 11/27A—U. S. Immigration Policy After World War II. Because an instructor may revisit a topic days or even weeks after introducing it, this suggestion will help you gather all your notes on the same topic when it is time to study.

- If your instructor jumps from topic to topic during a single class, it may help to start a new page for each new topic.

- Some students prefer to use only one side of the notepaper because this can make notes easier to read. Others prefer to use both sides, which can be a more economical paper-saving option. Choose what works best for you.

- Record whatever your instructor emphasizes. See Figure 9.1 for more details about how an instructor might call attention to particular information.

- Write down all key terms and definitions. If, for example, your instructor is discussing the stages of mental development in children, as defined by psychologist Jean Piaget, your notes would probably mention such terms as *sensorimotor* and *preoperational*.

How to pick up on instructors' cues. **FIGURE 9.1**

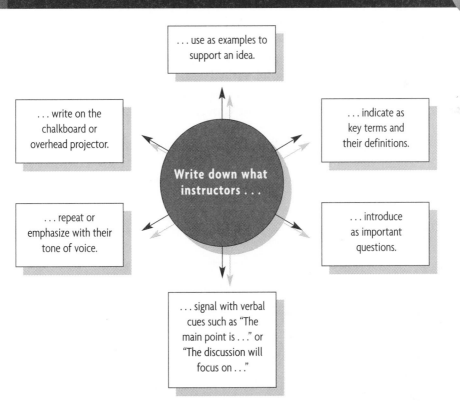

... use as examples to support an idea.

... write on the chalkboard or overhead projector.

... indicate as key terms and their definitions.

Write down what instructors ...

... repeat or emphasize with their tone of voice.

... introduce as important questions.

... signal with verbal cues such as "The main point is ..." or "The discussion will focus on ..."

- Avoid writing out every word your instructor says. If you use short phrases instead of full sentences, you will save yourself a lot of time and trouble. For example, write "German—nouns capitalized" instead of "In the German language, all nouns are capitalized"; "Abraham Lincoln was elected president in the year 1860" becomes "Lincoln—elec. Pres. 1860."

- Continue to take notes during class discussions and question-and-answer periods. What your fellow students ask about may help you as well.

- Write down all questions raised by the instructor; the same questions may appear on a test.

- Leave one or more blank spaces between points. This white space will help you review your notes because information will be in self-contained segments. (This suggestion does not apply if you are using a think link.)

- Draw pictures and diagrams that help illustrate ideas.

- Write quickly but legibly, perhaps using a form of personal short-hand (see the section on shorthand on p. 248 of this chapter).

- Indicate material that is especially important with a star, underlining, a highlighter pen, a different color pen, or capital letters.

- If you don't understand something, leave space and place a question mark in the margin. Then take advantage of your resources—ask the instructor to explain it after class, discuss it with a classmate, or consult your textbook—and fill in the blank when the idea is clear.

- Take notes until the instructor stops speaking. If you stop writing a few minutes before the class is over, you might miss critical information.

- Make your notes as legible and organized as possible—you can't learn from notes that you can't read or understand. Don't be so fussy, however, that you miss information while you are dotting every "i"

EXPERT INSIGHT

Take Notes to Cement Your Learning

The act of writing reinforces learning. You learn by listening, but you double that learning if you take notes at the same time. Taking notes forces you to think about concepts as you select and transcribe the instructor's thoughts. Like a high performance automobile, you're running on all eight cylinders instead of on just two.

STEPHEN REID, PROFESSOR OF ENGLISH,
COLORADO STATE UNIVERSITY

and crossing every "t." Remember that you can always rewrite and improve your notes.

- Consider that your notes are not all of what you need to learn. Using your text to add to your notes after class makes a superior, "deeper and wider" body of information to study.

REVIEW AND REVISE YOUR NOTES

Even the most comprehensive notes in the world won't do you any good unless you review them. The crucial act of reviewing helps you solidify the information in your memory so that you can recall it and use it. It also helps you link new information to information you already know, which is a key step in building new ideas. The best review strategy includes planning your review schedule, thinking critically, using print sources, summarizing, and working with a study group.

Plan a Review Schedule

As you learned in Chapter 8, one of the memory strategies involves the timing of your reviews. Reviewing right after the lecture but not again until the test, reviewing here and there without a plan, or cramming it all into one crazy night will not allow you to make the most of your abilities. Do yourself a favor by trying to plan your time as strategically as possible.

REVIEW WITHIN A DAY OF THE LECTURE. If you can, plan your first review for some time during the day following the lecture. Reviewing while the material is still fresh in your mind will help you to remember it more effectively. You don't have to sit down for two hours and focus on every word—just set some time aside to reread your notes and perhaps write questions and comments on them. If you know you have an hour between classes, for example, that would be an ideal time to work in a quick review.

REVIEW REGULARLY. Try to schedule certain times during the week for reviewing the notes from that week's class meetings. For example, if you know you always have from 2 P.M. to 5 P.M. free every Tuesday and Thursday afternoon, you can plan to review notes from two of your courses on Tuesday and notes from two others on Thursday. Having a routine helps assure that you will be looking at your material on a regular basis.

REVIEW WITH AN EYE TOWARD TESTS. When you know you have a test coming up, step up your efforts. Schedule longer review sessions, call a meeting of your study group, and review more frequently. As you may recall from the memory chapter, shorter sessions of intense review work interspersed with breaks may be more effective than long hours of continuous studying.

Read and Rework Using Critical Thinking

The critical-thinking mind actions will help you make the most of your notes.

- *Recall.* Read your notes to learn the information, clarify points, write out abbreviations, and fill in missing information.

- *Similarity.* Consider what similar facts or ideas the information brings to mind. Write them in the margins or white space on the page if they are helpful to you.

- *Difference.* Consider how the information differs from what you already know. Is there a discrepancy you should examine? If something seems way off base, could you have written it down inaccurately?

- *Cause and effect.* Look at how ideas, facts, and statements relate to one another. See if any of them have cause-and-effect relations. You might even want to use another color pen to draw a line linking related ideas or facts on the page.

- *Example to idea.* Think about what new ideas you can form from the information in your notes. If any come to mind, write them in your notes or on a separate page. If particular information seems to fit together more specifically than your notes initially indicate, you may want to add headings and subheadings, and insert clarifying phrases or sentences.

- *Idea to example.* Think carefully about the ideas in your notes. What do they mean? See if the examples in your notes support or negate them. If you have no examples in your notes as written, add them as you review.

- *Evaluation.* Use your evaluation skills to select and underline or highlight the most important ideas and information. Think about why they are important and make sure you understand them as completely as possible.

Revise Using Print Sources

Revising and adding to your notes using material from your print sources (books and other required reading for your course) is one of the best ways to build your understanding and link new information to information you already know. Try using critical-thinking actions to add on to your notes in the following ways:

- Brainstorm and write down examples from other sources that illustrate central ideas in your notes.

- After evaluating the important ideas in your reading, highlight or rewrite the ones that also appear in your notes.
- Think of similar facts or ideas from the reading that will help you understand your notes.
- Consider what in your class notes might differ from your reading, and why.
- Write down any new ideas that come up when reviewing your notes.
- Look at cause-and-effect relations between material from your notes and reading material. Note how ideas, facts, and examples relate to one another.

Summarize

Writing a summary of your notes is another important review technique. Summarizing involves critically evaluating which ideas and examples are most important and then rewriting the material in a shortened form, focusing on those important ideas and examples.

You may prefer to summarize as you review, with the notes in front of you. If you are using the Cornell system (see p. 244), you would summarize in the space you have saved at the bottom of the page. Other ideas include summarizing on a separate page that you insert in your loose-leaf binder, or summarizing on the back of the previous page (if you only take notes on one side of the paper).

Another helpful review technique is to summarize your notes from memory after you review them. This will give you an idea of how well you have retained the information. You may even want to summarize as you read, then summarize from memory, and compare the two summaries.

Work with Study Groups

Study groups can be a useful way to review notes because group members can benefit from one another's different perspectives and abilities. For example, if you happened to focus well on one particular part of the lec-

If you recopy your notes to prepare for a test, don't simply copy them over in a neater form. That's a passive activity. A more active strategy involves summarizing as you recopy.

PAUL EGGEN,
PROFESSOR OF EDUCATION, UNIVERSITY OF NORTH FLORIDA

EXPERT INSIGHT

Summarize as You Recopy Notes

ture and lost concentration during another, a fellow student may have been taking good notes on the part you missed. See Chapter 12 for more on effective studying in groups.

What Note-Taking System Should You Use?

You will benefit most from the system that feels most comfortable to you and makes the most sense for the type of content covered in any given course. For example, you might take notes in a different style for a history class than for a foreign language class, or use a different system during a work-related planning meeting than for a professional conference. As you consider each system, remember your learning style from Chapter 2. Everyone has a different learning and working style, so don't wedge yourself into a system that doesn't work for you. The most common note-taking systems include outlines, the Cornell system, and think links.

TAKING NOTES IN OUTLINE FORM

When a reading assignment or lecture seems well organized, you may choose to take notes in outline form. When you use an outline, you construct a line-by-line representation, with certain phrases set off by varying indentations, showing how ideas relate to one another and are supported by facts and examples.

Formal versus Informal Outlines

Formal outlines indicate ideas and examples with Roman numerals, capital and lowercase letters, and numbers. The rules of formal outlines require at least two headings on the same level. That is, if you have a IIA, you must also have a IIB. Similarly, if you have a IIIA1, you must also have a IIIA2. In contrast, informal outlines show the same relations but replace the formality with a system of consistent indenting and dashes. Figure 9.2 shows the difference between the two outline forms. Because making a formal outline can take time, many students find that using informal outlines is better for in-class note taking. Figure 9.3 shows how a student has used the structure of a formal outline to write notes on the topic of civil rights legislation.

When you use an outline to write class notes, you may have trouble when an instructor rambles or jumps from point to point. The best advice in this case is to abandon the outline structure for the time being. Focus instead on taking down whatever information you can and on drawing connections between key topics. After class, try to restructure your notes and, if possible, rewrite them in outline form.

FIGURE

9.2

FORMAL OUTLINE	INFORMAL OUTLINE

I. Topic
First Main Idea
A. Major supporting fact
B. Major supporting fact
   1. First reason or example
   2. Second reason or example
     a. First supporting fact
     b. Second supporting fact
 	
II. Second Main Idea
A. Major supporting fact
   1. First reason or example
   2. Second reason or example
B. Major supporting fact
	Topic
	First Main Idea
	—Major supporting fact
	—Major supporting fact
	   —First reason or example
	   —Second reason or example
	     —First supporting fact
	     —Second supporting fact
	
	Second Main Idea
	—Major supporting fact
	   —First reason or example
	   —Second reason or example
	—Major supporting fact

Sample formal outline.

FIGURE

9.3

Civil Rights Legislation: 1860–1968

I. Post-Civil War Era
  A. Fourteenth Amendment, 1868: equal protection of the law for all citizens
  B. Fifteenth Amendment, 1870: constitutional rights of citizens regardless of race, color, or previous servitude
II. Civil Rights Movement of the 1960s
  A. National Association for the Advancement of Colored People (NAACP)
    1. Established in 1910 by W.E.B. DuBois and others
    2. Legal Defense and Education fund fought school segregation
  B. Martin Luther King Jr., champion of nonviolent civil rights action
    1. Led bus boycott: 1955-1956
    2. Marched on Washington, D.C.: 1963
    3. Awarded NOBEL PEACE PRIZE: 1964
    4. Led voter registration drive in Selma, Alabama: 1965
  C. Civil Rights Act of 1964: prohibited discrimination in voting, education, employment, and public facilities
  D. Voting Rights Act of 1965: gave the government power to enforce desegregation
  E. Civil Rights Act of 1968: prohibited discrimination in the sale or rental of housing

Guided Notes

From time to time, an instructor may give you a guide, usually in the form of an outline, to help you take notes in the class. This outline may be on the board, on an overhead projector, or on a page that you receive at the beginning of the class.

Although guided notes help you follow the lecture and organize your thoughts during class, they do not replace your own notes. Because they are more of a basic outline of topics than a comprehensive coverage of information, they require that you fill in what they do not cover in detail. If your mind wanders because you think that the guided notes are all you need, you may miss important information.

When you receive guided notes on paper, write directly on the paper if there is room. If not, use a separate sheet and write on it the outline categories that the guided notes suggest. If the guided notes are on the board or overhead, copy them, leaving plenty of space in between for your own notes.

USING THE CORNELL NOTE-TAKING SYSTEM

The Cornell note-taking system, also known as the T-note system, was developed more than 45 years ago by Walter Pauk at Cornell University and is now in use throughout the world.[1] The system is successful because it is simple—and because it works. It consists of three sections on ordinary notepaper:

- *Section 1*, the largest section, is on the right. Record your notes here in informal outline form, or in whatever form is most comfortable for you.
- *Section 2*, to the left of your notes, is the *cue column*. Leave it blank while you read or listen; then fill it in later as you review. You might fill it with comments that highlight main ideas, clarify meaning, suggest examples, or link ideas and examples. You can even draw diagrams. Many students use this column to raise questions that they will ask themselves when they study. By placing specific questions in the cue column, you can help yourself focus on critical details and understand meaning.
- *Section 3*, at the bottom of the page, is known as the *summary area*. Here you use a sentence or two to summarize the notes on the page. Use this section during the review process to reinforce concepts and provide an overview of what the notes say.

When you use the Cornell system, create the note-taking structure before class begins. Picture an upside-down letter *T* as you follow these directions, and use Figure 9.4 as your guide.

- Start with a sheet of standard loose-leaf paper. Label it with the date and title of the lecture.

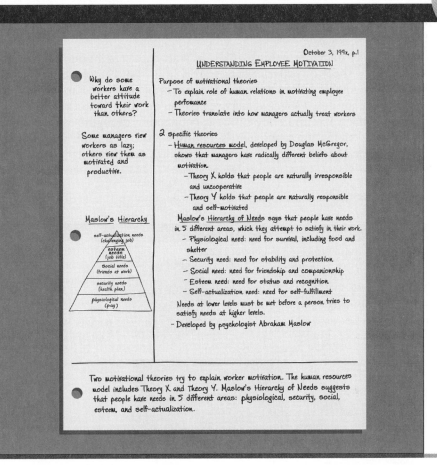

- To create the *cue column*, draw a vertical line about 2 1/2 inches from the left side of the paper. End the line about 2 inches from the bottom of the sheet.
- To create the *summary area*, start at the point where the vertical line ends (about 2 inches from the bottom of the page) and draw a horizontal line that spans the entire paper.

Figure 9.4 shows how a student used the Cornell system to take notes in a business course.

CREATING A THINK LINK

A *think link*, also known as a mind map, is a visual form of note taking. When you draw a think link, you diagram ideas by using shapes and lines that link ideas and supporting details and examples. The visual design makes the connections easy to see, and the use of shapes and pictures extends the material beyond just words. Many learners respond well to the power of visualization. You can use think links to brainstorm ideas for paper topics as well.

One way to create a think link is to start by circling your topic in the middle of a sheet of paper. Next, draw a line from the circled topic and write the name of one major idea at the end of the line. Circle that idea also. Then, jot down specific facts related to the idea, linking them to the idea with lines. Continue the process, connecting thoughts to one another by using circles, lines, and words. Figure 9.5 shows a think link on social stratification (a sociology concept) that follows this particular structure.

FIGURE

9.5

Sample think link.

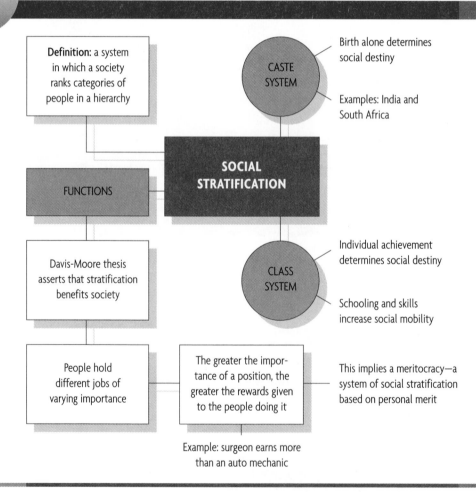

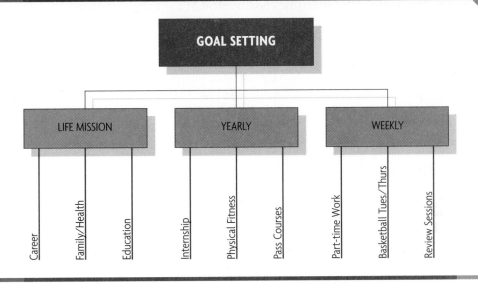

You can design any kind of think link that feels comfortable to you. Different examples include stair steps showing connected ideas that build toward a conclusion, or a tree shape with roots as causes and branches as effects. Figure 9.6 shows a type of think link sometimes referred to as a "jellyfish."

A think link may be difficult to construct in class, especially if your instructor talks quickly. In this case, use another note-taking system during class. Then, make a think link as part of the review process.

OTHER VISUAL NOTE-TAKING STRATEGIES

Several other note-taking strategies will help you organize your information and are especially useful to visual learners. These strategies may be too involved to complete quickly during class, so you may want to use them when taking notes on a text chapter or when rewriting your notes for review.

TIME LINES.   A time line can help you organize information—such as dates of French Revolution events or eras of different psychology practices—into chronological order. Draw a vertical or horizontal line on the page and connect each item to the line, in order, noting the dates.

TABLES.   You will notice tables throughout this text that show information through vertical or horizontal columns. Use tables to arrange information according to particular categories.

HIERARCHY CHARTS. Charts showing the hierarchy of information can help you understand that information in terms of how each piece fits into the hierarchy. A hierarchy chart could show levels of government, for example, or levels of scientific classification of animals and plants.

Once you choose a note-taking system, your success will depend on how well you use it. Personal shorthand will help you make the most of whatever system you choose.

How Can You Write Faster When Taking Notes?

When taking notes, many students feel that they can't keep up with the speaker. Using some personal shorthand (not standard secretarial shorthand) can help you push your pen faster. *Personal shorthand* refers to abbreviations and shortened words in addition to the act of replacing words or parts of words with symbols. Because you are the only intended reader, you can misspell and abbreviate words in ways that only you understand.

The only danger with shorthand is that you might forget what your writing means. To avoid this problem, review your shorthand notes while your abbreviations and symbols are fresh in your mind. If there is any confusion, spell out words as you review.

Here are some suggestions that will help you master this important skill:

1. Use the following standard abbreviations in place of complete words:

w/	with	cf	compare, in comparison to
w/o	without	ff	following
→	means; resulting in	Q	question
←	as a result of	p.	page
↑	increasing	*	most importantly
↓	decreasing	<	less than
∴	therefore	>	more than
∵	because	=	equals
≈	approximately	%	percent
+ or &	and	△	change
−	minus; negative	2	to; two; too
NO. or #	number	vs	versus; against
i.e.	that is	e.g.	for example
etc.	and so forth	c/o	care of
ng	no good	lb	pound

2. Shorten words by removing vowels from the middle of words:

prps	=	purpose
lwyr	=	lawyer
cmptr	=	computer

3. Substitute word beginnings for entire words:

assoc	=	associate; association
info	=	information
subj	=	subject

4. Form plurals by adding "s" to shortened words:

prblms	=	problems
drctrys	=	directories
prntrs	=	printers

5. Make up your own symbols and use them consistently:

b/4	=	before
4tn	=	fortune
2thake	=	toothache

6. Use standard or informal abbreviations for proper nouns such as places, people, companies, scientific substances, events, and so on:

D.C.	=	Washington, D.C.
H_2O	=	water
Moz.	=	Wolfgang Amadeus Mozart

7. If you know you are going to repeat a particular word or phrase often throughout the course of a class period, write it out once at the beginning of the class and then establish an abbreviation that you will use in the rest of your notes. For example, if you are taking notes on the rise and fall of Argentina's former first lady Eva Peron, you might start out by writing "Eva Peron (EP)" and then use "EP" throughout the rest of the class period.

Finally, throughout your note taking, remember that the primary goal is for you to generate materials that help you learn and remember information. No matter how sensible any note-taking strategy, abbreviation, or system might be, it won't do you any good if it doesn't help you reach that goal. Keep a close eye on what works for you and stick to it.

If you find that your notes aren't comprehensive, legible, or focused enough, think critically about how you might improve them. Can't read your notes? You might just have been too sleepy, or you might have a handwriting issue. Lots of confusing gaps in the information? You might be distracted in class, have an instructor who jumps around in the lecture, or have a deeper lack of understanding of the course material. Put your problem-solving skills to work and address your note-taking issues, brainstorming solutions from the variety of strategies in this chapter. With a little time and effort, your notes will truly become a helpful learning tool in school and beyond.

Gestalt

The German word *gestalt* refers to a whole that is greater than the sum of its parts. When you can think in terms of *gestalt*, you are able to see both the whole picture and how each individual part contributes to it. To refer to a common phrase, *gestalt* is seeing the whole forest as well as individual trees.

Think of this concept as you consider how note taking can help you build your knowledge and store of information. When you're reading your notes, ask yourself, "Do I truly understand the material, or am I just trying to cram facts into my head?" As important as the individual facts and examples may be, the *gestalt* is what helps the individual parts of your notes gain a new and important meaning as a whole.

Study Skills in Action

Test Competence

MEASURING WHAT YOU'VE LEARNED

MULTIPLE CHOICE. *Circle or highlight the answer that seems to fit best.*

1. The benefits of taking notes include all of the following **except**
   A. help with organizing your study materials.
   B. making you an active listener.
   C. generating material to review for a test.
   D. showing your instructor that you are busy.

2. As you prepare to take class notes, you should
   A. sit next to another student who takes good notes.
   B. hold off looking at the assigned reading material.
   C. choose a note-taking system that suits the instructor's style, the course material, and your learning style.
   D. choose a note-taking system you've used in other classes.

3. As you record information in your notes, you should
   A. take down every word the instructor says.
   B. avoid using shorthand because it may be difficult to read later on.
   C. avoid leaving too much white space on the page.
   D. record all key terms and definitions, especially those the instructor emphasizes.

4. It is a mistake to close your notebook during the question and answer period because
   A. your instructor may assume you are not paying attention.
   B. critical facts often emerge during this exchange.
   C. the class is not officially over until you are dismissed.
   D. you may need to rewrite your notes.

5. Reviewing your notes is important for all of the following reasons **except**

   A. you are solidifying information in your memory so you can recall it later.

   B. the process helps keep you alert and focused.

   C. you are making connections between new information and the information you already have.

   D. through review, you may build new ideas.

6. As part of your reviewing schedule, you should consider

   A. how you can best use your notes to prepare for exams.

   B. when you can find a full day to review all of your notes at once.

   C. when you can borrow and copy the notes from another student in your class.

   D. when you can spend a night cramming for exams.

7. You should consider using a formal or informal outline for note taking if

   A. your instructor tends to jump from point to point.

   B. your instructor tends to present material in an organized, logical manner.

   C. you learned to use an outline in high school and are comfortable with it.

   D. the other students around you are using an outline.

8. Guided notes are

   A. a complete set of class notes provided by the teacher.

   B. instructions on how to take effective notes.

   C. a basic outline of the key points an instructor plans to make in a lecture.

   D. another name for the course outline you receive at the beginning of the semester.

9. The Cornell note-taking system includes all of the following elements **except**

   A. a space to record your notes from class.

   B. a space for any comments your instructor wants to make about your notes.

   C. a cue column to be used during review sessions.

   D. a summary area to summarize and reinforce the concepts on the page.

10. A *think link* is an especially effective note-taking system for

    A. visual learners.

    B. disorganized people.

    C. students who are tired of using outlines.

    D. students who want to make note taking a more creative process.

TRUE/FALSE. *Place a T or an F beside each statement to indicate whether you think it is true or false.*

1. _____ A table can be a helpful summary tool as you review your class notes.

2. _____ There is one correct form of personal shorthand.

3. _____ When you review your notes, just try to learn what's on the page and avoid critical thinking.

4. _____ When you share your notes in a study group, you are benefiting from the perspectives and abilities of other students.

5. _____ The cue column in the Cornell note-taking system is a space for clarifying comments and questions, examples and ideas.

Brain Power

BUILDING VOCABULARY FITNESS

The paragraphs below are taken from the current media. Read the paragraph, noting the context of the vocabulary words shown in bold type. Next, for each vocabulary word (reprinted in the left-hand column), highlight the word or phrase in column A, B, or C that is the most similar in meaning. Finally, on a separate sheet of paper, solidify your understanding of these words by using each in a sentence of your own.

Satire came easier in the 1960s when the "hip" and the "square" were definable **blocs** in American society, and most people knew on which side they belonged. Subsequently, several social ground swells converged to blur the **distinctions.** The triumph of popular culture made it no longer possible to distinguish between high and low art. And the doctrine of political correctness along with the rise of multiculturalism prevented aspiring satirists from heaping **scorn** on once easy targets.

    At the same time, the human potential and recovery movements ushered in a mass **therapeutic** culture, institutionalizing a nonjudgmental "I'm O.K., You're O.K." social doctrine. This touchy-feely ethos has helped pathologize the misanthropy that has traditionally been the **well-**

spring of satire; it has also **tainted** the **venting** of contempt, snobbery and critical scorn with an aura of psychic ill health, not to mention "elitism."

From "Satire Is Dying For Our Sins," by Stephen Holden, *The New York Times*, Sunday, June 18, 2000, p. AR–13.

Vocabulary Words

	A	B	C
1. **blocs**	groups	labels	people
2. **distinctions**	individuals	awards	contrasts
3. **scorn**	ridicule	criticism	praise
4. **therapeutic**	psychological	healing	personal
5. **wellspring**	energy	source	health
6. **tainted**	decorated	spoiled	encouraged
7. **venting**	discharging	heating	gathering

Strategic Thinking

GETTING THE BIG PICTURE

Answer the following questions on a separate piece of paper or in a journal.

Imagine you are a consultant who helps businesses improve their operations. You are in a meeting with the governing board—the leaders and owners—of a particular company. They tell you that each one will spend 20 minutes or so presenting to you the facts about the company, the issues that they are facing now, and the ideas about the future. How will you take notes? Describe your materials, how you will decide which note-taking style is best for each speaker, and any other strategies that you would use in order to record your information as comprehensively as possible. Also describe the steps you will take after the meeting to transform your notes from raw data into the building blocks of your report.

NOTES

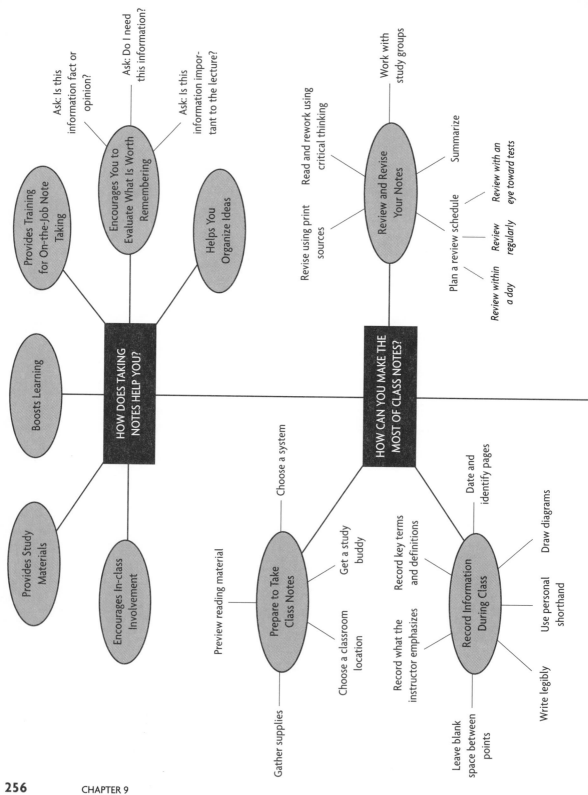

HOW DOES TAKING NOTES HELP YOU?

Boosts Learning

Provides Study Materials

Encourages In-class Involvement

Provides Training for On-the-Job Note Taking

Encourages You to Evaluate What Is Worth Remembering
- Ask: Is this information fact or opinion?
- Ask: Do I need this information?
- Ask: Is this information important to the lecture?

Helps You Organize Ideas

HOW CAN YOU MAKE THE MOST OF CLASS NOTES?

Review and Revise Your Notes
- Read and rework using critical thinking
- Work with study groups
- Summarize
- Review with an eye toward tests
- Plan a review schedule
  - Review regularly
  - Review within a day
- Revise using print sources

Prepare to Take Class Notes
- Choose a system
- Get a study buddy
- Preview reading material
- Choose a classroom location
- Gather supplies

Record Information During Class
- Date and identify pages
- Record key terms and definitions
- Draw diagrams
- Record what the instructor emphasizes
- Use personal shorthand
- Write legibly
- Leave blank space between points

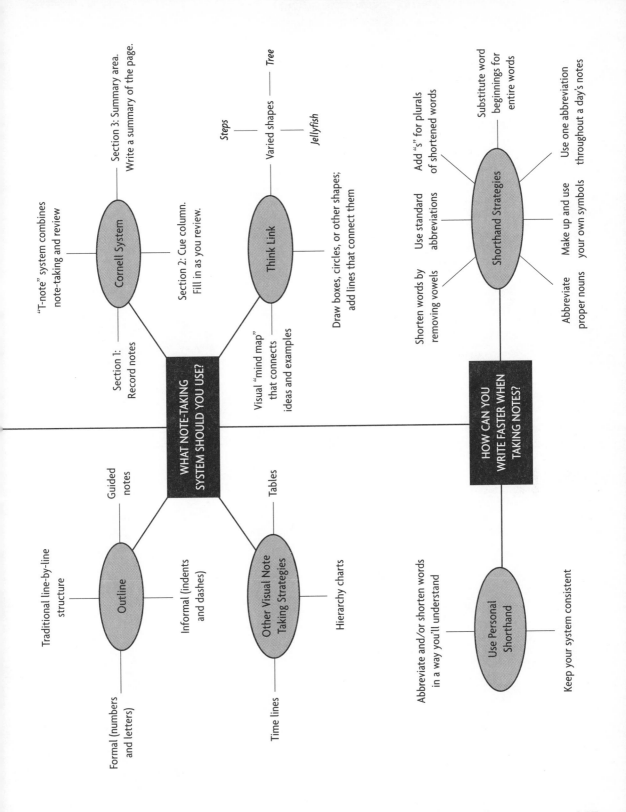

WHAT NOTE-TAKING SYSTEM SHOULD YOU USE?

Cornell System
- "T-note" system combines note-taking and review
- Section 1: Record notes
- Section 2: Cue column. Fill in as you review.
- Section 3: Summary area. Write a summary of the page.

Think Link
- Visual "mind map" that connects ideas and examples
- Draw boxes, circles, or other shapes; add lines that connect them
- Varied shapes
  - Steps
  - Tree
  - Jellyfish

Outline
- Traditional line-by-line structure
- Guided notes
- Informal (indents and dashes)
- Formal (numbers and letters)

Other Visual Note Taking Strategies
- Tables
- Hierarchy charts
- Time lines

HOW CAN YOU WRITE FASTER WHEN TAKING NOTES?

Shorthand Strategies
- Add "s" for plurals of shortened words
- Substitute word beginnings for entire words
- Use standard abbreviations
- Use one abbreviation throughout a day's notes
- Make up and use your own symbols
- Shorten words by removing vowels
- Abbreviate proper nouns

Use Personal Shorthand
- Abbreviate and/or shorten words in a way you'll understand
- Keep your system consistent

RESEARCH

As a worker in the "Information Age," your job is likely to involve gathering, evaluating, and disseminating information and data. For example, if you're part of an Internet start-up, you'll be spending hours on the Web trying to learn how your competitors present their products, including their marketing and technology strategies. This type of research is not unusual in our 21st century economy. In fact, one of the most important skills for any career is the ability to find the information you need to do your job. In school, you prepare for this task in nearly every class you take, as you search for information, evaluate its usefulness, compile it in a form that suits your goal, and present it—in essay, paper presentation, or lab experiment—to your instructors and fellow students.

The library and Internet are your main sources of information. This chapter will help you learn how to use both to find the information that you need. At the end of the chapter, you will be able to answer these questions:

- How can you make the most of your library?
- How do you use a search strategy to conduct research?
- How can you do research on the Internet?

DOING LIBRARY AND INTERNET RESEARCH

TAPPING INTO THE WORLD OF INFORMATION

> *"The human mind is our fundamental resource."*
>
> **John F. Kennedy**

How Can You Make the Most of Your Library?

A library is a home for information; consider it the "brain" of your college. Libraries contain a world of information—from every novel Salman Rushdie ever wrote to scholarship and financial aid directories to online job listings to medical journal articles on breast cancer research. It's all there waiting for you; your job is to find what you need as quickly and efficiently as you can.

START WITH A ROAD MAP

Most college libraries are bigger than high school and community libraries. You may feel lost on your first visit, or even a few visits after that. Make your life easier right away by learning how your library is organized. Although every library has a different layout, all libraries have certain areas in common:

- *Reference area.* Here you'll find reference books, including encyclopedias, public- and private-sector directories, dictionaries, almanacs, and atlases. You'll also find librarians or other library employees who can help direct you to the information you need. Computer terminals, containing the library's catalog of holdings, as well as online bibliographic and full-text databases, are usually part of the reference area.

- *Book area.* Books—and, in many libraries, magazines and journals in bound or boxed volumes—are stored in the *stacks*. A library with "open stacks" will allow you to search for materials on your own. In a "closed-stack" system, a staff member will retrieve materials for you.

- *Periodicals area.* Here you'll find recent issues of popular and scholarly magazines, journals, and newspapers. Most college libraries collect *periodicals* (magazines, journals, and newspapers published on a regular basis throughout the year), ranging from *Time* to *Advertising Age* to the *New England Journal of Medicine*. Because you usually cannot check out unbound periodicals, you may find photocopy machines nearby, where you can copy the pages that you need.

- *Audio/visual materials areas.* Many libraries have specialized areas for video, art and photography, and recorded music collections.

- *Computer areas.* Computer terminals, linked to databases and the Internet, are increasingly found in libraries and may be scattered throughout the building or set off in special areas. You may be able to access these databases and the Internet from the college's computer labs and writing centers, or even from your own computer if you have one.

- *Microform areas.* Most libraries have microform reading areas or rooms. Microforms are materials printed in reduced size on film, either *microfilm* (a reel of film) or *microfiche* (a sheet or card of film), that is read through special viewing machines. Many microform reading machines can print hard copies of stored images and text.

To learn about your college library, take a library tour or a training session. You might also ask for a pamphlet that describes the layout, and then take some time for a self-tour. Almost all college libraries offer some kind of orientation on how to use their books, periodicals, databases, and Internet hookups. If your school has a network of libraries, including one or more central libraries and other smaller, specialized libraries, explore each one you intend to use.

LEARN HOW TO CONDUCT AN INFORMATION SEARCH

The most successful and time-saving library research involves following a specific *search strategy*—a step-by-step method for finding information that takes you from general to specific sources. Starting with general sources usually works best because they provide an overview of your research topic and can lead you to more specific information and sources. For example, an encyclopedia article on the archaeological discovery of the Dead Sea Scrolls—manuscripts written between 250 B. C. and A. D. 68 that trace the roots of Judaism and Christianity—may mention that one of the most important books on the subject is *Understanding the Dead Sea Scrolls*, edited by Hershel Shanks (New York: Random House, 1992). This book, in turn, will lead you to 13 experts who wrote text chapters.

Defining your exact topic is critical to the success of your search. Although "the Dead Sea Scrolls" may be too broad for your research paper, narrower topic possibilities may include the following:

- How the Dead Sea Scrolls were discovered by Bedouin shepherds in 1947
- The historical origins of the scrolls
- The process archaeologists used to reconstruct scroll fragments

Conducting a Keyword Search

A *keyword search*—a search for information through the use of specific words and phrases related to the information—will help you narrow your topic. Use your library's computer database for keyword searches. For example, instead of searching through the broad category *Art*, you can use a keyword search to narrow your focus to *French Art* or more specifically to *French Art in the nineteenth century*.

Keyword searches are relatively easy because they use natural language, rather than specialized classification vocabulary. Table 10.1 includes some tips that will help you use the keyword system. The last three entries, describing how to use "or," "and," and "not" to narrow searches, describe what is called Boolean logic.

As you search, keep in mind that

- Double quotes around a word or phrase will locate the term exactly as you entered it ("financial aid").
- Using upper or lower case will not affect the search (*Scholarships* will find *scholarships*).
- Singular terms will find the plural (*scholarship* will find *scholarships*).

TABLE 10.1

How to perform an effective keyword search.

IF YOU ARE SEARCHING FOR	DO THIS	EXAMPLE
A word	Type the word normally.	aid
A phrase	Type the phrase in its normal word order (use regular word spacing) or surround the phrase with double quotation marks.	financial aid or "financial aid"
Two or more keywords without regard to word order	Type the words in any order, surrounding the words with quotation marks (use "and" to separate the words).	"financial aid" and "scholarships"
Topic A or topic B	Type the words in any order (use "or" to separate the words).	"financial aid" or "scholarships"
Topic A but not topic B	Type topic A first and then topic B (use "not" to separate the words).	"financial aid" not "scholarships"

How Do You Use a Search Strategy to Conduct Research?

Knowing where to look during each phase of your search will help you find information quickly and efficiently. A successful search strategy often starts with general reference works, then moves to more specific reference works, books, and periodicals (see Figure 10.1). Your search may also involve the use of electronic sources such as the Internet; you will learn more about Internet research in the second half of this chapter.

USE GENERAL REFERENCE WORKS

Begin your research with *general reference works*. These works cover hundreds—and sometimes thousands—of different topics in a broad, nondetailed way. General reference guides are often available online or on CD-ROM.

Among the works that fall into the general reference category are these:

- Encyclopedias such as the multivolume *Encyclopedia Americana* and the single-volume *New Columbia Encyclopedia*
- Almanacs such as the *World Almanac* and *Book of Facts*
- Yearbooks such as the *McGraw-Hill Yearbook of Science and Technology* and the *Statistical Abstract of the United States*
- Dictionaries such as *Webster's New World College Dictionary*

Library search strategy.

FIGURE

10.1

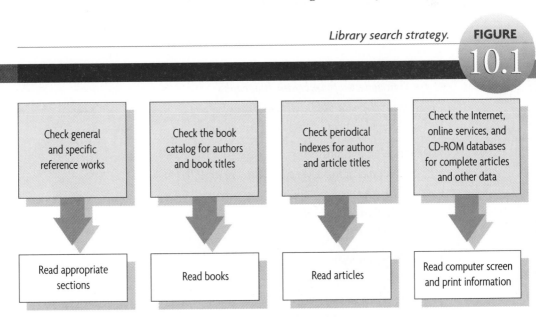

- Biographical reference works such as *American Writers, The New York Times Biographical Service, Webster's Biographical Dictionary,* and *Who's Who* (Various *Who's Who* editions are published for different geographic regions and fields, including art and music, finance, law, literature, and medicine.)
- Bibliographies such as *Books in Print* (especially the *Subject Guide to Books in Print*)

Scan these sources for an overview of your topic. Bibliographies at the end of encyclopedia articles may also lead to other important sources.

SEARCH SPECIALIZED REFERENCE WORKS

After you have an overview of your topic, *specialized reference works* will help you find more specific facts. Specialized reference works include encyclopedias and dictionaries that focus on a narrow field. Although the entries you find in these volumes are short summaries, they focus on critical ideas and on the keywords you will need to conduct additional research. Bibliographies that accompany the articles point to the names and works of recognized experts. Examples of specialized reference works, organized by subject, include the following:

1. Fine Arts (including music, art, film, television, and theatre)
   - *International Cyclopedia of Music and Musicians*
   - *Oxford Companion to Art*
   - *International Encyclopedia of Film*
   - *International Television Almanac*
   - *The McGraw-Hill Encyclopedia of World Drama*

2. History
   - *Dictionary of American Biography*
   - *Encyclopedia of American History*
   - *New Cambridge Modern History*

3. Science and Technology
   - *Encyclopedia of Computer Science and Technology*
   - *The Encyclopedia of Biological Sciences*
   - *The McGraw-Hill Encyclopedia of Science and Technology*
   - *Grzimek's Animal Life Encyclopedia*

4. Social Sciences
   - *Dictionary of Education*
   - *Encyclopedia of Psychology*
   - *International Encyclopedia of the Social Sciences*

5. Current Affairs
   - *Social Issues Resources Series (SIRS)*
   - *Great Contemporary Issues Series*
   - *Facts on File*

BROWSE THROUGH BOOKS ON YOUR SUBJECT

Use the *library catalog* to find books and other materials on your topic. The catalog tells you which publications the library owns and where they can be found. Before computers, most library catalogs consisted of endless cards filed in tiny drawers. Today most of these "card catalogs" have been replaced by online computer catalogs. When general and specialized reference works lead to a dead end, the catalog may provide a good topic overview.

Many school libraries now offer students the ability to search the card catalog and other databases from personal computers, enabling them to pull up full-text articles, abstracts, and other information from the comfort of their rooms. You can also reserve books via your personal computer and find them waiting for you at the library.

The library catalog contains a list of every library holding, searchable by author, title, and subject. For example, a library that owns *The Artist's Way: A Spiritual Path to Higher Creativity* by Julia Cameron may list the book in the author catalog under Cameron, Julia (last name first); in the title catalog, under *Artist's Way* (articles such as *the*, *a*, and *an* are dropped from the beginnings of titles and subjects); in the subject catalog under "Creative Ability—problems, exercises," "Self-actualization—psychology," and "Creation—literary, artistic." If you are using a keyword search, you may be able to find this book using "Art" and "Creativity" or "Art" and "Spirituality."

Library Classification Systems

Each catalog listing refers to the library's classification system, which tells you exactly where the publication can be found. Getting to know your library's system will help save time and trouble in your research because you will quickly know where to go to find what you need. The Dewey Decimal and Library of Congress systems are among the most common classification systems.

THE DEWEY DECIMAL SYSTEM classifies materials into 10 major subject categories (see Figure 10.2) and assigns each library holding a specific *call number*. For example, publications with call numbers between 100 and 199 deal with philosophy. Successive numbers and decimal points divide each major category into subcategories. The more specific the call number, the more targeted your search. For example, a book with a call number of 378 falls into the general social science category and into the subcategory of higher education. Student finances, a narrower topic, uses the call number 378.3.

FIGURE
10.2

The Dewey Decimal System.

CALL NUMBER	MAIN CLASSIFICATION CATEGORY
000–99	General works
100–199	Philosophy
200–299	Religion
300–399	Social sciences
400–499	Languages
500–599	Natural sciences
600–699	Technology and applied sciences
700–799	Fine arts
800–899	Literature
900–999	History and geography

THE LIBRARY OF CONGRESS SYSTEM uses a letter-based classification system to divide library holdings according to subject categories (see Figure 10.3). Each category is divided further into specialized subgroups through the addition of letters and numbers.

Become familiar with these classification systems. The more you know about how a library is organized, the more you can focus your research and avoid hours of needless effort.

FIGURE
10.3

The Library of Congress Subject Classification System.

CALL LETTER	MAIN CLASSIFICATION CATEGORY	CALL LETTER	MAIN CLASSIFICATION CATEGORY
A	General works	N	Fine arts
B	Philosophy and religion	P	Language–Literature (nonfiction)
C	History–Auxiliary sciences	Q	Sciences
D	History–Topography	R	Medicine
E–F	American history–Topography	S	Agriculture
G	Geography–Anthropology	T	Technology
H	Social sciences	U	Military science
J	Political sciences	V	Naval science
K	Law	Z	Bibliography and library science
L	Education	P–Z	Literature (fiction)
M	Music		

USE PERIODICAL INDEXES TO SEARCH FOR PERIODICALS

Because of their frequent publication, periodicals are a valuable source of current information. *Journals* are periodicals written for readers with special knowledge and expertise. Whereas *Newsweek* magazine may run a general-interest article on AIDS research, the *Journal of the American Medical Association* may print the original scientific study and direct the article to physicians and scientists. Many libraries display periodicals that are up to a year or two old and convert older copies to microfilm or microfiche. Some libraries also bind recent issues into volumes.

Periodical indexes will lead you to specific articles. There are many different indexes; only a few are mentioned here. One of the most widely used for general information is the *Reader's Guide to Periodical Literature*, available on CD-ROM and in book form. The *Reader's Guide* indexes articles from more than 240 general-interest magazines and newspapers. Many libraries also carry the *Reader's Guide Abstracts*, which includes article summaries.

You'll discover other general periodical indexes within the *Infotrac* family of databases (available online or on CD-ROM), including:

- *Magazine Index Plus*—an index, summaries, and full text of recent general-interest periodicals
- *Health Reference Center*—an index, summaries, and full text of journal articles, reference books, and pamphlets on health and medicine
- *General Business File*—an index, summaries, and full text of recent business and trade journals with company information and investment analysts' reports.

Another periodical database family—Ebsco Host—catalogs general and health-related periodicals.

Indexing information is listed in the *Standard Periodical Directory, Ulrich's International Periodicals Directory*, and in *Magazines for Libraries*, edited by Bill Katz. In addition, each database lists the magazines and periodicals it indexes. Because there is no all-inclusive index for technical, medical, and scholarly journal articles, you'll have to search indexes that specialize in such narrow subject areas as history, art, and psychology. Such indexes also include *abstracts* (article summaries), and can be found in electronic or book form. Here are just a few of the indexes you may find in your research:

ABI/Inform	Education Index
Applied Science and Technology	ERIC (Educational Resources Information Center)
Art Index	Film Literature Index
BIOSIS Previews	General Science Index
Business Periodicals Index	Hispanic American Periodicals Index
Child Development Abstracts and Bibliography	Historical Index

Humanities Index	Psychological Abstracts
Index Medicus	PsycINFO
Index to Legal Periodicals	Public Affairs Information Index
Index to United States Government Periodicals	Social Science Citation Index
Music Index	Social Science Index
Modern Language Association Bibliography	Women Studies Abstracts

You'll also find separate newspaper indexes at your library in print, microform, CD-ROM, or online. Some include many different newspapers, whereas others index a single publication:

Chicago Tribune Index	Christian Science Monitor Index
Dow Jones Index	National Newspaper Index
Index To Black Newspapers	Newspaper Abstracts OnDisc
Newsbank	New York Times Index
Wall Street Journal Index	Washington Post Index

Almost no library owns all the publications listed in these and other specialized indexes. However, journals that are not part of your library's collection or that are not available in full-text form online may be available through an interlibrary loan. The *interlibrary loan* is a process by which you can have your library request materials from another library. You can then use the materials at your library, but must return them by a specified date. Interlibrary loans can be helpful, but the amount of time you will have to wait for the materials can be unpredictable and may stretch out for weeks.

ASK THE LIBRARIAN

Librarians are information experts who can provide valuable assistance in solving research problems. They can help you locate unfamiliar or hard-to-find sources, navigate computer catalogs and databases, and uncover shortcuts in your research.

Say, for example, you are researching a gun-control bill that is currently before Congress, and you want to contact organizations on both sides of the issue. The librarian may lead you to the *Encyclopedia of Associations*, which lists the National Rifle Association, a pro-gun lobbying organization, and Handgun Control Inc., a gun-control group. By calling or e-mailing these groups or visiting their websites, you will get their information on current legislation.

Note that librarians are not the only helpful people in the library. For simplicity's sake, this book will use the word *librarian* to refer to both librarians and other staff members who are trained to help.

Among the specific services librarians provide are the following.

SEARCH SERVICES. Here are some tips on getting the best advice:

- *Be prepared.* Know what you're looking for so that you can make a specific request. Instead of asking for information on the American presidency, focus on the topic you expect to write about in your American history paper—for example, how President Franklin D. Roosevelt's physical disability may have affected his leadership during World War II.

- *Be willing to reach out.* Don't feel you have to do it all yourself. Librarians will help you, whether with basic sources or more difficult problems. Asking questions is a sign of willingness to learn, not weakness.

- *Ask for help when you can't find a specific source*—for example, when a specific book is not on the shelf. The librarian may direct you to another source that will work just as well.

INFORMATION SERVICES. Most libraries answer phone inquiries that can be quickly researched. For example, if you forget to write down the publisher and date of publication of Renee Blank and Sandra Slipp's book, *Voices of Diversity: Real People Talk about Problems and Solutions in a Workplace Where Everyone Is Not Alike*, call a staff member with the title and author.

INTERLIBRARY LOANS. If a publication is not available in your library, the librarian can arrange for an interlibrary loan.

USE CRITICAL THINKING TO EVALUATE EVERY SOURCE

If all information were equal, you could trust the accuracy of every book and article, and information from the Internet home page of the National Aeronautics and Space Administration (NASA) would have the same value as information from "Bob's Home Page on Aliens and Extraterrestrials." Because that isn't the case, use critical-thinking skills to evaluate research sources. Here are some critical-thinking questions to ask about every source:

- *Is the author a recognized expert?* A journalist who writes his first article on child development may not have the same credibility as an author of three child-development texts.

- *Does the author write from a particular perspective?* An article evaluating liberal democratic policies written by a Republican conservative would almost certainly have a bias.

- *Is the source recent enough for your purposes?* Whereas a history text published in 1990 on the U. S. Civil War will probably be accurate in the year 2000, a 1990 analysis of current computer technology will be hopelessly out-of-date at the turn of the century.

- *Are the author's sources reliable?* Where did the author get the information? Check the bibliography and footnotes not only for the number of sources listed but also for their quality. Find out whether they are reputable, established publications. If the work is based on *primary evidence*, the author's original work or direct observation, does solid proof support the conclusions? If it is based on *secondary evidence*, an analysis of the works of others, are the conclusions supported by evidence?

- *Have content experts reviewed articles submitted to academic and scientific journals before they were published?* Recognized journals have panels of experts who analyze the merits of every article's academic research before accepting the material for publication. For example, the editorial board of the *New England Journal of Medicine*, one of the country's leading medical journals, is made up of physicians who analyze every article's scientific merits and publish only those that meet the highest standards.

Critical-thinking skills are especially important when using the Internet. Accepting information you find there at face value—no matter the source—is often a mistake and may lead to incorrect conclusions.

The library is one of your college's most valuable resources, so take advantage of it. Your library research and critical-thinking skills will give you the ability to collect information, weigh alternatives, and make decisions. These skills will last a lifetime.

Some careers also require that you know how to do library research effectively; you may need to find a particular article in *The Washington Post* that reviewed your pharmaceutical company's latest drug, for example, or you may need to locate materials on depression for use in your counseling center. Your library research skills will help you research effectively. More

EXPERT INSIGHT

Be a Tenacious Researcher

Being a researcher is like being a bulldog. Research takes tenacity, it takes time, it takes sweat. Sometimes you'll be lucky and find exactly what you're looking for—it's right there and it's over and done with. In my experience, that doesn't happen too often. Whether you're researching a paper in history or English, or trying to uncover some information for a math or chemistry problem, it's going to take time and effort. My observation is that the more research that's done up front, the better the results at the end.

WAYNE KUNA, INVENTOR AND ENTREPRENEUR

and more often, though, workplace research takes place on the Internet because access is so widespread—and because the Internet portal is only as far as your computer.

How Can You Do Research on the Internet?

The *Internet* is a worldwide computer network that links businesses, universities, governments, and people. A miracle of technology, it can connect you to endless sources of information instantaneously—all while you sit in front of your computer terminal.

The Internet is becoming a frequently used research tool on college campuses. According to a survey of 1,200 students by Student Monitor, college students are spending an average of 8.1 hours online each week, and more than 44 percent of these students reported that researching was their highest-priority online activity.[1] With its speed and accessibility, the Web appeals to today's technology-oriented, time-crunched college students.

Because of its widespread reach through the ever-increasing sea of information, the Internet can be a helpful research tool—if used wisely. Like any tool, it has its advantages and disadvantages. The information in this section will help you to make the most of its good points and avoid the pitfalls.

THE BASICS

With a basic knowledge of the Internet, you can access facts and figures; read articles and other written materials; download files, software, and images; send typed messages electronically to others; and even "talk" to people in real time by typing messages that pop up on the screen as soon as you send them. The following is some information that you should know.

ACCESS. Users access the Internet through Internet Service Providers (ISPs). Some ISPs are commercial, such as America Online or Earthlink. Others are linked to companies, colleges, and other organizations. When you sign up with an ISP, you are given (or can choose) a *screen name*, which is the "address" that others can use to send you mail or files.

INFORMATION LOCATIONS. Much of the information on the Internet is displayed on "web pages" or "websites," individual locations in cyberspace developed by companies, government agencies, organizations, or individuals. Together, these sites are referred to as the *World Wide Web*. By visiting particular websites, you can do extensive research on any topic as well as buy, sell, and market products. Other "locations" where information resides include newsgroups (collections of messages from people interested in a particular topic), FTP (File Transfer Protocol) sites (such sites provide the means for you to download files), and other non-web sites that give you access to databases or library holdings (often stored by universities and government agencies using a system called "Gopher").

FINDING LOCATIONS.   Another kind of online address is the string of text and numbers that identifies a site on the Internet. These strings are called *URLs* (universal resource locators). You can type in a URL to access a specific site. On any given website you might also find a *hyperlink*—a URL that appears underlined and in a highlighted color—that you can click on to go directly to the location it lists.

One of the problems of the Internet is that it is an immense, constantly growing sea of information from sources of every level of reliability, not easily navigated by even the most savvy researcher. Now that you have some basic knowledge, explore how to search for information.

SEARCH DIRECTORIES AND SEARCH ENGINES

You will almost always need to use a system, or "tool," to find and select websites and other information locations likely to have the information you need. Usually, you will use either a *search directory* or a *search engine* to locate information or websites. Some details about the systems you will use and how to use them follows.

Search Directories

A search directory is an index of websites that allows you to search for topics using keywords. Its searching capabilities are limited to websites only. Search directories are basically large collections of websites sorted by category, much in the way that the Yellow Pages organizes business telephone numbers.

When searching, you might want to start with a search directory first because the results may be more manageable than with a search engine (search engines can produce a large number of "hits"—occurrences of your keyword). Some of the most popular and effective search directories include (names and URLs):

- Yahoo (http://www.yahoo.com)
- Galaxy (http://galaxy.einet.net/galaxy.html)
- Snap (http://www.snap.com)
- Excite (http://www.excite.com)
- Magellan (http://mckinley.com)

Each search directory has its own particular features. Some have different search options (simple search, advanced search); some are known for having strong lists of sites for particular topics; some have links that connect you to lists of sites that fall under particular categories. The search directory's website will help you learn how to best use the directory.

Search Engines

Slightly different than search directories, a search engine searches for keywords through the entire Internet—newsgroups, websites, and other resources—instead of just websites. This gives you wider access but may yield an enormous list of hits unless you know how to limit your search effectively.

Some useful search engines include:

- AltaVista (http://altavista.com)
- HotBot (http://www.hotbot.com)
- Lycos (http://www.lycos.com)
- GoTo (http://www.goto.com)
- Ask Jeeves (http://www.askjeeves.com)

As with search directories, each search engine has its own set of resources and its own particular helpful search tools and guides.

Search Strategy

Although any search may take you in a unique direction, start with this basic search strategy when researching online.

1. Think carefully about what you want to locate. Professor Eliot Soloway of the University of Michigan School of Education recommends that you first phrase your search in the form of a question, for example, What vaccines are given to children before the age of 5? Then he advises you to consider what the important words in that question are (vaccines, children, before the age of 5). Write them down; then write down other words you can think of that may be related to those words (chicken pox, tetanus, polio, shot, pediatrics, and so on). This will give you a useful collection of words to use in different combinations as you search.[2]

2. Use a search directory to isolate a list of sites under your desired topic or category. Save the sites that look as though they might have information useful to you (most Internet service providers have a way for you to save or "bookmark" sites that you want to be able to find again).

3. Explore these sites to get a general idea of what's out there. If by chance your search is fairly general and the directory takes you

where you need to go, you're in luck. More often in academic research situations, though, you will need to dig deeper and range farther. Use what you have found in the search directory to note useful keywords and information locations.

4. Move on to a search engine to narrow your search. Use your keywords in a variety of ways to come up with as many possibilities as you can.

   - Vary their order if you are using more than one. (For example, search under *education, college, statistics* and *statistics, education, college.*)

   - Use *Boolean operators.* The words "and," "not," and "or" limit your search specifically (see Table 10.1). You can also use plus or minus signs in a similar way—a plus sign will include the word (dogs +terriers) while a minus sign will exclude it (dogs -terriers). Make sure you have no space between the sign and the word to which it refers.

   - Put quotation marks around a word or phrase that you want to find *exactly as it appears* (for this reason, be sure your spelling is correct). For example, typing the words *The Cold War* may find documents that mention any one of those words in any context, but "The Cold War" will only find documents that include that exact phrase.

5. Evaluate the list of links that pop up. If there are too many, narrow your search by using more keywords or by being more specific with your keywords (*Broadway* could become *Broadway musical theatre* or *Broadway* AND *"fall season"* AND *2001*). If there are too few or none that seem useful, broaden your search by using fewer or different keywords.

6. Bookmark the links that you think you will be able to use. This will enable you to go right back to them without having to go through the search process again.

7. When you think you are done, choose another search directory or search engine and perform your search again—just to be sure. Because different systems have access to different information, you never know what may appear.

NON-WEB RESOURCES

The web is not your only source of information. Newsgroups and Gopher can also help you achieve your research goals.

Newsgroups

Usenet, the system of *newsgroups,* is a series of "bulletin boards" where users can type in messages and "post" them on the newsgroup. Then other users can read posts and respond to them. Posts are grouped in "threads" (a thread is a series of posts that follow, and are in response to, one particular topic or post). Like chat rooms, newsgroups focus on individual topics—and there are thousands, from silent film stars to modern architecture to text fonts.

When you search newsgroups, you may want to post a question to the newsgroup and start a new thread, or look at the titles of existing threads to see if your question has already been discussed there. Chances are, the more specific your question, the better your chances of getting a coherent answer. Looking through threads may ultimately reward you with information; on the downside, however, it often takes a good deal of time and patience because you can only search post by post within a thread that may be as long as a few hundred posts.

Be careful to choose your newsgroups carefully when researching. Many newsgroups are more recreational than information-focused. For example, if you are looking for information on plants, *sci.bio.botany* will probably be more of a pertinent scientific resource ("Second European Symposium on Aerobiology" reads one thread) than *rec.gardens.edible* (with threads like "couple of green tomatoes"). Every newsgroup has a helpful FAQ (Frequently Asked Questions list) that you should read before you post. You may also want to "lurk" a while (read posts without posting yourself) to get a better sense of what the newsgroup is all about.

Gopher Searches

There are over 5,500 known Gopher servers, or sites, mostly located on campuses or at government agencies (the name comes from the mascot of the University of Minnesota, where the Gopher system was developed). These servers contain data and archived writings available to the public for searching and retrieval. The data is arranged much like in a library, with keywords that refer to sections, divided repeatedly into subsections, even-

During school you're given research assignments, theme papers, and so on. The research skills that you learn in school are directly transferable to what you do at work. Work projects may involve interviewing people, researching on the web, library research, taking a look at costs, providing input on support levels, and more. All of this is basic research.

These basic skills—being inquisitive and using the library, the Internet, and other people to uncover information—will do well for you in school and later on in life.

VICTOR YIPP, COMMONWEALTH EDISON

EXPERT INSIGHT

Build Research Skills for the Real World

tually arriving at the smallest segments of information. Gopher is not as flashy as the World Wide Web, and many former users of Gopher have transferred their material to websites. However, quite a few institutions only offer their information through Gopher.

Particular tools are useful for searching Gopher sites. One is called *Veronica*, which helps to match your keywords to long and detailed Gopher entries. Veronica does for your Gopher search what a search engine does for your website search—it helps you sort through the vast amounts of information. You can access Veronica through your ISP. Look for "Gopher Worldwide" to find a list of the servers, organized by continent, country, and organization.

BE A CRITICAL RESEARCHER

Researching on the Internet is not without its problems. The Internet has millions of web pages and sites containing information from a huge variety of sources—everything from the federal government to random individuals creating sites from their home computers. No one sorts through the sites and decides which are valid, current, or important enough to stay—anyone can make any kind of information available. That leaves it up to you to evaluate the truth and usefulness of the information you find.

If you are informed about the potential pitfalls and do your best to avoid them, you will get the most from your time and effort. Critical thinking is the key to making sure you get valid information from Internet resources. Watch for the following issues.

CHANGING INFORMATION.   Change is swift and rampant on the Internet— new information arrives every day, and old information may or may not be removed or updated. This makes it difficult to know if the information you find is the most valid and current available. Floyd H. Johnson, at a conference on Society and the Future of Computing, commented on the changeable nature of information on the Internet. He identifies two change-based issues[3]:

- *Fluidity of information.* What is available one day when you surf the Internet may not be available the next. Even if it is available, it may have changed overnight. URLs routinely work one week and then are completely inaccessible the next.
- *Aging of information.* With the rapid changes taking place in today's world, many people and organizations have neither the time nor the personnel to keep their websites or Gopher sites updated. Dates on sites are often obscure or nonexistent. Therefore, you may access— and mistakenly use—outdated information without knowing it.

VALIDITY OF INFORMATION.   As a researcher, you need to carefully evaluate the validity of the information you find. Johnson also identifies four validity-based issues[4]:

- *Authority.* Authorship of Internet information is often difficult to determine. It isn't easy to distinguish an experienced, credentialed professor from a random prankster.
- *Authenticity.* Nothing stops any author of an Internet document from lying about who they are or what credentials they have.
- *Security/Ownership.* Anyone can copy someone else's material and put it on the Web, claiming it as their own, without being caught.
- *Documentation.* Because it is such a new phenomenon, there are no established standards for citing Internet resources.

TECHNOLOGICAL PROBLEMS. Technology is great—when it works. Ideally, you should be able to access the information you want in the blink of an eye. Unfortunately, however, this is not always the case. Your modem speed may be slow for the searching you are doing. Your ISP may have technical difficulties that prevent you from logging on, make you wait a long time to access sites, or result in your being disconnected from the service without warning. Websites may be inaccessible because they have moved, have been deleted, are having tech trouble, or are simply too busy and cannot handle the overload. It can be incredibly frustrating to find what you think is the perfect site for your research, only to be met with "Cannot connect" or "Unable to find."

The answer to all of these problems lies in your critical-thinking ability. Consider them to be challenges that you have the power to meet. Address them using the following strategies[5]:

EVALUATE THE SOURCE. Note the website name and the organization that creates and maintains the site where you have located the information. Is the organization reputable? Is it known as an authority on the topic you are researching? If you are not sure of the source, the URL will usually give you a clue. For example, URLs ending in *.edu* originate at an educational institution, and *.gov* sites originate at government agencies.

EVALUATE THE AUTHOR. Look carefully to find out who exactly wrote the article or gathered and compiled the data. Again, think about whether this author is reliable and reputable in the field (refer back to the material on evaluating library sources on p. 269). What are the author's credentials? If you cannot find any indication of credentials or affiliation, that may be a warning in and of itself.

EVALUATE THE MATERIAL. Can you tell if the material is valid and accurate? Evaluate it the way you would evaluate any other material you read (see Chapters 4 and 6 for more detail on how to critically evaluate reading material). See if sources are noted and if you trust them. Is the source a published document (newspaper article or professional journal article), or is it simply one person's point of view? Can you verify the data by comparing it to any other material? Pay attention, also, to the general quality of the material. Text that has errors in grammar or spelling, is poorly organized, or contains mistaken names or dates is likely to be unreliable.

Perhaps your best bet is to combine library and Internet resources. Remember that the library is laid out using an established system and may be more navigable than the tangle of Internet sites. Plus, library employees are there to help you in person, and sometimes that kind of one-on-one assistance can be more valuable than any hyperlink or Boolean operator. You might want to seek out library materials to help you verify the authenticity of what you discover on the Internet.

Your awake mind is your greatest asset in researching on the Internet. Take advantage of the wealth of material it has to offer you—but take your time and be picky. Your work is only as strong as the materials with which you build it. If you work to make sure your research is valid and comprehensive, your work will reflect that care.

Testa dura

An Italian parent might use this phrase, literally meaning "hardhead," to describe the attitude of a stubborn child. People who are single-mindedly determined to have something or do something and won't give up until they have reached the goal might be seen as hardheaded. Even though the phrase is often used in a somewhat negative way, there are some positive aspects to being a *testa dura*. The accompanying determination, strength, and patience can make hardheadedness a useful trait.

Think of the concept of *testa dura* as you pursue your research goals. Research can take you down paths that lead to dead ends and information that is useless to you. Libraries can be overwhelming; the Internet can connect you with sources that are neither accurate nor reputable. When you are tempted to give up, or to use information that is substandard, make the decision to be hardheaded. Stay the course; take the time to press on and exhaust every resource until you have found what will truly make your work the best it can be. The determination of *testa dura* will take you far.

Study Skills in Action

Test Competence

MEASURING WHAT YOU'VE LEARNED

MULTIPLE CHOICE. *Circle or highlight the answer that seems to fit best.*

1. The periodical area in the library holds
   A. the latest books listed in the library's card catalog.
   B. sequels to films in the library's video collection.
   C. reference works, including encyclopedias.
   D. recent issues of popular and scholarly magazines, journals, and newspapers.

2. A keyword search relies on
   A. a well-developed, extensive knowledge of your subject.
   B. your ability to identify specific words and phrases related to your subject.
   C. knowing how to "key" information into the computer.
   D. your mastery of specialized classification vocabulary.

3. A library search strategy will take you from
   A. specific reference works to general reference works.
   B. general reference works to specific reference works.
   C. encyclopedias to almanacs.
   D. encyclopedias to the Internet.

4. You should seek help from a librarian
   A. only after you've spent hours researching with little success.
   B. only when you can't find a particular source.
   C. when you're having trouble navigating the library's computer databases.
   D. early or late in the day when the librarian is more available.

5. Using critical thinking to evaluate sources involves investigating all of the following **except**
   A. the level of expertise of the author.
   B. how the material is coded in the library.
   C. the reliability of the source.
   D. whether the source is updated.

6. Which of the following is **not** a commonly used Internet abbreviation?
   A. ITP
   B. WWW
   C. FTP
   D. URL

7. College students who use computers consider which of the following their highest priority activity?
   A. chatting
   B. sending e-mail
   C. conducting online research
   D. sending digital photographs

8. All of the following are search engines **except**
   A. AltaVista
   B. Lycos
   C. HotBot
   D. Magellan

9. A usenet newsgroup is
   A. a chat room.
   B. a World Wide Web site.
   C. a series of virtual bulletin boards.
   D. an Internet user's manual.

10. When evaluating the validity of information you find on the Internet, you should look at all of the following **except**
    A. the authenticity of the information.
    B. the authority of the author.
    C. how well the article is written.
    D. the author's documentation of sources.

TRUE/FALSE. *Place a T or an F beside each statement to indicate whether you think it is true or false.*

1. _____ To learn about your school's library, it is a good idea to take a library tour.

2. _____ General reference works usually yield few additional research leads.

3. _____ The library card catalog will help you find all the cataloged material in the library's collection.

4. _____ The *Reader's Guide to Periodical Literature* indexes specialized, academic journals.

5. _____ Internet sources are not always reliable.

Brain Power

BUILDING VOCABULARY FITNESS

The paragraphs below are taken from the current media. Read the paragraph, noting the context of the vocabulary words shown in bold type. Next, for each vocabulary word (reprinted in the left-hand column), highlight the word or phrase in column A, B, or C that is the most similar in meaning. Finally, on a separate sheet of paper, solidify your understanding of these words by using each in a sentence of your own.

> Play comes in many forms—**solitary,** social and physical. In humans it can be a purely mental activity. Its key identifying feature is its apparent lack of serious purpose or immediate goal.
>
> But dig deeper and there is much to be learned from play: the biology of play has implications for the way people and organizations behave in many **spheres,** including the business world. In particular, play has something to say about **innovation** and job satisfaction. . . .
>
> Play is **quintessentially** associated with having fun, the **antithesis** of work. . . . Many businesses have noticed that playful, happy people are more motivated, more loyal and more productive. Some companies, including The Body Shop, have even incorporated fun into their mission statements. It follows then that a business wanting to identify areas with **incipient** problems should look where people have stopped playing and laughing.
>
> From "Why All Work and No Play Can Be Bad for Business," by Patrick Bateson and Paul Martin, *The Financial Times*, April 8, 2000, p. Weekend FT IX. Copyright © Patrick Bateson. Used with permission of the author.

Vocabulary Words

	A	B	C
1. **solitary**	done alone	done quietly	emotional
2. **spheres**	classrooms	environments	marketplaces
3. **innovation**	job satisfaction	risk-taking	positive change
4. **quintessentially**	characteristically	sometimes	barely
5. **antithesis**	bedrock	converse	spirit
6. **incipient**	budding	systemic	serious

Strategic Thinking

GETTING THE BIG PICTURE

Answer the following questions on a separate piece of paper or in a journal.

Think of a time you spent researching a topic in the library. What parts of the library search strategy did you use? What role did the Internet play in your research? How did you use your critical-thinking skills to evaluate sources? Did you ask the librarian for help? What steps can you take to improve the efficiency and reliability of your research? How do you think acquiring solid research skills will impact the work you do in your chosen career?

NOTES

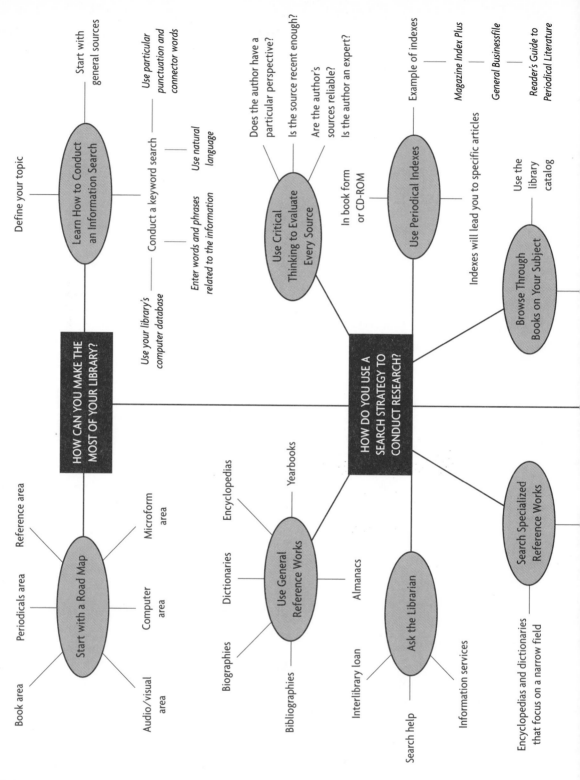

HOW CAN YOU MAKE THE MOST OF YOUR LIBRARY?

Learn How to Conduct an Information Search
- Define your topic
- Start with general sources
- Conduct a keyword search
  - Use particular punctuation and connector words
  - Use natural language
  - Enter words and phrases related to the information
- Use your library's computer database

Start with a Road Map
- Reference area
- Book area
- Periodicals area
- Computer area
- Microform area
- Audio/visual area

HOW DO YOU USE A SEARCH STRATEGY TO CONDUCT RESEARCH?

Use Critical Thinking to Evaluate Every Source
- Does the author have a particular perspective?
- Is the source recent enough?
- Are the author's sources reliable?
- Is the author an expert?

Use Periodical Indexes
- Example of indexes
  - Magazine Index Plus
  - General Businessfile
  - Reader's Guide to Periodical Literature
- In book form or CD-ROM
- Indexes will lead you to specific articles

Browse Through Books on Your Subject
- Use the library catalog

Use General Reference Works
- Encyclopedias
- Yearbooks
- Dictionaries
- Almanacs
- Biographies
- Bibliographies

Ask the Librarian
- Interlibrary loan
- Search help
- Information services

Search Specialized Reference Works
- Encyclopedias and dictionaries that focus on a narrow field

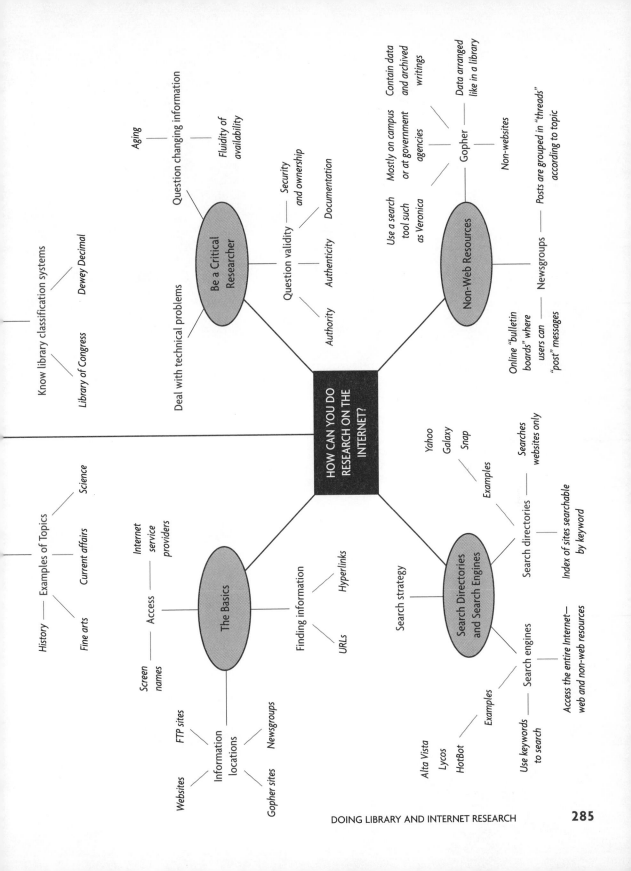

HOW CAN YOU DO RESEARCH ON THE INTERNET?

Be a Critical Researcher
- Know library classification systems
  - Dewey Decimal
  - Library of Congress
- Deal with technical problems
- Question changing information
  - Aging
  - Fluidity of availability
- Question validity
  - Security and ownership
  - Documentation
  - Authenticity
  - Authority

Non-Web Resources
- Gopher
  - Contain data and archived writings
  - Data arranged like in a library
  - Non-websites
  - Use a search tool such as Veronica
  - Mostly on campus or at government agencies
- Newsgroups
  - Posts are grouped in "threads" according to topic
  - Online "bulletin boards" where users can "post" messages

The Basics
- Access
  - Examples of Topics
    - History
    - Fine arts
    - Current affairs
    - Science
  - Internet service providers
  - Screen names
- Finding information
  - Hyperlinks
  - URLs
- Information locations
  - Websites
  - FTP sites
  - Gopher sites
  - Newsgroups

Search Directories and Search Engines
- Search strategy
- Search directories
  - Examples
    - Yahoo
    - Galaxy
    - Snap
  - Searches websites only
  - Index of sites searchable by keyword
- Search engines
  - Use keywords to search
  - Examples
    - Alta Vista
    - Lycos
    - HotBot
  - Access the entire Internet—web and non-web resources

EXPRESS

Words, joined to form ideas, are tools that have enormous power. Whether you write a research paper, a short essay, a memo to a supervisor, or an extensive report about your field for a trade journal, words allow you to take your ideas out of the realm of thought and give them a form that other people can read and consider. In class or at work, writing well will help you truly understand what you take in and express what you learn, showing the potential of your mind.

This chapter will help you learn how to use words to construct understandable ideas. At the end of the chapter, you will be able to answer these questions:

- Why does good writing matter?
- What are the elements of effective writing?
- What is the writing process?

EFFECTIVE WRITING
COMMUNICATING YOUR MESSAGE
THROUGH THE WRITTEN WORD

"Clear a space for the writing voice . . . you cannot will this to happen. It is a matter of persistence and faith and hard work. So you might as well just go ahead and get started."

Anne Lamott

Why Does Good Writing Matter?

In school, almost any course you take will require you to communicate your knowledge and thought processes by writing essays or papers. To express yourself successfully, you need good writing skills. Knowing how to write and express your ideas is essential outside school as well. Those who see your writing, whether instructors, supervisors, or coworkers, judge your thinking ability based on what you write and how you write it. Good writing skills will help you achieve the goals you set out to accomplish with each writing task, whether it is educational, professional, or personal.

Your knowledge of reading and critical thinking are essential to your writing. First of all, reading the work of other writers helps you learn words, experience concepts, and discover the different ways that a writer can put words together to express ideas. In addition, critical reading generates new ideas you can use in your writing. Secondly, a clear thought process is the best preparation for a well-written document. Your critical-thinking skills will help you organize ideas so that your readers can understand them.

You may consider writing to be more of a final product of your study efforts than a study skill on its own. However, it is most emphatically a study skill, and a very important one. Writing is an essential ingredient in how you take in information and how you retain it as well as how you express it. When you write well, your notes are comprehensive and understandable. When you write well, you fulfill expectations on essay tests (as you will see in Chapter 13). When you write well, you solidify knowledge as you rewrite notes, write summaries, and compile study sheets in preparation for tests.

To keep things simple, this chapter focuses primarily on the writing of an essay. However, the skills involved can apply to nearly any writing situation you encounter in your studies or your career. As you read, ask critical-thinking questions about how you would apply what you are learning: "How might I use freewriting for an essay test? How might brainstorming help me in a study group session? How will knowing my audience help me write a grant proposal for my organization?"

The written documents you leave with a company may be your most lasting calling card. If your documents are incorrect, messy, or poorly organized, they will leave a negative impression. No matter how well you do in a face-to-face meeting, your cover letter, resume, and other work-related documents are a record that memorializes who you are. Make sure it is your best work.

JUNE BROWN, OLIVE-HARVEY COLLEGE

EXPERT INSIGHT

Leave a Lasting Impression at Job Interviews with Your Writing

What Are the Elements of Effective Writing?

Every writing situation is different, depending on three elements. Your goal is to understand each element before you begin to write:

- *Your purpose.* What do you want to accomplish with this particular piece of writing?
- *Your topic.* What is the subject about which you will write?
- *Your audience.* Who will read your writing?

Figure 11.1 shows how these elements depend on one another. As a triangle needs three points to be complete, a piece of writing needs these three elements. Consider purpose and audience even before you begin to plan. Topic will come into play during the planning stage (the first stage of the writing process).

The three elements of writing. **FIGURE**

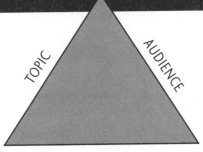

PURPOSE

WRITING PURPOSE

Writing without having a clear purpose is like driving without deciding where you want to go. You'll get somewhere, but chances are it won't be the right place. Therefore, when you write, always decide what you want to accomplish before you start. Although there are many different writing purposes, the two you will most commonly use for school and on the job are to inform and to persuade.

The purpose of *informative writing* is to present and explain ideas. A research paper on how hospitals use donated blood to save lives informs readers without trying to mold opinions. The writer presents facts in an unbiased way, without introducing a particular point of view. Most newspaper articles, except on the opinion and editorial pages, are examples of informative writing.

Persuasive writing has the purpose of convincing readers to adopt your point of view. For example, as the health editor of a magazine, you write a column attempting to persuade readers to give blood. Examples of persuasive writing include newspaper editorials, business proposals, and books and magazine articles with a point of view.

KNOWING YOUR AUDIENCE

In almost every case, a writer creates written material so that others can read it. The writer and audience are partners in this process. Knowing who your audience is will help you communicate successfully.

Key Questions About Your Audience

In school, your primary audience is your instructors. For many assignments, instructors will want you to assume that they are typical readers. Writing for "typical readers" usually means that you should be as complete as possible in your explanations. You may also write for "informed readers" who know a great deal about your topic. At work, your audience may be coworkers, supervisors, customers or clients, or others. In every case, ask yourself some or all of the following questions to help you define your readers' needs:

- What are my readers' ages, cultural backgrounds, interests, and experiences?
- What are their roles? Are they instructors, students, employers, customers?
- How much do they know about my topic? Are they experts in the field or beginners?
- Are they interested, or do I have to convince them to read what I write?
- Can I expect my audience to have open or closed minds?

After you answer the questions about your audience, take what you have discovered into consideration as you write.

Your Commitment to Your Audience

Your goal is to communicate—to organize your ideas so that readers can follow them. Suppose, for example, you are writing an informative research paper for a nonexpert audience on using Internet job banks to get a job. One way to accomplish your goal is to first explain what these employment services are and the kinds of help they offer, then describe each service in detail, and finally conclude with how these services will change job hunting in the twenty-first century.

Effective and successful writing involves following the steps of the writing process.

What Is the Writing Process?

The writing process provides an opportunity for you to state and refine your thoughts until you have expressed yourself as clearly as possible. Critical thinking plays an important role every step of the way. The four main parts of the process are planning, drafting, revising, and editing.

PLANNING

Planning gives you a chance to think about what to write and how to write it. Planning involves brainstorming for ideas, defining and narrowing your topic by using *prewriting strategies* (techniques for generating ideas about a topic and finding out how much you already know before you start), conducting research if necessary, writing a thesis statement, and writing a working outline. Although these steps are listed in sequence, in real life the steps overlap one another as you plan your document.

Open Your Mind Through Brainstorming

Whether your instructor assigns a partially defined topic (novelist Amy Tan) or a general category within which you make your own choice (women authors), you should brainstorm to develop ideas about what you want to write. Brainstorming is a creative technique that involves generating ideas about a subject without making judgments (see p. 90).

First, let your mind wander. Write down anything on the assigned subject that comes to mind, in no particular order. Then, organize that list into an outline or think link that helps you see the possibilities more clearly. To make the outline or think link, separate list items into general ideas

FIGURE

11.2

Part of a brainstorming outline.

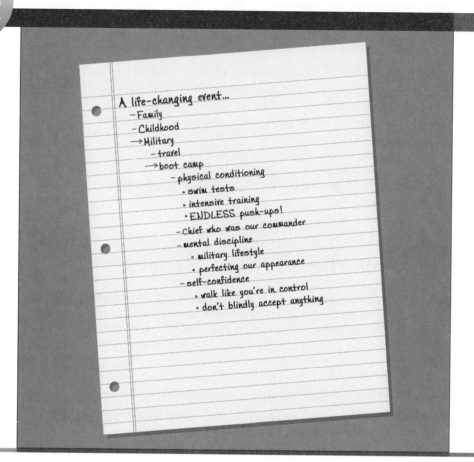

A life-changing event...
- Family
- Childhood
→ Military
  - travel
→ boot camp
    - physical conditioning
      • swim tests
      • intensive training
      • ENDLESS push-ups!
    - Chief who was our commander
    - mental discipline
      • military lifestyle
      • perfecting our appearance
    - self-confidence
      • walk like you're in control
      • don't blindly accept anything

or categories and subideas or examples. Then associate the subideas or examples with the ideas they support or fit. Figure 11.2 shows a portion of an outline that student Michael B. Jackson constructed from his brainstorming list. The assignment is a five-paragraph essay on a life-changing event. Here, only the subject that Michael eventually chose is shown broken down into different ideas.

Narrow Your Topic Through Prewriting Strategies

When your brainstorming has generated some possibilities, narrow your topic. Focus on the subideas and examples from your brainstorming session. Because they are relatively specific, they will be more likely to point you toward possible topics. Choose one or more subideas or examples that you like and explore them by using prewriting strategies such as brainstorming, freewriting, and asking journalists' questions.[1] Prewriting strategies will help you decide which of your possible topics you would most like to pursue.

BRAINSTORMING.   The same process you used to generate ideas will also help you narrow your topic further. Generate thoughts about the possibility you have chosen and write them down. Then, organize them into categories, noticing any patterns that appear. See if any of the subideas or examples seem as if they might make good topics.

FREEWRITING.   Another technique that encourages you to put ideas on paper as they occur to you is called *freewriting*. When you freewrite, you write whatever comes to mind without censoring ideas or worrying about grammar, spelling, punctuation, or organization. Freewriting helps you think creatively and gives you an opportunity to begin weaving in information you know. Freewrite on the subideas or examples you have created to see if you want to pursue any of them. Here is a sample of freewriting:

> Boot camp for the Coast Guard really changed my life. First of all, I really got in shape. We had to get up every morning at 5 A.M., eat breakfast, and go right into training. We had to do endless military-style push-ups—but we later found out that these have a purpose, to prepare us to hit the deck in the event of enemy fire. We had a lot of aquatic tests, once we were awakened at 3 A.M. to do one in full uniform! Boot camp also helped me to feel confident about myself and be disciplined. Chief Marzloff was the main person who made that happen. He was tough but there was always a reason. He got angry when I used to nod my head whenever he would speak to me, he said that made it seem like I was blindly accepting whatever he said, which was a weakness. From him I have learned to keep an eye on my body's movements when I communicate. I learned a lot more from him too.

ASKING JOURNALISTS' QUESTIONS.   When journalists begin work on a story, they ask themselves Who? What? Where? When? Why? and How? You can use these *journalists' questions* to focus your thinking. Ask these questions about any subidea or example to discover what you may want to discuss.

Who?	Who was at boot camp? Who influenced me the most?
What?	What about boot camp changed my life? What did we do?
When?	When in my life did I go to boot camp, and for how long? When did we fulfill our duties?
Where?	Where was camp located? Where did we spend our day-to-day time?
Why?	Why did I decide to go there? Why was it such an important experience?
How?	How did we train in the camp? How were we treated? How did we achieve success?

As you prewrite, keep an eye on paper length, assignment due date, and any other requirements (such as topic area or purpose). These requirements influence your choice of a final topic. For example, if you have a month to write an informative 20-page paper on a learning disability, you might discuss the symptoms, effects, and treatment of attention deficit disorder (ADD). If you have a week to write a five-page persuasive essay, you might write about how elementary students with ADD need special training. If you are writing about ADD for a professional journal, you may also have a word limit and a due date to get your work in before the publishing deadline.

Prewriting will help you develop a topic broad enough to give you something with which to work but narrow enough to be manageable. Prewriting also helps you see what you know and what you don't know. If your assignment requires more than you already know, you may need to do research.

Conduct Research

Some college writing, such as an opinion essay or exam essay, will rely on what you already know about a subject. In these cases, prewriting strategies may generate all the ideas and information you need. In other writing situations, outside sources are necessary. Try doing your research in stages. In the first stage, look for a basic overview that can lead to a thesis statement. In the second stage, go into more depth, tracking down information that will help you fill in gaps and complete your thoughts. Chapter 10 goes into detail about how to research effectively.

Write a Thesis Statement

Your work up until this point has prepared you to write a thesis statement, the central message you want to communicate. The thesis statement states your subject and point of view, reflects your writing purpose and audience, and acts as the organizing principle of your paper. It tells your readers what they should expect to read. Here is an example from Michael's paper:

Topic	Coast Guard boot camp
Purpose	To inform
Audience	Instructor with unknown knowledge about the topic
Thesis statement	Chief Marzloff, our Basic Training Company Commander at the U. S. Coast Guard Basic Training Facility, shaped my life through physical conditioning, developing my self-confidence, and instilling strong mental discipline.

A thesis statement is just as important in a short document, such as a letter, as it is in a long paper. For example, when you write a job application letter, a clear thesis statement will help you tell the recruiter why you deserve the job.

Write a Working Outline

The final step in the preparation process is writing a working outline. Use this outline as a loose guide instead of a final structure. As you draft your paper, your ideas and structure may change many times. Only by allowing changes and refinements to occur can you get closer and closer to what you really want to say. Some students prefer a more formal outline structure, while others like to use a think link. Choose whatever form suits you best.

Create a Checklist

Use the checklist in Table 11.1 to make sure your preparation is complete. Under Date Due, create your own writing schedule, giving each task an intended completion date. Work backward from the date the assignment is due and estimate how long it will take to complete each step. Refer to Chapter 3 for time-management skills that will help you schedule your writing process.

As you develop your schedule, remember that you'll probably move back and forth between tasks. You might find yourself doing two and even three things on the same day. Stick to the schedule as best you can, while balancing the other demands of your busy life, and check off your accomplishments on the list as you complete them.

DRAFTING

Some people aim for perfection when they write a first draft. They want to get everything right—from word choice to tone to sentence structure to paragraph organization to spelling, punctuation, and grammar. Try to

Preparation checklist.

TABLE 11.1

DATE DUE	TASK	COMPLETED
	Brainstorm	
	Define and narrow	
	Use prewriting strategies	
	Conduct research if necessary	
	Write thesis statement	
	Write working outline	
	Complete research	

resist this tendency because it may lead you to shut the door on ideas before you even know they are there.

A *first draft* involves putting ideas down on paper for the first time—but not the last. You may write many different versions of the assignment until you do one you like. Each version moves you closer to communicating exactly what you want to say in the way you want to say it. It is as if you started with a muddy pond and gradually cleared the mud away until your last version became a clear body of water, showing the rocks and the fish beneath the surface. Think of your first draft as a way of establishing the pond before you start clearing it up.

The process of writing a first draft includes freewriting, crafting an introduction, organizing the ideas in the body of the paper, formulating a conclusion, citing sources, and soliciting feedback. When you think of drafting, it might help you to imagine that you are creating a kind of "writing sandwich." The bottom slice of bread is the introduction, the top slice is the conclusion, and the sandwich stuffing is made of central ideas and supporting examples (see Figure 11.3).

Freewriting Your Draft

If the introduction, body, and conclusion are the three parts of the sandwich, freewriting is the process of searching the refrigerator for the ingredients and laying them all on the table. Take everything that you have

FIGURE 11.3   *The "writing sandwich."*

developed in the planning stages and freewrite a very rough draft. Don't censor yourself. For now, don't consciously think about your introduction, conclusion, or structure within the paper's body. Focus on getting your ideas out of the realm of thought and onto the paper, in whatever form they prefer to be at the moment.

When you have the beginnings of a paper in your hands, you can start to shape it into something with a more definite form. First, work on how you want to begin.

Writing an Introduction

The introduction tells your readers what the rest of the paper will contain. A thesis statement is essential. Here, for example, is a draft of an introduction for Michael's paper about the Coast Guard. The thesis statement is underlined at the end of the paragraph:

> Chief Marzloff took on the task of shaping the lives and careers of the youngest, newest members of the U. S. Coast Guard. During my eight weeks in training, he was my father, my instructor, my leader, and my worst enemy. He took his job very seriously and demanded that we do the same. <u>The Chief was instrumental in conditioning our bodies, developing our self-confidence, and instilling mental discipline.</u>

When you write an introduction, you might try to draw the reader in with an anecdote—a story that is related to the thesis. You can try other *hooks* (elements that catch the reader's attention and encourage him to want to continue to read), including a relevant quotation, dramatic statistics, a pertinent story, and questions that encourage critical thinking. Whatever strategy you choose, link it to your thesis statement.

After you have an introduction that seems to set up the purpose of your paper, make sure the body fulfills that purpose.

Creating the Body of a Paper

The body of the paper contains your central ideas and supporting evidence. *Evidence*—proof that informs or persuades—consists of the facts, statistics, examples, and expert opinions that you know or have gathered during research.

Look at the array of ideas and evidence in your draft in its current state. Think about how you might group certain items of evidence with the particular ideas they support. Then, try to find a structure that helps you to organize such evidence groups into a clear pattern. Here are some strategies to consider.

- *Arrange ideas by time.* Describe events in order or in reverse order.
- *Arrange ideas according to importance.* You can choose to start with the idea that carries the most weight and move to ideas with less value or

influence. You can also move from the least important to the most important idea.

- *Arrange ideas by problem and solution.* Start with a specific problem; then discuss one or more solutions.

Writing the Conclusion

Your conclusion is a statement or paragraph that communicates that your paper is complete. Summarize the information that is in the body of your paper and critically evaluate what is important about it. Try one of the following strategies:

- Summarize main points (if material is longer than three pages)
- Relate a story, statistic, quote, or question that makes the reader think
- Call the reader to action
- Look to the future

As you work on your conclusion, try not to introduce new facts or restate what you feel you have proved ("I have successfully proven that violent cartoons are related to increased violence in children"). Let your ideas as they are presented in the body of the paper speak for themselves. Readers should feel that they have reached a natural point of completion.

Crediting Authors and Sources

When you write a paper using any materials other than your own thoughts and recollections, the ideas you gathered in your research become part of your own writing. This does not mean that you can claim these ideas as your own or fail to attribute them to someone. To avoid *plagiarism*—the act of using someone else's exact words, figures, unique approach, or specific reasoning without giving appropriate credit—you need to credit authors for their ideas and words.

Writers own their writings just as a computer programmer owns a program that she designed or a photographer owns an image that he created. A piece of writing and its ideas are the writer's products, or "intellectual property." Using an idea, phrase, or word-for-word paragraph without crediting its author is the same as using a computer program without buying it or printing a photograph without paying the photographer. It is just as serious as any other theft and may have unfavorable consequences. Most colleges have stiff penalties for plagiarism, as well as for any other cheating offense.

To avoid plagiarism, learn the difference between a quotation and a paraphrase. A *quotation* refers to a source's exact words, which are set off from the rest of the text by quotation marks. A *paraphrase* is a restatement of the quotation in your own words, using your own sentence structure.

QUOTATION

"The most common assumption that is made by persons who are communicating with one another is . . . that the other perceives, judges, thinks, and reasons the way he does. Identical twins communicate with ease. Persons from the same culture but with a different education, age, background, and experience often find communication difficult. American managers communicating with managers from other cultures experience greater difficulties in communication than with managers from their own culture."[2]

UNACCEPTABLE PARAPHRASE

(The underlined words are taken directly from the quoted source.)

When we communicate, we assume that the person to whom we are speaking perceives, judges, thinks, and reasons the way we do. This is not always the case. Although identical twins communicate with ease, persons from the same culture but with a different education, age, background, and experience often encounter communication problems. Communication problems are common among American managers as they attempt to communicate with managers from other cultures. They experience greater communication problems than when they communicate with managers from their own culture.

ACCEPTABLE PARAPHRASE

Many people fall into the trap of believing that everyone sees the world exactly as they do and that all people communicate according to the same assumptions. This belief is difficult to support even within our own culture as African-Americans, Hispanic-Americans, Asian-Americans, and others often attempt unsuccessfully to find common ground. When intercultural differences are thrown into the mix, such as when American managers working abroad attempt to communicate with managers from other cultures, clear communication becomes even harder.

Restatement means to completely rewrite the idea, not just to remove or replace a few words. A paraphrase may not be acceptable if it is too close to the original. Figure 11.4 demonstrates these differences.

Plagiarism often begins by accident when you research. You may forget to include quotation marks around a word-for-word quotation from the source, or you may intend to cite it or paraphrase but never find the time to do so. To avoid forgetting, try writing something like "Quotation from original; rewrite later" next to quoted material, and note at that time the specifics of the original document (title, author, source, page number), so you don't spend hours trying to locate it later.

Even an acceptable paraphrase requires a citation of the source of the ideas within it. Take care to credit any source that you quote, paraphrase, or use as evidence. To credit a source, write a footnote or endnote that describes it. Use the format preferred by your instructor. Writing handbooks such as the *Modern Language Association* (MLA) *Handbook* contain acceptable formats.

Solicit Feedback

Having one or more pairs of eyes look over your work is one of the most valuable steps you can take when writing any kind of paper. It is difficult to have perspective on your writing when you are in the midst of a project—another person, however, will have more of a chance to be objective. Make an appointment with your instructor and show your draft to him or her. Ask a classmate, a friend, or a coworker to take a look. Perhaps you can look over a draft in return.

If you have ideas about the issues you find particularly difficult or confusing when you write, ask your readers to look for specific things. Ask them if there are any sections that they cannot understand, and have them explain why. Ask if any sections don't seem linked to the rest of the paper, if any information seems unimportant, or if any information is missing that should be included. Be open-minded about the comments you receive from your readers—consider each one carefully and then make a decision about what changes you intend to make.

Continue Your Checklist

Create a checklist for your first draft (see Table 11.2). The elements of a first draft do not have to be written in order. In fact, many writers prefer to write the introduction after they complete the body of the paper, so the introduction will reflect the paper's content and tone. Whatever order you choose, make sure your schedule allows you to get everything done—with enough time left over for revisions.

TABLE 11.2 *First draft checklist.*

DATE DUE	TASK	COMPLETED
	Freewrite a draft	
	Plan and write the introduction	
	Organize the body of the paper	
	Include research evidence in the body	
	Plan and write the conclusion	
	Check for plagiarism and rewrite passages to avoid it	
	Credit your sources	
	Solicit feedback	

REVISING

When you revise, you critically evaluate the word choice, paragraph structure, and style of your first draft. Any draft, no matter how good, can always be improved. Be thorough as you add, delete, replace, and reorganize words, sentences, and paragraphs. You may want to print out your draft and then make notes and corrections on the hard copy before you make changes on the word processed version. Figure 11.5 shows a paragraph from Michael's first draft, with revision comments added.

Sample first draft with revision comments.

FIGURE

11.5

Of the changes that ~~happened to us,~~ [military recruits undergo] the physical

transformation is the ~~biggest.~~ [most evident] ~~When we arrived at the~~ [Too much ↗]

~~training facility, it was January, cold and cloudy. At the~~

~~time,~~ [Maybe— upon my January arrival at the training facility,] I was a little thin, but I had been working out and

thought that I could physically do anything. Oh boy, was

I wrong! The Chief said to us right away: "Get down,

maggots!" [← his trademark phrase] Upon this command, we [were] all to drop to the

ground and do [endless] military-style push-ups. Water survival

tactics were also part of the training ~~that we had to~~

~~complete.~~ [unnecessary] Occasionally, my dreams of home were

interrupted at 3 a.m. when we had a surprise aquatic

test. Although we ~~didn't feel too happy about~~ [resented] this

sub-human treatment at the time, we learned to [mention how chief was involved]

appreciate how the conditioning was turning our bodies

into fine-tuned machines. [say more about this (swimming in uniform incident?)]

In addition to revising on your own, some classes may include peer review (having students read one another's work and offer suggestions). A peer reviewer can tell you what comes across well and what seems confusing. Having a different perspective on your writing is extremely valuable. Even if you don't have an organized peer-review system, you may want to ask a classmate to review your work as a favor.

The elements of revision include being a critical writer, evaluating paragraph structure, and checking for clarity and conciseness.

Being a Critical Writer

Critical thinking is as important in writing as it is in reading. Thinking critically when writing will help you move beyond restating what you have researched and learned. Of course, your knowledge is an important part of your writing. What will make your writing even more important and unique, however, is how you use critical thinking to construct your own new ideas and knowledge from what you have learned.

One key to critical writing is asking the question "So what?" For example, if you were writing a piece on nutrition, you might discuss a variety of good eating habits. Asking "So what?" could lead into a discussion of why these habits are helpful, or, what positive effects they have. If you were writing a paper on egg imagery in the novel *All the King's Men* by Robert Penn Warren, you might list all the examples of it that you noticed. Then, asking "So what?" could lead you to evaluate why that imagery is so strong and what idea you think those examples convey.

Another key, if your paper contains an argument, is to make sure that the argument is well-constructed and convincing. Using what you know about arguments from the discussion in Chapter 4, think through your ideas and provide solid support for them with facts and examples.

Use the mind actions to guide your revision. As you revise, ask yourself questions that can help you think through ideas and examples, come up with your own original insights about the material, and be as complete and clear as possible. Here are some examples of questions you may ask:

- Are these examples clearly connected to the idea?
- Are there any similar concepts or facts I know of that can add to how I support this?
- What else can I recall that can help to support this idea?
- In evaluating any event or situation, have I clearly indicated the causes and effects?
- What new idea comes to mind when I think about these examples or facts?
- How do I evaluate any effect, fact, or situation? Is it good or bad, useful or not?

- What different arguments might a reader think of that I should address here?

Finally, critical thinking can help you evaluate the content and form of your paper. As you start your revision, ask yourself the following questions:

- Will my audience understand my thesis and how I've supported it?
- Does the introduction prepare the reader and capture attention?
- Is the body of the paper organized effectively?
- Is each idea fully developed, explained, and supported by examples?
- Are my ideas connected to one another through logical transitions?
- Do I have a clear, concise, simple writing style?
- Does the paper fulfill the requirements of the assignment?
- Does the conclusion provide a natural ending to the paper?

Evaluating Paragraph Structure

Think of your paragraphs as miniversions of your paper, each with an introduction, a body, and a conclusion. Make sure that each paragraph has a *topic sentence* that states the paragraph's main idea. (A topic sentence does for a paragraph what a thesis statement does for an entire paper.) The rest of the paragraph should support the idea with examples and other evidence. Although some topic sentences may occur just after the first sentence of a paragraph, or even at the end, most occur at the beginning. An example follows:

> <u>Chief Marzloff played an integral role in the development of our self-confidence.</u> He taught us that anything less than direct eye contact was disrespectful to both him and ourselves. He encouraged us to be confident about our own beliefs and to think about what was said to us before we decided whether to accept it. Furthermore, the Chief reinforced self-confidence through his own example. He walked with his chin up and chest out, like the proud parent of a newborn baby. He always gave the appearance that he had something to do and that he was in complete control.

Examine how your paragraphs flow into one another by evaluating your use of transitions. For example, words like *also*, *in addition*, and *next* indicate that another idea is coming. Similarly, *finally*, *as a result*, and *in conclusion* tell readers a summary is on its way.

Checking for Clarity and Conciseness

Aim to say what you want to say as clearly and concisely as you can. Try to eliminate extra words and phrases. Rewrite wordy phrases in a more straightforward, conversational way. For example, you can write "if" instead of "in the event that," or "now" instead of "at this point in time."

The writing process gives you time to begin thinking about ideas and letting them float around in your mind for an hour or perhaps several days. But writing your first draft, putting it away, and coming back to it with fresh eyes takes discipline. If you write a paper the night before it is due, there is no time to reflect on your work, synthesize your ideas, or weave them in and out as you would a lovely tapestry. All you can do is just get it down and hand it in.

LYNN QUITMAN TROYKA,
QUEENSBOROUGH COMMUNITY COLLEGE, CUNY

EXPERT INSIGHT

**Take Time
for the
Writing Process**

EDITING

In contrast to the critical thinking of revising, *editing* involves correcting technical mistakes in spelling, grammar, and punctuation, as well as checking style consistency for such elements as abbreviations and capitalizations. Editing comes last, after you are satisfied with your ideas, organization, and style of writing. If you use a computer, you might want to use the grammar-check and spellcheck functions to find mistakes. A spell-checker helps, but you still need to check your work on your own. Although a spell-checker won't pick up the mistake in the following sentence, someone who is reading for sense will:

They are not hear on Tuesdays.

Look also for *sexist language*, which characterizes people according to their gender. Sexist language often involves the male pronoun *he* or *his*. For example, "An executive often spends hours each day going through his electronic mail" implies that executives are always men. A simple change will eliminate the sexist language: "Executives often spend hours each day going through their electronic mail," or, "An executive often spends hours each day going through electronic mail." Try to be sensitive to words that leave out or slight women. *Mail carrier* is preferable to *mailman; student* to *coed.*

Proofreading is the last editing stage and happens after your paper is in its final form. Proofreading means reading every word and sentence to make sure they are accurate. Look for technical mistakes, run-on sentences, and sentence fragments. Look for incorrect word usage and unclear references.

Teamwork can be a big help as you edit and proofread because another pair of eyes may see errors that you didn't notice on your own. If possible, have someone look over your work. Ask for feedback on what is clear and what is confusing. Then, ask the reader to edit and proofread for errors.

DATE DUE	TASK	COMPLETED
	Check the body of the paper for clear thinking and adequate support for ideas	
	Finalize introduction and conclusion	
	Check word spelling, usage, and grammar	
	Check paragraph structure	
	Make sure language is familiar and concise	
	Check punctuation and capitalization	
	Check transitions	
	Eliminate sexist language	
	Get feedback from peers or instructor	

A Final Checklist

You are now ready to complete your revising and editing checklist. All the tasks listed in Table 11.3 should be complete when you submit your final paper. Figure 11.6 shows the final version of Michael's paper.

Sample final version of paper. **FIGURE 11.6**

March 19, 2001
Michael B. Jackson

BOYS TO MEN

His stature was one of confidence, often misinterpreted by others as cockiness. His small frame was lean and agile, yet stiff and upright, as though every move were a calculated formula. For the longest eight weeks of my life, he was my father, my instructor, my leader, and my worst enemy. His name is Chief Marzloff, and he had the task of shaping the lives and careers of the youngest, newest members of the U.S. Coast Guard. As our Basic Training Company Commander, he took his job very seriously and demanded that we do the same. Within a limited time span, he conditioned our bodies, developed our self-confidence, and instilled within us a strong mental discipline.

Of the changes that recruits in military basic training undergo, the physical transformation is the most immediately evident. Upon my January arrival at the training facility, I was a little thin, but I had been working out and thought that I could physically do anything. Oh boy, was I wrong!

(continued)

FIGURE

11.6

Sample final version of paper, continued.

The Chief wasted no time in introducing me to one of his trademark phrases: "Get down, maggots!" Upon this command, we were all to drop to the ground and produce endless counts of military-style push-ups. Later, we found out that exercise prepared us for hitting the deck in the event of enemy fire. Water survival tactics were also part of the training. Occasionally, my dreams of home were interrupted at about 3 a.m. when our company was selected for a surprise aquatic test. I recall one such test that required us to swim laps around the perimeter of a pool while in full uniform. I felt like a salmon swimming upstream, fueled only by natural instinct. Although we resented this sub-human treatment at the time, we learned to appreciate how the strict guidance of the Chief was turning our bodies into fine-tuned machines.

Beyond physical ability, Chief Marzloff also played an integral role in the development of our self-confidence. He would often declare in his raspy voice, "Look me in the eyes when you speak to me! Show me that you believe what you're saying!" He taught us that anything less was an expression of disrespect. Furthermore, he appeared to attack a personal habit of mine. It seemed that whenever he would speak to me individually, I would nervously nod my head in response. I was trying to demonstrate that I understood, but to him, I was blindly accepting anything that he said. He would roar, "That is a sign of weakness!" Needless to say, I am now conscious of all bodily motions when communicating with others. The Chief also reinforced self-confidence through his own example. He walked with his square chin up and chest out, like the proud parent of a newborn baby. He always gave the appearance that he had something to do, and that he was in complete control. Collectively, all of the methods that the Chief used were all successful in developing our self-confidence.

Perhaps the Chief's greatest contribution was the mental discipline that he instilled in his recruits. He taught us that physical ability and self-confidence were nothing without the mental discipline required to obtain any worthwhile goal. For us, this discipline began with adapting to the military lifestyle. Our day began promptly at 0500 hours, early enough to awaken the oversleeping roosters. By 0515 hours, we had to have showered, shaved, and perfectly donned our uniforms. At that point, we were marched to the galley for chow, where we learned to take only what is necessary, rather than indulging. Before each meal, the Chief would warn, "Get what you want, but you will eat all that you get!" After making good on his threat a few times, we all got the point. Throughout our stay, the Chief repeatedly stressed the significance of self-discipline. He would calmly utter, "Give a little now, get a lot later." I guess that meant different things to all of us. For me, it was a simple phrase that would later become my personal philosophy on life. The Chief went to great lengths to ensure that everyone under his direction possessed the mental discipline required to be successful in boot camp or in any of life's challenges.

Chief Marzloff was a remarkable role model and a positive influence on many lives. I never saw him smile, but it was evident that he genuinely cared a great deal about his job and all the lives that he touched. This man single-handedly conditioned our bodies, developed our self-confidence, and instilled a strong mental discipline that remains in me to this day. I have not seen the Chief since March 28, 1992, graduation day. Over the years, however, I have incorporated many of his ideals into my life. Above all, he taught us the true meaning of the U.S. Coast Guard slogan, "Semper Peratus" (Always Ready).

Your final paper reflects all the hard work you put in during the writing process. Ideally, when you are finished, you have a piece of work that is in a clearly readable format, shows your writing ability, and most importantly communicates interesting and important ideas. Writing is speaking using the written word—take the time and effort to make your ideas known.

Suà

Suà is a Shoshone Indian word, derived from the Uto-Aztecna language, meaning "think." Whereas much of the Native-American tradition in the Americas focuses on oral communication, written languages have allowed Native-American perspectives and ideas to be understood by readers outside the Native-American culture. The writings of Leslie Marmon Silko, J. Scott Momaday, and Sherman Alexis have expressed important insights that all readers can consider.

Think of *suà*, and of how thinking can be communicated to others through writing, every time you begin to write. The power of writing allows you to express your own insights so that others can read them and perhaps benefit from knowing them. Explore your thoughts, sharpen your ideas, and remember the incredible power of the written word.

Study Skills in Action

Test Competence

MEASURING WHAT YOU'VE LEARNED

MULTIPLE CHOICE. *Circle or highlight the answer that seems to fit best.*

1. Writing is considered a study skill for all of the following reasons **except**
   A. writing skills enable you to take effective notes.
   B. writing skills give you the ability to effectively complete essay tests.
   C. writing skills prepare you to write letters to friends.
   D. writing skills help you solidify your knowledge as you prepare for tests.

2. Identifying your purpose for writing helps you
   A. choose a topic.
   B. understand your audience.
   C. write without grammatical mistakes.
   D. focus on what you want your document to accomplish.

3. Making a commitment to your audience enables you to
   A. provide the reader with the appropriate level of information to foster communication.
   B. exhibit an extensive and unique knowledge of your topic.
   C. focus on the needs of the reader instead of your purpose for writing.
   D. use your document as the basis for a speech.

4. The writing process includes all of the following **except**
   A. planning.
   B. drafting.
   C. typing.
   D. revising and editing.

5. A creative technique that involves generating ideas about a topic, without judgment, is known as
   A. planning.
   B. drafting.
   C. brainstorming.
   D. evaluating.

6. A thesis statement does all of the following **except**
   A. explains your writing style.
   B. tells readers what they should expect from your written presentation.
   C. links together your topic, purpose, and commitment to your audience.
   D. appears near the beginning of your document.

7. A first draft must
   A. have no spelling or punctuation errors.
   B. be ready to show to your instructor.
   C. have exactly the right tone.
   D. create the initial structure and content of your document.

8. Possible strategies for effectively organizing the body of a paper include all of the following **except**
   A. arranging ideas as they occur to you.
   B. arranging ideas by time.
   C. arranging ideas according to importance.
   D. arranging ideas by problem and solution.

9. Avoiding plagiarism includes all of the following **except**
   A. setting off quotes with quotation marks.
   B. citing sources of quotes or paraphrases.
   C. avoiding the use of any ideas from research sources.
   D. paraphrasing important ideas.

10. Revising enables you to do all of the following **except**
   A. fine tune your first draft.
   B. finish the writing process and hand your document to your instructor.
   C. rewrite and strengthen sections of your draft.
   D. use your critical-thinking skills to evaluate your first draft.

TRUE/FALSE. *Place a T or an F beside each statement to indicate whether you think it is true or false.*

1. _____ Critical writers refocus on their thesis and audience during the revision process.

2. _____ Editing involves identifying information gaps in your draft and conducting new research.

3. _____ Checklists help you keep track of all the elements in the writing process.

4. _____ Every document involves persuasive writing.

5. _____ Freewriting is the time in the writing process to pay attention to grammar and spelling.

Brain Power

BUILDING VOCABULARY FITNESS

The paragraphs below are taken from the current media. Read the paragraph, noting the context of the vocabulary words shown in bold type. Next, for each vocabulary word (reprinted in the left-hand column), highlight the word or phrase in column A, B, or C that is the most similar in meaning. Finally, on a separate sheet of paper, solidify your understanding of these words by using each in a sentence of your own.

A scientific panel was convened by the National Research Council to resolve a mysterious **discrepancy** between two conflicting sets of temperature data: Although measurements recorded by land-based instruments have shown a marked increase in Earth's surface temperature over the past two decades, satellite and weather-balloon measurements taken during the same period reveal little warming in the sky above . . .

Said panel chairman John Wallace, an atmospheric scientist at the University of Washington: "There really is a difference between temperatures at the two levels that we don't fully understand." But he went on to state **emphatically** that this **variance** "in no way **invalidates** the conclusion that the Earth's temperature is rising." . . . .

The panel steered clear of the question of why Earth is getting warmer. Many scientists, as well as most **environmentalists,** are convinced that carbon dioxide and atmospheric **pollutants** are responsible.

From "So It's Not the Humidity," by Laura Tangley, *U.S. News & World Report,* January 24, 2000, p. 49.

Vocabulary Words

Vocabulary Words	A	B	C
1. **discrepancy**	disappearance	inconsistency	excess
2. **emphatically**	softly	angrily	adamantly
3. **variance**	difference	variety	rule
4. **invalidates**	affirms	nullifies	strengthens
5. **environmentalists**	politicians	scientists	conservationists
6. **pollutants**	contaminants	breezes	storms

Strategic Thinking

GETTING THE BIG PICTURE

Answer the following question on a separate piece of paper or in a journal.

With the speed at which technology is developing, writing instructions for how to use various products is a very important skill. Effective instructions allow people to use a product efficiently and happily. Poor instructions create confusion, often result in misuse that creates problems, and lose customers who might have bought again in the future. Using your writing skills, write a description of how to use some kind of machine or electronic device that is important to your work either at school or at your job. Make clarity your top priority.

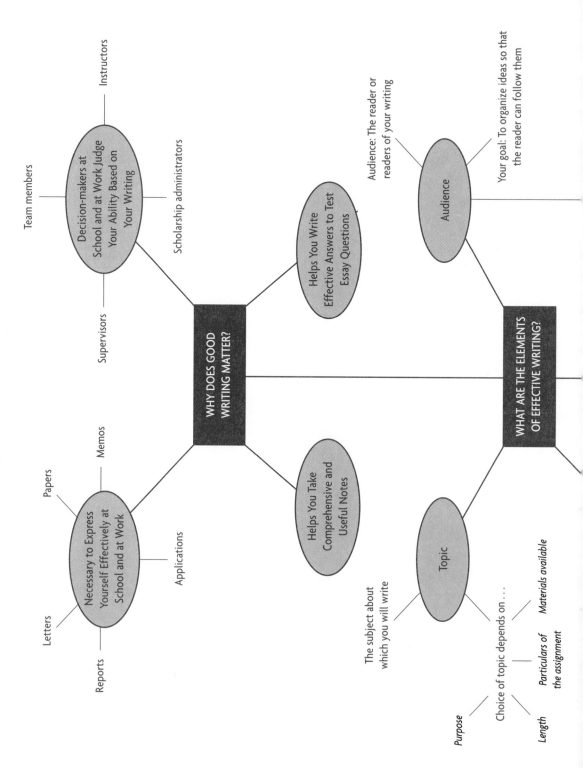

Reports

Letters

Papers

Memos

Applications

Necessary to Express
Yourself Effectively at
School and at Work

Team members

Supervisors

Decision-makers at
School and at Work Judge
Your Ability Based on
Your Writing

Scholarship administrators

Instructors

**WHY DOES GOOD
WRITING MATTER?**

Helps You Write
Effective Answers to Test
Essay Questions

Helps You Take
Comprehensive and
Useful Notes

**WHAT ARE THE ELEMENTS
OF EFFECTIVE WRITING?**

Audience

Audience: The reader or
readers of your writing

Your goal: To organize ideas so that
the reader can follow them

Topic

The subject about
which you will write

Choice of topic depends on . . .

Materials available

Particulars of
the assignment

Purpose

Length

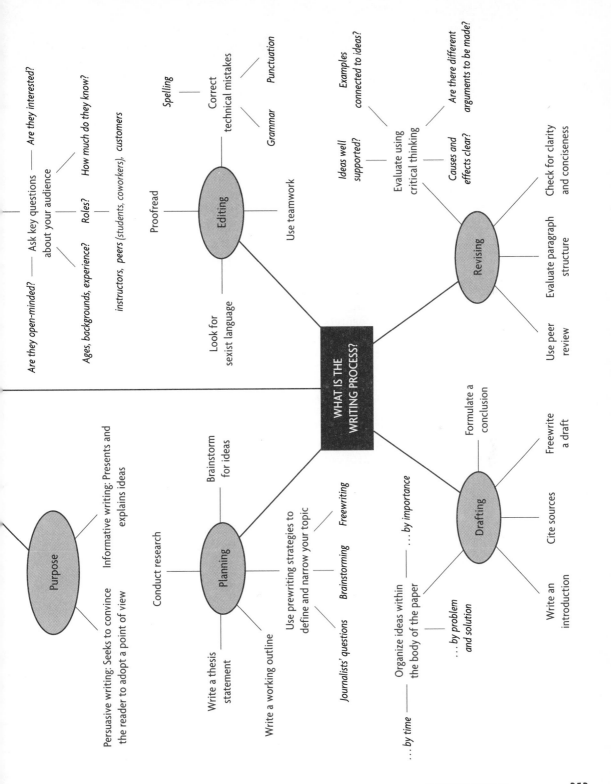

WHAT IS THE WRITING PROCESS?

Purpose
- Persuasive writing: Seeks to convince the reader to adopt a point of view
- Informative writing: Presents and explains ideas

Are they open-minded? — Ask key questions about your audience — Are they interested?

How much do they know?

Roles? — instructors, peers (students, coworkers), customers

Ages, backgrounds, experience?

Editing
- Proofread
- Correct technical mistakes
  - Spelling
  - Grammar
  - Punctuation
- Use teamwork
- Look for sexist language

Revising
- Evaluate using critical thinking
  - Ideas well supported?
  - Examples connected to ideas?
  - Causes and effects clear?
  - Are there different arguments to be made?
- Check for clarity and conciseness
- Evaluate paragraph structure
- Use peer review

Planning
- Brainstorm for ideas
- Conduct research
- Use prewriting strategies to define and narrow your topic
  - Freewriting
  - Brainstorming
  - Journalists' questions
- Write a thesis statement
- Write a working outline

Drafting
- Formulate a conclusion
- Freewrite a draft
- Cite sources
- Organize ideas within the body of the paper
  - ... by importance
  - ... by time
  - ... by problem and solution
- Write an introduction

Making Connections

The following multiple-choice, true/false, fill-in-the-blank, matching, and essay questions will reinforce the concepts you learned in the three chapters that make up Part III, *Notes, Research, and Writing: Interpreting and Expressing Ideas*, and will build critical-thinking skills as well. Whereas the end-of-chapter objective quizzes focus mainly on material from that particular chapter, many of the following questions encourage you to compare material from different chapters and find ways that different ideas connect. Recognizing the key relations between ideas will help you master and use knowledge in the most effective way.

MULTIPLE CHOICE. *Circle or highlight the answer that seems to fit best.*

1. Skills employed by effective writers include all of the following **except**
   A. recording information in an accessible way.
   B. performing the prewriting strategies in order.
   C. organizing thoughts on paper even under time pressure.
   D. focusing on key concepts.

2. Of these aspects of the planning process for writing, the link between effective writing and critical thinking is clearest in
   A. researching.
   B. asking journalists' questions.
   C. freewriting.
   D. writing a thesis statement.

3. Having clear research goals will help with all of the following **except**
   A. conducting an efficient keyword search.
   B. pointing you to general and specific reference works that are likely to contain relevant information.
   C. giving you the skill to do research on the Internet.
   D. helping you reject irrelevant information.

4. The *main* reason notes on research sources are often easier to take than lecture notes is

   A. you can take research notes any hour of the day or night.

   B. the process of taking research notes is largely in your control; there is no need to adjust to the instructor's presentation style.

   C. you can spend hours or even days taking notes on every research source.

   D. your handwriting is likely to be better when you take research notes than when you take lecture notes.

5. Effective time-management skills are

   A. unrelated to the writing process.

   B. important to writing a clear thesis statement and supporting it with examples.

   C. essential during revision and editing.

   D. tools that will help you get through the writing process on schedule.

TRUE/FALSE. *Place a T or an F beside each statement to indicate whether you think it is true or false.*

1. _____ Revising and editing checklists are no longer important after you write a few papers.

2. _____ The main advantage of receiving guided notes from your instructor is that you do not have to take your own class notes.

3. _____ When you review your notes, you should enhance their effectiveness by using critical thinking.

4. _____ You are unlikely to use the library research computer skills you are learning in college after you graduate.

5. _____ How you present your ideas in writing may have a major influence on your success at work.

FILL-IN-THE-BLANK. *Complete the following sentences with the appropriate word(s) or phrase(s) that best reflect what you learned in Part III. Choose from the items that follow each sentence.*

1. Like having a clear purpose for reading, having a clear purpose for writing gives _____ to your work. (understanding, interest, direction)

2. When attending a meeting in the workplace, you will _____ need to take notes. (frequently, rarely, never)

3. Reviewing class notes in a systematic way will help you _____ the information in your memory. (disregard, find fault with, solidify)

4. When you approach a librarian for research help, you should expect him or her to _____ your efforts. (take charge of, guide, criticize)

5. Periodicals are likely to contain more _____ information than books. (comprehensive, interesting, current)

6. When you conduct Internet research, it is especially important to be _____ as you use critical thinking to evaluate every source. (media literate, honest, sensitive)

7. Writing without an understanding of your _____ will almost always lead to _____. (topic/writing success, audience/poor communication, research/a disorganized presentation)

8. _____ encourages you to put your _____ ideas on paper and is an important part of the _____ process. (Freewriting/ uncensored/planning, Editing/polished/ planning, Researching/ censored/editing)

9. The act of using someone else's exact words, figures, unique approach, or specific reasoning without giving appropriate credit is known as _____. (cheating, dishonesty, plagiarism)

10. When you correct technical mistakes in spelling, grammar, and punctuation, you are _____ your document. (revising, editing, planning)

MATCHING. *Match each item in the left-hand column to an item in the right-hand column by writing the letter from the right that corresponds best to the number on the left.*

1. _____ formal outline

A. restatement of a quotation in your own words

2. _____ informal outline

B. central message you want to communicate in a written document

3. _____ Cornell note-taking system

C. an organizational tool that links ideas through the use of Roman numerals, capital and lowercase letters, and numbers

4. _____ think link

D. T-note system

5. _____ library search strategy

E. use of specific words and phrases to conduct effective library research

6. _____ keyword search

F. a comprehensive index of magazines and newspapers

7. _____ *Reader's Guide to Periodic Literature*

G. mind map

8. _____ thesis statement

9. _____ first draft

10. _____ paraphrase

H. method for finding information that takes you from general to specific sources

I. first, unpolished attempt to put your ideas on paper

J. an organizational tool that shows a hierarchy of ideas through a system of consistent indenting and dashes

Essay Question

Carefully read the following excerpt from Society: The Basics, *5th Ed., by John J. Macionis, a college textbook published by Prentice Hall, and then answer the essay question that follows. This exercise will help you focus on the meaning of the selection, apply your personal knowledge and experiences to the reading, organize your ideas, and communicate your thoughts effectively in writing.*

Before you begin writing your essay, it is a good idea to spend a few minutes planning. Try brainstorming possible approaches, writing a thesis statement, and jotting down your main thoughts in the form of an outline or think link. Because most essay tests are timed, limit the time you take to write your response to no more than one-half hour. This will force you to write quickly and effectively as it prepares you for actual test conditions.

SEEING INDIVIDUALITY IN SOCIAL CONTEXT

Perhaps the most compelling evidence of how social forces affect human behavior comes from the study of suicide. What could be a more personal "choice" than taking one's own life? But Emile Durkheim (1858–1917), a pioneer of sociology, showed that social forces are at work even in an isolated act of self-destruction.

From official records in and around his native France, Durkheim found some categories of people were more likely than others to take their own lives. Specifically, he found that men, Protestants, wealthy people, and the unmarried each had higher suicide rates than women, Catholics and Jews, the poor, and married people. Durkheim explained the differences in terms of social integration. Categories of people with strong social ties had low suicide rates while more individualistic people had high suicide rates.

In the male-dominated societies studied by Durkheim, men certainly had more autonomy than women. But whatever its advantages, autonomy also contributed to social isolation and a higher suicide rate. Likewise, individualistic Protestants were more prone to suicide than traditional Catholics and Jews whose rituals foster stronger social ties. The wealthy had more freedom than the poor but, once again, at the cost of a higher suicide rate. Finally, can you see why single people-compared to married people, were also at greater risk?

A century later, statistical evidence still supports Durkheim's analysis. . . . In 1995, there were 12.9 recorded suicides for every 100,000 white people, almost twice the rate for African Americans (6.7). For both races, suicide is more common among men than among women. White men (21.4) are four times more likely than white women (4.8) to take their own lives. Among African Americans, the rate for men (11.9) is six times that for women (2.0). Following Durkheim's logic, the higher suicide rate among white people and men reflects their greater wealth and freedom. Conversely, the lower rate among women and people of color follows from their limited social choices. Just as in Durkheim's day, we can see social patterns in suicide, the most personal of actions.

Source: Excerpted from John J. Macionis, *Society: The Basics,* 5th Ed., Upper Saddle River, NJ: Prentice Hall, 2000, pp. 3–4.

ESSAY QUESTION. What you have just read illustrates a sociological perspective—the ability of sociologists to see general patterns in the behavior of particular individuals. Using your personal background as a point of reference, discuss how broad and narrow social forces affect the way you and your family live. Then, analyze whether the effect of social forces on your behavior gives you a greater or lesser sense of personal power and control.

Teamwork

STUDY GROUP NOTES EVALUATION. Choose one particular meeting of this class from the last two weeks. Join with two or three other classmates, all of whom were in class that day, and make a temporary study group. Each of you should make enough photocopies of your own notes to pass around one copy to each of the other group members.

First, look over the sets of notes on your own. Think about:

- Readability of handwriting
- Information covered
- Note-taking systems used
- Clarity of the ideas and examples

Then, gather again and talk through the four topics together, one by one. Approach the notes as though you were in a study group session.

- Can you read each other's handwriting? If not, the information won't be of much use to you.
- Did you cover the same information? If someone missed a topic, someone else can help them fill in the blanks.
- Did you use the same or different note-taking systems? You might gather insight from the way someone else structures their notes.
- Could you understand what the notes were saying? If you are confused about something in your own notes, someone else might have a helpful perspective. If you don't understand someone else's notes, together you can figure out what information is confusing or missing.

Finally, come up with one change you plan to make in your note-taking based on your study group session. If you have more than one, make a list. For each change, if you have time, write a paragraph about how you plan to put the change into action.

TESTING, TECHNOLOGY, AND COMPETENCY

CREATING YOUR FUTURE

P A R T

IV

A test is a measure of ability at that moment. Whether or not the test goes well, however, your need to do what the test measures will continue. If you know that you will continue to use the skills that you are being tested on and if you remember that owning the skills is more important than getting a perfect score, you may have a more positive attitude toward the test and retain more of what you learned. Approaching tests in this way is crucial in your working life as well, for two reasons: One, you may encounter tests in the workplace—for example, to gain a teaching or medical certification, to show proficiency in a computer language, or to demonstrate skill level in operating machinery. Two, on the job you will need to use the information you are tested on.

As you will see in this chapter, successful test taking involves effective preparation, conquering fears, paying attention to details, and learning from mistakes. At the end of the chapter, you will be able to answer these questions:

- How can preparation help improve test scores?
- How can you conquer test anxiety?
- How can studying with others help you succeed?
- What general strategies can help you succeed on tests?
- How can you learn from test mistakes?

TEST TAKING

DEVELOPING A WINNING STRATEGY FOR TEST SUCCESS

> *"The essence of knowledge is,*
> *having it, to use it."*
>
> **Confucius**

How Can Preparation Help Improve Test Scores?

Like a runner who prepares for a marathon by exercising, eating right, taking practice runs, and getting enough sleep, you can take steps to master your exams. The primary step, occupying much of your preparation time, is to listen when material is presented, read carefully, and study until you know the material that will be on the test. In this sense, staying on top of your class meetings, readings, and assignments over the course of the semester is one of the best ways to prepare yourself for tests. Other important steps are the strategies that follow.

IDENTIFY TEST TYPE AND MATERIAL COVERED

Before you begin studying, find out as much as you can about the type of test you will be taking and what it will cover. Try to identify:

- The type of questions on the test. Will they be objective (multiple choice, true/false, sentence completion), subjective (essay), or a combination?
- The topics the test will cover. Will it cover everything since the semester began, or will it be limited to a narrower topic?
- The material you will be tested on. Will the test cover only what you learned in class and in the text, or will it also cover outside readings?

Your instructors or coworkers may answer these questions for you. Even though they may not reveal specific test questions, they might let you know the question format or information covered. Some instructors may even drop hints throughout the semester about possible test questions, either directly ("I might ask a question on this subject on your next exam") or more subtly ("One of my favorite theories is . . . ").

Here are a few other strategies for predicting what may be on a test.

USE SQ3R TO IDENTIFY IMPORTANT IDEAS AND FACTS.   Often, the questions you write and ask yourself when you read assigned materials may be part of the test. Textbook study questions are also good candidates.

TALK TO PEOPLE WHO TOOK THE COURSE OR TEST BEFORE.   Try to find out how difficult the tests are, whether they focus more on assigned readings or notes, what materials are usually covered, and what types of questions are used. Ask also about instructors' preferences. If you learn that the instructor pays close attention to factual and grammatical accuracy, for example, study accordingly. If he or she has a special appreciation for neatness, writing carefully and cleanly will make an impression.

EXAMINE OLD TESTS IF INSTRUCTORS MAKE THEM AVAILABLE IN CLASS OR ON RESERVE IN THE LIBRARY.   Old tests help to answer the following questions:

- Does the instructor focus on examples and details, general ideas and themes, or a combination?
- Can you do well through straight memorization or does the material require critical thinking?
- Are the questions straightforward or confusing and sometimes tricky?
- Do the tests require the integration of facts from different areas to draw conclusions?

If you can't get copies of old tests and your instructor doesn't give too many details about the test, use clues from the class to predict test questions. After taking the first exam in the course, you will have more information about what to expect in the future.

CHOOSE STUDY MATERIALS

Once you have identified as much as you can about the subject matter of the test, choose the materials that contain the information you need to study. Save time by making sure that you aren't studying anything extraneous. Go through your notes, your texts, related primary source materials, and any handouts; then, set aside any materials you don't need.

CREATE AN ORGANIZED STUDY PLAN AND SCHEDULE

Use your time-management skills to set a schedule that will help you feel as prepared as you can be. Consider all the relevant factors—the materials you need to study, how many days or weeks until the test date, and how much time you can study each day. If you establish your schedule ahead of time and write it in your date book, you will be much more likely to follow it.

Schedules vary widely according to the situation. For example, if you have three days before the test and no other obligations during that time, you might set two 2-hour study sessions during each day. On the other hand, if you have two weeks before a test, classes during the day, and work three nights a week, you might spread out your study sessions over the nights you have off during those two weeks.

A checklist, like the one in Figure 12.1, will help you get organized and stay on track as you prepare for each test. Use a checklist like this to assign specific tasks to particular study times and sessions. That way, not only will you know when you have time to study, but you will also have defined your goals for that study session.

PREPARE THROUGH CAREFUL REVIEW

Thorough review of your materials will give you the best shot at remembering the contents. Use the following strategies when you study.

USE SQ3R. The reading method you studied in Chapter 6 provides an excellent structure for reviewing your reading materials.

- *Surveying* will give you an overview of topics.
- *Questioning* will help you focus on important ideas and determine what the material is trying to communicate.
- *Reading* (or, in this case, rereading) will remind you of the ideas and supporting information.
- *Reciting* will help you anchor the concepts in your head.
- *Reviewing* tasks such as quizzing yourself on the Q-stage questions, summarizing sections you have highlighted, making flash cards for important concepts, and constructing a chapter outline will help you solidify your learning so that you will be able to use it at test time and beyond.

REVIEW YOUR NOTES. Recall the section in Chapter 9 on note taking for making your notes a valuable after-class reference. Use the following techniques to effectively review notes:

- *Time your reviews carefully.* Review notes for the first time within a day of the lecture, if you can, and then review again closer to the test day.
- *Mark up your notes.* Reread them, filling in missing information, clarifying points, writing out abbreviations, and highlighting key ideas.
- *Organize your notes.* Consider adding headings and subheadings to your notes to clarify the structure of the information. Rewrite them using a different organizing structure—a think link if you have originally written them in longhand, for example, or an outline if you originally used a think link.

Course: _____ Teacher: _____

Date, time, and place of test: _____

Type of test (e.g., Is it a midterm or a minor quiz?): _____

What the instructor has told you about the test, including the types of test questions, the length of the test, and how much the test counts toward your final grade: _____

_____

_____

_____

Topics to be covered on the test in order of importance:

1. _____
2. _____
3. _____
4. _____
5. _____

Study schedule, including materials you plan to study (e.g., texts and class notes) and dates you plan to complete each:

Material   Date of Completion

1. _____
2. _____
3. _____
4. _____
5. _____

Materials you are expected to bring to the test (e.g., your textbook, a sourcebook, a calculator): _____

_____

Special study arrangements (e.g., plan study group meetings, ask the instructor for special help, get outside tutoring):

_____

_____

Life-management issues (e.g., make child-care arrangements, rearrange work hours): _____

_____

_____

Source: Adapted from Ron Fry, *"Ace" Any Test,* 3rd ed. (Franklin Lakes, NJ: Career Press, 1996), 123–124.

- *Summarize your notes.* Evaluate which ideas and examples are most crucial, and then rewrite your notes in shortened form, focusing on those ideas and examples. Summarize your notes in writing or with a summary think link. Try summarizing from memory as a self-test.

THINK CRITICALLY.   Using the techniques from Chapter 4, approach your test preparation as an active, critical thinker, working to understand material rather than just to repeat facts. As you study, try to connect ideas to examples, analyze causes and effects, establish truths, and look at issues from different perspectives.

Those who grade your tests often look for evidence that you can link seemingly unrelated ideas into logical patterns. As you study, try to explore concepts from different perspectives and connect ideas and examples that on the surface appear to be unrelated. Although you'll probably find answers to these questions in your text or class notes, you may have to work at putting different ideas together. Critical thinking takes work but may promote a greater understanding of the subject and probably a higher grade on the exam.

Critical thinking is especially important for essay tests that ask you to develop and support a thesis. Prepare by identifying three or four potential essay questions and write out your responses.

TAKE A PRETEST

Use questions from your textbook to create your own pretest. Most textbooks, although not all, will include such questions at the end of the chapters. If your course doesn't have an assigned text, develop questions from your notes and from assigned outside readings. Choose questions that are likely to be covered on the test; then answer them under testlike conditions—in quiet, with no books or notes to help you (unless your exam is open-book), and with a clock telling you when to quit. Try to come as close as you can to duplicating the actual test situation.

EXPERT INSIGHT

Take a Pretest

The best way to get ready for an exam is to give yourself a pretest. Put yourself in your instructor's shoes and ask yourself this question: "If I were testing my class, what kinds of questions would be fair and productive to ask on this examination?" Just framing these questions puts you ahead of the game.

SONIA POWELL, OLIVE-HARVEY COLLEGE

PREPARE PHYSICALLY

When taking a test, you often need to work efficiently under time pressure. If your body is tired or under stress, you might not think as clearly or perform as well as you usually do. If you can, avoid staying up all night. Get some sleep so that you can wake up rested and alert. Adequate sleep can actually help cement your study recall by reducing interference from other memories. If you tend to press the snooze button in your sleep, try setting two alarm clocks and placing them across the room from your bed.

Eating right is also important. Sugar-laden snacks will bring up your energy, only to send you crashing back down much too soon. Also, too much caffeine can add to your tension and make it difficult to focus. Eating nothing will leave you drained, but too much food can make you sleepy. The best advice is to eat a light, well-balanced meal before a test. When time is short, grab a quick-energy snack such as a banana, orange juice, or a granola bar.

MAKE THE MOST OF LAST-MINUTE STUDYING

Last-minute studying, or *cramming*, often results in information going into your head and popping right back out shortly after. Study conditions, however, aren't always ideal. Sometimes a busy week may leave you only a few hours to prepare for a big exam. Nearly every student crams sometime during college. If you have a tight schedule, use these hints to make the most of your study time:

- Go through your flash cards, if you have them, one last time.
- Focus on crucial concepts; don't worry about the rest. Resist going through your notes or textbook page by page.
- Create a last-minute study sheet. On a single sheet of paper, write down key facts, definitions, formulas, and so on. Try to keep the material short and simple. If you prefer visual notes, use think links to map out ideas and their supporting examples.
- Arrive early. Study the sheet or your flash cards until you are asked to clear your desk.
- While it is still fresh in your mind, record any helpful information on a piece of scrap paper. Do this before looking at any test questions. Review this information as needed during the test.

After your exam, evaluate the effects cramming had on your learning. Even if you passed, you might remember very little of the material. This low level of retention won't do you much good in the real world where you have to actually make use of information instead of just recalling it for a test. Think about how you can plan strategically to start earlier and improve the situation next time.

How Can You Conquer
Test Anxiety?

A certain amount of stress can be a good thing. Your body is alert, and your energy motivates you to do your best. For some students, however, the time before and during an exam can be miserable. Many students have experienced some level of test anxiety at some time during their studies. A bad case of nerves that makes it hard to think or remember, *test anxiety* can also cause physical symptoms such as sweating, nausea, dizziness, headaches, and extreme fatigue. Work through test anxiety by dealing with its two primary aspects: preparation and attitude.

PREPARE EFFECTIVELY

Preparation is the basic defense against anxiety. The more confident you feel about your knowledge of the material, the more you'll feel able to perform on test day. In this way, you can consider all of the preparation and study information in this chapter as test-anxiety assistance. Also, finding out what to expect on the exam will help you feel more in control. Seek out information about what material will be covered, the question format, the length of the exam, and the points assigned to each question.

Making and following a detailed study plan will help you build the kind of knowledge that can help you fight off anxiety. Divide the plan into a series of small tasks. As you finish each one, you will build your sense of accomplishment, confidence, and control.

Preparation is all about action. Instead of sitting and worrying about the test, put your energy toward concrete, active steps that will help you succeed.

BUILD A POSITIVE ATTITUDE

Although good preparation will help build your confidence, maintaining a positive *attitude* toward testing is as important as studying. Here are some key ways to maintain an attitude that will help you.

SEE THE TEST AS AN OPPORTUNITY TO LEARN. Sometimes students or workers see a test as an opportunity to fail. Turn this around by focusing on learning. See that a test is an opportunity to show what you have learned, as well as to learn something new about the material and about test taking itself.

SEE THE TEST AS A SIGNPOST. It's easy to see a test as a contest to be won or lost. If you pass, or "win" the contest, you might feel no need to retain what you've learned. If you fail, or "lose" the contest, you might feel no need to try again. However, if you see the test as a signpost along the way to a greater goal, you may be more likely to try your best, learn from the experience, and move on. A test is only a small part of your life, and your grade does not reflect your ability to succeed.

GIVE YOUR INSTRUCTOR A POSITIVE ROLE.   Your instructors don't want to make you miserable. They test you to give you an opportunity to grow and to demonstrate what you have accomplished. They test you so that, in rising to this challenge, you will become better prepared for challenges outside of school. Don't hesitate to engage your instructors in your quest to learn and succeed—go to their office hours and take the time to clarify material and issues with them before tests.

SEEK STUDY PARTNERS WHO CHALLENGE YOU.   Your anxiety may get worse if you study with someone who feels just as anxious and unprepared as you do. Find someone who can inspire you to do your best.

SET YOURSELF UP FOR SUCCESS.   Try not to expect failure before you even start. Expect progress of yourself. Take responsibility for creating a setting for success through your preparation and attitude. Know that you are ultimately responsible for the outcome.

PRACTICE RELAXATION.   When you feel test anxiety coming on, take some deep breaths, close your eyes, and visualize positive mental images related to the test, such as getting a good grade and finishing confidently, with time to spare. Do whatever you have to do to ease muscle tension—stretch your neck; tighten and then release your muscles; even take a trip to the restroom to do a couple of forward bends.

These strategies will help in most every test anxiety situation. Students returning to college later in life, however, may have particular anxieties surrounding test taking that require additional attention.

TEST ANXIETY AND THE RETURNING STUDENT

If you're returning to school after 5, 10, or even 20 years, you may wonder if you can compete with younger students or if your mind is still able to learn new material. To counteract these feelings of inadequacy, focus on how your life experiences have given you useful skills. For example, managing work and a family requires strong time-management, planning, and communication skills that can help you plan your study time, juggle school responsibilities, and interact with students and instructors.

In addition, life experiences give you examples through which you can understand ideas in your courses. For example, your relationships may help you understand psychology concepts, managing your finances may help you understand economics or accounting practices, and work experience may give you a context for what you learn in a business management course. If you let yourself feel positive about your knowledge and skills, you may improve your ability to achieve your goals.

Parents who have to juggle child care with study time can find the challenge especially difficult just before a test. Here are some suggestions that might help:

- *Tell your children why this test is important.* Discuss the situation in concrete terms that they can understand. For example, a better education and job for you might mean for them a better home, more money to plan outings and vacations, more time to spend as a family, and a happier parent (you).

- *Explain the time frame.* Tell them your study schedule and when the test will occur. Plan a reward after your test—going for ice cream, seeing a movie, or having a picnic.

- *Keep children active while you study.* Stock up on games, books, and videos. If a child is old enough, have her invite a friend to play.

- *Find help.* Ask a relative or friend to watch the children during study time, or arrange for your child to visit a friend. Consider trading baby-sitting hours with another parent, hiring a baby-sitter who will come to your home, or enrolling your child in a day-care center.

If you talk to other students about your test anxiety, you will probably find that you are not alone in your concerns. In fact, working with others as you prepare for your tests is one of the best ways to solidify knowledge and reduce anxiety at the same time.

How Can Studying with Others Help You Succeed?

Everything you know and will learn comes from your interaction with the outside world. Often this interaction takes place between you and one or more people. You learn from listening to them, reading what they write, observing them, and trying what they do. In school you listen to instructors and other students, you read materials that people have written, and you model yourself after the behavior and ideas of those whom you most trust and respect.

Learning takes place the same way in your career and personal life. Today's workplace puts the emphasis on work done through team effort. Companies value the ideas, energy, and cooperation that results from a well-coordinated team.

When preparing for an exam, taking advantage of the opportunity to interact with your fellow students will greatly enrich your learning. Together you will know more, and retain more, than you would alone.

STRATEGIES FOR STUDY GROUP SUCCESS

Not all study groups work the same way. The way you operate your group may depend on the group's personalities, the subject you study, the location of the group, and the size of the group. No matter what your particular group's situation, though, certain general strategies will help.

- *Choose a leader for each meeting.* Rotating the leadership helps all members take ownership of the group. Be flexible. If a leader has to miss class for any reason, choose another leader for that meeting.

- *Set meeting goals.* At the start of each meeting, compile a list of questions you want to address. When preparing for a test, focus specifically on what the test will cover.

- *Adjust to different personalities.* Respect and communicate with members whom you would not necessarily choose as friends. The art of getting along will serve you well in the workplace, where you don't often choose your coworkers.

- *Share the workload.* The most important factor is a willingness to work, not a particular level of knowledge.

- *Set a regular meeting schedule.* Try every week, every two weeks, three times the week before a test, or whatever the group can manage.

- *Create study materials for one another.* Give each group member the task of finding a piece of information to compile, photocopy, and review for the other group members.

- *Help each other learn.* One of the best ways to solidify your knowledge of something is to teach it to someone else. Have group members teach certain pieces of information; make up quizzes for each other; go through flash cards together.

- *Pool your note-taking resources.* Compare notes with your group members and fill in any information you don't have. Try other note-taking styles: If you generally use outlines, rewrite your notes in a think link. If you tend to map out ideas in a think link, try recompiling your notes using the Cornell method (see Chapter 9 for more on note taking).

Research has shown that if learning is presented in a social setting and if your emotions are involved in that learning, you are likely to retain the information. So the frustration that you feel when your study group can't solve a difficult problem and the elation you experience when you finally succeed will help you remember and internalize what you learn.

DON PIERCE, EXECUTIVE DIRECTOR OF EDUCATION, HEALD COLLEGES

EXPERT INSIGHT

Use Study Groups to Help You Remember

BENEFITS OF WORKING WITH OTHERS

Studying with a partner or in a group usually brings positive results, such as shared knowledge, solidified knowledge, increased motivation, and increased teamwork ability.

- *Shared knowledge.* Each student has a unique body of knowledge and individual strengths. Students can learn from one another. To have individual students pass on their knowledge to each other in a study group requires less time and energy than for each of those students to learn all of the material alone.

- *Solidified knowledge.* Study group members don't just help each other gather knowledge, they also help each other solidify and retain it. When you discuss concepts or teach them to others, you reinforce what you know and strengthen your critical thinking. Part of the benefit comes from simply repeating information aloud and rewriting it on paper, and part comes from how you think through information in your mind before you pass it on to someone else.

- *Increased motivation.* When you study by yourself, you are accountable to yourself alone. In a study group, however, others will see your level of work and preparation, which may increase your motivation.

- *Increased teamwork ability.* The more you understand the dynamics of working with a group and the more experience you have at it, the more you will build your ability to work well with others. This is an invaluable skill for the workplace, and it will contribute to your personal marketability.

You now have many different test preparation strategies at your fingertips. Evaluate them to see which ones suit you best. When you have prepared by using the strategies that work for you, you are ready to take your exam. Now you can focus on methods to help you succeed when the test begins.

What General Strategies Can Help You Succeed on Tests?

Even though every test is different, there are general strategies that will help you handle almost all tests, including short-answer and essay exams.

WRITE DOWN KEY FACTS

Before you even look at the test, write down any key information—including formulas, rules, and definitions—that you studied recently or even just before you entered the test room. Use the back of the question sheet or a piece of scrap paper for your notes (be sure it is clear to your instructor that this scrap paper didn't come into the test room already filled in). Recording this information right at the start will make forgetting less likely.

BEGIN WITH AN OVERVIEW OF THE EXAM

Although exam time is precious, spend a few minutes at the start of the test to get a sense of the kinds of questions you'll be answering, what type of thinking they require, the number of questions in each section, and their point values. Use this information to schedule your time. For example, if a two-hour test is divided into two sections of equal point value—an essay section with four questions and a short-answer section with sixty questions—you can spend an hour on the essays (15 minutes per question) and an hour on the short-answer section (one minute per question).

As you make your calculations, think about the level of difficulty of each section. If you think you can handle the short-answer questions in less than an hour and that you'll need more time with the essays, rebudget your time that way.

READ TEST DIRECTIONS

Although it seems obvious, reading test directions carefully can save you trouble. For example, although a history test of 100 true-or-false questions and one essay may look straightforward, the directions may tell you to answer 80 of the 100 questions or that the essay is an optional bonus. If the directions indicate that you are penalized for incorrect answers—meaning that you will lose points instead of simply not gaining points—avoid guessing unless you're fairly certain. These questions may do damage, for example, if you earn two points for every correct answer and lose one point for every incorrect answer.

When you read directions, you may learn that some questions or sections are weighted more heavily than others. For example, the short-answer questions on a test may be worth 30 points, whereas the essays are worth 70. In this case, it's smart to spend more time on the essays than on the short answers. To stay aware of the specifics of the directions, circle or underline key words and numbers.

WORK FROM EASY TO HARD

Begin with the parts or questions that seem easiest to you. One advantage of this strategy is that you will tend to take less time to answer the questions you know well, leaving more time to spend on the questions that may require increased effort and thinking. If you like to work through questions in order, mark difficult questions as you reach them and return to them after you answer the questions you know.

Another advantage of answering easier questions first is that knowing the answers can boost your confidence, helping you to continue to believe in yourself when you work on more difficult sections.

WATCH THE CLOCK

Keep track of how much time is left and how you are progressing. You may want to plan your time on a piece of scrap paper, especially if you have one or more essays to write. Wear a watch or bring a small clock with you to the test room. A wall clock may be broken, or there may be no clock at all.

Some students are so concerned about time that they rush through the test and have time left over. In such situations, it's easy to leave early. The best move, however, is to take your time. Stay until the end so that you can refine and check your work; it couldn't hurt, and it might help.

MASTER THE ART OF INTELLIGENT GUESSING

When you are unsure of an answer on a short-answer test, you can leave it blank or you can guess. In most cases, provided that you are not penalized for incorrect answers, guessing will help you. "Intelligent guessing," writes Steven Frank, an authority on student studying and test taking, "means taking advantage of what you do know in order to try to figure out what you don't. If you guess intelligently, you have a decent shot at getting the answer right."[1]

First, eliminate all the answers you know—or believe—are wrong. Try to narrow your choices to two possible answers; then choose the one you think is most likely to be correct. Strategies for guessing the correct answer in a multiple-choice test will be discussed in Chapter 13.

When you check your work at the end of the test, ask yourself whether you would make the same guesses again. Chances are that you will leave your answers alone, but you may notice something that will make you change your mind—a *qualifier* (a word that affects the meaning of another word or word group), a remembered fact that will enable you to answer the question without guessing, or a miscalculated step in a math problem.

FOLLOW DIRECTIONS ON MACHINE-SCORED TESTS

Machine-scored tests require that you use a special pencil to fill in a small box on a computerized answer sheet. When the computer scans the sheet, it can tell whether you answered the questions correctly.

Taking these tests requires special care. Use the right pencil (usually a number 2) and mark your answer in the correct space. Periodically, check the answer number against the question number to make sure they match. If you mark the answer to question 4 in the space for question 5, not only will you get question 4 wrong, but your responses for every question that follows will be off by a line. One way to avoid getting off track is to put a small dot next to any number you skip and plan to return to it later on.

Neatness counts on these tests because the computer can misread stray pencil marks or partially erased answers. If you mark two answers to a question and only partially erase one, the computer will read both responses and charge you with a wrong answer. Completely fill each answer space and avoid any other pencil marks that could be misinterpreted by the computer.

USE CRITICAL THINKING TO AVOID ERRORS

Critical thinking can help you work through each question thoroughly and avoid errors. The following are some critical-thinking strategies to use during a test.

- *Recall facts, procedures, rules, and formulas.* Base your answers on the information you recall. Think carefully to make sure you recall it accurately.

- *Think about similarities.* If you don't know how to attack a question or problem, consider any similar questions or problems that you have worked on in class or while studying.

- *Notice differences.* Especially with objective questions, items that seem different from the material you have studied may indicate answers you can eliminate.

- *Think through causes and effects.* For a numerical problem, think about how you plan to solve it and see if the answer—the effect of your plan—makes sense. For an essay question that asks you to analyze a condition or situation, consider both what caused it and what effects it has.

- *Find the best idea to match the example or examples given.* For a numerical problem, decide what formula (idea) best applies to the example or examples (the data of the problem). For an essay question, decide what idea applies to, or links, the examples given.

- *Support ideas with examples.* When you put forth an idea in an answer to an essay question, be sure to back up your idea with an adequate number of examples that fit.

- *Evaluate each test question.* In your initial approach to any question, decide what kinds of thinking will best help you solve it. For example, essay questions often require cause-and-effect and idea-to-example thinking, whereas objective questions often benefit from thinking about similarities and differences.

How Can You Learn From Test Mistakes?

The purpose of a test is to see how much you know, not merely to achieve a grade. Making mistakes, or even failing a test, is human. Rather than ignoring mistakes, examine them and learn from them as you learn from mistakes on the job and in your relationships. Working through your mistakes will help you avoid repeating them again on another test— or outside school life. The following strategies will help.

TRY TO IDENTIFY PATTERNS IN YOUR MISTAKES. Look for the following:

- *Careless errors.* In your rush to complete the exam, did you misread the question or directions, blacken the wrong box on the answer sheet, inadvertently skip a question, or use illegible handwriting?

- *Conceptual or factual errors.* Did you misunderstand a concept or never learn it in the first place? Did you fail to master certain facts? Did you skip part of the assigned text or miss important classes in which ideas were covered?

IF YOU HAVE TIME, TRY TO REWORK THE QUESTIONS YOU GOT WRONG. Based on the feedback from your instructor or other test administrator, try to rewrite an essay, recalculate a math problem by starting from the original question, or redo the questions that follow a reading selection. If you see patterns of careless errors, promise yourself that you'll be more careful in the future and that you'll save time to double-check your work. If you pick up conceptual and factual errors, rededicate yourself to better preparation.

AFTER REVIEWING YOUR MISTAKES, FILL IN THE KNOWLEDGE GAPS. If you made mistakes on questions because you didn't know or understand them, develop a plan to comprehensively learn the material. Solidifying your knowledge can help you in exams further down the road, as well as in life situations that involve the subject matter you're studying. You might even consider asking to retake the exam, if you have the time to do so. The score might not count, but you may find that focusing on learning rather than on grades can improve your knowledge and build self-respect.

TALK TO YOUR INSTRUCTORS. You can learn a lot from consulting an instructor about specific mistakes you made or about subjective essays on which you were marked down. Respectfully ask the instructor who graded the test for an explanation of grades or comments. In the case of a subjective test where the answers are often not clearly right or wrong, ask for specifics about what you could have done to have earned a better grade. Take advantage of this opportunity to find out solid details about how you can do better next time.

IF YOU FAIL A TEST COMPLETELY, DON'T THROW IT AWAY. First, know that many students have been in your shoes and that you have room to grow and improve. Then try to understand why you failed by reviewing and analyzing your errors. This is especially important for an essay test. Whereas most objective questions are fact-based and clearly right or wrong, subjective questions are in large part subject to the opinion of the grader.

Sine qua non

Although the Latin language is no longer commonly used, it is one of the most dominant ancestors of modern English, and many Latin words and phrases have a place in the English language. The Latin phrase *sine qua non* (pronounced sihn-ay kwa nahn) means, literally, "without which not." Translated into everyday language, a sine qua non is "an absolutely indispensable or essential thing."

Think of true learning as the sine qua non of test taking. When you have worked hard to learn ideas and information, taking it in and using different techniques to review and retain it, you will be able to take tests successfully, confident that you have the knowledge necessary to answer the required questions. Focus on knowledge so that test taking becomes not an intimidating challenge but an opportunity to show what you know.

Study Skills in Action

Test Competence

MEASURING WHAT YOU'VE LEARNED

MULTIPLE CHOICE. *Circle or highlight the answer that seems to fit best.*

1. A typical test given in one of your courses measures
   A. your self-worth.
   B. how much you will ever know about a topic.
   C. your proficiency at a moment in time.
   D. general IQ.

2. To predict what will be on a test you can use all of the following strategies **except**
   A. reread your class notes as often as you can before the test.
   B. use SQ3R to identify important ideas and facts.
   C. try to find out what the test will be like from people who took the course before.
   D. examine old tests.

3. Which of the following is **not** a good source to use when developing pretest questions?
   A. your textbook
   B. your class notes
   C. assigned outside readings
   D. the course description you received at the start of the semester

4. Cramming includes all of the following **except**
   A. plagiarizing for an open-book test.
   B. reviewing flash cards.
   C. creating a last-minute study sheet.
   D. writing helpful information on a piece of scrap paper at the start of the test.

5. Test anxiety refers to

   A. the uncertainty you feel when you haven't studied for a test.

   B. the uncertainty you feel when you have to take a test with a teacher you don't like.

   C. the uncertainty you feel when you don't like the coursework on which the test is based.

   D. the mental and physical symptoms of stress that appear before a test.

6. To achieve a positive attitude before a test, you should

   A. see the test as an opportunity to learn and experience success.

   B. tell yourself that the grade you get doesn't matter.

   C. get yourself keyed up with intense studying and caffeine.

   D. realize that once you take a test the results are final and you can't do anything about them.

7. Test anxiety may be especially difficult for returning students because

   A. they often see themselves as less prepared because they have taken a break.

   B. the study methods they learned years ago no longer work.

   C. they tend to be less committed than students who didn't take a break.

   D. they have already earned money, so they no longer need to focus on taking tests.

8. All of the following are strategies for a successful study group **except**

   A. choosing group members who are your friends.

   B. choosing a leader for each meeting.

   C. creating study materials for one another.

   D. pooling your notes.

9. Spending a few minutes at the start of a test getting an overview is important because

   A. you're certain to have plenty of time to complete the exam.

   B. you can get a general sense of whether you will probably pass or fail.

   C. you can get an idea of the type of questions you face and how to approach them.

   D. you can decide which questions you have no hope of answering.

10. To identify patterns in your mistakes on a test, keep an eye out for

    A. questions that you have time to rework.

    B. subjective and objective questions.

    C. evidence that the test was incorrectly graded.

    D. both careless and conceptual errors.

TRUE/FALSE. *Place a T or an F beside each statement to indicate whether you think it is true or false.*

1. _____ Because study schedules shift so often, it's a waste of time to create one before an exam.

2. _____ The reading method SQ3R will help you study for tests.

3. _____ Most instructors will allow you to bring your last minute study sheet into the testing room.

4. _____ One of the most difficult challenges returning students must face during their test preparation time is managing their child-care responsibilities.

5. _____ The teamwork skills you develop in study groups aren't useful after you graduate.

Brain Power

BUILDING VOCABULARY FITNESS

The paragraphs below are taken from the current media. Read the paragraph, noting the context of the vocabulary words shown in bold type. Next, for each vocabulary word (reprinted in the left-hand column), highlight the word or phrase in column A, B, or C that is the most similar in meaning. Finally, on a separate sheet of paper, solidify your understanding of these words by using each in a sentence of your own.

We work more hours than any other country in the advanced industrial world . . . We work the equivalent of an amazing eight weeks a year longer than the average Western European. Nor is this a case of the **downtrodden** masses. It's the bosses, the managers, and the professionals who are working more—wired into **perpetual** motion by the pager, cell phone, and laptop. And no one . . . seems to be griping. Today, over 80 percent of people at work say they are satisfied with their jobs. Noel Coward's **aphorism** seems to have come true: "Work is much more fun than fun." . . . .

    Paradox prevails. Some thought it progress when the first capitalist factory owners took work out of the household, its prime **locus** for hundreds of years, and moved it to the plant floor, creating a new world of mass wage employment and productions. . . . Now it appears it is the factory's turn. In a neat back-to-the-future twist, work is being done more and more today in the home.

From "Whistling While We Work," by Mortimer B. Zuckerman, *U.S. News & World Report*, January 24, 2000, p. 72.

Vocabulary Words	A	B	C
1. **downtrodden**	subjugated	rewarded	appreciated
2. **perpetual**	temporary	continuous	occasional
3. **aphorism**	advice	creation	saying
4. **paradox**	contradiction	insanity	calm
5. **prevails**	fails	lasts	triumphs
6. **locus**	nest	map	focal point

Strategic Thinking

GETTING THE BIG PICTURE

Answer the following question on a separate piece of paper or in a journal.

Feelings similar to test anxiety can come up in all kinds of life and work situations. Consider this chapter's advice on how to overcome test anxiety. In what other situation in your life, perhaps on the job or in an interview, might these strategies come in handy? Describe one such situation, and tell which strategies would help you most and why.

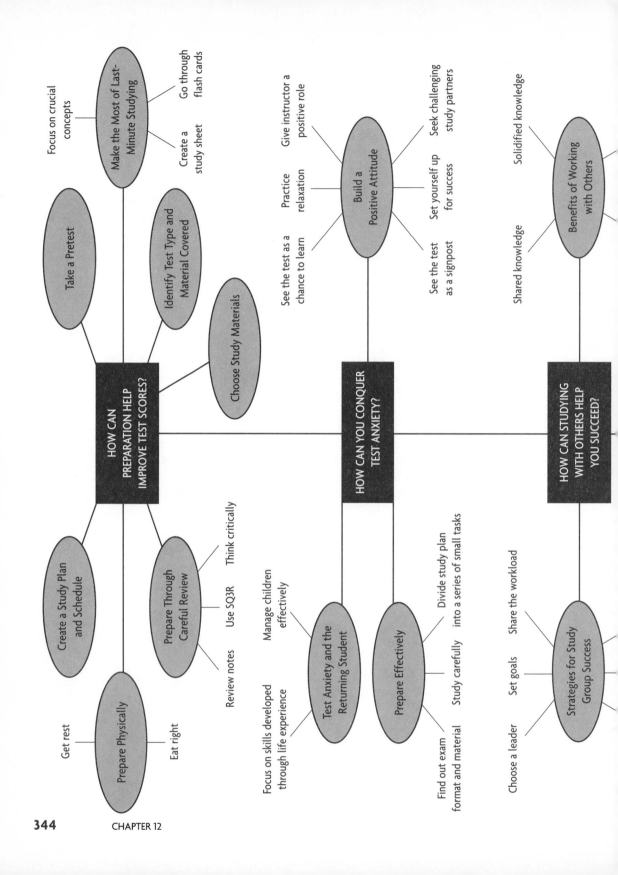

HOW CAN PREPARATION HELP IMPROVE TEST SCORES?

Take a Pretest

Make the Most of Last-Minute Studying
- Focus on crucial concepts
- Create a study sheet
- Go through flash cards

Identify Test Type and Material Covered

Choose Study Materials

Create a Study Plan and Schedule

Prepare Through Careful Review
- Review notes
- Use SQ3R
- Think critically

Prepare Physically
- Get rest
- Eat right

HOW CAN YOU CONQUER TEST ANXIETY?

Build a Positive Attitude
- Practice relaxation
- See the test as a chance to learn
- Give instructor a positive role
- Set yourself up for success
- Seek challenging study partners
- See the test as a signpost

Test Anxiety and the Returning Student
- Focus on skills developed through life experience
- Manage children effectively

Prepare Effectively
- Find out exam format and material
- Study carefully
- Divide study plan into a series of small tasks

HOW CAN STUDYING WITH OTHERS HELP YOU SUCCEED?

Benefits of Working with Others
- Shared knowledge
- Solidified knowledge

Strategies for Study Group Success
- Choose a leader
- Set goals
- Share the workload

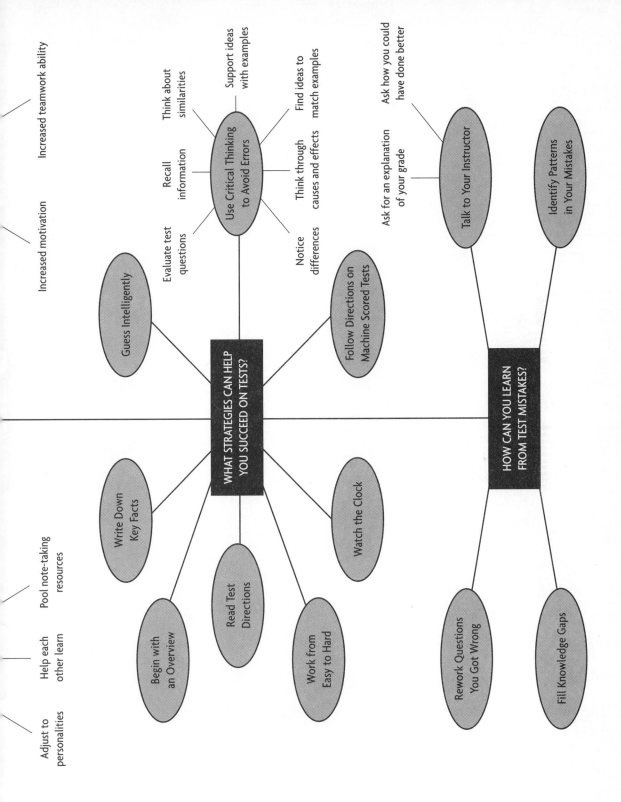

Increased teamwork ability

Increased motivation

Pool note-taking resources

Help each other learn

Adjust to personalities

WHAT STRATEGIES CAN HELP YOU SUCCEED ON TESTS?

Guess Intelligently

Evaluate test questions

Use Critical Thinking to Avoid Errors

- Think about similarities
- Support ideas with examples
- Find ideas to match examples
- Think through causes and effects
- Notice differences
- Recall information

Follow Directions on Machine Scored Tests

Write Down Key Facts

Begin with an Overview

Read Test Directions

Work from Easy to Hard

Watch the Clock

HOW CAN YOU LEARN FROM TEST MISTAKES?

Talk to Your Instructor

- Ask how you could have done better
- Ask for an explanation of your grade

Identify Patterns in Your Mistakes

Rework Questions You Got Wrong

Fill Knowledge Gaps

APPLY

13

Your exams are preparation for life. When you get a job, act as a volunteer, or even work through your family budget, you'll have to apply what you know and put your skills into action—exactly what you do when you take an academic test. Much as life hands you special challenges that require different responses, the tests you take while in college require different strategies for success. How you prepare for an oral exam, for example, will be quite different from how you would prepare for an objective test with multiple choice and true/false questions. The key is to be ready and to be versatile in any situation—test taking or otherwise. With that ability to adapt, you can embrace and manage the changes of the 21st century.

This chapter will provide you with strategies tailored to objective, essay, and oral examinations. At the end of the chapter, you will be able to answer these questions:

- How can you master objective tests?
- How can you master essay questions?
- How can you master oral exams?

SHOWING WHAT YOU KNOW
TAKING OBJECTIVE, ESSAY, AND ORAL EXAMINATIONS

> *"The secret of a leader lies in the tests he has faced over the whole course of his life and the habit of action he develops in meeting those tests."*
>
> **Gail Sheehy**

How Can You Master Objective Tests?

Although the goal of all test questions is to discover how much you know about a subject, every type of question has a different way of doing so. Answering different types of questions is part science and part art. The strategy changes according to whether the question is objective or subjective.

For objective questions—short-answer questions that test your ability to recall, compare, and contrast information—you choose or write a short answer you believe is correct, often making a selection from a limited number of choices. Multiple-choice, true-or-false, matching, and fill-in-the-blank questions fall into this category.

MULTIPLE-CHOICE QUESTIONS

Multiple-choice questions are the most popular type of question on standardized tests. The following strategies can help you answer them:

READ THE DIRECTIONS CAREFULLY.   In the rush to get to work on a question it is easy to read directions too quickly or to skip them. Directions, however, can be tricky. For example, although most test items ask for a single correct answer, some give you the option of marking several choices that are correct. For some tests, you might be required to answer only a certain number of the questions.

READ EACH QUESTION THOROUGHLY.   Then look at the choices and try to answer the question. This strategy will reduce the possibility that the choices will confuse you.

UNDERLINE THE QUESTION'S KEYWORDS AND PHRASES.   If the question is complicated, try to break it down into small sections that are easy to understand.

PAY ATTENTION TO CERTAIN WORDS. For example, it is easy to overlook negatives in a question ("Which of the following is *not* . . .").

ELIMINATE THOSE ANSWERS THAT YOU KNOW OR SUSPECT ARE WRONG. Your goal is to leave yourself with two possible answers, which would give you a fifty-fifty chance of making the right choice. The following are questions you can ask as you eliminate choices:

- Is the choice accurate in its own terms? If there's an error in the choice—for example, a term that is incorrectly defined—the answer is wrong.
- Is the choice relevant? An answer may be accurate, but it may not relate to the essence of the question.
- Are there any qualifiers? Absolute qualifiers like *always, never, all, none,* or *every* often signal an exception that makes a choice incorrect. For example, the statement that "normal children always begin talking before the age of two" is an untrue statement; although most normal children begin talking before age two, some start later. Analysis has shown that choices containing conservative qualifiers *(often, most, rarely, or may sometimes be)* are often correct.
- Do the choices give clues? Does a puzzling word remind you of a word you know? If you don't know a word, does any part of the word—its prefix, suffix, or root—seem familiar? (See Chapter 5 for information on the meanings of common prefixes, suffixes, and roots.)

LOOK FOR PATTERNS. THEN, MAKE AN EDUCATED GUESS. The ideal is to know the material so well that you don't have to guess, but that isn't always possible. Test-taking experts have found patterns in multiple-choice questions that may help you. Here is their advice:

- Consider the possibility that a choice that is more *general* than the others is the right answer.
- Consider the possibility that a choice that is *longer* than the others is the right answer.
- Look for a choice that has a middle value in a range (the range can be from small to large or from old to recent). It is likely to be the right answer.
- Look for two choices that have similar meanings. One of these answers is probably correct.
- Look for answers that agree grammatically with the question. For example, a fill-in-the-blank question that has an *a* or *an* before the blank gives you a clue to the correct answer.

READ EVERY WORD OF EVERY ANSWER. Instructors have been known to include answers that are almost right, except for a single word. Focus especially on qualifying words such as *always, never, often,* and *frequently.*

READ THE QUESTIONS FIRST WHEN KEYED TO A LONG READING PASSAGE. This will help you, when you read the passage, to focus on the information you need to answer the questions.

Here are some examples of the kinds of multiple-choice questions you might encounter in an Introduction to Psychology course[1] (the correct answer follows each question):

1. Arnold is at the company party and has had too much to drink. He releases all of his pent-up aggression by yelling at his boss, who promptly fires him. Arnold normally would not have yelled at his boss, but after drinking heavily he yelled because

   A. parties are places where employees are supposed to be able to "loosen up."
   B. alcohol is a stimulant.
   C. alcohol makes people less concerned with the negative consequences of their behavior.
   D. alcohol inhibits brain centers that control the perception of loudness.

   (The correct answer is C)

2. Which of the following has not been shown to be a probable cause of or influence in the development of alcoholism in our society?

   A. intelligence
   B. culture
   C. personality
   D. genetic vulnerability

   (The correct answer is A)

3. Geraldine is a heavy coffee drinker who has become addicted to caffeine. If she completely ceases her intake of caffeine over the next few days, she is likely to experience each of the following **except**

   A. depression.
   B. lethargy.
   C. insomnia.
   D. headaches.

   (The correct answer is C)

TRUE-OR-FALSE QUESTIONS

True-or-false questions test your knowledge of facts and concepts. Read them carefully to evaluate what they truly say. If you're stumped, guess (unless you're penalized for wrong answers).

Look for qualifiers in true-or-false questions—such as *all*, *only*, and *always* (the absolutes that often make a statement false) and *generally*, *often*, *usually*, and *sometimes* (the conservatives that often make a statement true)—that can turn a statement that would otherwise be true into one that is false or vice versa. For example, "The grammar rule 'I before E except after C' is always true" is false, whereas "The grammar rule 'I before E except after C' is usually true" is true. The qualifier makes the difference.

Here are some examples of the kinds of true-or-false questions you might encounter in an Introduction to Psychology course. The correct answer follows each question:

Are the following questions true or false?

1. Alcohol use is clearly related to increases in hostility, aggression, violence, and abusive behavior. (True)

2. Marijuana is harmless. (False)

3. Simply expecting a drug to produce an effect is often enough to produce the effect. (True)

4. Alcohol is a stimulant. (False)

MATCHING QUESTIONS

Matching questions ask you to match the terms in one list with the terms in another list, according to directions. For example, the directions may tell you to match the names of different countries with the explorers who discovered them. Or you may be asked to match a communicable disease with the pathogen that usually causes it. The following strategies will help you handle these questions:

- *Make sure you understand the directions.* The directions will tell you whether each answer can be used only once or any number of times.

- *Work from the column that has the longest entries.* Working from the column with the longest phrases will save precious moments because you won't have to continually reread the longer items as you attempt to find the right matches. You'll be looking at each long phrase only once as you scan the column with the shorter phrases for the match.

- *Start with the matches you know.* On your first run-through, mark these matches immediately with a penciled line, waiting to make your final choices until you've completed all the items. Keep in mind that if you can use an answer only once, you may have to change many answers if you reconsider any of your original choices.

- *Tackle the matches you're not sure of last.* On your next run-through, focus on the more difficult matches. Look for clues and relations you might not have thought of at first. Think back to your class lectures, notes, and study sessions and try to visualize the correct response.

Consider the possibility that one of your sure-thing answers is wrong. If one or more phrases seem to have no correct answer, look back at your easy matches to be sure that you did not jump too quickly. See if another phrase can be used instead, thus freeing up an answer for use in another match.

FILL-IN-THE-BLANK QUESTIONS

Fill-in-the-blank questions, also known as sentence completion questions, ask you to supply one or more words or phrases with missing information that will complete the sentence. Here are some strategies that will help you make the right choices:

BE LOGICAL. Make sure the answer you choose completes the sentence in a logical way. Reread the sentence from beginning to end to be sure you're satisfied that it is factually and grammatically correct and that it makes sense. Few instructors will intentionally mislead you by manipulating the sentence's grammatical structure.

NOTE THE LENGTH AND NUMBER OF THE BLANKS. Use length and number of blanks as important clues, but not as absolute guideposts. If two blanks appear right after one another, the instructor is probably looking for a two-word answer. If a blank is longer than usual, the correct response may require this additional space. However, if you are certain of a one-word answer for a multiple-blank space, go with that answer. Trust your knowledge and instincts.

PAY ATTENTION TO HOW BLANKS ARE SEPARATED. If there is more than one blank in a sentence and the blanks are widely separated, treat each one separately. Answering each as if it were a separate sentence-completion question will minimize your stress as it increases the likelihood that you will get at least one of the answers correct. Here is an example:

> When Toni Morrison was awarded the _____ prize for
> Literature, she was a professor at _____ University.

In this case and in many other cases, your knowledge of one answer has little impact on your knowledge of the other answer.

THINK OUT OF THE BOX. If you can think of more than one correct answer, put them both down. Your instructor may never have thought of one of your responses and award you extra credit for your assertiveness and creativity.

MAKE A GUESS. If you are uncertain of an answer, make an educated guess. Use qualifiers like may, sometimes, and often to increase the chance that your answer is at least partially correct. Have faith that after hours of studying, the correct answer is somewhere in your subconscious mind and that your guess is not completely random.

One way to avoid test anxiety is to learn the material very well, and then spend time teaching that material to yourself or to another person. This will help you become aware of what you really understand and—just as importantly—what you don't understand. Since you're not in an actual testing situation, you can open the book again and say, "I am not quite sure I understand that distinction. Let me double check and make sure."

When you can teach yourself in this way or teach a roommate—if he or she is willing—or even say the material out loud to your baby sister or your dog, you know that you have mastered the concepts. Your goal is to communicate the key ideas in a chapter with confidence and without opening the book.

CHARLES G. MORRIS, PROFESSOR OF PSYCHOLOGY, UNIVERSITY OF MICHIGAN

EXPERT INSIGHT

Teach Yourself Key Concepts Before a Test

How Can You Master Essay Questions?

Subjective questions demand the same information recall as objective questions, but they also require you to plan, organize, draft, and refine a written response. They may also require more extensive critical thinking and evaluation. All essay questions are subjective. Although some guidelines will help you choose the right answers to both types of questions, part of the skill is learning to "feel" your way to an answer that works.

An essay question allows you to express your knowledge and views on a topic in a much more extensive manner than any short-answer question can provide. With the freedom to express your views, though, comes the challenge to both exhibit knowledge and show you have command of how to organize and express that knowledge clearly.

STRATEGIES FOR ANSWERING ESSAY QUESTIONS

Using the following steps will help you make the most of your time and resources when answering essay questions. Many of these essay-test guidelines reflect the methods you should use when you approach any writing assignment (see Chapter 11). The difference here is that you are writing under time pressure and that you are working from memory.

1. *Start by reading the questions.* Decide which to tackle (if there's a choice). Then focus on what each question is asking and the mind actions you will need to use. Read the directions carefully and do everything that you are asked to do. Some essay questions may contain more than one part.

2. *Watch for action verbs.* Certain verbs can help you figure out how to think. Table 13.1 explains some words commonly used in essay questions. Underline these words as you read the question, clarify what they mean, and use them to guide your writing.

3. *Budget your time and begin to plan.* Create an informal outline or think link to map your ideas and indicate examples you plan to cite in support. (See Chapter 9 for a discussion of these organizational devices.) Avoid spending too much time on introductions or flowery language.

4. *Write your essay.* Start with a thesis statement or idea that states in a basic way what your essay will say (see Chapter 11 for a discussion of thesis statements). Then devote one or more paragraphs to the main points in your outline. Back up the general statement that starts each paragraph with evidence in the form of logical connections, examples, statistics, and so on. Make sure the support you provide is clearly linked to each paragraph's topic statement. Use simple, clear language in the body of the essay, and look back at your outline to make sure you are covering everything. Wrap it up with a conclusion that is short and to the point.

5. *Reread and revise your essay.* Look for ideas you left out, ideas you didn't support with enough examples, and sentences that might confuse the reader. Check for mistakes in grammar, spelling, punctuation, and usage. No matter what you are writing about, having a command of these factors will make your work more complete and impressive.

Neatness is a crucial factor in your essay writing. Try to write legibly; if your instructor can't read your ideas, it doesn't matter how good they are. You might consider printing and skipping every other line if you know your handwriting is problematic. Avoid writing on both sides of the paper because it will make your handwriting even harder to read. You may even want to discuss the problem with the instructor. If your handwriting is so poor that it will be a hardship for the instructor to read, ask about the possibility of taking the test on a laptop computer or typewriter.

Here are some examples of essay questions you might encounter in an Interpersonal Communication course. In each case, notice the action verbs from Table 13.1.

1. Summarize the role of the self-concept as a key to interpersonal relationships and communication.

2. Explain how internal and external noise affects the ability to listen effectively.

TABLE

13.1

Analyze	Break into parts and discuss each part separately.
Compare	Explain similarities and differences.
Contrast	Distinguish between items being compared by focusing on differences.
Criticize	Evaluate the positive and negative effects of what is being discussed.
Define	State the essential quality or meaning. Give the common idea.
Describe	Visualize and give information that paints a complete picture.
Discuss	Examine in a complete and detailed way, usually by connecting ideas to examples.
Enumerate/List/Identify	Recall and specify items in the form of a list.
Explain	Make the meaning of something clear, often by making analogies or giving examples.
Evaluate	Give your opinion about the value or worth of something, usually by weighing positive and negative effects, and justify your conclusion.
Illustrate	Supply examples.
Interpret	Explain your personal view of facts and ideas and how they relate to one another.
Outline	Organize and present the sub-ideas or main examples of an idea.
Prove	Use evidence and argument to show that something is true, usually by showing cause and effect or giving examples that fit the idea to be proven.
Review	Provide an overview of ideas and establish their merits and features.
State	Explain clearly, simply, and concisely, being sure that each word gives the image you want.
Summarize	Give the important ideas in brief.
Trace	Present a history of the way something developed, often by showing cause and effect.

3. Describe three ways that body language affects interpersonal communication. (Figure 13.1 shows an essay that responds effectively to this question.)

WHY GOOD WRITING MATTERS

In order to express yourself successfully in your responses to essay questions, you need good writing skills. Imagine that, as part of an essay exam, students have been asked to write a letter convincing a prospective employer in the television industry that they should be chosen for an open internship position. Parts of two students' responses are shown in Figure 13.2.

FIGURE

13.1

Response to an essay question.

QUESTION: Describe three ways that body language affects interpersonal communication.

Body language plays an important role in interpersonal communication and helps shape the impression you make, especially when you are making a first impression. Two of the most important functions of body language are to contradict and reinforce verbal statements. When body language contradicts verbal language, the message conveyed by the body is dominant. For example, if a friend tells you that she is feeling "fine," but her posture is slumped, her eye contact minimal, and her facial expression troubled, you have every reason to wonder whether she is telling the truth. If the same friend tells you she is feeling fine and she is smiling, walking with a bounce in her step, and has direct eye contact, her body language is accurately reflecting and reinforcing her words.

The nonverbal cues that make up body language also have the power to add shades of meaning. Consider this statement: "This is the best idea I've heard all day." If you were to say this three different ways—in a loud voice while standing up, quietly while sitting with arms and legs crossed and looking away, and while maintaining eye contact and taking the receiver's hand— you might send three different messages.

Finally, the impact of nonverbal cues can be greatest when you meet someone for the first time. Although first impressions emerge from a combination of nonverbal cues, tone of voice, and choice of words, nonverbal elements (cues and tone) usually come across first and strongest. When you meet someone, you tend to make assumptions based on nonverbal behavior such as posture, eye contact, gestures, and speed and style of movement.

In summary, nonverbal communication plays a crucial role in interpersonal relationships. It has the power to send an accurate message that may belie the speaker's words, offer shades of meaning, and set the tone of a first meeting.

FIRST STUDENT

I am a capable student who'se interests are many. I like the news business so much so that I want you to offer me the internship with your company.

My experience will impress you, as I'm sure you will agree I am a reporter for the college news station, and I can be a reporter for you as well. If you let me try. Instructors who know my work like my style. I prefer to think of myself as an individual with a unique style that nothing can match.

I want the summer internship because it will put me at the center of the action. At this point in my education, I deserve the chance to learn from the masters of the business.

I look forward to hearing from you and to the news that I got the internship.

SECOND STUDENT

From the time I was 8 years old, I was hooked on the news. Instead of watching cartoons on television, I watched Tom Brokaw, Dan Rather, and Peter Jennings. I celebrated the day that CNN started a 24-hour all-news network.

It seemed like a natural step to go into the news business. I started in high school as a reporter, and then I became editor-in-chief of the school paper. As a college freshman, I am majoring in broadcast journalism, and I am also working at the school TV station. Even though I'm starting at the bottom, I believe that there's a learning opportunity around every corner. By the time I take on my first reporting assignment next year, I feel that my knowledge and experience will have grown. I hope it will be enough to make me a competent journalist.

Your internship program will help me learn the news business in an environment I never dreamed of experiencing until later in my career. I look forward to hearing from you and to the possibility of working for your station this summer.

If you were the employer, which candidate would you choose? If you were the instructor, which student would earn the better grade on the essay question? The second student's letter is well written, persuasive, logical, and error free. In contrast, the first student's letter is not thought through clearly and has technical errors. Good writing quality gives the edge to student #2.

As this hypothetical example demonstrates, the ability to write essays clearly and well can make a huge difference in your ability to succeed on essay tests and, ultimately, in life. Your instructors judge your thinking ability based on what you write in your essays (content) and how you write it (your style and grammar). Likewise, your supervisors in work situations will form ideas of your abilities in large part from seeing how well you write job application letters, resumes, business proposals and reports, memos to coworkers, and letters to customers and suppliers. Plus, as with an essay test situation, you will often have very little time to prepare for and accomplish your on-the-job writing tasks.

Keep the following in mind as you work to use the level of writing that good essays require:

- *Good writing depends on and reflects clear ideas.* A clear thought process is the best preparation for a well-written essay, and a well-written essay shows the reader a clear thought process. Clarity is especially important when time is short and you don't have the luxury of taking a day or two to mull over the structure of a paper.

- *Good writing depends on reading.* The more you expose yourself to the work of other writers, the more you will develop your ability to express yourself well. Not only will you learn more words and ideas, but you will also learn about all the different ways that a writer can put words together in order to *express* ideas.

- *Good writing depends on critical thinking.* When you read and think critically, you generate new ideas that you can use in your writing. Most essay questions will ask you to go beyond recall and to express the ideas that have formed in your mind from what you have read and studied.

THE WRITING PROCESS DURING AN ESSAY TEST

What you know about the writing process from Chapter 11 will also serve you in an essay test situation. Writing an answer to an essay test question is like taking the writing process and telescoping it into a matter of minutes. You follow the same steps, but spend far less time and energy on each.

Try not to skip any of these steps when writing an answer to an essay question on a test, even if your time is very short. When you skip the planning step, for example, your work may lack structure. If you skip the editing step, your work may exhibit spelling or grammar errors.

Before you start, plan out your time so that you have an estimate of how much time you can spend on each stage. Based on your knowledge of how you work, decide which stages need more time than others (some students might need more planning time, for example, while others might plan quickly but need more time to do the actual writing). Say that you have one hour in which to complete three questions. Assuming twenty minutes per question, you might assign five minutes for planning, ten for drafting, three for revising, and two for editing. Bring a watch with you so that you can keep track of the time as you work.

Planning

Brainstorming and freewriting are two effective ways of getting your ideas down on paper in a limited period of time. Use a piece of scrap paper and jot down everything that comes to mind when you think of the question, either in a freewriting-style paragraph, a freeform think link, or an informal brainstorming outline.

From what you have generated, come up with a thesis statement. Then construct a slightly more organized outline or think link that will help you define the structure of your essay.

Drafting

Unlike writing a paper, in which you can go through a series of drafts before writing your final version, the answer you draft is usually the one you hand in. If you have taken enough time and care with your planning stage, you will have enough material with which to construct a suitable answer.

Don't take too much time or space on an elaborate introduction or conclusion. Lay out your thesis statement concretely and then get right to the evidence that backs up your statement. Pay close attention to how you organize your ideas and how well you support them with examples. Finally, end with a brief and basic conclusion.

Pay attention to the test directions when drafting your answer. Your essay may need to be of a certain length, for example, or may need to take a certain form (a particular number of paragraphs or a particular format such as a business letter).

Revising

Take a few moments to evaluate your word choice, paragraph structure, and style. Although you may not have the time or opportunity to rewrite your whole answer, you can certainly improve it with minor deletions or additions in the margin. If you find a hole in your work—an idea without support, for example, or some unnecessary information—evaluate the situation. If the change would make an important improvement, it may be worth marking up your paper somewhat. Be as neat as you can when making last-minute changes.

As you check over your essay, ask yourself these questions:

- Does your essay begin with a clear thesis statement, and does each paragraph start with a strong topic sentence that supports the thesis?
- Have you provided the support necessary in the form of examples, statistics, and relevant facts to prove your argument?
- Are your logical connections sound and convincing?
- Have you covered all the points in your original outline?
- Is your conclusion an effective wrap-up?
- Does every sentence effectively communicate your point?

Editing

Finally, do one last check for punctuation, spelling, grammar, and elements such as capitalizations and abbreviations. Mistakes in these areas call attention to themselves and distract from the sense of your answer. Likewise, a technically correct paper makes a good impression even before the instructor considers the ideas that are expressed.

Not all exams are written. In certain situations, you may have to give the answers to exam questions orally.

Read every essay question very carefully. Look for performance words, especially action verbs, that tell you how to approach the question. Slow down and look for words like *compare, recognize, analyze, identify.* It may help to copy these words in the margin. Between the performance words are the content words—what you're being asked about.

I always tell students to try to find a unique way into the question that not everybody is going to use. For example, if you are asked the causes of World War II, you may want to state and compare them to the causes of World War I. That's the way to get a higher grade and use your best critical-thinking skills.

Use a Specific Essay Question Strategy

KIM FLACHMANN, PROFESSOR OF ENGLISH,
CALIFORNIA STATE UNIVERSITY AT BAKERSFIELD

How Can You Master Oral Exams?

In an oral exam, your instructor asks you to present verbally your responses to exam questions or to discuss a preassigned topic. Exam questions may be similar to the essay questions on written exams. They may be broad and general, or they may focus on a narrow topic, which you are expected to explore in depth.

You may have never had an oral exam; depending on your course of study and particular needs, you may never have one in school. Don't let that tempt you to skip this section of the chapter. Being well-versed in the skills involved in taking an oral examination has several benefits.

ORAL EXAMS REQUIRE SKILLS USEFUL IN PUBLIC SPEAKING. If you master the skills in this section, you will be well-prepared for any kind of public speaking. Whether you address your class with a presentation of a project, your coworkers with a revised fitness plan for the health club where you are a trainer, or a community group with a message about local safety issues, you need to be able to get your point across clearly, concisely, and in a manner that grabs the attention of your audience. Oral exams, like public speaking, give you the chance to show your understanding of a topic and your ability to present it logically.

ORAL SKILLS ARE CRUCIAL TO CAREER SUCCESS. In the work place, employees are often asked to present information in meetings and through public speaking to members of their work teams, clients and other business associates, and supervisors who are looking for a summary of a completed project or an update on a project in progress. Often, situations requiring oral exam skills, such as ease of speaking and think-on-your-feet capability, will come up without warning. The more comfortable you are with these skills, the more successfully you will handle your boss dropping by for a surprise meeting, an unexpected phone call where you have to give details of your latest research, or a situation where a group of readers questions the conclusions you made in an article you wrote.

ORAL EXAMS ARE ESSENTIAL FOR STUDENTS WITH PARTICULAR LEARNING DISABILITIES. Some students have a learning style or disability that limits their capacity to express themselves effectively in writing. Such students need to take all of their exams orally. If you have a learning disability that fits into this category, be sure to speak with your advisor and your instructors to set up a system of taking exams that works for you.

PREPARATION STRATEGIES

Because oral exams require that you speak logically and succinctly with little time to organize your thoughts, your instructors will often give you the exam topic in advance and may even allow you to bring your notes to the exam room. Other instructors ask you to study a specified topic and then ask directed questions during the exam. Your challenge is to prepare effectively, just as you would for a written exam, as you practice your oral presentation skills.

Speaking in front of others—even an audience of one, your instructor—involves developing a presentation strategy before you enter the exam room:

- *Learn your topic.* Study for the exam until you have mastered the material. Nothing can replace subject-mastery as a confidence booster.
- *Plan your presentation.* Dive into the details. Brainstorm your topic if it is preassigned, narrow it with the prewriting strategies you learned in Chapter 11, determine your central idea or argument, and write an outline that will be the basis of your talk. If the exam uses a question-and-answer format, make a list of the most likely questions the instructor will ask, and formulate the key points of your responses.
- *Use clear thinking.* Illustrate ideas with examples, and show how examples lead to ideas. Try to formulate an effective beginning and ending that focus on the exam topic.
- *Draft your thoughts.* To get your thoughts organized for the exam, make a draft, using "trigger" words or phrases that will remind you of what you want to say.

PRACTICE YOUR PRESENTATION

The element of performance distinguishes speaking from writing. As in any performance, practice is essential. Use the following strategies to guide your efforts:

- *Know the parameters.* How long do you have to present your topic? Make sure you stick to the guidelines your instructor gives you. Where will you be speaking? Be aware of the physical setting—where your instructor will be sitting, and what you may have around you to use, such as a podium, table, chair, or white board.

- *Use index cards or notes.* If your instructor doesn't object, bring note cards to the presentation. However, keep them out of your face; it's tempting to hide behind them.

- *Pay attention to the physical.* Your body positioning, your voice, and what you wear contribute to the impression you make. Look good and sound good. Walk around if you like to talk that way, and try to make eye contact with your instructor. Never forget that you are speaking *to* your instructor so use nonverbal cues to acknowledge his presence and engage him in your talk.

- *Do a test run with friends or alone.* If possible, practice in the room where you will speak. Audiotape yourself practicing, and use the tapes to evaluate yourself. Pay special attention to eliminating crutch words and expressions, such as *like, you know,* and *um.*

- *Time your practice sessions.* This will help you determine whether to add or cut material. If you are given your exam topic in advance, make sure you can say everything you want to say in the allotted time. During the exam, monitor your rate of speech to make sure it is not too rapid. Nervous speakers have the tendency to race through a presentation, which minimizes its effect.

- *Try to be natural.* Use words you are comfortable with to express concepts you know. Don't try to impress your instructor with big words that sound stiff and formal. Rather, be yourself as you show your instructor your knowledge and enthusiasm for the topic.

BE PREPARED FOR QUESTIONS

After your formal presentation, your instructor may ask you questions about the exam topic. Your responses and the way you handle the questions will affect your grade. Here are some strategies for answering questions effectively:

- *Take the questions seriously.* The exam is not over until the question-and-answer period ends.

- *Jot down keywords from the questions.* This is especially important if the question has several parts, and you intend to address one part at a time.

- *Ask for clarification.* If you don't understand a question, ask the instructor to rephrase it. Your goal is to answer the question the instructor asks.
- *Think before you speak.* Take a moment to organize your thoughts and to write down keywords for the points you want to cover. An organized answer will impress your instructor.
- *Answer only part of a question if that's all you can do.* Emphasize what you know best and impress the instructor with your depth of knowledge.
- *Be calm if you don't know an answer.* Although you may take it for granted that you may not be able to answer all the questions on a written exam, you may panic when a question you can't answer comes your way on an oral exam. Simply tell the instructor that you don't know the answer to the question and move onto the next.

HANDLING YOUR NERVES DURING AN EXAM

Taking an oral exam is similar to giving a speech or business presentation. All eyes are on you as you communicate your message. If you respond with a bad case of nerves—also known as speech tension—there are things you can do to help yourself:

- *Be physically and mentally fit.* Get a good night's sleep before the exam so you'll speak with energy. Avoid drinking too much coffee or any alcohol.
- *Keep your mind on your presentation, not on yourself.* Focus on what you want to say and how you want to say it, not on yourself.
- *Take deep breaths right before you begin, and have a bottle of water handy.* Deep breathing will calm you, and the water will quench your parched mouth.
- *Visualize your own success.* Create a powerful mental picture of yourself acing the exam. Then, visualize yourself speaking with knowledge, confidence, and poise.
- *Establish eye contact with your instructor and realize that he or she wants you to succeed.* You'll relax when you feel that your instructor is on your side. Often students are given oral exams by instructors who have been extremely supportive, either as advisors or informally, in their process through a course or through the completion of a major. Such instructors may have a special interest in the success of their students.

Finally, in addition to the special challenge of having to present your knowledge verbally, oral exams demand the use of your other test-taking skills. Engage what you know about writing and organizing your thoughts whenever you prepare for an oral exam.

Kente

The African word *kente* means "that which will not tear under any condition." *Kente* cloth is worn by men and women in African countries like Ghana, Ivory Coast, and Togo. There are many brightly colored patterns of *kente*, each unique, each an opportunity for self-expression by the wearer.

Think of how this concept applies to taking tests. Like the cloth, all people are unique, with different strengths as students. Likewise, tests and test questions are unique and require different approaches and skills. See tests as unique opportunities to express what you know in your own particular way. Paying attention to the particular skills required for any testing situation, and bringing your own unique perspective to your work on tests, can help you succeed and build the kind of knowledge that will stay with you long after you have turned in your test.

Study Skills in Action

Test Competence

MEASURING WHAT YOU'VE LEARNED

MULTIPLE CHOICE. *Circle or highlight the answer that seems to fit best.*

1. An example of an *objective question* is one that
   A. measures your ability to differentiate one object from another.
   B. allows the use of open-book materials during the test.
   C. asks you to select from a limited number of choices.
   D. requires you to plan, organize, draft, and refine a written response.

2. A strategy that is **not** advised for making an educated guess on a multiple-choice question is to
   A. look for a choice with a middle value in a range.
   B. look for a shorter choice.
   C. look for a choice that agrees grammatically.
   D. look for a more general choice.

3. Which of the following is an example of an *absolute qualifier?*
   A. always
   B. seldom
   C. frequently
   D. almost

4. When working through a matching question
   A. work from the column that has the shortest entries.
   B. start with the matches you do not know.
   C. after you make a choice, resist the temptation to change your answer at the end of the test.
   D. tackle the matches you're not sure of after you mark the matches you know.

5. Essay questions fall into all the following categories **except**
   A. objective questions
   B. subjective questions
   C. important questions
   D. critical-thinking questions

6. When answering an essay question
   A. spend most of your time on the introduction because the grader will see it first.
   B. skip the planning steps if your time runs short.
   C. use the four steps of the writing process but take less time for each step.
   D. write your essay and then rewrite it on another sheet or booklet.

7. Good writing skills on essay tests depend on all of the following factors **except**
   A. clear ideas and thinking.
   B. writing quickly so that you have time to revise.
   C. continual exposure to the writing of others.
   D. critical thinking.

8. The one activity you probably will **not** have time for during an essay test is
   A. planning your essay.
   B. drafting your essay.
   C. drafting an alternate essay as a backup.
   D. revising and editing your essay.

9. One way in which oral examination skills will prove useful after graduation is that
   A. you will often take oral exams on the job.
   B. you need to be prepared to speak in front of people at any time.
   C. many jobs require you to make presentations to work teams, clients, and others.
   D. planning is essential to any profession.

10. Which of the following is **not** a useful oral exam strategy?
    A. Jotting down keywords from the questions.
    B. Answering only those questions you feel like answering.
    C. If you don't understand a question, asking for clarification.
    D. Answering only part of a question if that's all you can do.

TRUE/FALSE. *Place a T or an F beside each statement to indicate whether you think it is true or false.*

1. _____ Fill-in-the-blank questions are also known as sentence completion questions.

2. _____ The verbs *define, describe, discuss,* and *explain* all have the same meaning on essay tests.

3. _____ Brainstorming and freewriting are two important planning tools during an essay test.

4. _____ During an oral exam, focus exclusively on your subject and ignore your presentation method.

5. _____ It is unusual for students to get nervous before and during an oral exam.

Brain Power

BUILDING VOCABULARY FITNESS

The paragraphs below are taken from the current media. Read the paragraph, noting the context of the vocabulary words shown in bold type. Next, for each vocabulary word (reprinted in the left-hand column), highlight the word or phrase in column A, B, or C that is the most similar in meaning. Finally, on a separate sheet of paper, solidify your understanding of these words by using each in a sentence of your own.

> During intermission [at my first opera in New York's Lincoln Center], I **eavesdropped** on conversations in the lobby; most had nothing to do with opera or the performance at hand. Old friends caught up with one another; new acquaintances chatted about the weather . . . For the most part, the women in line for the ladies' room held their tongues. But as I returned to my seat, I heard a man in standing room explain some aspect of the opera to two of his friends. He seemed to be an **aficionado,** his friends mere **novices.** I regretted not apprenticing my twenty-year-old self in a similar fashion. . . .
>
> I plan to spend the remainder of the winter and the whole of the spring listening to my growing CD collection and asking everyone I meet about their opera experiences. Of course, being in New York imposes certain limitations on my **demographics.** Maybe cyberspace should be my next stop. There must be tons of chatlines devoted to opera **buffs.**

From "A Twentysomething at the Opera," by Kelli Rae Patton, *Opera News,* June 2000, pp. 12 and 14.

Vocabulary Words	A	B	C
1. **eavesdropped**	listened in	dismissed	interrupted
2. **aficionado**	dilettante	knowledgeable fan	critic
3. **novices**	beginners	experts	priests
4. **demographics**	finances	networking contacts	transportation
5. **buffs**	haters	fans	singers

Strategic Thinking

GETTING THE BIG PICTURE

Answer the following questions on a separate piece of paper or in a journal.

Think about the career area you are in or plan to be in. In this career you may encounter one or more tests—tests for entry into the field (such as the medical boards), tests on particular equipment (such as a proficiency test on Microsoft Word), or tests that are necessary to move you to the next level of employment (such as a technical certification test). Research and describe any test(s) involved in your particular field, and whether they are objective, subjective, or even oral. Finally, describe the test-taking strategies that you think will best serve you in your quest to succeed on those tests.

NOTES

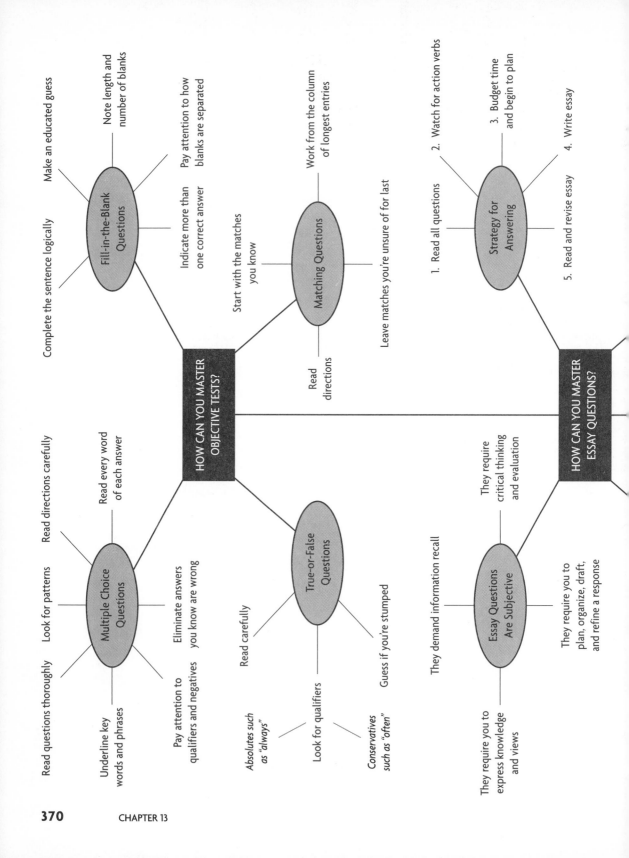

HOW CAN YOU MASTER OBJECTIVE TESTS?

Fill-in-the-Blank Questions
- Complete the sentence logically
- Make an educated guess
- Note length and number of blanks
- Pay attention to how blanks are separated
- Indicate more than one correct answer

Matching Questions
- Start with the matches you know
- Work from the column of longest entries
- Leave matches you're unsure of for last
- Read directions

Multiple Choice Questions
- Read directions carefully
- Read every word of each answer
- Look for patterns
- Read questions thoroughly
- Underline key words and phrases
- Pay attention to qualifiers and negatives
- Eliminate answers you know are wrong

True-or-False Questions
- Read carefully
- Look for qualifiers
  - Absolutes such as "always"
  - Conservatives such as "often"
- Guess if you're stumped

HOW CAN YOU MASTER ESSAY QUESTIONS?

Strategy for Answering
1. Read all questions
2. Watch for action verbs
3. Budget time and begin to plan
4. Write essay
5. Read and revise essay

Essay Questions Are Subjective
- They require critical thinking and evaluation
- They demand information recall
- They require you to plan, organize, draft, and refine a response
- They require you to express knowledge and views

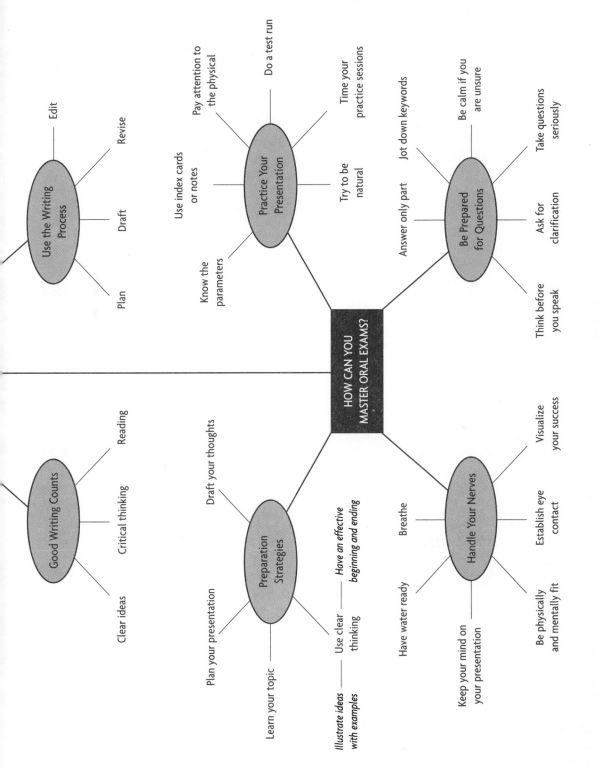

Use the Writing Process
- Edit
- Revise
- Draft
- Plan

Good Writing Counts
- Reading
- Critical thinking
- Clear ideas

Practice Your Presentation
- Pay attention to the physical
- Do a test run
- Time your practice sessions
- Use index cards or notes
- Try to be natural
- Know the parameters

Be Prepared for Questions
- Be calm if you are unsure
- Jot down keywords
- Take questions seriously
- Answer only part
- Ask for clarification
- Think before you speak

Preparation Strategies
- Draft your thoughts
- Have an effective *beginning and ending*
- Use clear thinking
- Illustrate ideas with examples
- Plan your presentation
- Learn your topic

Handle Your Nerves
- Visualize your success
- Establish eye contact
- Breathe
- Be physically and mentally fit
- Have water ready
- Keep your mind on your presentation

HOW CAN YOU MASTER ORAL EXAMS?

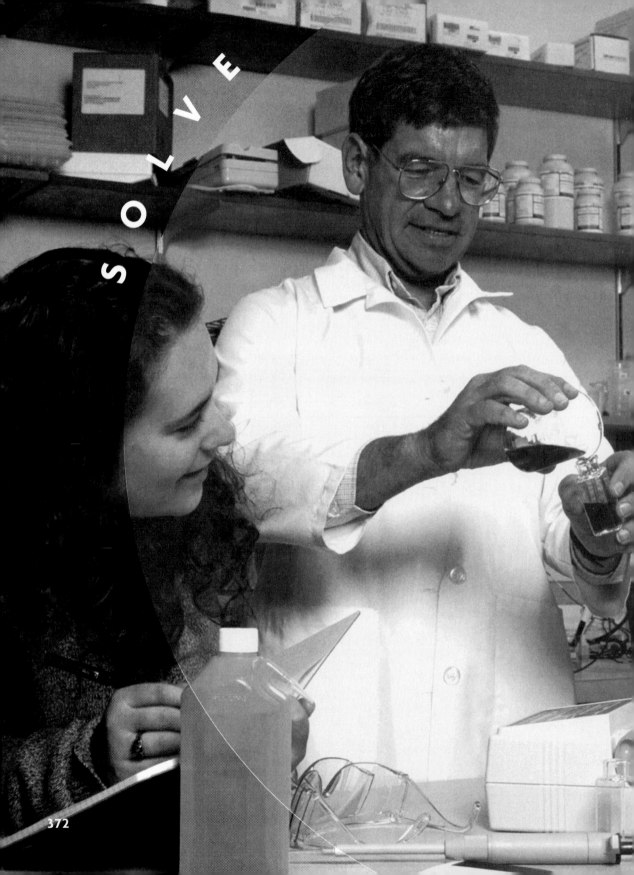

SOLVE

W

hen asked about math
or science, many students reply by saying "I hate math," or "I was never any good
at math and science." With the growing technology of today's world, however, a basic
knowledge of *quantitative thinking,* or thinking in
terms of measurable quantities—including math, science, and computer technology—is as necessary as the
ability to read and write. Along with leadership skills,
quantitative thinking is a large part of what employers look
for in their most promising and promotable hires.

This chapter will look at the need for quantitative thinking in today's technologically changing and competitive
world. At the end of the chapter, you will be able to answer
these questions:

- Why do you need to be able to think quantitatively?
- How can you master math basics?
- How can you overcome math anxiety?
- What techniques will improve your performance
  on math tests?
- What do learning math and learning science
  have in common?
- What basics should you know about
  computers?

QUANTITATIVE LEARNING CHAPTER 14

QUANTITATIVE LEARNING
BECOMING COMFORTABLE WITH
MATH, SCIENCE, AND TECHNOLOGY

> *"People seldom see the halting and painful steps by which the most significant success is achieved."*
>
> **Annie Sullivan**

Why Do You Need to be Able to Think Quantitatively?

Quantitative thinking goes far beyond a math course or two that you take in school and then put aside. Working with numbers is a crucial skill for the modern world, both in terms of the growth of technology and the importance of problem solving. Math is, at heart, a problem-solving discipline—the single most important skill that math develops and reinforces is the ability to think critically. Consider the following examples of problems requiring quantitative thinking that you might encounter:

- You make $2,000 per month in your job. How do you determine how you allocate your money to pay your bills?
- You want to carpet your house. However, many of the rooms and hallways are not regularly shaped. How do you determine how much carpet you need to buy?
- You are trying to schedule your classes for next semester. Each of your classes is only offered at certain times. How do you go about making the best possible schedule?

The level of quantitative competency needed will vary depending on your specific career goals and objectives, but everyone will need some minimum amount of skill. These skills can be broadly broken down into the following areas.

- *Arithmetic.* Many everyday tasks require arithmetic (numerical computations such as addition, subtraction, multiplication, and division, plus fractions and other ratios). You are using arithmetic when you calculate how much tuition you can cover in a semester or figure out what to tip in a restaurant.
- *Algebra.* A knowledge of algebra—in which letters representing unknown quantities are combined into equations according to the rules of arithmetic—is needed almost as frequently as arithmetic. You use algebra when you figure out the interest on a loan or compute

your GPA. Algebra involves determining an unknown value using known values.

- *Geometry.* The most important uses of geometry occur in determining areas and volumes. However, geometric ideas occur in many other forms. Examples of geometry in everyday life include determining how closely you can pass a car and packing a suitcase so that it can close.

- *Probability and Statistics.* A knowledge of basic probability (the study of the chance that a given event will occur) and statistics (collection, analysis, and interpretation of numerical data) is needed for understanding the relevance and importance of the overwhelming amount of statistical information you encounter. For example, if a woman reads breast cancer statistics, her statistical and probability knowledge can help her determine her risk of getting the disease. Careers such as actuarial or genetic science demand a strong background in these subjects, and some areas of business, economics, and engineering require some skills as well.

- *Calculus and Differential Equations.* Calculus and differential equations are needed for most engineering fields, business and economics, physics, and astronomy. Any problem in which a rate of change is needed involves calculus and differential equations. Many problems that involve work, water pressure, areas, and volumes also use calculus.

Certainly not every student will need to master calculus. The basics, however, will be of use to everyone.

How Can You Master Math Basics?

Certain thinking strategies will help improve your ability to think quantitatively. Mastering math basics involves a critical approach to the classroom, the textbook, studying and homework, and word problems.

THE CLASSROOM

In taking a math class, as with any other class, the two most important factors are being in class and being prepared. If you build your base of declarative and procedural knowledge before class by reading about the topic being covered that day, you will have a context in which to ask questions about the material. Asking questions will allow you to think critically about the important aspects of the material and help you retain and apply it. When you take notes, focus on the central ideas and connect supporting examples to those ideas.

THE TEXTBOOK

Instead of just reading through math material, interact with it critically as you go. Keep a pad of paper nearby and take note of the examples as you read. If steps are left out, as they often are, work them out on your pad. Draw sketches as you read to help visualize the material. Try not to move on until you understand the example and how it relates to the central ideas. Write down questions you want to ask your instructor or fellow students.

Also, note what formulas are given. Evaluate whether these formulas are important and recall whether the instructor emphasized them. Be aware that in some classes you are responsible for all formulas, while in others, the instructors will provide them to you. Read the material to prepare you for any homework assigned to you.

STUDYING AND HOMEWORK

Following class, it is crucial to review your notes as soon as possible. Fill in missing steps in the instructor's examples before you forget them. When reviewing notes, have the book alongside and look for similarities and differences between the lecture information and the book. Then work on the homework.

Because math focuses on problem solving, doing a lot of problems is critical. Do not expect to complete every problem without effort. To fight frustration, stay flexible. If you are stuck on a problem, go on to another one. Sometimes you need to take a break to clear your head.

If you have done the assigned homework but still aren't sure about the method, then do some other problems. Doing a lot of problems will give you a base of examples that will help to clarify ideas (math concepts and formulas) for you. Plus, doing a group of problems similar to one another will help you apply the ideas to similar problems on other assignments and on tests.

Study groups can facilitate quantitative thinking. Other peoples' perspectives can often help you break through a mental block. Even if your math classes have smaller lab sessions, try to set up study groups outside of class. Do as much of your homework as you can and then meet to discuss the homework and work through additional problems. Be open to other perspectives, and don't hesitate to ask them to explain their thought processes in detail.

WORD PROBLEMS

Because word problems are the most common way you will encounter mathematics throughout your life, the ability to solve them is a necessary skill. Word problems can be tough, however, because they force you to translate between two languages—English and mathematics. Although math is a precise language, English and other living languages are not so precise. This difference in precision makes the process of translating more difficult.

Steps to Solving Word Problems

Translating English or any other language to math takes a lot of practice. George Polya, in his 1945 classic, *How To Solve It*, devised a four-step method for attacking word problems.[1] The basic steps reflect the general problem-solving process you explored in Chapter 4.

1. *Understand the individual elements of the problem.* Read the problem carefully. Understand what it is asking. Know what information you have. Know what information is missing. Draw a picture, if possible. Take the given information and translate it from words into mathematical language (numbers, symbols, formulas).

2. *Name and explore potential solution paths.* Think about similar problems that you understand and how those were solved. Consider whether this problem is an example of a mathematical idea that you know. In your head, try out different ways to solve the problem to see which may work best.

3. *Carry out your plan.* Choose a solution path and solve the problem. Check each of your steps.

4. *Review your result.* Check your answer, if possible. Make sure you've answered the question the problem is asking. Does your result seem logical in the context of the problem? Are there other ways to do the problem?

Different problem-solving strategies will be useful to you when solving word problems. You use your critical-thinking skills both by evaluating which strategy will work best on a given problem and by applying the strategy itself. The following section lays out several problem-solving strategies by working through different types of word problem examples.[2]

Problem-Solving Strategies

STRATEGY 1: LOOK FOR A PATTERN. G. H. Hardy (1877–1947), an eminent British mathematician, described mathematicians as makers of patterns and ideas. The search for patterns is one of the best strategies in problem solving. When you look for a pattern, you think inductively, observing a series of examples and determining the general idea that links the examples together.

Example: Find the next three entries in the following:

a. 1, 2, 4, ___, ___, ___
b. O, T, T, F, F, S, S, ___, ___, ___

Solutions to Example:

a. When trying to identify patterns, you may find a different pattern than someone else. This doesn't mean yours is wrong. Example 1a actually has several possible answers. Here are two:

1. Each succeeding term of the sequence is twice the previous term. In that case, the next three values would be 8, 16, 32.
2. The second term is 1 more than the first term and the third term is 2 more than the second. This might lead you to guess the fourth term is 3 more than the third term, the fifth term is 4 more than the fourth term and so on. In that case, the next three terms are 7, 11, 16.

b. Example 1b is a famous pattern that often appears in puzzle magazines. The key to it is that "O" is the first letter of <u>o</u>ne, "T" is the first letter of <u>t</u>wo, and so on. Therefore, the next three terms would be E, N, and T for <u>e</u>ight, <u>n</u>ine, and <u>t</u>en.

STRATEGY 2: MAKE A TABLE. A table can be used to help organize and summarize information. This may enable you to see how examples form a pattern that leads you to an idea and a solution.

Example: How many ways can you make change for a half dollar using only quarters, dimes, nickels, and pennies?

Solution to Example: You might construct several tables and go through every possible case. You could start by seeing how many ways you can make change for a half dollar without using a quarter, which would produce the following tables:

Quarters	0	0	0	0	0	0	0	0	0	0	0	0	0	0	0	0	0	0
Dimes	0	0	0	0	0	0	0	0	0	0	0	1	1	1	1	1	1	1
Nickels	0	1	2	3	4	5	6	7	8	9	10	0	1	2	3	4	5	6
Pennies	50	45	40	35	30	25	20	15	10	5	0	40	35	30	25	20	15	10

Quarters	0	0	0	0	0	0	0	0	0	0	0	0	0	0	0	0	0	0
Dimes	1	1	2	2	2	2	2	2	2	3	3	3	3	3	4	4	4	5
Nickels	7	8	0	1	2	3	4	5	6	0	1	2	3	4	0	1	2	0
Pennies	5	0	30	25	20	15	10	5	0	20	15	10	5	0	10	5	0	0

There are 36 ways to make change for a half dollar without using a quarter. Using one quarter results in this table:

Quarters	1	1	1	1	1	1	1	1	1	1	1	1
Dimes	0	0	0	0	0	0	1	1	1	1	2	2
Nickels	0	1	2	3	4	5	0	1	2	3	0	1
Pennies	25	20	15	10	5	0	15	10	5	0	5	0

Using one quarter, you get 12 different ways to make change for a half dollar. Lastly, using two quarters, there's only one way to make change for a half dollar. Therefore, the solution to the problem is that there are 36+12+1=49 ways to make change for a half dollar using only quarters, dimes, nickels, and pennies.

STRATEGY 3: IDENTIFY A SUBGOAL. Breaking the original problem into smaller and possibly easier problems may lead to a solution to the original problem. This is often the case in writing a computer program.

Example: Arrange the nine numbers 1, 2, 3, . . . , 9 into a square subdivided into nine sections in such a way that the sum of every row, column, and main diagonals is the same. This is what is called a magic square.

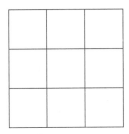

Solution to Example: Because each number will go into one of the squares, the sum of all the numbers will end up being three times the sum of any given row, column, or main diagonal. The sum of 1+2+3+4+5+6+7+8+9=45. Therefore, each row, column, and main diagonal needs to sum to 45/3=15. Now you need to see how many ways you can add three of the numbers from 1 to 9 and get 15. In doing this, you should get:

9 + 1 + 5 = 15	8 + 3 + 4 = 15
9 + 2 + 4 = 15	7 + 2 + 6 = 15
8 + 1 + 6 = 15	7 + 3 + 5 = 15
8 + 2 + 5 = 15	6 + 4 + 5 = 15

Now, looking at your magic square, notice that the center position will be part of four sums (a row, a column, and the two main diagonals). Looking back at your sums, you see that 5 appears in four different sums, therefore 5 is in the center square.

Now in each corner, the number there appears in 3 sums (row, column, and a diagonal). Looking through your sums, you find that 2, 4, 6, and 8 each appear in three sums. Now you need to place them in the corners in such a way that your diagonals add up to 15.

2		6
	5	
4		8

Then to finish, all you need to do is fill in the remaining squares to get the needed sum of 15 for each row, column, and main diagonal. The completed square is as follows:

2	7	6
9	5	1
4	3	8

STRATEGY 4: EXAMINE A SIMILAR PROBLEM. Sometimes a problem you are working on has similarities to a problem you've already read about or solved. In that case, it is often possible to use a similar approach to solve the new problem.

Example: Find a magic square using the numbers 3, 5, 7, 9, 11, 13, 15, 17, and 19.

Solution to Example: This problem is very similar to the example for Strategy 3. Approaching it in the same fashion, you find that the needed row, column, and main diagonal sum is 33. Writing down all the possible sums of three numbers to get 33, you find that 11 is the number that appears 4 times, so it is in the center.

	11	

The numbers that appear three times in the sums and will go in the corners are 5, 9, 13, and 17. This now gives you:

13		17
	11	
5		9

Finally, completing the magic square gives you:

13	3	17
15	11	7
5	19	9

STRATEGY 5: WORK BACKWARDS.   With some problems, you may find it easier to start with the perceived final result and work backwards.

Example: In the game of "Life," Carol had to pay $1,500 when she was married. Then she lost half the money she had left. Next, she paid half the money she had for a house. Then, the game was stopped, and she had $3,000 left. How much money did she start with?

Solution to Example: Carol ended up with $3,000. Right before that she paid half her money to buy a house. Because her $3,000 was half of what she had before her purchase, she had 2($3,000)=$6,000 before buying the house. Prior to buying the house, Carol lost half her money. This means that the $6,000 is the half she didn't lose. So, before losing half her money, Carol had 2($6,000)=$12,000. Prior to losing half her money, Carol had to pay $1,500 to get married. This means she had $12,000+$1,500=$13,500 before getting married. Because this was the start of the game, Carol began with $13,500.

STRATEGY 6: DRAW A DIAGRAM.   Drawing a picture is often an aid to solving problems, especially for visual learners. Although pictures are especially useful for geometrical problems, they can be helpful for other types as well.

Example: There were 20 people at a round table for dinner. Each person shook hands with the person to his immediate right and left. At the end of the dinner, each person got up and shook hands with everybody except the people who sat on his immediate right and left. How many handshakes took place after dinner?

Solution to Example: To solve this with a diagram, it might be a good idea to examine several simpler cases to see if you can determine a pattern of any kind that might help. Starting with two or three people, you can see there are no handshakes after dinner because everyone is adjacent to everyone else.

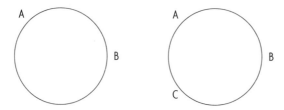

Now in the case of four people, we get the following diagram, connecting those people who shake hands after dinner:

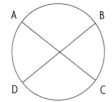

In this situation, you see there are two handshakes after dinner, AC and BD. In the case of five people, you get this picture:

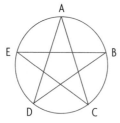

In this case, you have five after-dinner handshakes, AC, AD, BD, BE, and CE. Looking at one further case of six people seated around a circle gives the following diagram:

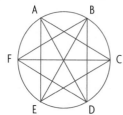

In this diagram, there are now a total of nine after-dinner hand-shakes, AC, AD, AE, BD, BE, BF, CE, CF, and DF. In noticing from the diagrams what is happening, you realize that if there are N people, each person would shake N–3 people's hands after dinner (they don't shake their own hands or the hands of the two people adjacent to them.) Because there are N people that would lead to N(N–3) after-dinner handshakes. However, this would double count every handshake because AD would also be counted as DA. Therefore, this is twice as many actual handshakes. So, the correct number of handshakes is [N(N–3)]/2. So finally, if there are 20 people, there would be 20(17)/2=170 after-dinner handshakes.

STRATEGY 7: TRANSLATE WORDS INTO AN EQUATION. This is often used in algebra.

Example: A farmer needs to fence a rectangular piece of land. He wants the length of the field to be 80 feet longer than the width. If he has 1,080 feet of fencing available, what should the length and width of the field be?

Solution to Example: The best way to start this problem is to draw a picture of the situation and label the sides.

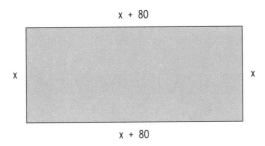

x + 80

x

x

x + 80

Let x represent the width of the field and x+80 represent the length of the field. The farmer has 1,080 feet of fencing and he will need 2x+2(x+80) feet of fencing to fence his field. This gives you the equation:

$$2x + 2(x + 80) = 1080$$

Multiplying out:
$$2x + 2x + 160 = 1080$$

Simplifying and Subtracting 160:
$$4x = 920$$

Dividing by 4:
$$x = 230$$

Therefore,
$$x + 80 = 310$$

As a check, you find that
$$2(230) + 2(310) = 1080.$$

These sample problems are designed to boost your ability to think critically through some basic math strategies. If they have made you feel anxious, however, you will benefit from some information about math anxiety.

How Can You Overcome Math Anxiety?

Math anxiety describes any of several high-stress, uncomfortable feelings that appear in relation to quantitative thinking. Math anxiety is often as a result of common misconceptions about math (such as the notion that people are born with or without an ability to think quantitatively, or the idea that real quantitative thinkers solve problems quickly in their heads). Some students feel that they can't do any math at all, and as a result may give up without asking for help. Use the questionnaire in Figure 14.1 to get an idea of your math anxiety level.

FIGURE 14.1   *Explore your math anxiety.*

Answer the following statements by marking a number from 1 (Disagree) to 5 (Agree).

1. _____ I don't like math classes, and haven't since high school.

2. _____ I do okay at the beginning of a math class, but I always feel it will get to the point where it is impossible to understand.

3. _____ I can't seem to concentrate in math classes. I try, but I get nervous and distracted and think about other things.

4. _____ I don't like asking questions in math class. I'm afraid that the teachers or the other students will think I'm stupid.

5. _____ I stress out when I'm called on in math class. I seem to forget even the easiest answers.

6. _____ Math exams scare me far more than any of my other exams.

7. _____ I can't wait to finish my math requirement so that I'll never have to do any math again.

Scoring Key:

28–35:   You suffer from full-blown math anxiety.
21–27:   You are coping, but you're not happy about mathematics.
14–20:   You're doing okay.
7–13:   So what's the big deal about math? You have very little problem with anxiety.

Source: Freedman, Ellen (March 1997). *Test Your Math Anxiety* [online]. Available: http://fc.whyy.org/CCC/alg1/anxtest.htm (March 1998).

Math anxiety most commonly occurs right before or during an exam. As a student gets ready to take a test or reads a particular problem on a test, he experiences rising anxiety or even what can be described as "blanking out." This can happen during exams for other subjects, but seems to occur especially often with tests involving quantitative thinking.

The best way to overcome test-time anxiety is to practice quantitative thinking and thereby increase your confidence. Keeping up with your homework, attending class, preparing well for tests, and doing extra problems will help you feel confident because it increases your familiarity with the material. Figure 14.2 shows additional ways to reduce math anxiety.

Even though math anxiety is a real problem, students must take some responsibility for their responses to quantitative thinking. You can't change the math experiences you have had in the past, but you can make choices about how to respond to quantitative material from here on out. Some of your responsibilities as a quantitative thinker include:[3]

- To attend all classes and do homework
- To seek extra help when necessary, from an instructor, tutor, or fellow student
- To speak up in class when you have questions
- To be realistic about your abilities and to work to improve them
- To approach math with an open mind, not assuming the worst

Ten ways to reduce math anxiety. **FIGURE 14.2**

1. Overcome your negative self-image about math.

2. Ask questions of your teachers, your friends, and seek outside assistance.

3. Math is a foreign language—practice it often.

4. Don't study mathematics by trying to memorize information and formulas.

5. READ your math textbook.

6. Study math according to your personal learning style.

7. Get help the same day you don't understand something.

8. Be relaxed and comfortable while studying math.

9. "TALK" mathematics. Discuss it with people in your class. Form a study group.

10. Develop a sense of responsibility for your own successes and failures.

Source: Freedman, Ellen (March 1997). *Ten Ways to Reduce Math Anxiety* [online]. Available: http://fc.whyy.org/CCC/alg1/reduce.htm (March 1998).

Finally, along with being a responsible student, you also have rights regarding your mathematical learning. These include:[4]

- The right to learn at your own pace
- The right to ask questions
- The right not to understand
- The right to be treated as a competent person
- The right to believe you are capable of thinking quantitatively

Besides working to control your math anxiety, several other techniques will help you do your very best when you are tested on your math skills.

What Techniques Will Improve Your Performance on Math Tests?

In addition to the general strategies for test-taking that you have explored, here are several other techniques that can help you achieve better results on math exams.

- *Read through the exam first.* When you first get an exam, read through every problem quickly. Make notes on how you might attempt to solve the problem if something occurs to you immediately.
- *Analyze problems carefully.* Categorize problems according to what type they are. Take all the "givens" into account, and write down any formulas, theorems, or definitions that apply before you begin your calculations. Focus on what you want to find or prove, and take your time—precision demands concentration. If some problems seem easier than others, do them first in order to boost your confidence.
- *Estimate before you begin to come up with a "ballpark" solution.* Work the problem and check the solution against your estimate. The two answers should be close. If they're not, recheck your calculations. You may have made a simple calculation error.
- *Break the calculation into the smallest possible pieces.* Go step-by-step and don't move on to the next step until you are clear about what you've done so far.
- *Recall how you solved similar problems.* Past experience can give you valuable clues to how a particular problem should be handled.
- *Draw a picture to help you see the problem.* This can be a diagram, a chart, a probability tree, a geometric figure, or any other visual image that relates to the problem at hand.
- *Be neat.* When it comes to numbers, mistaken identity can mean the difference between a right and a wrong answer. A 4 that looks like a 9, for example, can mean trouble.

- *Use the opposite operation to check your work.* When you come up with an answer, work backward to see if you are right. Use subtraction to check your addition; use division to check multiplication, and so on.

- *Look back at the questions to be sure you did everything that was asked.* Did you answer every part of the question? Did you show all the required work? Be as complete as you possibly can.

All the strategies you are learning aren't just useful in your math classes. Many science classes have a mathematical element that will require you to use your math knowledge.

What Do Learning Math and Learning Science Have in Common?

Many of the issues you face in mathematics also occur in science. Therefore, many of the strategies discussed about mathematics will also be effective in the sciences. Sciences such as chemistry, physics, and astronomy are quite often problem-solving courses. There are also classes in geology, anthropology, and biology that fall into this category. The math strategies you have explored will be applicable to these sciences.

For example, in beginning chemistry, you will usually have to balance chemical equations. This may involve writing an equation, drawing a diagram, or perhaps working backwards. In physics, the study of forces involves applying problem-solving strategies developed from vector calculus. In fact, the most common strategy to solve force problems involves drawing a diagram called a force diagram. The key thing to remember is that although these strategies are listed as mathematical strategies, the actual process of applying them is far more wide-ranging, helping you to develop into a critical thinker and problem solver.

Beyond the necessity of gaining problem-solving skills, the change from high school to college science is quite similar to the change in mathematics courses.

- *The pace of the courses will be faster.* Quite often, what was done in a year in high school will be done in a semester or less in college.

- *The assignments will be considered crucial.* However, your instructor may not collect them often, if at all. You are responsible for staying current.

- *The classes may be more focused on theories and ideas.* Your class periods may devote more time to proving and deriving theorems. There may be less time spent on examples and problems.

- *The class size might be considerably larger.* You may be in classes taught in large auditoriums with several hundred people enrolled. Your classes may also be organized differently. You may have a lecture sec-

**See How
Math and
Science
Are Linked**

EXPERT INSIGHT

Leonardo da Vinci believed that you can't call anything real science if it can't be demonstrated mathematically. Math is the empowering skill that underlies all science. Without it, you can't succeed as a scientist. The scientific process depends on your ability to analyze, interpret, and attach meaning to data, so math and science are intrinsically linked.

DON PIERCE, EXECUTIVE DIRECTOR OF EDUCATION, HEALD COLLEGES

tion, a recitation section or discussion section (often led by a teaching assistant), and possibly a lab section.

- *The expectations of the instructors might be different.* You may be expected to understand and be able to apply the concepts and principles. Skill in manipulating symbols or memorizing facts may be de-emphasized.
- *You may be expected to be technologically proficient.* This could mean using graphing calculators or software such as Mathematica or Maple (mathematical packages), Minitab or SAS (statistical packages), or course-specific software.

Of course, your science courses will go beyond basic mathematical operations. Many of these courses, however, will hinge on mathematical principles. Thinking mathematically will help you understand specific operations and apply them to the more general scientific knowledge you learn.

Furthermore, both math and science have relevance to all of your other subjects. Mathematical operations, because of their problem-solving essence, are pure critical thinking. Simply learning math and science, and putting your brain through the paces of problem solving, builds the kind of critical-thinking ability that you can apply to problem solving in any subject—examples include finding ways for different people to communicate in a sociology course, writing an analysis of an event in a history course, reconciling two different philosophical perspectives in a philosophy course, or finding a solution to a technological problem in a computer course.

What Basics Should You Know About Computers?

As the world continues to become more technologically complicated, the role of computers becomes increasingly prevalent. In almost every job, knowledge of basic computer use is a necessity. On campus, computer use is more and more widespread—and more and more crucial for academic success. "The computer has . . . become the portal through which students do everything they need to do on campus," says Lisa Guernsey in *The New York Times*. "Using the Internet, they register for classes, turn in assignments, order books, browse the library catalog, listen to music, talk to friends, read the news, write papers, play games, pay bills, watch movies and carry on heated political discussions."[5]

The *Student Monitor* reports that in the fall of 1999 students spent an average of 7.2 hours per week using computers—and an average of 8.1 hours in the spring of 2000.[6] Although much of this time is spent writing, Internet usage comprises a large percentage of computer time. Instructors report that most courses require students to use the Internet in some way, whether to access a web page where they can read the syllabus, research online for assignments, take interactive quizzes, or communicate with instructors and fellow students on topics pertinent to the course.[7]

These statistics demonstrate to you how important your command of basic computer use is now and will be in the future. Computer basics fall into four general categories: Word processing, databases and spreadsheets, the Internet, and e-mail.

WORD PROCESSING

The ability to use a computer to write letters, papers, briefs, and so on is now a requirement at most institutes of higher learning. Many businesses also require the use of these skills. There are many word-processing software programs, and each has its own quirks. Two of the most commonly used are Microsoft Word and Word Perfect. Besides composing documents, features such as a spell check and a grammar checker are extremely useful.

DATABASES AND SPREADSHEETS

The ability to organize and store large volumes of information and data has always been important in most businesses. The easiest way to do this is through the use of some type of computer software for managing databases and spreadsheets. Again, there are many software programs specifically designed to handle, organize, and analyze large volumes of information. Some of the more common programs are Lotus, Symphony, and Microsoft Excel. A knowledge of one or more of these is becoming increasingly beneficial for most careers in business and science, as well as for maintaining personal finance records on a home computer.

THE INTERNET

The Internet, a large worldwide network of connected businesses, universities, governments, and people, is expanding continually. The ability

EXPERT INSIGHT

When you begin your job search, highlight your technology skills on your resume. Many companies now require job applicants to demonstrate these skills in a meaningful way during job interviews. For example, you may be asked to bring examples of written work that you've done on a word processor from qualitative courses, such as English or philosophy. Your interviewers may also want to see examples of your quantitative work, such as a spreadsheet model from an economics or math course. And they may ask you to pull up your personal Internet home page or demonstrate your mastery of Internet research.

Be prepared for these requests. And start now to build a portfolio of technology projects from your academic career.

DAN COOPER, MARIST COLLEGE

Be Prepared to Demonstrate Your Technology Skills

to use the Internet allows you to access the world and communicate with others almost instantaneously. You can now do extensive research on any topic as well as buy, sell, and market products on the Internet. It will be hard to be well prepared for the workforce if you have no Internet experience. Refer to Chapter 10 for more information on researching on the Internet.

E-MAIL

The ability to communicate electronically is rapidly becoming a challenge to the U. S. Postal Service. The major advantage is the speed at which electronic mail (e-mail) can be sent, received, and responded to. If your college has an e-mail system in place, you may be required to communicate with your instructor using e-mail, submit homework via e-mail, and even take exams via e-mail. To learn about e-mail, many schools offer some type of orientation. Every student who has access to e-mail should spend time becoming proficient in electronic communication.

The use of computers in composing letters, desktop publishing, maintaining databases, keeping spreadsheets, working on the Internet, communicating by e-mail, and numerous other tasks will make computer literacy a requirement in the job market. The more capable you are of learning and using various computer systems, the more employable you will be.

al-Khowârizmî

Mohammed ibn Musa al-Khowârizmî was an Arabic astronomer who lived around 825. An 1857 Latin translation of a book no longer existing in the original begins "Spoken has Algoritmi . . ." Hence his name had become Algoritmi, from which was derived the present word *algorithm*. An algorithm is a series of steps used to solve a particular problem in mathematics or the sciences. Many computer software programs are simply strings of algorithms used to do certain functions.

For those of you who don't know Arabic, this word may seem completely out of your realm of knowledge. Just as if you were to study Arabic or any other language, however, success in math boils down to steady work and focus. When you put your mind to it, you can become as fluent in math, science, and technology as you are in your native language.

Study Skills in Action

Test Competence

MEASURING WHAT YOU'VE LEARNED

MULTIPLE CHOICE. *Circle or highlight the answer that seems to fit best.*

1. Strategies that are helpful when studying a math textbook include
   A. speed reading.
   B. skimming.
   C. scanning.
   D. working problems.

2. The first step in solving word problems is to
   A. carry out a plan.
   B. name and explore potential solution paths.
   C. understand the individual elements of the problem.
   D. review your results.

3. Problem solving strategies include all of the following **except**
   A. making a table.
   B. asking your instructor for help.
   C. looking for a pattern.
   D. examining a similar problem.

4. Drawing a diagram as a strategy for mathematical problem solving can be especially helpful to
   A. interpersonal learners.
   B. intrapersonal learners.
   C. musical–rhythmic learners.
   D. visual learners.

5. Strategies to overcome math anxiety include all of the following **except**
   A. avoiding courses with any mathematical content.
   B. seeking help from your instructor or working with a tutor or classmate.
   C. asking questions in class.
   D. being conscientious about your responsibilities to do your home-work and attend class.

6. Estimating is an important tool when taking math tests because
    A. it allows you to complete a problem with very little actual work.
    B. it helps you think how you solved similar problems.
    C. most instructors will accept an estimated answer if it is close to the actual answer.
    D. estimating may help you come up with a ballpark solution that you can compare with your final answer.

7. In general, science courses are characterized by all of the following **except**
    A. a focus on examples and problems rather than theories and ideas.
    B. a faster pace.
    C. larger classes.
    D. the expectation that you will have basic technology skills.

8. Common database and spreadsheet programs include all of the following **except**
    A. Microsoft Excel.
    B. Microsoft Word.
    C. Symphony.
    D. Lotus.

9. The ability to use the Internet is important in business for all of the following reasons **except**
    A. the Internet gives users the ability to communicate almost instantaneously with people all over the world.
    B. the Internet gives users access to research data.
    C. the Internet gives companies the ability to reach customers by way of their virtual storefronts.
    D. Internet games and chat rooms are welcome diversions during the workday.

10. The primary reason e-mail has replaced ground mail is
    A. e-mail does not require postage.
    B. e-mail does not require a company letterhead.
    C. e-mail is almost instantaneous and increases productivity.
    D. e-mail is not permanent.

TRUE/FALSE. *Place a T or an F beside each statement to indicate whether you think it is true or false.*

1. _____ Probability refers to the study of the chance that a given event will occur.

2. _____ When approaching a word problem, you should avoid thinking about similar problems you have encountered in the past.

3. _____ By helping to organize and summarize problem information, tables help you see how examples form a pattern, and this may lead you to the solution.

4. _____ Math anxiety, which describes the stress people feel when confronted with quantitative problems, is a problem you are born with.

5. _____ When you finish all the problems on a math test, resist the temptation to check your answers because you may introduce new errors.

Brain Power

BUILDING VOCABULARY FITNESS

The paragraphs below are taken from the current media. Read the paragraph, noting the context of the vocabulary words shown in bold type. Next, for each vocabulary word (reprinted in the left-hand column), highlight the word or phrase in column A, B, or C that is the most similar in meaning. Finally, on a separate sheet of paper, solidify your understanding of these words by using each in a sentence of your own.

"Most people assume that a company's personality matches its CEO's personality," says [Sandy] Fekete, 43, founder of Fekete + Company, a marketing-communications firm based in Columbus, Ohio. "But that's not true. An organization has its own ways of being."

Fekete's job is to help her clients understand their company's personality—its strengths and its weaknesses. Her main tool is a **diagnostic** called, appropriately, "Companies are People, Too.". . . So far, people in 63 organizations ranging from museums to construction firms to medical practices have put pen to paper to **scrutinize** their companies' personalities. . . .

It may sound like psychobabble, but the idea behind the tool is fairly simple: An organization, like a person, has preferred ways of focusing energy, gathering information, making decisions, and structuring work. Once people inside an organization understand those preferences, argues Fekete, they can do a better job of **articulating** ways to work and to communicate. Some of her clients even elect "keepers of the personality"—volunteers who make sure that their organization is clear about the **attributes** it **prizes.**

"Change comes from awareness," Fekete says. "Once you figure out who you are, you can begin to **differentiate** yourself from your competitors."

Reprinted from "Companies Are People, Too," by Anna Muoio, *Fast Company*, July 2000, #36, p. 44. All rights reserved. To subscribe, call 800-542-6029 or visit www.fastcompany.com.

Vocabulary Words

	A	B	C
1. **diagnostic**	medical exam	investigative test	poll
2. **scrutinize**	identify	examine	criticize
3. **articulating**	clearly expressing	discovering	effectively improving
4. **attributes**	employees	successes	qualities
5. **prizes**	values highly	earns easily	wins frequently
6. **differentiate**	wean	praise	separate

Strategic Thinking

GETTING THE BIG PICTURE

Answer the following question on a separate piece of paper or in a journal.

Numbers are part of your life no matter what your academic focus. Carefully consider where your school experience or work life requires you to work well with numbers—it could be a class, your personal finances, data at work, or other situations. Describe what strategies from this chapter seem like they will help you make the most of your ability to think quantitatively.

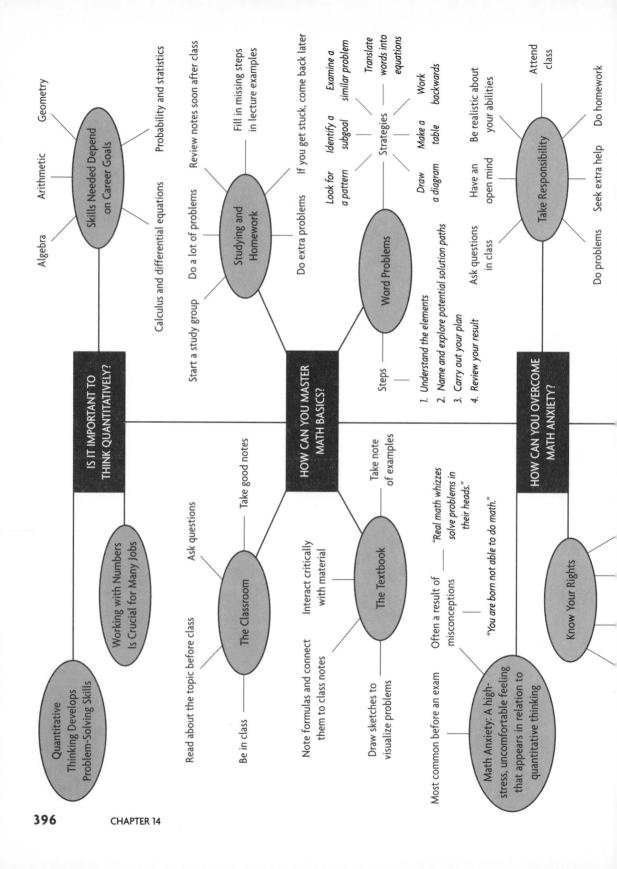

IS IT IMPORTANT TO THINK QUANTITATIVELY?

Skills Needed Depend on Career Goals
- Geometry
- Probability and statistics
- Arithmetic
- Algebra
- Calculus and differential equations

Quantitative Thinking Develops Problem-Solving Skills

Working with Numbers Is Crucial for Many Jobs

HOW CAN YOU MASTER MATH BASICS?

Studying and Homework
- Review notes soon after class
- Fill in missing steps in lecture examples
- If you get stuck, come back later
- Do a lot of problems
- Do extra problems
- Start a study group

Word Problems

Steps
1. Understand the elements
2. Name and explore potential solution paths
3. Carry out your plan
4. Review your result

Strategies
- Examine a similar problem
- Translate words into equations
- Identify a subgoal
- Work backwards
- Look for a pattern
- Make a table
- Draw a diagram

The Classroom
- Take good notes
- Ask questions
- Read about the topic before class
- Be in class

The Textbook
- Take note of examples
- Interact critically with material
- Note formulas and connect them to class notes
- Draw sketches to visualize problems

HOW CAN YOU OVERCOME MATH ANXIETY?

Take Responsibility
- Attend class
- Do homework
- Be realistic about your abilities
- Have an open mind
- Ask questions in class
- Seek extra help
- Do problems

Math Anxiety: A high-stress, uncomfortable feeling that appears in relation to quantitative thinking
- Most common before an exam
- Often a result of misconceptions
- "Real math whizzes solve problems in their heads."
- "You are born not able to do math."

Know Your Rights

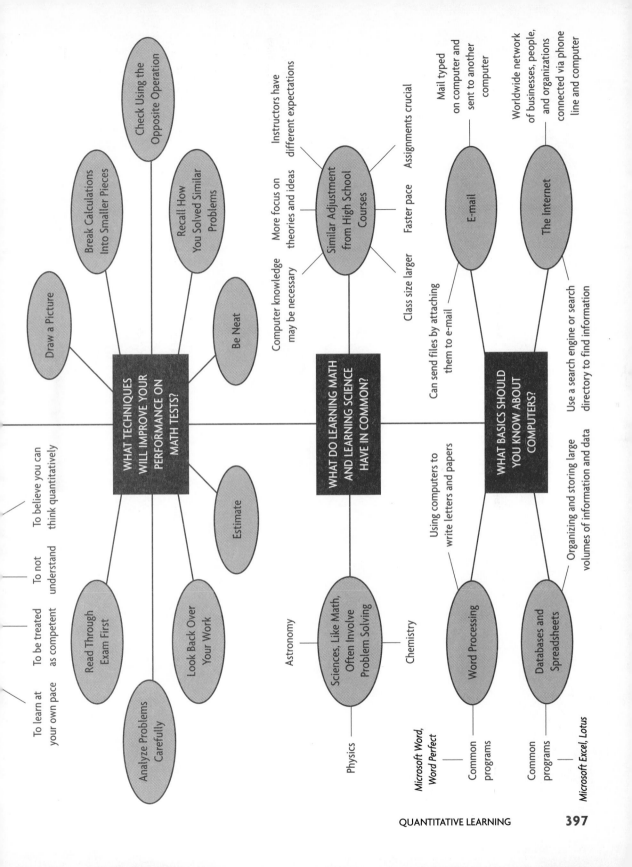

WHAT TECHNIQUES WILL IMPROVE YOUR PERFORMANCE ON MATH TESTS?

- Draw a Picture
- Break Calculations Into Smaller Pieces
- Check Using the Opposite Operation
- Recall How You Solved Similar Problems
- Be Neat
- Estimate
- Look Back Over Your Work
- Analyze Problems Carefully
- Read Through Exam First

- To learn at your own pace
- To be treated as competent
- To not understand
- To believe you can think quantitatively

WHAT DO LEARNING MATH AND LEARNING SCIENCE HAVE IN COMMON?

- Similar Adjustment from High School Courses
  - Instructors have different expectations
  - More focus on theories and ideas
  - Assignments crucial
  - Faster pace
  - Class size larger
  - Computer knowledge may be necessary

- Sciences, Like Math, Often Involve Problem Solving
  - Astronomy
  - Chemistry
  - Physics

WHAT BASICS SHOULD YOU KNOW ABOUT COMPUTERS?

- E-mail
  - Mail typed on computer and sent to another computer
  - Can send files by attaching them to e-mail

- The Internet
  - Worldwide network of businesses, people, and organizations connected via phone line and computer
  - Use a search engine or search directory to find information

- Word Processing
  - Using computers to write letters and papers
  - Common programs — *Microsoft Word, Word Perfect*

- Databases and Spreadsheets
  - Organizing and storing large volumes of information and data
  - Common programs — *Microsoft Excel, Lotus*

As you come to the end of your work in this course, you have built both the knowledge you need to choose the most effective study strategies and the skills to put those strategies to work. Now you have more power to decide what directions you want your life to take. With the effort to learn throughout your life and to remain flexible, you can adjust goals, make the most of successes, and work through failures. With an exploration of the big picture of what you want and who you want to be in your life, you can realize your educational, professional, and personal dreams, embracing the challenges and opportunities of the new century along the way.

This chapter will help you plan how to use study skills as you build the life you envision. At the end of the chapter, you will be able to answer these questions:

- Why is college just the beginning of lifelong learning?
- How can you adjust to change?
- What will help you handle success and failure?
- How can you live your mission?

MOVING AHEAD
MAKING TODAY'S STUDY SKILLS THE FOUNDATION FOR TOMORROW'S SUCCESS

> *"And life is what we make it, always has been, always will be."*
>
> **Grandma Moses**

Why Is College Just the Beginning of Lifelong Learning?

As you learned in the first chapter, today's world favors the student and worker who doesn't stop learning at graduation. Rapidly changing industries demand that workers keep up with new developments. The focus on information requires a constant effort to learn more each day. Increasing numbers of workers changing jobs means that people must retrain frequently.

There is more to lifelong learning than taking continuing education courses. In a general sense, lifelong learning means continually asking questions and exploring new ideas. Here are some lifelong learning strategies that can encourage you.

- *Investigate new interests.* When information and events catch your attention, take your interest one step further and find out more. If you are fascinated by politics, find out if your school has political clubs. If a friend of yours starts to take yoga, try a class. If you really like one portion of a particular class, see if there are other classes that focus on that topic.

- *Read books, newspapers, magazines, and other writings.* Reading opens a world of new perspectives. Ask your friends about books that have changed their lives. Stay current about your community, state, country, and the world by reading newspapers and magazines. A newspaper that has a broad scope, such as *The New York Times* or *Washington Post,* can be an education in itself. Explore religious literature, family letters, and Internet news groups and web pages.

- *Pursue improvement in your studies and in your career.* When at school, take classes outside your major if you have time. After graduation, continue your education both in your field and in the realm of general knowledge. Stay on top of ideas, developments, and new technology in your field by seeking out continuing education courses. Sign up for career-related seminars. Take single courses at a local college or community learning center. Some companies offer additional on-the-job training or pay for their employees to take courses that will improve their knowledge and skills. When you apply for jobs, you may want to ask about what kind of training or education the company offers or supports.

- *Find a mentor.* A mentor is a trusted advisor who will help you make academic and career decisions that are right for you. He will point you to important information and courses and introduce you to people who may help you reach your goal. Finding a mentor and nurturing the mentoring relationship can have an important influence on your entire life.

- *Delve into other cultures.* Visit the home of a friend who has grown up in a culture different from your own. Invite her to your home. Eat food from a country you've never seen. Initiate conversations with people of different races, religions, values, and ethnic backgrounds. Travel to different countries. Travel to different neighborhoods or cities near you—they may seem as foreign as another country. Take a course that deals with some aspect of cultural diversity.

Lifelong learning is the master key that unlocks every door you will encounter on your journey. If you keep it firmly in your hand, you will discover worlds of knowledge—and a place for yourself within them.

How Can You Adjust to Change?

Even the most carefully constructed plans can be turned upside down by change. Two ways to make change a manageable part of your life are to maintain flexibility and adjust your goals. These actions, which were introduced in Chapters 1 and 3, are at the heart of your successful adjustment throughout life.

MAINTAIN FLEXIBILITY

The fear of change is as inevitable as change itself. When you become comfortable with something, you tend to want it to stay the way it is, whether it is a place you live, a job, or the racial and cultural mix of people with whom you interact. Change may seem to have negative effects, and consistency positive effects. Think about your life right now. What do you wish would always stay the same? What changes have upset you and thrown you off balance?

You may have encountered any number of changes in your life to date, many of them unexpected—see Figure 15.1 for some examples. All of these changes, whether they seem good or bad, cause a certain level of stress. They also cause a shift in your personal needs, which may lead to changing priorities.

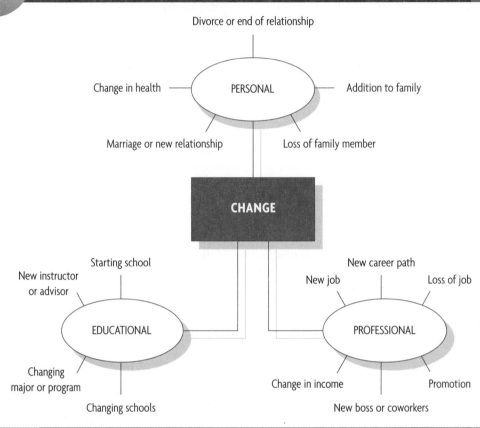

Change Brings Different Needs

Your needs can change from day to day, year to year, and situation to situation. Although you may know about some changes—such as school starting—ahead of time, others may take you completely by surprise, such as job loss. Even the different times of year bring different needs, for example, a need for extra cash around the holidays or additional child care when your children are home for the summer.

Some changes that shift your needs occur within a week or even a day. For example, an instructor may inform you that you have an end-of-week quiz, or your work supervisor may give you an additional goal. Such changes lead to new priorities. For example, if you lose a job, your loss of income may lead to priorities such as job hunting, reduction in spending, or training in a new career area.

Flexibility versus Inflexibility

When change affects your needs, flexibility will help you shift your priorities so that you address those needs. You can react to change with either inflexibility or flexibility, each with its resulting effects.

- *Inflexibility.* Not acknowledging a shift in needs and circumstance can cause trouble. For example, if you lose your job and refuse to take courses to update your skills, ignoring the need to remain competitive in an ever-changing job market, you can drive yourself into chronic under- or unemployment.
- *Flexibility.* Being flexible means acknowledging the change, examining your different needs, and addressing them in any way you can. Discovering what change brings may help you uncover positive effects. For example, a loss of a job can lead you to reevaluate your abilities and look for a job that suits you better. In other words, a crisis can spur opportunity, and you may learn that you want to adjust your goals in order to pursue it.

Sometimes you need time before you react to a major change. When you do decide you are ready, being flexible will help you cope with the negative effects and benefit from the positive effects.

ADJUST YOUR GOALS

Your changing life may result in the need to adjust goals accordingly. For example, a goal to graduate in four years may not be reasonable if economic constraints take you out of school for a while. Sometimes goals must change because they weren't appropriate in the first place. Some turn out to be unreachable; some don't pose enough of a challenge; others may be unhealthy for the goal setter or harmful to others.

Step One: Reevaluate

Before making adjustments in response to change, take time to reevaluate both the goals themselves and your progress toward them.

- *The goals.* First, determine whether your goals still fit the person you have become in the past week or month or year. Circumstances can change quickly. For example, dissatisfaction with a current major may result in some different ideas about educational goals.
- *Your progress.* If you feel you haven't gotten far, determine whether the goal is out of your range or simply requires more stamina than you had anticipated. As you work toward any goal, you will experience alternating periods of progress and stagnation. You may want to seek the support and perspective of a friend or counselor as you evaluate your progress.

Step Two: Modify

If after your best efforts it becomes clear that a goal is out of reach, modifying your goal may bring success. Perhaps the goal doesn't suit you. For example, an active, interpersonal learner might become frustrated while pursuing a detail-oriented, sedentary career such as computer programming.

Based on your reevaluation, you can modify a goal in two ways:

- *Adjust the existing goal.* To adjust a goal, change one or more aspects that define it—say, the time frame, due dates, or expectations. For example, a student adding a second major could adjust the anticipated graduation date, taking an extra year to complete her course work.
- *Replace it with a more compatible goal.* If you find that a particular goal does not make sense, try to find another that works better for you at this time. For example, a student could change a major entirely, redesigning his educational plan to fit the new goal. You and your circumstances never stop changing—your goals should reflect those changes.

The course of your life, and your progress toward goals, will often be unpredictable. When you stay open to unpredictability, you will be more aware of life's moments as they go by. Be an explorer: Focus on what is rather than what is supposed to be, and be willing to be surprised. Having the awareness and flexibility of an explorer will help you understand that both successes and failures are a natural part of your exploration.

What Will Help You Handle Success and Failure?

The perfect, trouble-free life is only a myth. The most wonderful, challenging, fulfilling life is full of problems to be solved and difficult decisions to be made. If you want to handle the bumps and bruises without losing your self-esteem, you should prepare to encounter setbacks along with your successes.

DEALING WITH FAILURE

Things don't always go the way you want them to go. Sometimes you may come up against obstacles that are difficult to overcome. Sometimes you will let yourself down or disappoint others. You may make mistakes or lose your motivation. All people do, no matter who they are or how smart or accomplished they may be. What is important is how you choose to deal with what goes wrong. If you can arrive at reasonable definitions of failure and success, accept failure as part of being human, and examine failure so that you can learn from it, you will have the confidence to pick yourself up and keep improving.

Measuring Failure and Success

Most people measure failure by comparing where they are to where they believe they should be. Because individual circumstances vary widely, so do definitions of failure. What you consider a failure may seem like a positive step for someone else. Here are some examples:

- Imagine that your native language is Spanish. You have learned to speak English well, but you still have trouble writing it. Making writing mistakes may seem like a failure to you, but to a recent immigrant from the Dominican Republic who knows limited English, your command of the language will seem like a success story.

- Having a job that doesn't pay you as much as you want may seem like a failure, but to someone who is having trouble finding any job, your job spells success.

Approach Failure Productively

No one escapes failure, no matter how hard she may try. Many an otherwise successful individual has had a problematic relationship, a substance-abuse problem, or a failing grade in a course.

You have choices when deciding how to view a failure or mistake. Pretending it didn't happen can deny you valuable lessons and may create more serious problems. Blaming someone else falsely assigns responsibility, stifling opportunities to learn. Blaming yourself can result in feeling incapable of success and perhaps becoming afraid to try.

By far the best way to survive a failure is to forgive yourself. Your value as a human being does not diminish when you make a mistake. Expect that you will do the best that you can within the circumstances of your life, knowing that getting through another day as a student, employee, or parent is a success in and of itself. Forgiving yourself opens you up to the possibilities of what you can learn from your experience.

Learning From Failure

Learning from your failures and mistakes involves thinking critically about what happened. First, evaluate what occurred and decide if it was within your control. It could have had nothing to do with you at all. You could have failed to get a job because someone else with equal qualifications was in line for it ahead of you. A family crisis that disrupted your sleep could have affected your studying, resulting in a failing test grade. These are unfortunate circumstances, but they are not failures.

On the other hand, something you did or didn't do may have contributed to the failure. If you decide that you have made a mistake, your next steps are to analyze the causes and effects of what happened, make any improvements that you can, and decide how to change your action or approach in the future.

For example, imagine that after a long night of studying, you forgot your part-time work-study commitment the next day.

- *Analyze causes and effects.* Causes: Your exhaustion and concern about the test caused you to forget to check your work schedule. Effects: Because you weren't there, a crucial curriculum project wasn't completed. An entire class and instructor who needed the project have been affected by your mistake.
- *Make any possible improvements on the situation.* You could apologize to the instructor and see if there is still a chance to finish up part of the work that day.
- *Make changes for the future.* You could set a goal to note your work schedule regularly in your date book—maybe in a bright color—and to check it more often. You could also arrange your future study schedule so that you will be less exhausted.

Think about the people you consider exceptionally successful. They didn't rise to the top without taking risks and making their share of mistakes. They have built much of their success on their willingness to recognize and learn from their shortfalls. You, too, can benefit from staying open to this kind of active, demanding, hard-won education. Learning involves change and growth. Let what you learn from falling short of your goals inspire new and better ideas.

Think Positively About Failure

When you feel you have failed, how can you boost your outlook?

- *Stay aware of the fact that you are a capable, valuable person.* Remind yourself of your successes, focusing your energy on your best abilities, and knowing that you have the strength to try again. Realize that your failure isn't a setback as long as you learn from it and rededicate yourself to excellence.
- *Share your thoughts and disappointment with others.* Everybody fails. When you confide in others, you may be surprised to hear them tell stories that rival your own. Exchange creative energy that can help you learn from failures, rather than having a mutual gripe session.
- *Look on the bright side.* At worst, you at least have learned a lesson that will help you avoid similar situations in the future. At best, there may be some positive results. If you fail a class, for example, you may discover that you need to focus on a subject that suits you better.

What you learn from a failure may, in an unexpected way, bring you around to where you want to be.

DEALING WITH SUCCESS

Success is the continual process of being who you want to be and doing what you want to do. Success is within your reach. Pay attention to the small things when measuring success. Although you may not feel successful until you reach an important goal you have set, each step along the way is a success. When you are trying to drop a habit of procrastinating on your papers, each time you complete a part of an assignment on schedule is positive. If you received a C on a paper and then earned a B on the next one, your advancement is successful.

Remember that success is a process. If you deny yourself the label of success until you reach the top of where you want to be, you will have a much harder time getting there. Just moving ahead toward improvement and growth, however fast or slow the movement, equals success.

Here are some techniques to manage your successes:

- *Appreciate yourself.* You deserve it. Take time to congratulate yourself for a job well done—whether it be a good grade, an important step in learning a new language, a job offer, a promotion, or graduation. Praise can give you a terrific vote of confidence.

- *Take your confidence on the road.* This victory can lead to others. Based on this success, you may be expected to prove to yourself and others that you are capable of continuing your successes and building on them. Show yourself and others that the confidence is well founded.

- *Stay sensitive to others.* There could be people around you who may not have been so successful. Remember that you have been in their place and they in yours, and the positions may change many times in the future. Enjoy what you have, work to build on it and not to take it for granted, and support others as they need it.

You are a unique human being with unique capabilities. It's important to define both failure and success in terms of your own goals and abilities, not those of others. This is especially crucial for students with learning disabilities.

REDEFINING FAILURE AND SUCCESS: LEARNING DISABILITIES

Whereas almost everyone has some measure of difficulty in some aspect of learning, people with learning disabilities have specifically diagnosed conditions that make certain kinds of learning difficult. Different disabilities have different effects—some cause reading problems, some create difficulties in math, some make it difficult to process heard language. Although only a small percentage of the student population has a diagnosable learning disability, these students deserve support that shows them they are as capable of success as any other student.

If you have a learning disability, it may be difficult to avoid feeling like you are experiencing constant failure. You may compare yourself to others, labeling as failure anything that does not live up to the examples set by students around you. You can beat this attitude, though, by becoming a strong advocate for your rights as a student with special needs, and by redefining failure and success in terms of your own accomplishments. Consider the following strategies.

- *Be informed about your disability.* The federal government, in Public Law 94–142, defines learning disabilities as follows: "Specific learning disability means a disorder in one or more of the basic psychological processes involved in understanding or in using language, spoken or written, which may manifest itself in an imperfect ability to listen, think, speak, read, write, spell, or to do mathematical calculations. The term includes such conditions as perceptual handicaps, brain injury, minimal brain dysfunction and dyslexia." A learning disability diagnosis results from specific testing done by a qualified professional, and may also involve documentation from instructors and family members.

- *Seek assistance from your school.* If you are officially diagnosed with a learning disability, you are legally entitled to particular aid. Armed with your test results and documentation about your disability, speak with your advisor about how you can secure specific accommodations that will help you learn. Among the services mandated by law for learning disabled students are testing accommodations (e.g., having extended time or computer availability), books on tape, and note-taking assistance (e.g., having a fellow student take notes for you or having access to the instructor's notes).

- *Know your needs.* The more you know about your disability, the more you will be able to seek the most appropriate assistance. Beyond legally mandated services, other services that may help learning disabled students include tutoring, study skills assistance, and counseling. If you understand your disability and can clearly explain what accommodations will help you and why, you will be able to make the most of what your school can offer you.

- *Build a successful attitude.* See your accomplishments in light of where you were before and how far you have come. Keep a list of your successes and refer to it often to reinforce positive feeling. Rely on people in your life who support you and see you as a capable person. Focus on what you do well, not just on what causes you difficulty. Know that the help you receive at school is deserved—it will give you the best possible chance to learn and grow.

How Can You Live Your Mission?

Think about your largest, most wide-ranging life goals. From them you may be able to derive your personal *mission*—a broad picture of who you want to be, what you want to do, and the principles by which you want to live. Your mission should change as the world changes and as you grow. It will continue to reflect your goals, values, and strengths if you live with integrity, create personal change, broaden your perspective, and work to achieve your personal best.

LIVE WITH INTEGRITY

You've spent time exploring who you are, how you learn, and what you value. Integrity is about being true to that self-portrait you have drawn while also considering the needs of others. Living with integrity will bring you great personal and professional rewards.

Having integrity puts your sense of what is right into day-to-day action. Figure 15.2 shows the building blocks of integrity—the principles by which a person of integrity strives to live. When you act with integrity, you earn trust and respect from yourself and from others. If people can trust you to be honest, to be sincere in what you say and do, and to consider the needs of others, they will be more likely to encourage you, support your goals, and reward your work. Integrity is a must for workplace success.

Building blocks of integrity. **FIGURE 15.2**

Integrity

| Honest representation of self and thoughts | Sincerity in word and action | Consideration of the needs of others |

meaning . . .

| You truthfully speak your mind and you seek accurate, true self-knowledge | You do what you say you will do | When making decisions, you take both your needs and the needs of others into account |

Think of situations in which a decision made with integrity has had a positive effect. Have you ever confessed to an instructor that your paper is late without a good excuse, only to find that despite your mistake you have earned the instructor's respect? Have extra efforts in the workplace ever helped you gain a promotion or a raise? Have your kindnesses toward a friend or spouse moved the relationship to a deeper level? When you decide to act with integrity, you can improve your life and the lives of others.

Most important, living with integrity helps you believe in yourself and in your ability to make good choices. A person of integrity isn't a perfect person but one who makes the effort to live according to values and principles, continually striving to learn from mistakes and to improve. Take responsibility for making the right moves, and you will follow your mission with strength and conviction.

CREATE PERSONAL CHANGE

How has your idea of who you are and where you want to be changed since you first opened this book? What have you learned about your values, your goals, and your styles of communication and learning? Consider how your goals have changed. As you continue to grow and develop, keep adjusting your goals to your changes and discoveries.

Stephen Covey says in *The Seven Habits of Highly Effective People*, "Change—real change—comes from the inside out. It doesn't come from hacking at the leaves of attitude and behavior with quick fix personality ethic techniques. It comes from striking at the root—the fabric of our thought, the fundamental essential paradigms which give definition to our character and create the lens through which we see the world."[1]

Examining yourself deeply in that way is a real risk, demanding courage and strength of will. Questioning your established beliefs and fac-

EXPERT INSIGHT

Start Every Day by Doing the Hardest Things First

Procrastination is a natural human trait. We all want to relax, enjoy, and put things off if we can. But it can also be a terrible problem.

One of Thomas Jefferson's rules for success was to do the worst things first. Go after the things that you're afraid to do, that you don't like to do, that you'd rather not do. Do them the first thing in the morning, if you can. You'll boost your self-image for the rest of the day, and you'll have a lot more pleasure from that point on.

ROB STEVENS, FINANCIAL ANALYST AND ENTREPRENEUR

ing the unknown are much more difficult than staying with how things are. When you face the consequences of trying something unfamiliar, admitting failure, or challenging what you thought you knew, you open yourself to learning opportunities. When you foster personal changes and make new choices based on those changes, you grow.

BROADEN YOUR PERSPECTIVE

Look wide, beyond the scope of your daily life. You are part of an international community and a global economy. In today's economically interconnected world, people all over are dependent on each other for products and services that are the necessities of life. What happens to the Japanese economy affects the prices of automobiles and electronic equipment sold in your neighborhood. The North American Free Trade Agreement (NAFTA) makes Mexico our special trading partner and affects the price of produce sold at your local market.

Globalization may affect the course of your career. If you take a job with a multinational corporation, you may find yourself working in Europe or Asia or the Middle East. Even if you never leave the United States, you will probably be doing business with people all over the world. You are an important link in the worldwide chain of human connection, communication, and interdependence that is creating a better world.

The twentieth century was marked by intense change. The industrial revolution transformed the face of farming, and inventions such as the telephone and television fostered greater communication. Labor unions organized, the civil rights movement struggled against inequality, and women fought for the right to vote.

Now, in the early years of this century, major shifts are happening once again. Computer technology is drastically changing every industry. The Internet and cable news networks spread information to people all over the world at a rapid rate. Many people continue to strive for equal rights. You are part of a world that is responsible for making the most of these developments. In making the choices that allow you to achieve your potential, you will make the world a better place.

AIM FOR YOUR PERSONAL BEST

Your personal best is simply the best that you can do, in any situation. It may not be the best you have ever done. It may include mistakes, for nothing significant is ever accomplished without making mistakes and taking risks. It may shift from situation to situation. As long as you aim to do your best, though, you are inviting growth and success.

Aim for your personal best in everything you do. As a lifelong learner, you will always have a new direction in which to grow and a new challenge to face. Seek constant improvement in your personal, educational, and professional life, knowing that you are capable of such improvement. Enjoy the richness of life by living each day to the fullest, developing your talents and potential into the achievement of your most valued goals.

改善

Kaizen is the Japanese word for "continual improvement." Striving for excellence, always finding ways to improve on what already exists, and believing that you can impact change are at the heart of the industrious Japanese spirit. The drive to improve who you are and what you do will help to provide the foundation of a successful future.

Think of this concept as you reflect on yourself, your goals, your life-long education, your career, and your personal pursuits. Create excellence and quality by continually asking yourself, "How can I improve?" Living by *kaizen* will help you to be a respected friend and family member, a productive and valued employee, and a truly contributing member of society. You can change the world.

Study Skills in Action

Test Competence

MEASURING WHAT YOU'VE LEARNED

MULTIPLE CHOICE. *Circle or highlight the answer that seems to fit best.*

1. Lifelong learning involves all of the following **except**
   A. keeping up with advancements in your chosen field.
   B. expecting someone else to tell you about new ideas you should learn.
   C. reading periodicals and books to learn new information and perspectives.
   D. learning about different cultures.

2. Being flexible in the face of change involves
   A. changing your direction when you encounter obstacles in your life and work.
   B. acknowledging the change and assessing what new needs it brings.
   C. reacting in a way that you have seen work for others.
   D. focusing on an aspect of your life not affected by the change.

3. You may need to adjust a goal if it is
   A. easily reached within a set period of time.
   B. not enough of a challenge or unhealthy for you.
   C. stretched over 10 years' time or more.
   D. requiring continual effort and stamina.

4. It is important to develop skills for handling failure because
   A. you are one of the few people who doesn't always succeed.
   B. failure happens more often than success.
   C. your friends and family expect you not to talk about your failures.
   D. failures can provide important learning opportunities for the future.

5. Developing self-confidence that you can build on in other situations is one of the key elements associated with

   A. learning from your successes.

   B. accepting your failures.

   C. getting an A in every course.

   D. maintaining consistent life goals.

6. If you have a learning disability, you should

   A. expect others to treat you the same as they do anyone else.

   B. demand that other people help you every time you encounter a problem.

   C. identify your disability and find out what services are available.

   D. expect to fail when first attempting any task or test.

7. Integrity is essential for workplace success because

   A. it enables you to get what you want.

   B. your boss expects you to be honest.

   C. electronic devices monitor your honesty.

   D. you earn trust and respect from others in the workplace.

8. Adjusting your goals involves risk for all of the following reasons **except**

   A. the process involves leaving comfortable situations behind as you open yourself up to change.

   B. you have to admit that your original goals were wrong.

   C. goal adjustment involves opening yourself up to new learning situations.

   D. goal adjustment often involves changing your fundamental attitudes and beliefs.

9. Workplace change in the twenty-first century is especially rapid for all of the following reasons **except**

   A. people feel it will be beneficial to start the century with new goals and attitudes.

   B. computer technology is transforming the workplace and changing the way companies do business.

   C. the world has a global economy that increases competition and innovation.

   D. women and minorities have greater opportunities than ever before to be agents of success.

10. Trying to achieve your personal best implies
    A. being perfect at everything you do.
    B. choosing goals and sticking with them no matter what happens.
    C. basing your belief in yourself on what others think of you.
    D. being a lifelong learner who seeks improvement in your personal, educational, and professional life.

TRUE/FALSE. *Place a T or an F beside each statement to indicate whether you think it is true or false.*

1. _____ Change can lead to the need to set new priorities.

2. _____ Inflexible people often do not recognize the implications of change.

3. _____ Forgiving yourself for making a mistake will not help you deal with failure.

4. _____ Successful people no longer need to be sensitive to others.

5. _____ The rights of learning disabled students are protected under federal law.

Brain Power

BUILDING VOCABULARY FITNESS

The paragraphs below are taken from the current media. Read the paragraph, noting the context of the vocabulary words shown in bold type. Next, for each vocabulary word (reprinted in the left-hand column), highlight the word or phrase in column A, B, or C that is the most similar in meaning. Finally, on a separate sheet of paper, solidify your understanding of these words by using each in a sentence of your own.

Do you remember the beautiful **penultimate** scene in Manhattan where Woody Allen is lying on his couch and talking into a tape recorder? He is writing a short story about people who are creating unnecessary, **neurotic** problems for themselves, because it keeps them from dealing with more unsolvable, terrifying problems about the universe.

He leads himself to the question, "Why is life worth living?" and to consider what makes it worthwhile for him: Groucho Marx, Willie Mays, the second movement of the Jupiter Symphony, Louis Armstrong's recording of "Potato Head Blues," Swedish movies, Flaubert's Sentimental Education, Marlon Brando, Frank Sinatra, the apples and pears by Cezanne, the crabs at Sam Wo's, and, finally, the showstopper: his love for Tracy's face.

(continued on p. 418)

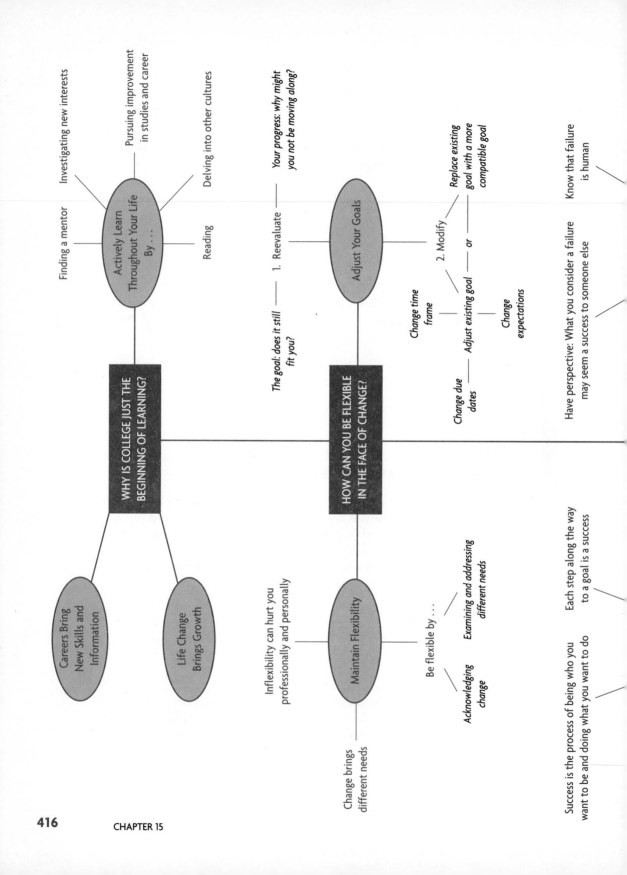

Investigating new interests

Pursuing improvement in studies and career

Finding a mentor

Actively Learn Throughout Your Life By . . .

Delving into other cultures

Reading

WHY IS COLLEGE JUST THE BEGINNING OF LEARNING?

Careers Bring New Skills and Information

Life Change Brings Growth

Your progress: why might you not be moving along?

The goal: does it still fit you?

1. Reevaluate

Adjust Your Goals

2. Modify

Replace existing goal with a more compatible goal

or

Adjust existing goal

Change time frame

Change expectations

Change due dates

HOW CAN YOU BE FLEXIBLE IN THE FACE OF CHANGE?

Know that failure is human

Have perspective: What you consider a failure may seem a success to someone else

Inflexibility can hurt you professionally and personally

Maintain Flexibility

Be flexible by . . .

Examining and addressing different needs

Acknowledging change

Change brings different needs

Each step along the way to a goal is a success

Success is the process of being who you want to be and doing what you want to do

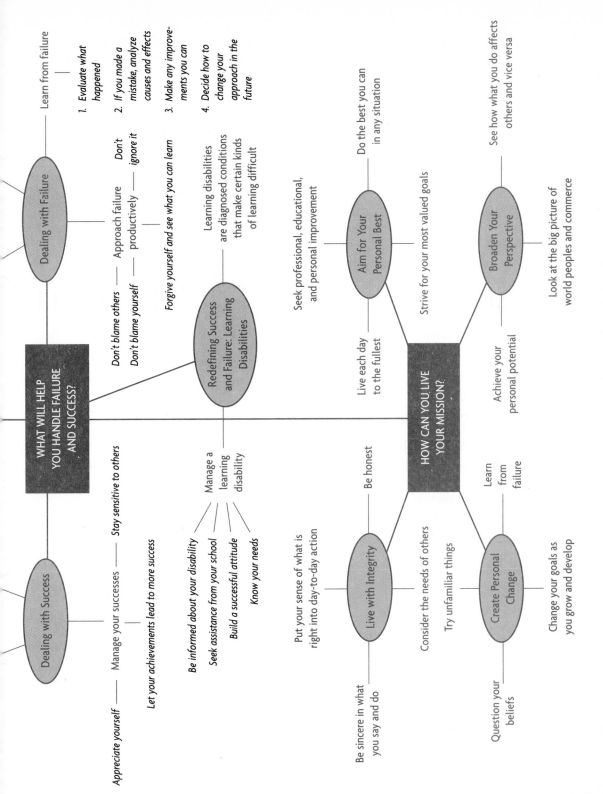

WHAT WILL HELP YOU HANDLE FAILURE AND SUCCESS?

Dealing with Failure

Learn from failure

Approach failure — productively

Don't blame others — Don't ignore it

Don't blame yourself

Forgive yourself and see what you can learn

1. Evaluate what happened
2. If you made a mistake, analyze causes and effects
3. Make any improvements you can
4. Decide how to change your approach in the future

Dealing with Success

Appreciate yourself — Manage your successes — Stay sensitive to others

Let your achievements lead to more success

Redefining Success and Failure: Learning Disabilities

Learning disabilities are diagnosed conditions that make certain kinds of learning difficult

Manage a learning disability

Be informed about your disability

Seek assistance from your school

Build a successful attitude

Know your needs

HOW CAN YOU LIVE YOUR MISSION?

Aim for Your Personal Best

Seek professional, educational, and personal improvement

Do the best you can in any situation

Strive for your most valued goals

Live each day to the fullest

Broaden Your Perspective

Look at the big picture of world peoples and commerce

See how what you do affects others and vice versa

Achieve your personal potential

Live with Integrity

Put your sense of what is right into day-to-day action

Be honest

Be sincere in what you say and do

Consider the needs of others

Create Personal Change

Learn from failure

Try unfamiliar things

Question your beliefs

Change your goals as you grow and develop

Each of us has our precious things, and as we care for them we locate the **essence** of our humanity. In the end, it is because of our great **capacity** for caring that I remain optimistic we will **confront** the dangerous issues now before us.

From "Why the future doesn't need us," © April 2000 by Bill Joy. This article originally appeared in *Wired*. Reprinted by permission of the author.

Vocabulary Words	A	B	C
1. **penultimate**	last	next to the last	first
2. **neurotic**	characterized by irrational thoughts	enormous	focused on others
3. **essence**	primary focus	ultimate nature	basic ideas
4. **capacity**	ability	tendency	possibility
5. **confront**	defeat	be in combat with	meet face-to-face

Strategic Thinking

GETTING THE BIG PICTURE

Answer the following questions on a separate piece of paper or in a journal.

Now it's time for the biggest of the big pictures. Consider your whole experience in this study-skills course. What have you learned that has had the biggest impact on how you live and work day-to-day? What ideas, strategies, or methods stand out to you as the most helpful? How are you a different student and worker for what you have accomplished this semester?

Making Connections

The following multiple-choice, true/false, fill-in-the-blank, matching, and essay questions will reinforce the concepts you learned in the four chapters that make up Part IV, *Testing, Technology, and Competency: Creating Your Future*, and will build critical-thinking skills as well. Whereas the end-of-chapter objective quizzes focus mainly on material from that particular chapter, many of the following questions encourage you to compare material from different chapters and find ways that different ideas connect. Recognizing key relations between ideas will help you master and use knowledge in the most effective way.

MULTIPLE CHOICE. *Circle or highlight the answer that seems to fit best.*

1. Stress reduction prior to a test is important for all of the following reasons **except**
   A. it reduces memory interference when you study.
   B. it enables you to effectively organize your study time.
   C. it gives you time to go to a movie or see friends.
   D. it clears your mind so you are receptive to the input from study group members.

2. You are more likely to suffer from test anxiety if you are
   A. unaware of your learning style.
   B. well prepared.
   C. on good terms with your instructor.
   D. a graduating senior.

3. One positive effect resulting from being both a student and a parent is
   A. a legitimate explanation for less-than-ideal performance.
   B. the ability to juggle multiple responsibilities.
   C. study assistance from school-age children.
   D. sympathy from instructors who are also parents.

4. You can improve your awareness and understanding of qualifiers on tests (words like *often*, *may*, and *sometimes*) by increasing your
   A. reading and goal setting.
   B. reading and math.
   C. reading and writing.
   D. writing and time management.

5. Drawing a diagram to solve a math problem is especially helpful for
   A. bodily–kinesthetic learners.
   B. verbal–linguistic learners.
   C. visual–spatial learners.
   D. musical learners.

TRUE/FALSE. *Place a T or an F beside each statement to indicate whether you think it is true or false.*

1. _____ A helpful method to solve math problems is to translate word problems into equations.

2. _____ Math anxiety comes from being born with a limited ability to do math.

3. _____ Many students find college-level math and science courses more difficult than high school level courses because the pace is faster and the content more theoretical.

4. _____ After setting your long-term goals, it is a sign of weakness to adjust them.

5. _____ Few people experience a major failure in their lives.

FILL-IN-THE-BLANK. *Complete the following sentences with the appropriate word(s) or phrase(s) that best reflect what you learned in Part IV. Choose from the items that follow each sentence.*

1. A trusted personal advisor who will help you make important academic and career decisions is known as a _____. (supervisor, mentor, friend)

2. A _____ person is likely to adjust his _____ in response to changing circumstances. (flexible/goals, inflexible/outlook, flexible/major)

3. A casualty of academic failure is often lowered _____. (personal priorities, self-esteem, academic schedules)

4. People with learning disabilities who experience continual _____ should request _____. (successes/accommodations, failure/accommodations, failure/scholarship money)

5. Taking a _____ will help prepare intellectually and _____ for the actual test. (review course/physically, course outline/psychologically, pretest/psychologically)

6. _____ prepare you for on-the-job _____. (Classroom lectures/ assignments, Study groups/work teams, Study groups/ computers)

7. It is important to be sensitive to _____ verbs on essay tests. (action, passive, static)

8. _____ exams require a thorough knowledge of a subject as well as effective _____ skills. (Written/oral presentation, True-false/ written presentation, Oral/oral presentation)

9. One of the best math problem-solving strategies is looking for a _____. (solution, clue, pattern)

10. The _____ is changing the way people communicate at school and work. (Internet, television, telephone)

MATCHING. *Match each item in the left-hand column to an item in the right-hand column by writing the letter from the right that corresponds best to the number on the left.*

1. _____ e-mail

2. _____ personal mission

3. _____ personal best

4. _____ cramming

5. _____ test anxiety

6. _____ qualifiers

7. _____ subjective questions

8. _____ objective questions

9. _____ databases

10. _____ inflexibility

A. last-minute studying

B. stress related to test taking

C. another name for electronic mail

D. failure to acknowledge a shift in life circumstances

E. short-answer test questions

F. an individual's greatest effort

G. broad picture of what you want to accomplish in your life

H. software programs that enable you to process large volumes of information

I. test questions that allow you to express your answers in essay form

J. words that have the potential to change the meaning of test questions

Essay Question

Carefully read the following excerpt from Life on Earth, *2nd Ed., by Teresa Audesirk, Gerald Audesirk, and Bruce E. Byers, a college textbook published by Prentice Hall, and then answer the essay question that follows. This exercise will help you focus on the meaning of the selection, apply your personal knowledge and experiences to the reading, organize your ideas, and communicate your thoughts effectively in writing.*

Before you begin writing your essay, it is a good idea to spend a few minutes planning. Try brainstorming possible approaches, writing a thesis statement, and jotting down your main thoughts in the form of an outline or think link. Because most essay tests are timed, limit the time you take to write your response to no more than one-half hour. This will force you to write quickly and effectively as it prepares you for actual test conditions.

LIVING THINGS REPRODUCE THEMSELVES

The *continuity of life* occurs because organisms reproduce, giving rise to offspring of the same type. The processes for producing offspring are varied, but the result—the perpetuation of the parents' genetic materials—is the same. The *diversity of life* occurs in part because offspring, although arising from the genetic material provided by their parents, are normally somewhat different from their parents. . . . The mechanism by which traits are passed from one generation to the next, through a "genetic blueprint," produces these variable offspring.

DNA is the Molecule of Heredity

All known forms of life use a molecule called **deoxyribonucleic acid,** or **DNA,** as the repository of hereditary information. Genes are segments of the DNA molecule. . . . An organism's DNA is its genetic blueprint or molecular instruction manual, a guide to both the construction and, at least in part, the operation of its body. When an organism reproduces, it passes a copy of its DNA to its offspring. The accuracy of the DNA copying process is astonishingly high: Only about one mistake occurs for every billion bits of information contained in the DNA molecule. But chance accidents to the genetic material also bring about changes in the DNA. The occasional errors and accidental changes, called **mutations,** are crucial. Without mutations, all life-forms might be identical. Indeed, there is reason to believe that, without mutations, there would be no life. Mutations in DNA are the ultimate source of genetic variations. These variations, superimposed on a background of overall genetic fidelity, make possible the final property of life, the capacity to evolve.

Source: Excerpted from Teresa Audesirk, Gerald Audesirk, and Bruce E. Byers, *Life on Earth*, 2nd Ed., Upper Saddle River, NJ: Prentice Hall, 2000, pp. 5–6.

ESSAY QUESTION.   Analyze and discuss why adaptive traits (traits that help the species cope with a difficult environment) that are the result of genetic mutations are likely to be passed on to the next generation while nonadaptive traits are not likely to be passed on.

Teamwork

EXAM STUDY GROUP.   When you study in a group for a particular exam, you can take advantage of the different skills and sets of knowledge that individual members bring to the group. Assemble a group of students in one of your courses. About a month before an exam, set up three group study sessions.

At the first session, spend most of the time making sure your notes are complete. If you have missed any days, get a copy of the notes taken by a group member. If you have any questions in your notes, see if someone else can help you answer them. At the end of this session, assign tasks to the group for the next session. You will maximize your energy if each group member accomplishes a particular task and then shares the information with the others. Tasks you can assign include:

- Finding out what the exam format will be and what material it will cover
- Talking to former students in the class, or of the instructor, and getting copies of old exams if they are available in the library
- Summarizing the central ideas and supporting examples of any reading materials—textbook chapters, articles, photocopied packets—that will be covered on the exam
- Summarizing notes from particular class periods when the instructor covered material that will be tested
- Researching strategies that will help to reduce test anxiety

At the second session, group members should present the information they have gathered to the rest of the group. Leave time for asking questions and clarifying information. In preparation for the third session, outside of the group meeting, members should go through their notes.

At the third session, think critically about your notes. Take the most important sets of notes and discuss them—present summaries, focus on key ideas and examples, connect ideas to related ideas, question the validity of information, connect causes to effects, and relate information in your notes to information in your readings. Keep an open mind and listen carefully to the ideas that come your way from fellow group members.

Answer Key

Answers for *Study Skills in Action*

CHAPTER 1

Test Competence: Measuring What You've Learned

MULTIPLE CHOICE

1. C   2. D   3. A   4. D   5. B   6. D   7. A   8. D   9. D   10. B

TRUE/FALSE

1. F   2. T   3. F   4. T   5. T

Brain Power: Building Vocabulary Fitness

1. A   2. C   3. C   4. B   5. A   6. A

CHAPTER 2

Test Competence: Measuring What You've Learned

MULTIPLE CHOICE

1. D   2. C   3. C   4. B   5. D   6. D   7. B   8. D   9. A   10. A

TRUE/FALSE

1. F   2. F   3. T   4. T   5. F

Brain Power: Building Vocabulary Fitness

1. C   2. A   3. B   4. B   5. A

CHAPTER 3

Test Competence: Measuring What You've Learned

MULTIPLE CHOICE

1. D   2. A   3. D   4. B   5. A   6. D   7. A   8. C   9. C   10. D

TRUE/FALSE

1. F   2. T   3. T   4. F   5. F

Brain Power: Building Vocabulary Fitness

1. A   2. C   3. A   4. B   5. C

CHAPTER 4

Test Competence: Measuring What You've Learned

MULTIPLE CHOICE

1. D   2. C   3. C   4. A   5. C   6. B   7. C   8. B   9. A   10. D

TRUE/FALSE

1. T   2. F   3. F   4. F   5. T

Brain Power: Building Vocabulary Fitness

1. A   2. B   3. A   4. B   5. C   6. A   7. B

CHAPTER 5

Test Competence: Measuring What You've Learned

MULTIPLE CHOICE

1. B   2. B   3. A   4. B   5. D   6. C   7. C   8. D   9. A   10. B

TRUE/FALSE

1. T   2. T   3. T   4. F   5. T

Brain Power: Building Vocabulary Fitness

1. A   2. B   3. C   4. A   5. C   6. A

CHAPTER 6

Test Competence: Measuring What You've Learned

MULTIPLE CHOICE

1. D   2. A   3. C   4. A   5. B   6. A   7. D   8. A   9. C   10. D

TRUE/FALSE

1. F   2. F   3. T   4. F   5. T

Brain Power: Building Vocabulary Fitness

1. C   2. C   3. B   4. A   5. B   6. A   7. C

CHAPTER 7

Test Competence: Measuring What You've Learned

MULTIPLE CHOICE

1. C   2. D   3. A   4. A   5. B   6. A   7. A   8. D   9. D   10. D

TRUE/FALSE

1. T   2. F   3. F   4. T   5. F

Brain Power: Building Vocabulary Fitness

1. B   2. B   3. A   4. B   5. C   6. C

CHAPTER 8

Test Competence: Measuring What You've Learned

MULTIPLE CHOICE

1. C   2. D   3. D   4. A   5. B   6. A   7. A   8. D   9. A   10. A

TRUE/FALSE

1. F   2. T   3. F   4. F   5. T

Brain Power: Building Vocabulary Fitness

1. B   2. A   3. B   4. B   5. C

CHAPTER 9

Test Competence: Measuring What You've Learned

MULTIPLE CHOICE

1. D   2. C   3. D   4. B   5. B   6. A   7. B   8. C   9. B   10. A

TRUE/FALSE

1. T   2. F   3. F   4. T   5. T

Brain Power: Building Vocabulary Fitness

1. A   2. C   3. A   4. B   5. B   6. B   7. A

CHAPTER 10

Test Competence: Measuring What You've Learned

MULTIPLE CHOICE

1. D   2. B   3. B   4. C   5. B   6. A   7. C   8. D   9. C   10. C

TRUE/FALSE

1. T   2. F   3. T   4. F   5. T

Brain Power: Building Vocabulary Fitness

1. A   2. B   3. C   4. A   5. B   6. A

CHAPTER 11

Test Competence: Measuring What You've Learned

MULTIPLE CHOICE

1. C   2. D   3. A   4. C   5. C   6. A   7. D   8. A   9. C   10. B

TRUE/FALSE

1. T   2. F   3. T   4. F   5. F

Brain Power: Building Vocabulary Fitness

1. B   2. C   3. A   4. B   5. C   6. A

CHAPTER 12

Test Competence: Measuring What You've Learned

MULTIPLE CHOICE

1. C   2. A   3. D   4. A   5. D   6. A   7. A   8. A   9. C   10. D

TRUE/FALSE

1. F   2. T   3. F   4. T   5. F

Brain Power: Building Vocabulary Fitness

1. A   2. B   3. C   4. A   5. C   6. C

CHAPTER 13

Test Competence: Measuring What You've Learned

MULTIPLE CHOICE

1. C   2. B   3. A   4. D   5. A   6. C   7. B   8. C   9. C   10. B

TRUE/FALSE

1. T   2. F   3. T   4. F   5. F

Brain Power: Building Vocabulary Fitness

1. A   2. B   3. A   4. B   5. B

CHAPTER 14

Test Competence: Measuring What You've Learned

MULTIPLE CHOICE

1. D   2. C   3. B   4. D   5. A   6. D   7. A   8. B   9. D   10. C

TRUE/FALSE

1. T   2. F   3. T   4. F   5. F

Brain Power: Building Vocabulary Fitness

1. B   2. B   3. A   4. C   5. A   6. C

CHAPTER 15

Test Competence: Measuring What You've Learned

MULTIPLE CHOICE

1. B   2. B   3. B   4. D   5. A   6. C   7. D   8. B   9. A   10. D

TRUE/FALSE

1. T   2. T   3. F   4. F   5. T

Brain Power: Building Vocabulary Fitness

1. B   2. A   3. B   4. A   5. C

Answers for *Skill Building*
(End-of-Part Exercises)

CHAPTERS 1–4

Making Connections

MULTIPLE CHOICE

1. D   2. A   3. B   4. C   5. D

TRUE/FALSE

1. F   2. F   3. F   4. F   5. F

FILL-IN-THE-BLANK

1. embraces
2. self-directed
3. learning
4. 8
5. learning styles
6. educational/career
7. time
8. questioning
9. persuade/examples
10. media/critical

MATCHING

1. D   2. F   3. H   4. A   5. E   6. I   7. B   8. J   9. G   10. C

CHAPTERS 5–8

Making Connections

MULTIPLE CHOICE

1. D   2. B   3. C   4. C   5. C

TRUE/FALSE

1. T   2. T   3. T   4. T   5. F

FILL-IN-THE-BLANK

1. pace
2. mnemonic devices/flash cards
3. slang
4. vocalizers/subvocalizers
5. critically
6. argument/perspective
7. Internet
8. partial hearing loss/learning disabilities
9. verbal signposts
10. acronyms

MATCHING

1. D   2. G   3. E   4. B   5. I   6. J   7. C   8. A   9. F   10. H

CHAPTERS 9–11

Making Connections

MULTIPLE CHOICE

1. B   2. B   3. C   4. B   5. D

TRUE/FALSE

1. F   2. F   3. T   4. F   5. T

FILL-IN-THE-BLANK

1. direction
2. frequently
3. solidify
4. guide
5. current
6. media literate
7. audience/poor communication
8. freewriting/uncensored/planning
9. plagiarism
10. editing

MATCHING

1. C   2. J   3. D   4. G   5. H   6. E   7. F   8. B   9. I   10. A

CHAPTERS 12–15

Making Connections

MULTIPLE CHOICE

1. C   2. A   3. B   4. C   5. C

TRUE/FALSE

1. T   2. F   3. T   4. F   5. F

FILL-IN-THE-BLANK

1. mentor
2. flexible/goals
3. self-esteem
4. failure/accommodations
5. pretest/psychologically
6. study groups/work teams
7. action
8. oral/oral presentation
9. pattern
10. Internet

MATCHING

1. C   2. G   3. F   4. A   5. B   6. J   7. I   8. E
9. H   10. D

Endnotes

Chapter 1

1. Cited in Colin Rise and Malcolm J. Nicholl, "Accelerated Learning for the 21st Century." New York: Dell, 1997, pp. 5–6.

2. Study cited in Susan Rosenblum, "Young Workers Name Lifelong Learning As Top Need for Economy of Future," *Nation's Cities Weekly*, September 6, 1999, p. 1.

3. David Raths, "Next-Century Skills," *InfoWorld*, April 19, 1999, p. 97.

4. Jay Palmer, "Marry Me A Little," *Barron's*, July 24, 2000, p. 25.

5. David Raths, "Next-Century Skills," *InfoWorld*, April 19, 1999, p. 97.

6. The following section is adapted from Claire Ellen Weinstein and Laura M. Hume, *Study Strategies for Lifelong Learning*. Washington, D.C.: American Psychological Association, 1998, pp. 10–12.

7. Rick Pitino, *Success is a Choice*. Broadway Books, 1997, p. 40.

8. Isaac Asimov, "My Own View," in *The Encyclopedia of Science Fiction*, Robert Holdstock, Ed. (1978).

9. National Institute for Literacy web site, http://www.nifl.gov/reders/!intro.htm#C

Chapter 2

1. Howard Gardner, *Multiple Intelligences: The Theory in Practice*. New York: HarperCollins, 1993, pp. 5–49.

2. Developed by Joyce Bishop, Ph.D., Psychology faculty, Golden West College, Huntington Beach, CA. Based on Howard Gardner, *Frames of Mind: The Theory of Multiple Intelligences*. New York: HarperCollins, 1993.

Chapter 3

1. Paul R. Timm, Ph.D., *Successful Self-Management: A Psychologically Sound Approach to Personal Effectiveness*. Los Altos, CA: Crisp Publications, Inc., 1987, pp. 22–41.

2. Ibid.

3. Jane B. Burka, Ph.D., and Lenora M. Yuen, Ph.D., *Procrastination: Why you do it and what to do about it.* Reading, MA: Perseus Books, 1983, pp. 21–22.

4. Jodi Wilgoren, "More Than Ever, First-Year Students Feeling the Stress of College," *The New York Times*, January 24, 2000, online.

5. Stephanie Armour, "Workplace Hazard Gets Attention," *USA Today*, May 5, 1998: B1.

6. Herbert, Benson, M.D., and Eileen M. Stuart, R.N., C. M. S., *The Wellness Book.* New York: Simon & Schuster, 1992, p. 292.

7. *Baltimore City Community College 1998–2000 Catalog.* Baltimore City Community College, Division of Planning and Advancement, 1996, p. 158.

Chapter 4

1. Frank T. Lyman, Jr., Ph.D., "Think-Pair-Share, Thinktrix, Thinklinks, and Weird Facts: An Interactive System for Cooperative Thinking." In *Enhancing Thinking Through Cooperative Learning*, Neil Davidson and Toni Worsham, Eds. New York: Teachers College Press, 1992, pp. 169–181.

2. Ben E. Johnson, *Stirring Up Thinking.* New York: Houghton Mifflin Company, 1998, pp. 268–270.

3. Sylvan Barnet and Hugo Bedau, *Critical Thinking, Reading, and Writing: A Brief Guide to Argument*, 2nd Ed. Boston: Bedford Books of St. Martin's Press, 1996, p. 43.

4. 1998 Center for Media Literacy.

Chapter 5

1. Kathryn Redway, *Be a Rapid Reader.* Chicago, IL: NTC Contemporary Publishing Group, 1991, p. 17.

2. Sherwood Harris, *The New York Public Library Book of How and Where to Look It Up.* Englewood Cliffs, NJ: Prentice Hall, 1991, p. 13.

3. See Harold Bloom, *How To Read and Why.* New York: Scribner, 2000.

4. George M. Usova, *Efficient Study Strategies: Skills for Successful Learning.* Pacific Grove, CA: Brooks/Cole Publishing, 1989, p. 45.

5. Grace J. Craig, *Human Development*, 7th Ed. Upper Saddle River, NJ: Prentice Hall, 1996, pp. 568–569.

6. Steven Moidel, *Speed Reading.* Hauppauge, NY: Barron's Educational Series, 1994, p. 18.

7. Ibid, pp. 18–25.

8. Ibid, p. 32.

Chapter 6

1. Francis P. Robinson, *Effective Behavior.* New York: Harper & Row, 1941.
2. John Mack Faragher, et al., *Out of Many*, 3rd Ed. (Upper Saddle River, NJ: Prentice Hall), p. xxxvii.
3. Sylvan Barnet and Hugo Bedau, *Critical Thinking, Reading, and Writing: A Brief Guide to Argument*, 2nd Ed. Boston: Bedford Books of St. Martin's Press, 1996, pp. 15–21.

Chapter 7

1. Information for this section from Darrell Huff, *How To Lie With Statistics.* New York: W.W. Norton, 1954, pp. 165–166, 278.

Chapter 8

1. Louis E. Boone and David L. Kurtz, *Contemporary Business Communication.* Upper Saddle River, NJ: Prentice Hall, 1994, p. 39.
2. Ralph G. Nichols, "Do We Know How to Listen? Practical Helps in a Modern Age," *Speech Teacher* (March 1961), pp. 118–124.
3. Ibid.
4. Herman Ebbinghaus, *Memory: A Contribution to Experimental Psychology*, transl. H. A. Ruger and C. E. Bussenius. New York: Teachers' College, Columbia University, 1885.
5. Philip Kotler and Gary Armstrong, *Marketing: An Introduction*, 4th Ed. Upper Saddle River, NJ: Prentice Hall, 1997, p. 201.

Chapter 9

1. Walter Pauk, *How to Study in College*, 5th Ed. Boston: Houghton Mifflin Company, 1993, pp. 110–114.

Chapter 10

1. Lisa Guernsey, "For the New College B.M.O.C., 'M' Is for 'Machine,'" *The New York Times*, August 10, 2000, p. G7.
2. Lori Leibovich, "Choosing Quick Hits Over the Card Catalog," *The New York Times*, August 10, 2000, p. G1.
3. Floyd H. Johnson (May 1996). "The Internet and Research: Proceed With Caution" [online]. Available: http://www.lanl.gov/SFC/96/posters.html#johnson (August 2000).
4. Ibid.
5. This material is based on Cynthia Leshin, "Researching Information and Student Resources on the Internet," *Keys to Effective Learning*, 2nd Ed. Upper Saddle River, NJ: Prentice Hall, 1999, pp. A-22–A-23.

Chapter 11

1. Analysis based on Lynn Quitman Troyka, *Simon & Schuster Handbook for Writers*. Upper Saddle River, NJ: Prentice Hall, 1996, pp. 22–23.
2. Philip R. Harris and Robert T. Moran, *Managing Cultural Differences*, 3rd Ed. Houston, TX: Gulf Publishing Company, 1991, p. 59.

Chapter 12

1. Steven Frank, *The Everything Study Book*. Holbrook, MA: Adams Media Corporation, 1996, p. 208.

Chapter 13

1. Many of the examples of objective questions used in this chapter are from Gary W. Piggrem, Test Item File for Charles G. Morris, *Understanding Psychology*, 3rd Ed. Upper Saddle River, NJ: Prentice Hall, 1996.

Chapter 14

1. George Polya, *How to Solve It*. London: Penguin, 1990.
2. This section is adapted from Rick Billstein, Shlomo Libeskind, and Johnny W. Lott, *A Problem Solving Approach to Mathematics for Elementary School Teachers*. Reading, MA: Addison-Wesley Longman, 1993, pp. 5–36. Reprinted by permission of Addison Wesley Longman.
3. Adapted from Kathy Acker (March 1997). "Math Anxiety Code of Responsibilities" [online]. Available: http://fc.whyy.org/CCC/alg1/code.htm (March 1998).
4. Sheila Tobias, *Overcoming Math Anxiety*. New York: W.W. Norton & Company, 1993, pp. 226–227.
5. Lisa Guernsey, "For the New College B.M.O.C., 'M' Is for 'Machine,'" *The New York Times*, August 10, 2000, p. G7.
6. Ibid.
7. Ibid.

Chapter 15

1. Stephen Covey, *The Seven Habits of Highly Effective People*. New York: Simon & Schuster, 1989, pp. 70–144, 309–318.

Index

OTHER TITLES OF INTEREST

OTHER TITLES OF INTEREST

KEYS TO SUCCESS: How to Achieve Your Goals, 3/e

Carol Carter

Joyce Bishop, Golden West College

Sarah Lyman Kravits

This best-selling text connects college skills with career and life success. With its learn-by-doing emphasis, it encourages students to think critically about their choices and goals.

NEW TO THIS EDITION:

- The critical thinking chapter is expanded and improved.
- Media literacy material discusses taking in and critically evaluating media information.
- Web exploration activities appear at the end of each part.
- Reading Room feature at end of each part features current issues.
- Updated critical thinking exercises appear at the end of each chapter.
- A global perspective is reflected in language and maps featured in chapter summaries.
- Revised end-of-chapter career/life applications include exercises incorporating critical thinking, teamwork, journaling, and career portfolio.
- Learning styles material has been revised and clarified.
- Time and goals chapter appears earlier in book.
- Material on using the library has been extensively revised and expanded.
- New and updated learning enhancement features include technology icons within each chapter, updated and improved tables and figures, and the Campbell Interest and Skill Inventory as an appendix.
- Annotated Instructor's Edition has been developed to assist instructors in the classroom. Includes eight different types of marginal annotations, intended to help enrich discussion.
- Updated Instructor's Manual contains materials organized according to the objectives and lessons of each chapter, including transparency masters, Test Item File questions, pre- and post-class evaluations, lecture guides, and excerpts from a wide variety of specialists.

© 2001, 464 pp., Paper (0-13-012883-X); (1288C-5)

SUPPLEMENTS:

Instructor's Manual: 0-13-018559-0; 1855J-2

Annotated Instructor's Edition: 0-13-018557-4; 1855G-9

Adopter's Resource Box: 0-13-055617-3

Companion Website

KEYS TO SUCCESS, Brief Edition, 2/e

This brief version of the best-selling text connects college skills with career and life success. With its learn-by-doing emphasis, it encourages students to think critically about their choices and goals. Includes the same core study skills content as *Keys to Success*, with less coverage of health and wellness issues.

FEATURES/BENEFITS:

UPDATE—Critical thinking chapter expanded and improved.

NEW—Media literacy material.

NEW—Web Connection. Web exploration activities appear at the end of each part, encouraging students to use the Web and Prentice Hall Super Site to build on what they've learned in that part's chapters.

NEW—Reading Room feature at end of each part. Each part has one Reading Room article, excerpted from the media, on a current issue.

NEW—Windows on the World. Formerly named Real World Perspectives, this question-and-answer interview feature appears in each chapter.

UPDATE—Diversity and Communication. Chapter 8 is revised with a critical thinking approach to diversity.

NEW—Additional pertinent topics. Information provided on oral presentations, technology, planning curriculum, and learning disabilities. Also, where the previous edition of *Keys Brief* had no wellness material, this edition contains a substantial wellness section in the final chapter.

UPDATE—Revised applications. Building Skills for College, Career, and Life Success exercises at the end of each chapter have been updated and streamlined. Because this book is used for shorter courses, the exercises are shorter than in *Keys* 3/e, to accommodate the resulting time crunch. Each set of exercises includes:

- One main integrated exercise that builds thinking, teamwork, strategy, and writing skills all at once
- Journal exercise (retained from *Keys* 3/e)
- Career Portfolio exercise (retained from *Keys* 3/e)

UPDATE—Career Portfolio (formerly entitled Personal Portfolio).

UPDATE—Learning Styles. Material has been revised and clarified.

NEW—Time and Goals chapter is earlier in the book.

UPDATE—The material on using the library has been extensively revised and expanded.

UPDATE—Visual learning. Current tables and figures have been updated and improved, and additional tables and figures added.

NEW—Campbell Interest and Skill Survey.

© 2001, 280 pp., Paper (0-13-030485-9)

SUPPLEMENTS:

Instructor's Manual: 0-13-011056-6

Adopter's Resource Box: 0-13-055617-3

Companion Website

KEYS TO EFFECTIVE LEARNING, 2/e

Carol Carter

Joyce Bishop, Golden West College

Sarah Lyman Kravits

This book focuses on developing effective learning techniques to help students excel in school, in their careers, and throughout their lives as lifelong learners. Unlike traditional study skills texts, this one emphasizes how students learn effectively by involving them in the active process of mastering their mental abilities and their personal confidence.

© 2000, 512 pp., Paper (0-13-012882-1)

SUPPLEMENTS:

Majoring in the Rest of Your Life—for Package Only: 0-13-098351-9

Instructor's Manual: 0-13-014370-7

Transparency Acetates: 0-13-917188-6

Companion Website

KEYS TO SCIENCE SUCCESS

Janet Katz, Gonzaga University

Sarah Lyman Kravits

Carol Carter

Proficiency in the sciences and an understanding of technological advances has become a must for students to excel, not only in the classroom but also in their careers. Based on the successful *Keys to Success*, this is the only text available for science majors.

© 2000, 352 pp., Paper (0-13-013305-1)

SUPPLEMENTS:

Instructor's Manual: 0-13-014384-7

KEYS TO ENGINEERING SUCCESS

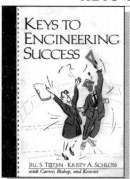

Jill S. Tietjen, University of Colorado at Boulder

Kristy A. Schloss, Schloss Engineered Equipment, Inc.

Carol Carter

Joyce Bishop, Golden West College

Sarah Lyman Kravits

Lively in format and filled with real-world vignettes, applications, and examples, this introduction to engineering is designed to keep students encouraged and motivated during their freshman year when they can't yet see how all the calculus, physics, and chemistry relates to their engineering education. The real-world vignettes and pictures capture not only the diversity of the profession, but of the engineers themselves, providing an overview of the various types of engineering as well as what working professionals do. The text also features extensive information on engineering-specific study skills, gives hints and suggestions on how to enhance one's college experience, and provides information on what resources to look for and where to find them.

© 2001, 360 pp., Paper (0-13-030482-4); (3048B-4)

SUPPLEMENTS:

Instructor's Manual: 0-13-030635-5; 3063E-7

KEYS TO BUSINESS SUCCESS

Martha Doran

Carol Carter

Sarah Lyman Kravits

Written for students majoring in business or considering a business major, this text demonstrates the necessity of business skills in any field, and incorporates real-world examples to illustrate the principles.

© 2000, 302 pp., Paper (0-13-013304-3)

SUPPLEMENTS:

Instructor's Manual: 0-13-014383-9

KEYS TO NURSING SUCCESS

Janet R. Katz, RN, MSN, RN,C, Washington State University, College of Nursing

Carol Carter

Joyce Bishop, Golden West College

Sarah Lyman Kravits

This innovative text/workbook is designed to help entry-level students understand the various aspects and opportunities of the profession of nursing, and to develop both the personal management and academic skills necessary to succeed in a nursing school program. It covers a full range of topics—from exploring the opportunities of the nursing profession; to discovering personal learning styles, values, and goals; to learning how to manage one's time, relationships, and money; to developing skills in reading, studying, critical thinking, note-taking and writing, listening, memory, test-taking, and lab work.

© 2001, 300 pp., Paper (0-13-019575-8); (1957E-0)

SUPPLEMENTS:

Instructor's Manual: 0-13-031542-7; 3154B-4

MAJORING IN THE REST OF YOUR LIFE: College and Career Secrets for Students

Carol Carter, Lynn Quitman Troyka

FEATURES:

- Conceptual thinking: Each chapter opens with a concept that is linked to the material in the chapter.
- Chapter-ending essays and readings: Provocative essays on topics from global competition to improving listening skills.
- Reading and writing connections: In addition to learning to think conceptually and learning to analyze their career and lives, students will be required to read and write effectively.
- Emphasis on skills needed for the 21st Century: With three unique chapters: Understanding Your Learning Style, Emotional Intelligence, and Becoming a Knowledge Worker.
- Profiles: Highlight opinions and experiences of recent graduates or individuals noteworthy for making a difference.

© 2000, 352 pp., Paper (0-13-013154-7)

SUPPLEMENTS:

Instructor's Manual: 0-13-014813-X

Reference Library

KEYS TO THINKING AND LEARNING:
Creating Options and Opportunities

Carol Carter

Joyce Bishop, Golden West College

Sarah Lyman Kravits

This text is designed to facilitate students' understanding of how they think and to enhance their power to apply their thinking ability.

FEATURES:

The *Keys to Success* critical thinking chapter is expanded to four chapters, with an extensive section on problem solving and added topics such as inductive and deductive thinking, truth and fallacy, and common errors in logic.

© 2000, Paper (0-13-086910-4)

KEYS TO COLLEGE STUDYING:
Becoming a Lifelong Learner

This study skills text provides a wide range of study strategies—all while effectively showing students how what they are working hard to accomplish now will help them succeed later in their careers.

FEATURES/BENEFITS:

- Comprehensive topics. Chapters address a wide range of study skills topics, including reading texts and literature, building vocabulary, using visual aids, taking notes, testing, doing library and internet research, writing, taking oral exams, and studying math.

- Career perspective. Each study skill is discussed in terms of how it will promote success for both in-school learning and on-the-job function.

- Adjusting to change. The first and last chapters "bookend" the study skills material with important perspective on the flexibility and strategy it takes to succeed in today's technology-driven, information-focused world.

- Learning styles. One full chapter presents two comprehensive assessments, Pathways to Learning (based on Multiple Intelligences theory) and Personality Spectrum (based on Myers-Briggs), which help the student develop self-knowledge that will help him or her select appropriate study strategies.

- Critical thinking. One full chapter teaches students the basic building blocks of thought, how to use them in critical thinking processes such as problem solving and thinking logically, and how to apply those processes to every other topic in the book.
- Applications. Study Skills In Action exercises at the end of each chapter include the following:
  - Test Competence: Measuring What You've Learned is an objective quiz with ten multiple-choice questions and five true/false questions.
  - Brain Power: Building Vocabulary Fitness is a vocabulary building exercise that culls words from current media sources.
  - Strategic Thinking: Getting the Big Picture is a short essay focused on applying the chapter's skills to the working world.
- End-of-part exercises. Segments at the end of the parts include additional objective test questions, an essay question, and a teamwork exercise.

© 2002, 430 pp., Paper (0-13-030481-6)

KEYS TO LIFELONG LEARNING:
College, Career, and Life Success Telecourse

Available from Dallas TeleLearning

FEATURING:

- Text
- Workbook
- Video
- Companion Web Exercises
- Essay Assessor
- Student Success Supersite

FULL VERSION EPISODES:

1. Education Today: Getting Started
2. Learning Styles: Using Your Strengths
3. Self-Awareness: Knowing Who You Are and What You Want
4. Goals and Values: Mapping Your Course
5. Time Management: Filling It All In
6. Critical Thinking: Tapping the Power of Your Mind
7. Clarity and Creativity: The Building Blocks of Understanding
8. Reading: Your Keys to Knowledge
9. Reading Between the Lines: Critical Reading
10. Do You Hear What I Hear?: Hone Listening Skills
11. The Memory Chip: Remembering Information
12. Note-Taking: The Skill of Getting It Down
13. Conducting Research: Learning From Others
14. Effective Writing: Communicating Your Message
15. The Writing Process: Steps To Successful Writing
16. Test Taking: Showing What You Know
17. The Art of Test-Taking: Mastering Any Test
18. Relating to Others: Appreciating Your Diverse World
19. Getting Along: Respecting Others
20. Skills for the 21st Century: Technology
21. Skills for the 21st Century: Math
22. Skills for the 21st Century: Science
23. Body and Mind: Personal Wellness
24. Managing Your Future: Reality Resources
25. Money Matters: Starting Out Right
26. Managing Change: Lifelong Journey

(Published by Prentice Hall, a division of Pearson Education, and distributed by Dallas TeleLearning, LeCroy Center for Educational Telecommunications, 9596 Walnut St., Dallas, TX 75243.) (0-13-085138-8)

THE CAREER TOOL KIT: Skills for Success, 3/e

Carol Carter

Gary Izumo

The Career Tool Kit is designed especially to help community college and vocational school students develop the skills and attitudes needed to successfully complete their educational program: search for, find, and win the job they want; transition smoothly from school to work; and build a long, happy, and successful working life. The book uses a user-friendly and visually appealing design.

FEATURES/BENEFITS

- Expanded self-assessment section.
- *NEW*—Expanded weaving of technology throughout—particularly in the Real People, Real Stories, Food for Thought, and Your Tool Kit at Work features.
- *NEW*—Workplace myths versus realities in every chapter.
- Important topics detail skills and attitudes that will help students while they are still in school.
- Self-awareness shows students how to search for and win the jobs that they want.
- All revised "Real People, Real Stories"
- School-to-work focus sharpened.

© 2001, 288 pp., Paper (0-13-088418-9); (8841H-9)

SUPPLEMENTS:

Instructor's Manual: 0-13-089415-4; 8941E-4